TWO PHILOSOPHERS

Ayn Rand Society Philosophical Studies
James G. Lennox and Gregory Salmieri, Editors

TWO PHILOSOPHERS
Aristotle and Ayn Rand

Edited by James G. Lennox and Gregory Salmieri

UNIVERSITY OF PITTSBURGH PRESS

Published by the University of Pittsburgh Press, Pittsburgh, Pa., 15260
Copyright © 2025, University of Pittsburgh Press
All rights reserved
Manufactured in the United States of America
Printed on acid-free paper
10 9 8 7 6 5 4 3 2 1

Cataloging-in-Publication data is available from the Library of Congress

Hardcover: 978-0-8229-4869-8
Paperback: 978-0-8229-6783-5

Cover photo of Ayn Rand by Arnold Newman Properties/Getty Images

Publisher: University of Pittsburgh Press, 7500 Thomas Blvd., 4th floor, Pittsburgh, PA 15260, United States, www.upittpress.org
EU Authorized Representative: Easy Access System Europe, Mustamäe tee 50, 10621 Tallinn, Estonia, gpsr.requests@easproject.com

CONTENTS

Preface   vii

Section I. Metaphysical Axioms

1. Axioms and Their Validation in Aristotle and Ayn Rand   5
JAMES G. LENNOX

2. Comments on "Axioms and Their Validation in Aristotle and Ayn Rand," by James G. Lennox: Grounding the Most Basic Principles   32
MICHAIL PERAMATZIS

3. Aristotle and Rand on "Being," "Existence," and the Primacy of Substances   45
JASON G. RHEINS

Section II. Universals and Concepts

4. Concepts and Essences in Aristotle and Ayn Rand   63
ALLAN GOTTHELF

5. Comments on "Concepts and Essences in Aristotle and Ayn Rand," by Allan Gotthelf   77
ANDREA FALCON

Section III. Foundations of Value Theory

6. Ayn Rand and Aristotle on Value and Choice   89
FRED D. MILLER JR.

7. "Man's Life" as the Standard of Value in the Ethics of Aristotle and Ayn Rand   111
GREGORY SALMIERI

8. Comments on "'Man's Life' as the Standard of Value in the Ethics of Aristotle and Ayn Rand," by Gregory Salmieri 148
JOSEPH KARBOWSKI

9. Thoughts on Ethical Methodology (In Response to Joseph Karbowski) 153
GREGORY SALMIERI

Section IV. Virtue and Character

10. Aristotle and Ayn Rand on the Unity of Virtue 165
NEERA K. BADHWAR

11. Comments on "Aristotle and Ayn Rand on the Unity of Virtue," by Neera K. Badhwar: Ayn Rand on Moral Virtue and Moral Character 202
BEN BAYER

12. Reply to Ben Bayer 231
NEERA K. BADHWAR

Section V. Spiritual Values: Art and Love

13. Ayn Rand's Aristotelian Literary Aesthetics 243
ROBERT MAYHEW

14. Love and Philosophy: Aristotelian versus Platonic 258
ALLAN GOTTHELF

15. Reflections on Allan Gotthelf's "Love and Philosophy" 276
GREGORY SALMIERI

Contributors 283

References 287

Index 301

PREFACE

"If there is a philosophical Atlas who carries the whole of Western civilization on his shoulders," Ayn Rand wrote, "it is Aristotle. He has been opposed, misinterpreted, misrepresented, and—like an axiom—used by his enemies in the very act of denying him. Whatever intellectual progress men have achieved rests on his achievements."[1] Such tributes to Aristotle in Rand's writing have led many readers to pick up his corpus. Over the decades a number of these readers, including some of the contributors to this volume, have gone on to become scholars of both Aristotle and Rand. It is high time, then, that there is a collection of essays on the relationship between these two philosophers.

This is the fourth collection in the Ayn Rand Society Philosophical Studies series. Its predecessors have dealt with aspects of Ayn Rand's ethical theory, epistemology, and political philosophy. As was the case with the first three volumes, much of the content of the present volume originated in presentations at meetings of the Ayn Rand Society of the American Philosophical Association. In particular, four of the chapters descend from a 2005 meeting on "Ayn Rand as Aristotelian," where James G. Lennox, Allan Gotthelf, Fred Miller, and Robert Mayhew presented papers and John Cooper served as chair.

Rand described the titles of the three parts of *Atlas Shrugged* as her "tribute" to Aristotle. Those titles are "Non-Contradiction," "Either-Or," and "A is A"—references to the axioms of Aristotelian logic, which both Aristotle and Rand regarded as metaphysical. This volume opens with a

1. "Review of J. H. Randall's Aristotle," *TON* (May 1963): 18.

section on such metaphysical axioms. James G. Lennox discusses Aristotle and Rand on the reference, function, and validation of metaphysical axioms. The paper originates from the 2005 session mentioned above, but a much expanded version was presented at a January 2020 ARS session along with comments by Michael Peramatzis, which are published with it here. This section concludes with a paper by Jason Rheins (occasioned by Lennox's) in which he explores the differences between Rand and Aristotle's conceptions of "existence" (or "being") and of metaphysics as the science that studies it.

In section II, "Universals and Concepts," we publish posthumously an essay by Allan Gotthelf, comparing Rand and Aristotle on the nature of concepts and essences. The paper originated in the 2005 session mentioned above. It is followed by comments that Andrea Falcon composed for this volume.

Section III, "Foundations of Value Theory," compares our two philosophers on some foundational issues in ethics. Fred Miller's chapter on the connection between "Value and Choice," began as his contribution to the 2005 session on Rand as Aristotelian. It is followed here by Gregory Salmieri's paper on "'Man's Life' as the Standard of Value." That paper was presented at a February 2020 meeting of the Ayn Rand Society where Joeseph Karbowski, in his capacity as commentator, pushed Salmieri on questions of philosophical method. Karbowski's comments are included here, followed by some "Thoughts on Ethical Methodology" that Salmieri authored in response.

"Virtue and Character" is the theme of a lively exchange between Neera Badhwar and Ben Bayer in Section IV, stemming from a 2021 online Society meeting based on Badhwar's paper on "Aristotle and Ayn Rand on the Unity of Virtue." Badhwar and Bayer clash over two, related questions: (1) Should virtues be thought of primarily as traits of character (as Aristotle and contemporary virtue-ethicists hold) or as value-oriented actions (the view Bayer attributes to Rand)? (2) Do Aristotle and Rand believe that genuine virtues constitute a unity, and if so, how do they each understand this unity?

The final section considers our two philosophers' views on two aspects of life that Rand described as dealing with spiritual values: art and love. The section opens with an essay by Robert Mayhew on the art about which the two philosophers had the most to say: literature. Mayhew's essay, which is descended from his presentation at the 2005 "Ayn Rand as Aristotelian" session, compares Aristotle's reflections on tragedy in his *Poetics* with Rand's essays on the nature and purpose of literature.

"Love and Philosophy: Platonic vs. Aristotelian" is a lecture that Allan Gotthelf presented on many occasions over the course of his career. Gotthelf draws heavily on Rand throughout the talk, treating her account of love as a "historic advance in the Aristotelian understanding of this fundamental aspect of human existence." The chapter is followed by a reflection by Gregory Salmieri, which draws out further connections between Objectivism and Gotthelf's interpretation of Aristotelian friendship.

It is our hope that this volume of essays will foster a deeper appreciation for Ayn Rand's place in the Aristotelian tradition and in the history of philosophy more generally.

TWO
PHILOSOPHERS

Section I
METAPHYSICAL AXIOMS

1
Axioms and Their Validation in Aristotle and Ayn Rand

JAMES G. LENNOX

> [Aristotle] has been opposed, misinterpreted, misrepresented, and—like an axiom—used by his enemies in the very act of denying him.
> AYN RAND, *THE VOICE OF REASON*

Ayn Rand's novel *Atlas Shrugged* portrays a world in collapse, a collapse being aided and hastened by the refusal of a number of key intellectuals, artists, inventors, and industrialists to contribute in any way to the irrationalism and exploitation sweeping the world. Among those on strike is a young man named Ragnar Danneskjöld, who majored in physics and philosophy in college and is preparing for a career teaching philosophy, but who emerges early in the novel as a modern-day pirate on the high seas, mysteriously restricting his piracy to ships carrying cargo paid for with government-expropriated wealth. Those who are interested in finding out why will have to read the novel. I mention this particular character here because of Ayn Rand's portrayal of him in a scene in the closing pages of *Atlas Shrugged*:

> Ragnar Danneskjöld lay stretched out on a couch, reading a volume of the works of Aristotle: "... for these truths hold good for everything that is, and not for some special genus apart from others. And all men use them, because they are true of being *qua* being.... For a principle which everyone must have who understands anything that is, is not a hypothesis.... Evidently then such a principle is the most certain of all; which

principle this is, let us proceed to say. It is, that the same attribute cannot at the same time belong and not belong to the same subject in the same respect." (*Atlas* 1167)

Danneskjöld is reading excerpts from the W. D. Ross translation of *Metaphysics* Γ.3, where Aristotle identifies the axiomatic status of the Principle of Non-Contradiction (PNC). Rand's decision to quote Aristotle in the closing scene of her magnum opus, and to select that quotation in particular, reveals a great deal both about her approach to philosophy and about her understanding of the relationship between her philosophy and Aristotle's.

Nor is this passage that novel's most obvious reference to the axioms of Aristotelian logic. *Atlas Shrugged* is divided into three parts, the titles of which are: "Non-Contradiction," "Either-Or," and "A Is A." As she acknowledged in the "About the Author" page at the end of the first edition: "[Aristotle's] definition of the laws of logic and of the means of human knowledge is so great an achievement that his errors are irrelevant by comparison" ("About the Author," *Atlas*).[1]

Although intended in part as an acknowledgment of Aristotle's achievement, these headings are also a key to the main themes of the novel's three parts. The first section is dominated by what appears to the two central characters in that part, Dagny Taggart and Hank Rearden, to be a contradiction[2]—those who have created America's greatest art, science, philosophy, and industry are abandoning it to its destroyers. At key moments they are challenged to question this apparent contradiction—on the grounds that, in reality, there are no contradictions. In the second section of the book a stark choice is revealed between two, diametrically opposed, philosophical approaches to the world, and it becomes increas-

---

1. It is important to note that in *Metaphysics* Γ Aristotle only discusses the Principles of Non-Contradiction and Excluded Middle. In an unpublished part of the Epistemology Workshops (Workshops 272), Rand, while answering a question about the relation of mathematical axioms to the Law of Identity, expresses her understanding of the relationship between it and these two principles: "I think the relationship is like between the law of identity and the other two laws of logic, which are only corollary restatements but they're restatements that are very valuable, epistemologically, as guidelines. But they in fact say the same thing" (see also Peikoff 1991, 119). I will return to the question of whether Aristotle recognizes, or comes close to recognizing, this point. But in *Atlas Shrugged*, Rand credits Aristotle with stating the Principle of Identity: "Centuries ago, the man who was—no matter what his errors—the greatest of your philosophers, has stated the formula defining the concept of existence and the rule of all knowledge: *A is A*. A thing is itself" (*Atlas* 1016).

2. Actually, many apparent contradictions. For an excellent discussion of them, see Ghate (2009, 2–19).

ingly clear that it is 'either-or.' Finally, in the last section, the culture dominated by one of those philosophical approaches is, as is inevitable, collapsing; and we are introduced to a hidden valley populated by people who live by the other philosophical approach and who are at peace with the Principle of Identity. Ragnar Danneskjöld is one of those people, and he is reading that passage from *Metaphysics* Γ while residing in that valley.

Ayn Rand thus pays tribute to Aristotle's identification and validation of fundamental axioms as a primary task of metaphysics, the science of being qua being, as one of his greatest philosophical achievements. Nevertheless, Ayn Rand's philosophical discussions of fundamental axioms are importantly different from Aristotle's. In the next two sections of this paper I will present their views on this topic somewhat independently, with respect to three distinct questions: (1) Reference: To what do axioms refer? (2) Function: What is their cognitive function? and (3) Validation: Can axioms be validated, and if so, how? In the third and fourth sections, I explore their similarities and differences on these three issues. Two conclusions will become clear in the process: first, Ayn Rand's position on this topic is fundamentally Aristotelian; and second, what is distinctive in her approach reflects distinctive and innovative features of her epistemology.

Aristotle on Axioms and Their Validation

It is implicit in the very first sentence of the *Posterior Analytics* that Aristotle's account of knowledge in the strict sense, *epistēmē haplōs*, will require some form of indemonstrable starting points. In the very first chapter he cites the Principle of Excluded Middle (PEM)—that "in every case either the affirmation or the denial is true" (*APo.* I.1 71a12–14)—as one such starting point. In chapter 2 he distinguishes two types of immediate starting points: posits and axioms. Of the latter, he notes that anyone who is to learn anything whatsoever must grasp (*echein*) them—and he feels it necessary to add, "for there are some things of this sort" (72a16–17).

The Unsatisfying Analytics *Answer*

These chapters make it clear, then, that there must be *indemonstrable* starting points of demonstration; the only validation for knowledge discussed in these chapters, however, is *demonstration*. How, then, are these indemonstrable starting points of demonstration to be validated? In *Analytics* I.3, Aristotle states this problem in the form of a dilemma: all scientific knowledge proceeds by demonstration; but demonstrations proceed from primitive and immediate starting points. Either our certainty about these rests on their being demonstrated, in which case they are not primitive and a regress looms (compare *Met.* Γ.4 1006a8–10); or it does not, in which case our alleged demonstrative knowledge rests on starting points that have not been justified (*APo.* I.3 72b8–12). Aristotle admits the validity of the challenge, but his only attempt at a reply here is to assert that there is "not only scientific knowledge (*epistēmē*) but a starting point (*archē*) of scientific knowledge as well, by which we come to know the definitions (*horoi*)" (72b23–25).³ The axioms, however, are *not* definitions, and so one might wonder about whether this starting point of knowledge (later identified as reason [*nous*; see *APo.* I.33 88b33–37, II.19 100b15]) is intended to be involved in grasping axioms as well as definitions. However one answers that question, the objection Aristotle is facing here is global and raises identical concerns regarding the validation of common axioms.⁴

Later in *Posterior Analytics* I.11, Aristotle discusses the logical axioms and to some extent clarifies their status. He argues that it is only in demonstrations of substitution instances of the PNC that the principle needs to be stated as a premise, and that it is only in the case of a *reductio* that it is necessary to posit PEM explicitly. PNC and PEM are not primarily *archai* in the sense of undemonstrated, primitive *premises* of demonstrations.⁵ Rather, they are presuppositions of demonstration itself. Syllogistic inference presupposes them; remove these starting points and anything (and therefore nothing) goes. But in neither chapter does Aristotle face the question of how we come to know these starting points of demonstration, nor what grounds we have for believing in them or in their axiom-

---

3. See also *Metaphysics* Γ.6 1011a12–13: "But as we said, this is what happens to them; for they search for an argument for things for which there is no argument. For the starting point of demonstration is not a demonstration."

4. The term *horos* here might have the sense it does at *Parts of Animals*: "for the enquiry into nature, too, there should be certain standards (*horoi*), such that by referring to them one can appraise the manner of its proofs, apart from the question of what the truth is" (*PA* I.1 639b13–16). The claim in *PA* I.1 is restricted to natural enquiry, but the characterization of the principles under consideration—standards by which to appraise the manner of proof, independently of considerations of the truth—also applies to PNC and PEM.

5. Some scholars such as Ross (1949, 531) and J. Lear (1980, 101–2) have made much of the terminological distinction between *ek* and *dia* at *APo.* I.11 76b10; but as Mignucci (1975, 141–43) and Barnes (1993, 139) have pointed out, Aristotle will use the preposition *ek* to discuss reasoning in accordance with the axioms and will even, rarely, refer to a common axiom as a *protasis* (premise). Less important than the terminology is the explicit claim of the *Analytics* that these axioms stand in a different relationship to demonstration than do, for example, the definitions and postulates of a science.

atic status.

Aristotle appears to address the problem of the validation of demonstrative starting points, including the logical axioms, in the final chapter (*APo.* II.19). The principles of both the crafts and the sciences, he explains, arise through a process that begins in perception and that involves the retention in memory of perceptions. Human beings have the ability to grasp something common ("whatever is present as one and the same in all of them") by means of comparing these many retained perceptions. We thus derive first level universals directly from perception: "for though one perceives the particular, perception is of the universal—of man, for instance, not of Callias the man" (*APo.* II.19 100a17–b1). Aristotle thus argues that "we come to know the primaries (*ta prōta*) by induction; for that is in fact how perception produces the universal in us" (100b4–6; *APr.* I.30, 46a17–27). The mental state that grasps the starting points of demonstration is, apparently, reason (*nous*), which is a starting point of scientific knowledge in a parallel sense to what it grasps being the starting point of demonstration, and induction is apparently its method.

Regrettably, Aristotle does not here distinguish among kinds of starting points, and the only example he gives in the relevant section of his chapter *APo.* II.19 describes a progression from the perception of particular entities such as individual men to a grasp of wider and wider universals (man, animal) under which they fall. The only reason to think that what is said here has any relevance to our grasp of common axioms such as PNC is the generality of Aristotle's conclusion. He appears to be providing an account of how, and by means of what cognitive faculty, we grasp *all* the starting points of demonstration.[6]

As far as I can see, this question is left without a satisfactory answer in the *Analytics*. This may be because Aristotle has an answer but recognizes it as a topic for another subject domain.[7] On the other hand, it may be (as Irwin tells it) that Aristotle realizes that the *Analytics* is, at least on this topic, a failed epistemological enterprise, and he takes a second shot at an answer, via "strong dialectic" in the *Metaphysics*.[8]

---

6. On the many different referents of *archē* in the *Analytics*, see Ferejohn 1991, 31–36; on *APo.* II.19 as providing the ultimate "justification" for PNC, see Bolton (1994, 351–54); against which see Irwin (1988, 179–98).

7. There is a hint in this direction in the *Analytics*: "And dialectic associates with all the sciences; and so would any [science] which attempted to give universal proofs of the common [axioms] (e.g. that everything is either asserted or denied, or that equals from equals leave equals, or any other [common axioms] of this sort)" (*APo.* I.11 77a29–31). Since this hypothetical discipline is being contrasted with dialectic, it cannot be dialectic that he has in mind.

8. See Irwin 1988, chs. 7–8. *APo.* I.11 also has hints pointing in this direction.

The More Satisfying Metaphysics Γ Answer

The Question of Reference

From the opening chapters of *Metaphysics* A, Aristotle is sending signals that he is on a quest for a new kind of science.[9] And the second puzzle (*aporia*) raised for consideration of this new kind of science in *Metaphysics* B is "whether it is for this science only to contemplate the first principles (*tas archas tas prōtas*) of substantial being (*tēs ousias*), or *also* [for it] to be concerned with the principles on the basis of which everyone proves, e.g. whether it is possible to assert and deny one and the same thing simultaneously or not, and about other such things" (*Met.* B.1 995b7–11). And when he takes up this puzzle for investigation at 996b27, he is explicit about these principles of proof: "I mean by demonstrative [principles] those common beliefs from which all [sciences] prove, e.g. that in all cases it is necessary either to assert or deny, and that it is impossible that something both be and not be simultaneously, and any other such premises: Is there a single science of these and of substantial being, or is there a different science [for each]; and if there is not a single science of both, which ought to be designated the one we are now seeking?" (*Met.* B.2 996b28–33). Why, one might ask, would this question even occur to Aristotle? Why would a science that investigates substantial being also investigate the sorts of postulates that mathematicians refer to as axioms?

It is an odd question for anyone inclined to see statements like the PNC as "laws of logic" or "laws of thought." But let us put this question into Aristotle's context. Parmenides (as quoted in Plato's *Sophist*, 237a, 258d) had proclaimed "Never will this prevail, that what is not is—bar your thought from that road of inquiry"—and drew from that proclamation the implication that the world of change familiar to us by perception must be illusory. Under the influence of Parmenides, Plato, in the *Republic*, has Socrates describe perceptible objects as "dualizing," neither "being" nor "not-being" (*Republic* V 479c3–4, 478e1–5), and draws from this the conclusion that such things cannot be objects of knowledge.

The philosophical world into which Aristotle enters when he joins the Academy is a world locked in a long-standing debate about appearance and reality, to which Aristotle proposes a radical solution. He insists that the senses provide us a direct awareness of being, and in so doing he

---

9. See also *Met.* A.2 982a5, b4, b8, 983a5, a21; *Met.* B.1 995a24, 2 996b3; and Broadie 2012, 51–55.

rejects the consensus epistemology of "appearance versus reality," a consensus for which his teacher Plato had become the most powerful exponent. When Aristotle opens his *Metaphysics* citing the delight humans take in their sensory awareness as evidence for his claim that all men by nature desire to know, he is striking out in a new direction. In his opening chapter he describes a continuous path to scientific knowledge that begins with perceptual awareness of particular substantial beings, a form of awareness we share with many other animals and which gives us the most accurate knowledge of particulars.

But scientific knowledge depends on demonstration, and demonstration depends on indemonstrable first principles. Many of those will take the form of basic concepts and their definitions, of course; but the very practice of demonstration presupposes that the propositions that make up their premises take one—*and only one*—side of a contradiction.[10] It cannot be the case that swimming simultaneously both belongs and does not belong to whales, or that 2R simultaneously belongs and does not belong to triangles.

In the first three (or four) books of our *Metaphysics*, I suggest, Aristotle is striving to distinguish inquiry into these sorts of issues, a special kind of wisdom that is primary over others because the "special sciences" presuppose it—in his terms, primary philosophy.[11] And he thus sees a defense of these axioms as part of an inquiry into the fundamental nature of reality—that is, as a proper subject for the science of being qua being.

But why would this science be the same science that investigates substantial being? After a long consideration of the fourteen puzzles (*aporiai*) about the subject at hand in *Met.* B, Aristotle opens *Met.* Γ by boldly asserting his answer to the previous book's first puzzle. "There is a science that studies being qua being and those things that belong to it in virtue of what it is" (*Met.* Γ.1 1003a21–22). He explains that it is a science not by virtue of there being a single genus that it investigates, but because there is a

10. "A proposition is one part of a contradictory pair, one thing said of one thing. It is dialectical if it assumes either part indifferently and demonstrative if it determinately assumes one part because it is true. A statement is one part of a contradictory pair. A contradictory pair is a pair between which, in their own right, there is nothing. The part of a contradictory pair which says something of something is an affirmation; the part which takes something from something is a negation" (Barnes translation, slightly modified, *APo.* I.2 72a8–14). There are a number of textual and interpretive issues raised by this passage that are not important here; on which see Barnes 1993, 98–99. There is important background to the distinctions drawn in this passage at *De Interpretation* 6–9.

11. For more detail on this topic, see the essays on *Met.* A.1 (by Cambiano) and *Met.* A.2 (by Broadie) in Steel (2012, 1–67).

primary category of being, substantial being (*ousia*), in relation to which everything else is said to be. One who studies being qua being, then, will focus primarily on the principles and causes of substantial being (*ousia*) (*Met.* Γ.2 1003a33–b23).[12] An interesting question to explore (on another occasion) is exactly what the relationship is between these principles and causes and the most secure truths that Aristotle refers to as common axioms. But this much is clear: an investigation into the topic of whether a being can simultaneously be and not be what it is, and into the principles and causes of substantial being are, in the context of fifth–fourth century Greek philosophy, intimately related investigations.

Metaphysics Γ.3 opens by reminding us of the *second* puzzle of *Met.* B: is it for one and the same science to discuss both substantial being and what the mathematicians call axioms, or are these two topics for two different sciences?[13] The answer, Aristotle claims, is now "apparent": "It is apparent that the investigation of these [*common axioms*] is also for a single science, that is, the science of the philosopher; for they belong to all beings and not to some distinct kind separate from others" (*Met.* Γ.3 1005a21–23).[14] And though he is now clear on this not being an appropriate subject for *Analytics*, he reiterates what he has asserted about the common axioms in *APo.* I.1–2: these principles are the most secure of all, they are non-hypothetical, and the student of any subject at all must come to his subject already knowing these principles (*Met.* Γ.3 1005b5–6, b13–17).

Finally, at *Metaphysics* Γ.3, 1005b18ff., the passage that Ragnar Danneskjöld is reading near the close of *Atlas Shrugged*, Aristotle gets around to identifying the most secure of axioms: "It is impossible for the same thing to belong and not belong to the same thing at the same time and in the same respect (and let as many other determinations as need to be

---

12. This topic is explored in more detail in Rheins's chapter, "The Subject of Ontology: Aristotle on the Focally Related Meanings of 'Being' and the Univocity of Rand's Axiomatic Concept of 'Existence,'" Chapter 3, below. See also *Met.* Z.1 1028b2–7: "Indeed, the question that was, is, and always will be asked and always will be puzzling, 'What is being?' (*ti to on*) is this question: 'What is substantial being?' (*tis tēs ousias*). For it is this that some say to be one and others more than one, and some say is limited and others unlimited; wherefore the greatest, first and essentially only thing for us to study is what is being in this sense."

13. For reasons of space I am omitting discussion of *Metaphysics* Γ.2, though when read against the backdrop of Plato's discussion of *megista genē* in the *Sophist*, it is of direct relevance to our topic.

14. See also *Met.* Γ.3 1005a27–29: "So since it is clear that they belong to all things qua being (for this is common to them), the study of these things too is for the one acquiring knowledge of being qua being."

added to deal with dialectical objections)" (*Met.* Γ.3 1005b19–21). The PNC (his focus in chs. 3–6) and the PEM (discussed in ch. 7) are universally applicable *because*:

- They "belong to all beings" (*Met.* Γ.3 1005a23)—that is, they identify facts true of all being
- They are used by everyone "because they are of being qua being, and each kind is a being" (1005a24–25)
- They are thus to be studied by the investigator of being qua being "because they belong to all things qua being" (1005a27–28)

Aristotle's fundamental argument for these axioms being investigated by the first philosopher is, then, not epistemic or logical but *metaphysical*. They are truths about all beings, just in so far as they are beings.

Thus, on the Reference Question, Aristotle and Rand agree: the common axioms are not conventions nor do they refer primarily to laws of thought: they identify fundamental aspects of reality, undeniable truths about being qua being.

The Question of Function

One of Aristotle's key tasks in *Metaphysics* Γ.3 is to identify five *epistemic properties* of PNC as a basic truth about being qua being:

1. It is the most firm, secure, or certain (*bebaiotatē*) of all starting points: (1005b10–12; see also 1005b17, 1011b13–15).
2. It is a principle about which it is impossible to be deceived (1005b13).
3. It is best known and non-hypothetical (1005b13–15).
4. It is a truth one must possess to understand anything about things that are (1005b15–18; recall *APo*. I.2 72a16–17).
5. And finally: "it is by its very nature an origin of all the other axioms" (*Met.* Γ.3 1005b33–34; likely he is thinking of mathematics).

That is, he aims to establish that the PNC provides the firmest possible foundation for reasoning of any kind—that is its function. But in order to play this role we have to be certain that it is best known and most secure; and common axioms have a distinctive problem in this respect, which is that all proof depends on them. They cannot be secured by demonstration.

Aristotle has provided, then, an explicit identification of a fundamental truth about being that all of us know implicitly, and he has made a number of second order or philosophical claims about its *epistemic func-*

tion as the most firm and certain foundation of knowledge. In the following chapter he appears to face up to the problem that was left unresolved in the *Posterior Analytics*: its validation.

The Question of Validation

In *Metaphysics* Γ.3 Aristotle so far has given us (1) explicit identification of a fundamental truth about being that all investigators know implicitly, and (2) assertions about its epistemic function as the most firm and certain foundation of knowledge. What he has not done is deal with the issue he left unresolved in the *Analytics*. Since it would be self-contradictory to expect demonstration of the indemonstrable starting points of demonstration, how are these starting points to be justified?

Telling his readers that they could not identify any principle as more worthy of being indemonstrable than PNC (*Met.* Γ.3 1006a11–12) is not in any sense a form of justification. Aristotle reminds us, however, that it shows a "lack of education" to expect there to be demonstration of everything, especially this most secure of all starting points. "Generally speaking, it is impossible for there to be demonstration of everything; for this would proceed to infinity, so in proceeding this way there would be no demonstration."[15] If, however, one ought not to seek a demonstration of certain things, they could not say which principle they deem to be more worthy of being such [i.e., indemonstrable]" (1006a7–12). But in *Metaphysics* Γ.4, after asserting this, he says something surprising: "It is possible to demonstrate in an elenctic manner (*apodeixai elenctikōs*) even about this [denying PNC] that it is impossible, if only the disputant says something" (1006a13–14).

To give an elenctic demonstration is to demonstrate by way of refutation. The practice is discussed in some detail in the work known as *Sophistical Refutations*, a discussion outlined with admirable clarity by Robert Bolton in his 1994 paper "Aristotle's Conception of Metaphysics as a Science." Bolton has shown convincingly that Aristotle is here using, in a very careful and precise way, the technique that is characterized as a form of *peirastic dialectic* in the *Sophistical Refutations*. Aristotle is not, in that case, out to prove any positive thesis. Indeed, from everything he says it is clear he thinks no proof of basic axioms is necessary or possible. Rather, the goal of chapter 4 is to provide a demonstrative refutation of

---

15. This is, of course, one of the objections to his account of scientific knowledge that he outlines at *APo.* I.3 72b8–16; it is just this objection that requires that there be a non-demonstrative way of knowing first principles, the issue he faces in *APo.* II.19.

PNC-deniers, those who state that it is possible for the same attribute to belong and not to belong to the same thing at the same time and in the same respect. It is a *dialectical* refutation in the sense that the opponent must say something and agree that it signifies one thing. If this minimal requirement is not fulfilled, one might as well be debating a begonia.[16] Nevertheless it is clear, upon reflection, that the refutation works only because it can be shown that, by committing to rational debate of the sort for which Aristotle's *Topics* provides "rules of engagement," the disputant has tacitly accepted what he claims to be denying—namely, PNC.

This reflection on what the parties to rational debate must tacitly accept—for which Alan Code has coined the apt term "meta-elenchus" (1987, 145)—takes up a good deal of the chapter, in fact. In this way we don't produce a question begging demonstration, but rather, since the PNC-denier is responsible for starting the discussion, we produce a refutation. It is a dialectical practice, and therefore (as its name implies) depends on an opponent making a statement that is capable of being refuted. In this case, however, the opponent need not say much! The only requirement is that he says something significant and that it signify one thing.[17] It will not be necessary for my purposes to go through the argument in detail. Bolton (1994, 334–35) lays out the argument in nine steps; Montgomery Furth (1986, commenting on Code 1986), provides an eight-step version. The argument operates via a denial of a "substitution instance" of PNC and forces the opponent to the conclusion that "it is not possible that the same thing at the same time is a man and not a man" (*Met.* Γ.4 1006b33–34). It is not, therefore, proving the truth of PNC but, rather, refuting its denial by using the techniques developed for doing so and relying on concessions made by the PNC-denier. As Aristotle puts it at one point: "While disowning reason, [the denier] submits to reason" (1006a26).[18] The technique draws out the implications of the disputant making a definite claim about a definite object.[19]

---

16. In *Metaphysics* Γ.5, Cratylus is reported to have decided "he ought to say nothing, and merely moved his finger" (1010a10–13). Apparently before reaching that decision, he stated that Heraclitus's claim that it is not possible to step into the same river twice was mistaken, since it is not possible to do so even once (a13–15).

17. For the detailed ways in which Aristotle here follows the strictures of proof by refutation discussed in *Sophistical Refutations*, see Bolton 1994, 335–36. As one example, Aristotle acknowledges that it would be illegitimate to insist that our opponent say that something either is or is not the case, since that would be a case of begging the question.

18. And see Lear (1980, 103–4).

19. This way of understanding the argument goes back at least to Alexander of Aphrodesias in his commentary on Aristotle *Metaphysics* (Hayduck, ed., 1891, 265.1–267.7); and

The method of validation that is developed in these chapters is redeployed for the Principle of Excluded Middle in chapters 7 and 8. In both cases, the validation of these principles is accomplished by showing that any attempt to articulate a denial of them is self-refuting.

The nature of this demonstration by refutation raises an interesting question about the intended audience of this text—and a passage in chapter 5 is helpful in thinking about that question. The context is a question addressed while discussing the consequences of Protagorean relativism. Aristotle distinguishes between the strategies to be used in arguing with two different sorts of opponent. "But the same mode of argument is not applicable to all; for some need persuasion and some need compulsion. For the ignorance of those who have accepted these ideas out of perplexity is easily remedied; for with them the reply is directed not to a stated position (*logos*) but to reasoning.[20] But the remedy for those who speak for the sake of a stated position is a refutation (*elenchos*) in terms of their statement and their words" (*Met.* Γ.5 1009a16–22).

Demonstration by refutation is not to be used against those who, by drawing faulty conclusions from puzzles about perception, conclude that things can be A and not-A at the same time. Much of Aristotle's chapters 5 and 6 is devoted to resolving such perplexities. Demonstration by refutation is to be used to force those who begin by denying PNC to conclude that their own *logos* commits them to it. In this way you establish its axiomatic status as the firmest of all starting points of demonstration.

But is this a genuine form of non-demonstrative validation for the principles?[21] No: it is an instance of what is sometimes referred to as reaffirmation through denial: any attempt to deny PNC or PEM must, in the end, affirm them. It establishes that PNC is axiomatic. As John Galt puts the point in *Atlas Shrugged*: "An axiom is a proposition that defeats its opponents by the fact that they have to accept it and use it in the process of any attempt to deny it" (*Atlas* 1040). That passage from Galt's speech will serve as a fitting segue into a discussion of Ayn Rand on axioms. We

---

is developed in Code (1986, 1987). A very different understanding of the argument and its relationship to that of *Posterior Analytics* can be found in Irwin (1988a, 179–98). Irwin's position is among the targets of Bolton (1994). Some interesting objections to Code 1986 can be found in Cohen 1986.

20. Out of context, of course, *logos* can mean many things; but here the context is elenctic disputation, for which one forces an opponent to take up a stated position on a topic.

21. I'm using the term "validation" in a way that has become standard in Objectivist literature. See Peikoff 1991, 8, quoted in my discussion of Rand on the question of validation, below.

will return to the question of validation when we compare the treatment of axioms in Aristotle and Rand, in the third section of this paper.[22]

Ayn Rand on Axiomatic Concepts

In notes in a philosophical notebook dated May 15, 1934, written when she was twenty-nine years old, Ayn Rand was reacting to José Ortega y Gasset's *The Revolt of the Masses*.[23] Very quickly—in a matter of two pages—her reactions move to broader questions of philosophical method, and specifically to questions of how to understand the relationship of philosophical abstractions to concretes. She complains about philosophers acting like mathematicians who are doing algebra as if they had forgotten its relationship to arithmetic—an interesting analogy in light of her theory of concepts, developed much later, in which she describes (proper) conceptual awareness as "the algebra of cognition" (*ITOE* 18). She pauses to reflect on these notes and expresses a sort of dissatisfaction with them but sees the importance of axioms for any area of knowledge, including philosophy: "[W]hat will [ultimately] come out of this is an arrangement of the whole in a logical system, proceeding from a few axioms in a succession of logical theorems. The axioms will be necessary—even mathematics has them—[because] you can't build something on nothing. The end result will be my 'Mathematics of Philosophy'" (*Journals* 72).

Taken out of context, these words have an almost Spinozistic ring. However, the context is critical—in these notes, Rand is expressing concerns about philosophers who act as if abstractions have no connection to the world of concrete particulars, what she would later refer to as "floating abstractions." To avoid this, the axioms she has in mind will need to be grounded in perception in some way. What is most important here, given her later understanding of axioms, is the early recognition of the epistemological necessity of axioms: you cannot build something on nothing; philosophy, like mathematics, needs an axiomatic foundation.

---

22. In anticipation of the discussion in section 4, the question of the validation of axioms in Ayn Rand, I remind the reader that Aristotle repeats a number of times that we come to know either by induction or by demonstration (*APo.* I.18ff., *APr.* II.23 68b13–14), and that we come to know first principles by induction (*APo.* II.19 100a4–5, *APr.* II.24 68b30–37). No exception is ever suggested for PNC or PEM. Since coming to know them by demonstration is explicitly ruled out, it would seem to commit Aristotle to the view that we come to know metaphysical axioms by induction—but he never explicitly says this, let alone explains how this would work.

23. The material I am using can be found in *Journals of Ayn Rand*, ed. David Harriman. The entirety of her journals are in the Archives at the Ayn Rand Institute.

At this stage of her philosophical development, however, she seems pulled in competing directions for that foundation. On the one hand, she rejects philosophical abstractions that cannot be shown to be based on and applicable to the concretes given to us in perception.[24] On the other hand, she sees that her model of logically ordered knowledge, mathematics, is based on highly abstract axioms upon which its proofs depend. The philosophical account of axioms presented in *Introduction to Objectivist Epistemology*, as we will see, integrates these two apparently conflicting insights.

The Question of Reference

She begins the *Introduction to Objectivist Epistemology* (*ITOE*), published initially in 1966 as a series of articles and then as a monograph, by declaring that "the issue of concepts . . . is philosophy's central issue." In the same paragraph she translates her early concern about the relation of abstractions to concretes into a question about concepts: "concepts are abstractions or universals, and everything that man perceives is particular, concrete. What is the relationship between abstractions and concretes? To what precisely do concepts refer in reality?" (*ITOE* 1). Concepts are abstractions; they refer to an unlimited number of similar entities or attributes.

Reality, however, consists of concrete particulars—the question of the connection of abstractions to concretes is translated into a question about conceptual reference. This starting point has two consequences for her view of axioms. First, in *ITOE* she presents a theory of concepts, and in that context she devotes a chapter to what she refers to as "axiomatic concepts" (*ITOE* 55–61). Second, a central concern in that chapter is to show how these concepts, the most abstract of all concepts, are related to the perceptually given. The primary axiomatic concepts are existence, identity and consciousness.[25] Their axiomatic status derives from their referents. "The units of the concepts 'existence' and 'identity' are every entity, attribute, action, event or phenomenon (including consciousness) that ex-

---

24. Using an extended metaphor that runs through this entry, where philosophical abstractions are thought of as algebraic and concretes as arithmetic, she worries that "in the field of philosophy today there is this tendency of considering the algebraic formula as final, and therefore philosophy has no practical significance or application" (Journals 71–72).

25. Looking forward to our comparison of Rand's conception of axioms with Aristotle's: two of these concepts (existence and identity) have a clear relationship to two concepts that are central to Aristotle's metaphysics—(1) 'being' and (2) 'what it is to be' or 'essence.' One of them, however (consciousness), does not. Its inclusion is of great historical significance and is the key to a number of Rand's philosophical innovations.

ists, has ever existed or will ever exist. The units of the concept 'consciousness' are every state or process of awareness that one experiences, has ever experienced or will ever experience" (56). To regard entities as "units" in Rand's sense is to focus on one or more of their attributes, to isolate them in virtue of how they are different from other entities, and then to integrate them in virtue of their similarities with respect to the attributes in focus. "*The ability to regard entities as units is man's distinctive method of cognition, which other species are unable to follow*" (6; italics in original).

Axiomatic concepts identify aspects of reality implicit in all knowledge—facts that are fundamentally given and directly perceived (*ITOE* 55). One can unpack these concepts in propositional form only by way of repetition: What is, *is*; it is *what it is*; and consciousness is the awareness of and the means of *identifying* what is. These most fundamental of all truths are incapable of proof, for all proof rests on them. Any attempt to establish them by a proof, Rand argues, would be self-contradictory (55). What one *can* prove is precisely that they are axiomatic, by showing that they are presupposed, even in attempts to deny them. On this point she and Aristotle are in complete agreement.

Their axiomatic status, then, derives from the aspects of reality they identify being self-evident in perception. But if their content is perceptually given, why are these concepts so abstract? This is, perhaps, their most puzzling feature. "Their peculiarity lies in the fact that they are perceived or experienced directly, but grasped conceptually. They are implicit in every state of awareness, from the first sensation to the first percept to the sum of all concepts. . . . [t]hese facts are contained in any single state of awareness; but what is added by subsequent knowledge is the epistemological need to identify them consciously and self-consciously" (*ITOE* 55–56).[26] Prior to the explicit formation of axiomatic concepts, Rand argues, they are implicit in every act of awareness. Underscoring their importance, this is a point she makes on the first page of the first chapter of *ITOE*:

> The building-block of man's knowledge is the concept of an "*existent*"—of something that exists, be it a thing, an attribute or an action. Since it is a concept, man cannot grasp it *explicitly* until he has reached the conceptual stage. But it is implicit in every percept (to perceive a thing is to perceive that it exists) and man grasps it implicitly on the perceptual level—i.e., he grasps the constituents of the concept "existent," the data which

26. This is her answer to the concerns she expressed in her philosophical notebook dated May 15, 1934. See *Journals*, 70–73.

are later to be integrated by that concept. It is this implicit knowledge that permits his consciousness to develop further. (5–6)[27]

The above description of the units of these concepts poses a prima facie problem, given the theory of concept-formation presented in the following chapters. For this theory argues that concepts are formed by integrating their referents through a process that crucially depends on differentiating those units from the units of other concepts that share a "conceptual common denominator" with them.[28] For example, one forms the concept "plate" by differentiating plates from other sorts of tableware (bowls, cups, saucers, etc.), according to their distinctive range of commensurable features of shape and function, and then integrating the plate-units into a single concept by omitting the measurable differences among them. Axiomatic concepts, however, cannot be formed by such a process. Rand faces this issue directly in *ITOE*, in the chapter devoted to axiomatic concepts. "Since axiomatic concepts are not formed by differentiating one group of existents from others, but represent an integration of all existents, they have no Conceptual Common Denominator with anything else. They have no contraries, no alternatives" (*ITOE* 58). What, then, is the nature of the distinctive cognitive process involved in explicitly grasping axiomatic concepts? The full answer to that question has two aspects. Part of the answer has to do with the peculiar nature of the abstraction involved in their case: "It [the abstraction involved in forming axiomatic concepts] is not the abstraction of an attribute from a group of existents, but of a basic fact from all facts. Existence and identity are *not attributes* of existents, they *are* the existents. Consciousness is an attribute of certain living entities, but it is not an attribute of a given state of awareness, it *is* that state" (56). From an epistemological standpoint, as

---

27. On the relationship between the concepts "existent" and "existence," see *ITOE* appendix, 241. The following personal anecdote may be of help in concretizing this move from implicit to explicit conceptual identification of axioms. I was driving my five-year-old daughter to kindergarten and (it began as a game) she said something like "a tree is a tree," to which I responded "and a car is a car," to which she replied "and a house is a house." After another minute or so of this, she paused—and then said, with a big smile on her face, "and everything is just what it is." At which point I realized that, for my daughter, the Principle of Identity had just gone from implicit to explicit status.

28. "Observe the multiple role of measurements in the process of concept-formation, in both of its two essential parts: differentiation and integration. Concepts cannot be formed at random. All concepts are formed by first differentiating two or more existents from other existents. All conceptual differentiations are made in terms of commensurable characteristics (i.e., characteristics possessing a common unit of measurement)" (*ITOE* 13).

she goes on to stress, the process of abstraction in the case of axiomatic concepts involves selective focus on metaphysical fundamentals. To conceptualize "existence" and "identity" (which Rand considers corollaries) is an act of abstraction because it requires a selective focus, not on an entity's size, color, shape, behavior, and so on, but on the fact that any object of awareness *is*, and is something *specific*.[29] "Consciousness" does not refer to a fundamental feature of "beings qua being"—it refers to a feature of a restricted class of beings. It is, however, equally fundamental to *knowledge*. Axiomatic concepts, then, refer to aspects of reality qua fundamental to every act of knowing. Their axiomatic status derives from the fact that the aspects of reality they identify are implicit in every act of awareness.

There is, moreover, an act of measurement-omission involved in the formation of axiomatic concepts. "The measurements omitted from axiomatic concepts are all the measurements of all the existents they subsume; what is retained, metaphysically, is only a fundamental fact; what is retained, epistemologically, is only one category of measurement, omitting its particulars: *time*—i.e., the fundamental fact is retained independent of any particular moment of awareness" (*ITOE* 56). In the discussions of this chapter in the Epistemology Workshops transcripts, selected portions of which are provided as an appendix to *ITOE*, one of the participants pressed Rand to elaborate on the distinction being made here between what is retained metaphysically and epistemologically. Her reply is helpful; it relates both to the topic of the referents of axiomatic concepts and to what Rand would characterize as their psychological and epistemological functions. That aspect of her reply will be taken up in the next section below. At this point, here is the relevant part of her response: "What I mean here by 'metaphysically' is: in reality, in existence—that is, focusing on the entities subsumed under the concept. By 'epistemologically' here I mean psychologically. In the process of cognition, what type of measurement do you retain when you deal with a concept that includes every existent?" (*ITOE* 256). In the process of forming an abstraction, as Rand understands it, one omits the exact measurements of the attribute in question but retains the category of measurement—for example, in forming the concept "length," one omits the different lengths of whatever objects one is comparing in forming the concept (pencils, rulers, fingers,

---

29. Why it is important to attend to those aspects of what one is aware of is the topic of the next section.

legs) but retains that attribute.[30] But what is of especial interest in the case of axiomatic concepts is the distinction between two different categories of what is retained in forming them: metaphysically, what is retained is simply the fact that the object of awareness *is* (something *specific*); epistemologically, what is retained is the category time. In order to delve into why Rand distinguishes these two aspects of abstraction and why, in particular, it is *temporal* measurements that are omitted psychologically, we need to turn to Rand's understanding of the function(s) of axiomatic concepts.

The Question of Function(s)

Early in the presentation of her account of concept-formation, Rand argues that *implicit* knowledge of these concepts—that is, awareness of the data that will later be integrated into these concepts—suffices for human beings to develop cognitively to the conceptual level (*ITOE* 6). Why, then, do we need to form these concepts at all—why must we make that knowledge explicit? Conveniently, for my purposes, Rand introduces the question of why it is important to identify axioms in conceptual terms immediately after summarizing their distinctive referential status: "Their peculiarity lies in the fact that they are perceived or experienced directly, but grasped conceptually. They are implicit in every state of awareness, from the first sensation to the first percept to the sum of all concepts. . . . [T]hese facts are contained in any single state of awareness; but what is added by subsequent knowledge is *the epistemological need* to identify them consciously and self-consciously" (55–56; emphasis added).

Before we explore the question of why subsequent knowledge creates an epistemological need to grasp the axiomatic concepts explicitly, I want to draw attention to a distinctive feature of Ayn Rand's philosophical method operative in this passage. Rather than assuming that explicit conceptual recognition of axioms is of value, she first asks, and then answers, the question "Why is explicit recognition of axioms necessary?" So too in her metaethics, her starting point is the question of whether human beings need a code of values—that is, an explicitly codified morality: "Let me stress this. The first question is not: What particular code of values should man accept? The first question is: *Does man need* values at

---

30. Rand spells out the process as she conceives it by imagining someone describing the process as they are experiencing it: "Length must exist in *some* quantity, but may exist in *any* quantity. I shall identify as 'length' that attribute of any existent possessing it which can be quantitatively related to a unit of length, without specifying the quantity" (*ITOE* 11).

all—and why?" (*VOS* 2). So then: what epistemological values are served by the identification of these fundamental facts in conceptual terms? In the Epistemology Workshops, one of the participants identified three functions of axiomatic concepts that he had concluded were identified by Rand in the chapter dealing with axiomatic concepts: "The first is the continuity function; the second is objectivity, in the sense of focusing on the distinction between existence and consciousness and on the independence of existence. And the third is the underscoring of primary facts" (*ITOE* 260–61). Rand agrees with this list, eventually adding a fourth function. Let's consider them, then, in order.

1. When asked by Rand to repeat the list, the first function is fleshed out by the questioner as "[e]nabling human consciousness to preserve continuity, the idea of continuity of existence and consciousness—the issue of psychological time-measurements" (*ITOE* 261).

This notion of "psychological time measurements" is briefly mentioned earlier (*ITOE* 56–57). Percepts are, she stresses, time-indexed—tied to a moment in time. One aspect of forming every concept, regardless of its referents, is ignoring the time stamp of the percepts that serve as the database for concept-formation. The concept "plate" refers to past, present, and future plates—it is not tied to the particular plates that served as the observational basis on which the concept was first formed. "It is only conceptual awareness that can grasp and hold the total of its experience—extrospectively, the continuity of existence; introspectively, the continuity of consciousness—and thus enable its possessor to project his course long-range. It is by means of axiomatic concepts that man grasps and holds this continuity, bringing it into his conscious awareness and knowledge" (*ITOE* 57).

The stress in this passage is on what the questioner referred to as the "continuity function." Notice, however, that there are two aspects to this continuity. Earlier, these aspects were identified as "metaphysical" and "epistemological." Here it is characterized in terms of whether the focus is on the continuity of *existence* (extrospection) or of *conscious experience* (introspection). Axiomatic concepts explicitly bring this continuity into focus. But in what respect does the formation of these concepts involve the retention of the category "time" while omitting its measurements—the "omission of psychological time measurements," as she puts it? And what role does that temporal aspect of forming these concepts play in underscoring the continuity of reality and of our awareness of reality?

To answer that we need to return to her response to the suggestion that axiomatic concepts serve a threefold function. "[A]xiomatic concepts have a wider function. Time is involved in them epistemologically or psychologically in a more important manner: they have to be held in your consciousness at all times. . . . [I]n all future processes of cognition the axiomatic concepts are directing that process. You cannot form another concept or utter a proposition without regard for your axiomatic concepts, once they have been consciously identified. They function implicitly up to the time of identification. Thereafter, they have to be explicit; they have to be automatized psychologically" (*ITOE* 257). Hold on to that point about the axiomatic concepts "directing that process"—we will return to that. Here I want to spotlight what this passage tells us about the continuity function of axioms—that they serve as constant reminders of what is implicit in all of our conceptual activity; the integration of past, present, and future, allowing us to project our thought into the future and into the past.

2. The second function of these concepts is as guardians of objectivity, as crucial reminders of the critical distinction that guarantees the possibility of objective knowledge—the distinction between consciousness and its object. "It is axiomatic concepts that identify the precondition of knowledge: the distinction between existence and consciousness, between reality and the awareness of reality, between the object and the subject of cognition. Axiomatic concepts are the foundation of objectivity" (*ITOE* 57). One of Ayn Rand's innovations regarding axioms, not found elsewhere in the Aristotelian tradition, is the inclusion of "consciousness" as an axiomatic concept, and of the priority of existence to consciousness, of the object of awareness to the awareness. Consciousness is epistemologically active, but metaphysically passive.[31] The first sentence of chapter 1 of *ITOE* states that "[c]onsciousness, as a state of awareness, is not a passive state, but an active process that consists of two essentials: differentiation and integration" (5; also 29, 81). But it is an awareness of what exists—it is an active process of *knowing* what is, not of *constituting* what is. The distinction between what is and our awareness of what is—and of the primacy of the latter in relationship to the former—is made explicit in her formulation of these axioms: existence is identity, consciousness is identification. They are the basis of one's commitment to objectivity.

3. The third role for axioms identified by the Workshop participant is

---

31. Rand never committed this formulation to writing, but Leonard Peikoff claimed that he owed this expression to her.

that of a standard and base for certainty, a reminder that every concept, in order to be cognitively useful, must be grounded in the awareness of what is, in fact. "[A]lthough they designate a fundamental metaphysical fact, axiomatic concepts are the products of an epistemological need—the need of a volitional, conceptual consciousness which is capable of error and doubt.... It is only man's consciousness, a consciousness capable of conceptual errors, that needs a special identification of the directly given" (*ITOE* 58). The axiomatic concepts, and the axioms at the base of both inductive and deductive reasoning, are reminders that we must check the products of our reasoning to ensure they are in tune with reality and do not harbor contradictions and inconsistencies. This becomes especially crucial as our knowledge becomes more abstract—further from perception, as Aristotle often puts it. Mistakes are easier to make and harder to detect as our conceptual knowledge grows, making the explicit identification of these concepts a critical epistemic need.

Rand agrees that all these functions are important but emphasizes the third, which she characterizes as "the confining of knowledge to reality, to existence, and delimiting it from nonexistence, imagination, falsehood, etc." She then concludes: "I would add one more that is also closely related, so it might be a restatement, but it is an important restatement: epistemological guidance" (*ITOE* 261). Earlier, we can now recall, she noted in passing that once, these concepts are formed, "in all future processes of cognition the axiomatic concepts are *directing* that process" (257, emphasis added). If one thinks about active, volitional, rational inquiry, the following brief remark about "the essence of ... human cognition" is a clear statement of the way these concepts serve this guiding and directing function. "They [the axiomatic concepts] sum up the essence of all human cognition: something *exists* of which I am *conscious*; I must discover its *identity*" (59).[32]

The Question of Validation

Objectivism distinguishes validation from proof: "'Validation' I take to be a broader term than 'proof,' one that subsumes any process of establishing an idea's relationship to reality, whether deductive reasoning, inductive reasoning, or perceptual self-evidence. In this sense, one can and

---

32. Notice that this statement mirrors Aristotle's distinction between a stage of inquiry where we seek to establish *that* something exists from a later stage of inquiry where we seek to establish *what it is* as the basis for explaining *why* it has the attributes that it does and behaves or changes as it does (*APo*. II.1, 2, 8, 10). For more on the epistemological functions of axioms, see Rheins 2016, 250–51, 257–60.

must validate every item of knowledge, including axioms. The validation of axioms, however, is the simplest of all: sense perception" (Peikoff 1991, 8).[33] Rand agrees with Aristotle that axioms cannot be directly proven, and a number of times she endorses the idea that lies behind the elenctic form of demonstration in *Metaphysics* Γ.4—that is, reaffirmation through denial.[34] As I noted while discussing the question of validation in Aristotle earlier, beyond reaffirmation through denial Aristotle says nothing explicit about validating PNC or PEM—however, he does explicitly claim that we know first principles through induction, and he does not make any exceptions for his metaphysical axioms.

Rand, however, has a theory of how axiomatic concepts (and thus axioms) are validated—the factual content of axiomatic concepts is perceptually self-evident, implicit in every act of perceptual awareness.

> One knows that axioms are true not by inference of any kind, but by sense perception. When one perceives a tomato, for example, there is no evidence that it exists, beyond the fact that one perceives it; there is no evidence that it is something, beyond the fact that one perceives it; and there is no evidence that one is aware, beyond the fact that one is perceiving it. Axioms are perceptual self-evidencies. There is nothing to be said in their behalf except: look at reality. . . . What philosophy does is to give an abstract statement of such self-evident facts. (Peikoff 1991, 8)

While, as we have seen, it is of fundamental importance for human beings to formulate axiomatic concepts explicitly, their factual basis is given in every act of awareness. Thus, while metaphysical axioms are not subject to proof, their axiomatic status can be proved by showing that any attempt to deny them depends on them—and their truth is validated perceptually.

Ayn Rand as Innovative Aristotelian

I will conclude my discussion by pointing to ways in which Ayn Rand's approach to metaphysical axioms is Aristotelian—and to ways in which it is a radically innovative development of Aristotelianism.

Agreements

Let us begin with a number of fundamental, and fundamentally important, areas of agreement. Like Aristotle, Ayn Rand considers axioms such as the PNC and PEM to be explicit identifications of fundamental facts

---

33. See also Binswanger 2014, 22–23 and Rheins 2016, 249–50.
34. See *ITOE* 55; *Atlas* 1015, 1040; Rheins 2016, 250.

about being. This view contrasts with the view of those who see them ultimately as arbitrary postulates of symbolic systems such as set theory. There is also fundamental agreement that anyone seeking to prove anything must accept, if only at some tacit level, PNC and PEM; and that any attempt to deny them is self-refuting. In Rand's terms, anyone who attempts to do so is guilty of "concept stealing"—that is, of using concepts that they have no right to. In Aristotle's words: "the well-known result for all such statements [denials of axioms] is that they do away with themselves" (*Met.* Γ.8 1012b14–16). In Rand's words: "an axiomatic concept . . . has to be accepted and used even in the process of any attempt to deny it" (*ITOE* 59). In the passage I selected as the epigraph to this paper, in fact, she analogizes Aristotle himself to an axiom on precisely this point: "*like an axiom*—[Aristotle is] used by his enemies in the very act of denying him" (*VOR* 6; emphasis added).

Differences

All of that being said, there are a number of significant differences in their treatment of philosophical axioms. First and foremost, unlike Aristotle, Rand begins, not with axiomatic propositions but with axiomatic *concepts*.[35] This decision reflects a general feature of her epistemology: concepts, not propositions, are the fundamental units of reason; propositions are tools for identifying relationships among previously formed concepts. The book she titled *Introduction to Objectivist Epistemology* is, therefore, largely a theory of concepts and their proper formation.

The previous section of this paper was, to a significant extent, devoted to explicating the chapter on Axiomatic Concepts in that book. She opens that chapter by stressing this distinctive feature of her understanding of axioms: "Axioms are usually considered to be propositions identifying a fundamental, self-evident truth. But explicit propositions as such are not primaries: they are made of concepts. The base of man's knowledge—of all other concepts, all axioms, propositions and thought—consists of axiomatic concepts" (*ITOE* 55). And once a reader reaches that chapter, another fundamental difference from Aristotle emerges: Even when stated in propositional form (e.g. Existence exists, A is A), Rand's primary axioms are *not* the Principles of Non-Contradiction and Excluded Middle.

---

35. As I noted earlier (and as is stressed in Michael Peramatzis's comments), in his discussion of the inductive ascent to first principles in *APo.* II.19, Aristotle uses concepts as his only examples. But he appears to restrict the term "axiom" to propositions such as PNC or PEM.

Rather, her primary axiomatic concepts are Existence, Identity, and Consciousness—and the associated axioms are that Existence exists, A is A, Consciousness is conscious.[36] She considers PNC and PEM to be *derivative corollaries* of the law of identity.[37] Notice, for example, how "identity" is explicated in this passage from John Galt's radio address in *Atlas Shrugged*: "Whatever you choose to consider, be it an object, an attribute or an action, the law of identity remains the same. *A leaf cannot be a stone at the same time, it cannot be all red and all green at the same time, it cannot freeze and burn at the same time.* A is A" (*Atlas* 1016; emphasis added). That is to say: a thing is what it is—and *therefore* it cannot simultaneously both be that thing and something else; and *therefore* it must be either one or the other. And the above quotation points to another distinctive feature of Rand's approach to axioms (though I will make a case that this is implicit in Aristotle): The law of causality is also a corollary of identity.[38] Because of what a leaf is, it cannot freeze and burn at the same time—given its nature, under certain circumstances it will freeze and under others it will burn.

Completing or Extending Aristotle?

In Galt's speech in *Atlas Shrugged*, without explicitly naming Aristotle, Rand pays tribute to him with the following words: "Centuries ago, the man who was—no matter what his errors—the greatest of your philosophers, has stated *the formula defining the concept of existence and the rule of all knowledge: A is A. A thing is itself.* You have never grasped the meaning of his statement. I am here to *complete* it: Existence is Identity, Consciousness is Identification" (*Atlas* 1016; emphasis added). There are two questions raised in this quotation that I want to close by considering:

(1) Did Aristotle state the formula identified in the first sentence?

(2) What precisely does Rand mean by saying that these last two statements—Existence is Identity, Consciousness is Identification—complete Aristotle's statement?

---

36. Rand identifies the Objectivist metaphysics by reference to these axioms in the following passage: "The primacy of existence (of reality) is the axiom that existence exists, i.e., that the universe exists independent of consciousness (of any consciousness), that things are what they are, that they possess a specific nature, an identity. The epistemological corollary is the axiom that consciousness is the faculty of perceiving that which exists—and that man gains knowledge of reality by looking outward" (*PWNI* 32).

37. See note 1, above.

38. This point is also stressed in H. W. B. Joseph's classic *An Introduction to Logic*. See also *Atlas* 1062; Peikoff 1991, 12–17; and Rheins 2016, 255–56.

1. As we saw in our discussion of *Metaphysics* Γ, Aristotle only explicitly identifies and defends two metaphysical axioms, the Principles of Non-Contradiction and of Excluded Middle. As noted earlier, it was Rand's view that these are corollaries of the Principle of Identity—that is, they are reformulations of the Principle of Identity and serve the purpose of providing epistemological norms for thought.[39]

Nowhere that I am aware of does Aristotle explicitly identify "A is A" as an axiomatic principle. However, although he does not explicitly identify certain concepts as axioms, a case can be made that two of Rand's axiomatic concepts—existence and identity—have clear precursors in two concepts that are central to Aristotle's metaphysics: "being" (*to on*) and "what it is to be" (*to ti ēn einai*), often translated "essence."[40] And these two metaphysical concepts are close in meaning to those that Rand links in the statement that, at the time of writing *Atlas Shrugged*, she viewed as a "completion" or "clarification" of Aristotle: Existence is Identity.[41]

2. In a biographical interview some years after this passage was written, Ayn Rand recounted a discussion about it with Leonard Peikoff: "I began to see that what I took as almost self-evident, was not self-evident at all. . . . Leonard [Peikoff] began to realize the importance of my statement that 'existence is identity,' and he explained to me in what sense no philosopher had claimed it, not in this form. I had thought of it as what I said in Galt's speech, that it's merely clarification of Aristotle. I began to realize in what way it isn't" (*Biographical Interviews*, 1960–1961). What Aristotle does clearly state is that every actual being, every existent thing, has a nature or identity, abstractly referred to as what it is to be that being.

Thus, while there is no passage I can think of in which Aristotle explicitly states the Principle of Identity, he does on many occasions state

---

39. There is a helpful formulation of this point in Rheins 2016: "The Law of Non-Contradiction takes the Law of Identity (that A is A) and extends it into a proscription against the denial of Identity. . . . The Law of Excluded Middle takes this one step further: if everything has a definite and non-contradictory identity, then for any well-defined attribute X, a given subject is either X or it is non-X (where that means anything other than X)" (251).

40. This nominalized phrase, as Aryeh Kosman has argued in some detail, is to be understood in relation to the answer to a more ordinary question about what something is. So, if I were to point to the being in the pot on my desk and ask "What is it?," someone might answer "a plant" or "an orchid." But those answers could well provoke another sort of question: "What is it to be a plant?" or "What is it to be an orchid?" That is, they could provoke a question about its nature or essence. In a perfectly natural sense, both sorts of question are about the identity of the being in the pot on my desk. See Kosman 2013, 151–63.

41. For more on this topic, see Peramatzis, chapter 2, and Rheins, chapter 3, in this volume.

what Rand takes to be alternative formulations of that principle: that entities have specific natures, and that to identify the nature of a thing is to identify what it is to be that thing.

What about "Consciousness is Identification"? Recall that one of Ayn Rand's axiomatic concepts, consciousness, does not have any apparent precursor in Aristotle. Its inclusion is of great historical significance and is the key to a number of Rand's philosophical innovations.

Consciousness as a state of awareness, is dependent on, and derivative of, that of which it is aware.

Clearly, Aristotle does not identify any such statement as an axiom. But there is a fundamental feature of his epistemology which supports the idea that this is a fundamentally Aristotelian axiom—the priority of the object of awareness to conscious awareness. And in fact, we can see this feature at work in *Metaphysics* Γ.5, in his refutation of Protagorean relativism: "it is impossible that the underlying subject that produces the perception does not exist, even without perception [existing]. *For perception is not of itself, but there is something different apart from perception which must be prior to perception*; for the mover is by nature prior to the moved, and this is no less true even if they are spoken of as corollaries" (*Met.* Γ.5 1010b30–11a3, emphasis added). Perception and its object are corollaries—but there is no perception without an object to be aware of—to act on the sense organ. In that sense, the object of perception is prior, and perception is the identification of what is. He makes a related point in the *De Anima*, in the process of contrasting perception with conceptual thought: "actual perception is of particulars, while knowledge is of universals; and these are somehow in the soul itself. For this reason, it is open to us to think when we wish, but perceiving is not similarly open to us; *for there must be the object of perception*" (*DA* II.5 417b21–25, emphasis added). We can, when we wish, think about our future actions, or about universals like "bird" or "triangle," because these abstractions reside in consciousness. But perception requires an object of awareness—without that, there is no perception. There is, then, a very real sense in which, in the statement "Consciousness is Identification," she is making explicit ideas that are implicit in Aristotle.

Other features of her view of metaphysical axioms are further examples of Ayn Rand as an Aristotelian innovator. I will close by mentioning just two.

1. As I pointed out earlier, a general feature of Ayn Rand's philosophical method is on display in her discussion of axiomatic concepts—her in-

sistence that we ask and answer the question of why human beings need to explicitly identify axiomatic concepts. As with a code of morality, it is crucial that we determine what it is about human nature that makes such identification necessary.

2. Her critical distinction between the metaphysical and the epistemological nature of axioms. Again, this is implicit in Aristotle's discussions—he sees PNC and PEM as identifying something fundamental about being qua being, and thus a proper subject for metaphysics; but he also recognizes them as presuppositions of all proof, and thus an appropriate subject for epistemology.

In all these respects, we see Ayn Rand as the Innovative Aristotelian.

2
Comments on "Axioms and Their Validation in Aristotle and Ayn Rand," by James G. Lennox
Grounding the Most Basic Principles
MICHAIL PERAMATZIS

In his extremely interesting and lucid paper Jim Lennox focuses on the following three questions about Aristotle's and Rand's views of common axioms:

(1) To what do axioms refer? This is to be understood as the question of what the nature of axioms is (e.g., concepts or propositions; metaphysical, epistemic, or logical) and what they apply to.

(2) Function: What role do axioms discharge in our cognitive apparatus, or how are they cognitively useful?

(3) Validation: How, if at all, can axioms be justified and/or grounded?

Jim points out that Aristotle does not clarify whether he is discussing concepts or propositions. While this is true generally speaking of Aristotle's discussion of principles in the *Posterior Analytics* and the *Metaphysics*, his examples of axioms in both works suggest that he takes them to be propositional principles or at least easily expressible in propositional form: it is necessary that F either belong or not belong to x; it is impossible that F both belong and not belong to x; it is necessary either to affirm or to deny F of x; and so on. At any rate, Jim's aim is to ascertain Aristotle's position as to whether axiomatic concepts are prior to propositional axioms or conversely.

In Jim's view, Aristotle addresses question (1) in *Metaphysics* Γ and suggests that axioms are propositions that have universal applicability—they are true of all beings insofar as they are—and they reveal universal truths about all beings insofar as they are. In this sense, axioms are metaphysical principles; they are not merely or primarily epistemic or logical principles, although in important senses they are principles of this sort too. It may be useful, at this juncture, to note that the notion of universality in Aristotle's discussion of the subject matter and principles of first philosophy (his term for our metaphysics) is ambiguous as between universality "in form," the universality characteristic of universal concepts or universal propositions (where, for instance, a concept such as *human* is universal or a proposition is universally quantified) and universality "in scope," the universality of an item that is a principle or cause of everything. The latter notion, of course, allows that a principle may be particular: for example, God is a universal principle in that God is a principle of everything. It seems reasonable to think that axioms are universal in both senses.

In the same context of *Metaphysics* Γ Aristotle also tackles question (2). Jim suggests that the cognitive functions of the axioms, especially PNC, are encapsulated in the following five epistemic features:

(i) Axioms are epistemically firm, with PNC being the firmest among them.
(ii) It is impossible to be deceived about them.
(iii) Nothing is prior to them; especially PNC is the ultimate, unhypothetical principle.
(iv) It is necessary to know the axioms, primarily PNC, if we are to know or even understand anything at all.
(v) PNC seems to be the principle of all other axioms.

Although, as Jim points out, Aristotle addresses question (3) first in the *Posterior Analytics*, he does not have a substantive answer in that treatise. He argues that axioms are primitive propositions that are indemonstrable, as there is nothing prior to them from which to demonstrate them. Further, he seeks to block the worries of infinite regress, circularity, and lack of justification by introducing a different mode of grasping the basic principles (presumably including the axioms): *nous* (intellect/intelligence or understanding). Jim also notes that Aristotle contrasts principles in the sense of basic demonstrative premises *from which* (*ex hōn*) demonstrable theorems are derived with axiomatic principles, which are not premises of demonstration. Rather, axioms have a different—presumably regulatory or grounding—role with respect to demonstration and perhaps deduction quite generally: they are that *through which* (*di' hōn*) demonstrations proceed.

In *Metaphysics* Γ, by contrast, Aristotle has a more elaborate answer to question (3). He continues to hold firm to the idea set out in the *Analytics* that the axioms are indemonstrable; indeed, he maintains that seeking to prove them shows a lack of education. He goes on, however, to add that it is possible to offer an elenctic demonstration pertaining to them, particularly PNC. Jim helpfully asks about the precise *demonstrandum* of this elenctic proof: is it PNC itself, or the fact that it is impossible to demonstrate everything, or rather the impossibility or incoherence of denying PNC? He contends (correctly in my view) that Aristotle's elenctic proof does not prove PNC itself, nor the fact that not everything is demonstrable, but is, rather, a refutation of any putative denier of PNC. The upshot of the proof is that such a denier cannot coherently deny PNC as the very denial of it presupposes it. Jim, however, maintains that this does not constitute a genuine form of non-demonstrative validation of PNC. Rather, it is a "reaffirmation through denial."

Turning to Rand, Jim observes that her initial thoughts on the foundations of our knowledge, particularly our knowledge of the axioms, are torn between radical empiricism and the model of mathematics, which uses highly abstract principles and concepts. Although in her initial discussion of question (1) and in *Atlas Shrugged* she construes the axioms as propositions, in the *Introduction to Objectivist Epistemology* she focuses on axiomatic concepts: existence, identity, and the (rather more epistemically laden) consciousness. The main question she engages with is the reference of such highly abstract concepts. How can they arise and become unified despite the fact that they refer to a manifold of concrete particulars given in perceptual experience?

Her answer to this last style-(3) question of validation is that existence and identity are justified by any and every past, present, and/or future existent (including mental existents). Consciousness, on the other hand, is justified by any and every past, present, and/or future act of experienced awareness. Indeed, she calls such particular justifying or grounding items "the units" of the relevant abstract concepts. Further, she maintains that from such axiomatic concepts we can proceed to form propositions only by repetition: for existence we get "what is, is," whereas for identity "it is what it is." Consciousness, on the other hand, is understood as the awareness of what is and the ability to employ ways to identify it. Although the propositions derived from our axiomatic concepts are indemonstrable, they can be validated only by refuting their denials and showing that their denials presuppose them—a conspicuously Aristotelian move.

In Jim's reading, Rand goes on to raise question (2): why do we need each concept we use, and ultimately why do we need to make explicit our axiomatic concepts? Her answer is fourfold. First, such concepts enable us to retain the idea of continuity of existence and consciousness. Second, they guarantee the fundamental distinction that underlies the possibility of objective knowledge, the distinction between consciousness and its object. Third, axiomatic concepts and our theorizing about them serve as standards of and grounds for our certainty: "[A]xiomatic concepts are the products of an epistemological need—the need of a volitional, conceptual consciousness which is capable of error and doubt" (*ITOE* 58). This idea may be betraying Cartesian worries about justification and certainty—worries that Aristotle, with his emphasis on explanation and understanding, may not share in similar measure. Finally, the fourth function of axiomatic concepts seems to be intimately linked to—or perhaps constitutes a more general formulation of—the second and third uses: they are "epistemological guides."

I shall raise five questions about Jim's analysis of, and comparison between, Aristotle's and Rand's views. In doing so, I shall also make a few more positive remarks that I cannot argue for in detail in the present context.

Question 1. Jim's discussion relies heavily on the distinction between concepts and propositions. Indeed, it looks as though Rand herself oscillated between propositional axioms and axiomatic concepts. Although this distinction is clear and important, it is worth asking whether Aristotle (or we) may have straightforward ways in which to bridge the gap between concepts and propositions. Aristotle often suggests that the principles of an axiomatic demonstrative science are non-propositional items such as the point, line, triangle, and so on (*APo*. I.7 75a42–b6, I.10 76b3–6, I.32 88a30–34). At other places he holds that, apart from the axioms, the principles comprise hypotheses, or propositions that posit the existence of certain items, and definitions, or propositions that specify the essence (or what-it-is) of such items (or, as the case may be, propositions that clarify what the corresponding terms signify [*APo*. I.1 71a11–17, I.2 72a14–24, I.10 76a31–36]).

Assuming that we have concepts of items such as the point or the line, why not think that the full grasp of a concept X just consists in understanding what X is? Further, why not think that in grasping X as non-empty we understand that things of type X exist? This is not to say that the concept-versus-proposition distinction collapses. It is simply to note that there is a natural way to move from concepts to propositions or conversely. This idea mirrors a point often made in connection with Plato's talk of knowledge or knowing: while he usually speaks of knowing X, there is no reason to understand his view of knowledge as acquaintance-based. Indeed, he normally supplements the locution "knowing X" with the subordinate clause "what it is" (e.g., *Euthyphro* 11a7–8, *Meno* 71b2–4, 72b1–2): to know X is to know of/about X what it is—a proposition specifying the essence of X.

Question 2. Following naturally from this point there is a question as to what Aristotle's project is in his discussion of Jim's questions (1) and (2). What is it to define or identify an axiom, especially PNC? In fact, is it even possible to define propositional items such as the axioms, and what would such a definition aim to achieve? We may think that the expression "definition of a proposition" borders on being a category mistake: for we normally take not propositions but things, terms, or concepts to be primarily definable. This is not an insurmountable difficulty. There does not seem to be any prima facie absurdity in thinking that we could define (for instance) a disjunction or a conjunction quasi-compositionally, in terms of its disjuncts or conjuncts together with the relevant operations of disjunction or conjunction, respectively. Generally, we could define a proposition in terms of its constituents plus their mode of combination—perhaps, to be faithful to Aristotelian spirit, by also insisting that their mode of combination is not just another constituent of the proposition (*Met.* Z.17 1041b11–25, H.3 1043b4–10).[1]

---

1. Aristotle himself argues that although primary (types of) object (such as substances) are definable in a primary way, yet non-substances too (such as accidental compounds) are definable in a derivative way: for example, a pale human is defined as some human or other who happens to be pale (*Met.* Z.4 1030a17–20, 27–32, 1030b4–13, Z.5 1030b26–28, 1031a7–11). Indeed, in such cases the definiens seems to codify a predicative proposition in which an attribute, being pale, is truly said to belong to an object (of a certain type), a human (Z.4 1030a14–17: *alla logos men estai hekastou kai tōn allōn ti sēmainei* [. . .] *hoti tode tō(i)de huparkhei*). At Z.4 1030a14–17, this point about "definitions" of non-substance items is framed in terms of accounts of what terms or phrases signify. Indeed, at this stage, Aristotle seems to be denying that non-substances have any proper definitions at all, as opposed to merely significatory accounts. But from Z.4 1030a17 onward, he goes on to argue that it is possible to think that while substances have a definition in the primary way, non-substances have a defi-

Aristotle too seems to think that there is nothing preventing us from defining propositional axioms such as PNC. In line with the views set out in the *Posterior Analytics* (see, e.g., I.1 71a11–17, I.2 72a14–24, I.10 76b3–22) about a basic non-propositional definiendum such as the unit, point, line, triangle, and so forth, he seeks to regiment the what-it-is of PNC to be able to use it as a basic principle: "That this sort of principle is the firmest of all is clear; what this is, let us say after these remarks" (*Met.* Γ.3 1005b17–19).

To begin addressing the question of how to define PNC, it is crucial to consider its initial formulation in the following passage: "It is impossible that the same item at the same time both belong and not belong to the same item, and in the same respect, together with as many further qualifications we could roughly specify in addition (*prosdihorisaimeth' an*), let them be roughly specified in addition (*estō prosdihōrismena*) against logical difficulties" (*Met.* Γ.3 1005b18–22). Although Aristotle does not explain how to fill in the required extra qualifications, it is reasonable to suppose that a proper definition of PNC would have to specify them. But is it possible to add those extra qualifications in the abstract—that is, without formulating an instance of PNC as it pertains to some or other specific type of object, with some or other definite attributes, respects, and such? My first suggestion is that we ought to return a negative response to this question.

My second suggestion is that Aristotle is aware of this point. In the passage just quoted, and generally in *Metaphysics* Γ.3, he consistently uses the terms *prosdihorizein* or *diohorizein* to describe our grasp and characterization of the qualifications needed to provide a determinate formulation of PNC (cf. 1005b23: *dihorismon*; b27: *prosdihōristhō*). These terms are formed from the verb *horizein* ("to define"), with the addition of the prepositional prefixes *pros* and/or *dia*. I submit that this initial formulation constitutes a first attempt at defining or explicating PNC. The preposition *pros* implies that we need additional qualifications if we are to define or explicate PNC—that is to say, if we are to render it determinate. By contrast, the preposition *dia* seems to have an attenuating function. It indicates that the extra qualifications offered at present— "at the same time . . . to the same item . . . in the same respect"—cannot yet be fully precise or complete. As it stands, the abstract formulation of PNC cannot by itself be a proper *horismos* (a fully determinate defini-

nition in a secondary or derivative way. Indeed, what his previous, stricter position deemed a mere significatory account, his subsequent, more liberal view may conceptualize as a definition in a secondary or derivative way. For further discussion, see Peramatzis 2010.

tion) but only a *dihorismos* (a rough approximation or looser description). Nor is my distinction between a merely rough or approximate *dihorismos* and a proper, precise, or strict *horismos* alien to Aristotle's conceptual resources. For a clear example of this distinction, it is useful to compare *Metaphysics* Γ.3 with Θ.6. While at *Met.* Θ.6 1048a25–27, he remarks that his discussion will give a rough description (*dihorismos*) of the nature and features of *energeia* (1048a26: *dihorisōmen ti te estin hē energeia kai poion ti*), at a35–37 he points out that we should not seek a definition (1048a36: *horon*) for everything but sometimes we should rest content with a looser account (or synoptic grasp; 1048a37: *sunhoran*) in terms of (for instance) analogy.

In *Metaphysics* Γ.4, by contrast, where Aristotle avails himself of the notions of substance and essence, he uses systematically the verbal forms *horizein* and *hōrismenon*, which suggest that a precise, fully determinate definition of the principle is possible. Indeed, this sort of definition relies on each term signifying a definite item (1006a24–25, a29–31: *to einai ē mē einai todi*; *ouk an pan houtōs kai mē houtōs ekhoi*; a31–32: *sēmainei hen*; 1006b1, b2–13, 1007a25–26, 1008a30–b4, b6). For, arguably, at this stage the notions of substance and essence enable us to use terms that signify something determinate (a certain "one" or unity and a "this"). If this is correct, the "extra" qualifications required in Γ.3 do not remain vague, rough, or approximate (mere *dihorismoi*) but are rendered precise and determinate (fully-fledged *horismoi*). In this proposal, the notions of substance and essence define or explicate PNC in that they precisify the required "extra" qualifications. Thus, for example, given the specific essence of a certain kind of object, these qualifications can be set out in a rigorous fashion and yield a fully determinate formulation of PNC.

Here is a speculative example of how substance and essence may be involved in defining or explicating a precise formulation of PNC. Suppose that a given instance of PNC refers to attributes such as colors and to subjects such as bodies or material substances. Using the notion of essence, we can plug in the claim that colors are essentially kinds of quality that belong to some bodily surface or other as their underlying subject. Moreover, because bodily surfaces are essentially magnitudes that belong to bodies, we can introduce the idea that, ultimately, colors are essentially types of quality that belong to the surface of some or other body. Using such essential truths about bodies or material substances, their surfaces, and being colored, we can formulate a determinate version of PNC in which a material substance cannot (at the same time) both be black and also not be black *with the extra qualification* "all over its surface."[2]

This point brings us back to my first suggestion. A formulation of PNC may not be fully determinate unless we invoke accounts that specify the (types of) object and feature it applies to in each case. Thus, the abstract formula "for any object, x, for any feature, F, it is impossible that x be both F and not F at the same time in the same respect . . . " contains an ellipsis that we cannot properly fill in—in Aristotle's jargon, we cannot specify the required extra qualifications—independently of, or before we supply, determinate values for x and F. It is important, then, to be able to provide determinate characterizations of the predicate- and subject-terms to offer a full and specific formulation of PNC: a definition or explication (*horismos*), as opposed to a rough characterization (*dihorismos*).

Moreover, this point may have implications for Aristotle's defense of PNC. Suppose that a dialectical opponent denies PNC by providing putative counterexamples to specific instances of PNC. For example, the op-

2. In cases of essentially changing types of object, such as larvae, the precise formula of PNC, with all the appropriate qualifications in place, would be sensitive to the essential truth that such living beings undergo a sort of transformation process. A caterpillar cannot at the same time be both a butterfly and not a butterfly, but it is (essentially) transforming into a butterfly. Indeed, we could introduce one of Aristotle's own arguments against PNC-deniers who are motivated by the indeterminate and apparently contradictory nature of perceptible, ever-changing beings (*Met.* Γ.5 1009a22–25, 30–36). A larva cannot be actually both a butterfly and not a butterfly, but it can be (and indeed is) potentially both a butterfly (as it is coming-to-be a butterfly and so may reach the completion stage of the relevant process) and not a butterfly (as it is not yet a butterfly and the process it is undergoing may be interrupted, inhibited, interfered with, and so on, before it reaches its completion stage). Perhaps, fuzzier phenomena, such as rain, may give rise to difficulties for this picture: after all, one might argue, it can be raining and not raining at the same time, if there is a slight drizzle. To this sort of case, an Aristotelian retort might be that the terms involved in a determinate version of PNC must signify one definite item. Even if the term "rain" signifies more than one item (perhaps because it is vague and/or multiply ambiguous), nothing prevents us from introducing different terms, each with one definite significatory account corresponding to the many significations of the initial vague or ambiguous term: "$rain_1$," "$rain_2$," . . . , "$rain_n$" for n significations of the term "rain" (*Met.* Γ.4 1006a34-b5). Politis (2004, 123–50) argues lucidly that Aristotle's phrase "extra qualifications" in the abstract formulation of PNC is extremely important. He also refers to Plato's discussion of the so-called Principle of Opposites at *Republic* IV, 436b9–437a8, which seems cognate with PNC. Plato's discussion is relevant to the question of how to specify some of the extra qualifications needed to make PNC determinate. Moreover, Politis holds that the view Aristotle takes to be implying the denial of PNC is that things are radically indeterminate (2004, 139). Similarly, he argues that Aristotle's defense depends on the claim that each term signifies one determinate item (150–53). Although my position is congenial to all these points, it develops them in light of the question as to whether and (if so) how Aristotle's argument shows that PNC depends on—that is, is defined or precisified in terms of—substance and essence.

ponent suggests that PNC does not apply to the case of a bodily surface and its color as the surface is both black and not black. To defuse such counterexamples, we ought to add extra qualifications to our abstract formulation of PNC, qualifications that cannot be set out without invoking determinate essences of specific types of object and feature. For instance, if the natures of bodily surface, body, and color suggest that the required extra qualification is "all over a body's surface," the precise definition of this instance of PNC is "it is impossible that any body be both black and not black all over its surface" or something along these lines.

Aristotle (or at least his argument) seems, therefore, to be committed to the idea that propositional axioms such as PNC cannot be fully or determinately defined or (in Jim's and Rand's terminology) cannot be identified without invoking the concept of essence: what a specific type of object, attribute, feature, or what have you is. Presumably, this would be cognate with Rand's concept of identity. Further, in his use of such essentialist resources in *Metaphysics Γ*, Aristotle also argues that denying PNC eliminates not only the concept of essence but also the concept of a substance, a determinate type of object that functions as the ultimate subject or underlier of true predications (*Met. Γ.*4 1007a20–b18). Without predication, however, the PNC-denier cannot even formulate their own denial of PNC—that is, that there is something that can be both *F* and not *F*. The concept of substance as an ultimate underlier of predication seems to invoke the notion of the existence of some object or other of a specific type. If this is correct, Aristotle's overall argument is also congenial to Rand's emphasis on the axiomatic concept of existence. Indeed, what undergirds such essentialist arguments in defense of PNC and against the possibility of coherently denying PNC is Aristotle's principle of what it is to signify one definite item: supposing that the term "human" signifies what-it-is-to-be a human (the "essence" of human), say, being a rational biped animal, then, if anything (x) should be a human, x ought to be a rational biped animal and cannot not be a rational biped animal (*Met. Γ.*4 1006a32–b20, 1007a23–31). This principle involves the concept of existence in the conditional's antecedent "if anything, x, should be a human": the condition is that *something is F* or *there is an F*. Moreover, the principle embeds the notion of essence, too, as it sets out signification in terms of the innocuous essentialist claim that a term "*F*" signifies a definite item in that it signifies what-it-is-to-be *F*.

My conclusion is twofold. First, in specifying the precise propositional formulation of PNC Aristotle himself seems to rely—implicitly or explicitly—on concepts such as existence and essence (Rand's "identity"). Jim and Rand would agree about this. I think that disagreement may arise about my second conclusion: the concepts of existence and essence (as already suggested in my discussion of Question 1, are not isolated from propositional items, nor are they proposition-free. F's existence is straightforwardly graspable and expressible in propositional format: there exists some F or other. Further, what-it-is-to-be F can be captured by an essential definition, a proposition such as what-it-is-to-be F is to be G (or: to be F is essentially to be G). Insofar as they presuppose propositions, however, the concepts of existence and essence are constrained by PNC and PEM just as every other proposition is. I shall return to this last point in my Question 4.

Question 3. My next question is about Rand's notion of identity as set out by Jim. First, there seems to be an important ambiguity inherent in this notion. Is Rand's concept of identity and the corresponding law of identity about individual items, the objects of reference, as (for example) in $a = b$? Or does she have in mind what theorists such as Russell, Whitehead, and Carnap call "intensional identity," as (for instance) in $F =_{def} G$ (or $F \equiv G$), perhaps also formulated with variables and bound with the universal quantifier? Resolving this ambiguity is important for tackling my second question about identity: does Aristotle introduce anywhere explicitly the concept of identity and/or does he invoke anything like the law of identity? At *Metaphysics* Z.17, 1041a16–20, he dismisses as trivial the question of whether X is X and formulates the principle that each thing is "indivisible" (non-distinct?) from itself. It should be noted, however, that this dismissal is indicative of his interests in that specific context, where he focuses on the inquiry into the essence of specific types of thing. Indeed, in *Topics* I.7, as well as in *Metaphysics* Δ.6 (esp. 1016b31–17a6), Δ.9, and I.3 (esp. 1054a32–b3), he discusses several notions of oneness or sameness, including numerical oneness or sameness. Similarly, in *Topics* VII he examines ways in which to test a putative definer's claim that two things are one and the same (primarily in number). Although, in such discussions, Aristotle focuses on notions that roughly approximate the modern concept of identity (and indeed even formulates principles that could be viewed as precursors to Leibniz's Law), he does not connect them to any of the axioms.

In *Metaphysics* Γ, by contrast, where he discusses PNC and PEM, he does not invoke such notions of sameness or oneness. But he does use the principle of determinate signification in the way I suggested earlier:

any nonvague or non-ambiguous term, for instance, "human," ought to signify one definite item, what-it-is-to-be a human, say, being a rational biped animal. As noted earlier, he sets out this principle as follows: if anything should be a human, this thing must be a rational biped animal; it cannot also not be a rational biped animal or be a not-rational-biped-animal (*Met.* Γ.4 1007a23–26).

This last formulation seems cognate with the Randian idea that each and every thing must be itself and cannot not be itself. Might the Aristotelian principle of determinate signification be not only the source of Rand's fascination with the axiomatic concept of identity and the law of identity but also the reason why she tends to take PNC and PEM as "derivative corollaries" of the law of identity, as Jim points out? Perhaps in her study of Aristotle's defense of PNC in *Metaphysics* Γ, Rand saw the connection between PNC and the principle of determinate signification but construed the latter as simply some version of the law of identity. Moreover, because of the pivotal role the principle of determinate signification plays in the defense of PNC, and her identification of this principle with the law of identity, perhaps she reached the conclusion that PNC is merely a corollary that is derived from the law of identity.

Whether these exegetical points about Rand are correct is an open question. It seems plausible to think, however, that the principle of determinate signification goes well beyond the law of identity: for it involves claims about the signification of terms and about the essence of the types of object referred to by such terms. Further, Aristotle does not think that PNC is derived as a corollary from any prior principle: for he takes PNC to be the absolutely fundamental, unhypothetical, and firmest of all principles.

Question 4. My fourth question returns to the issue of whether concepts or propositions are prior epistemically or in justification. In Jim's reading, it seems that Rand thinks the activity of conceptual identification underlies or grounds reason's propositional grasp of things' existence and essence. But is it necessary to think that either the conceptual or the propositional level is prior? Although the two levels are notionally distinct, do they mark any substantive division in our epistemic abilities? What would it be to grasp fully the concept of existence or essence without having any propositional understanding of them? Conversely, what would it be to have a propositional understanding of existence or essence without being able to grasp or apply the concepts of existence or essence to things that exist and have a certain nature?

More specifically, in the defense of PNC in *Metaphysics* Γ one might contend, as I have suggested, that there is some sort of foundational or justificatory collaboration between the axioms, especially PNC, and concepts such as "existence" and "essence" (perhaps the latter is encapsulated in the principle of determinate signification). We start from an indeterminate but determinable grasp of the propositional axiom of PNC, which is true of everything insofar as it exists. This is so, despite our lacking a fully precise specification of all the additional qualifications that are required to block any putative counterexamples offered by a PNC-denier. To achieve this latter demanding level of "definition" or "identification" we ought to invoke the concepts of "essence" and "substance" (or "identity" and "existence," in Rand's terminology). But this is not the bedrock. For such concepts not only feed back into the propositional axiom of PNC. They also are themselves expressible and graspable in terms of existential and definitional propositions. Moreover, insofar as they are equivalent to propositions, they are constrained by the basic propositional axioms PNC and PEM. This picture suggests a no-priority view, in which propositional axioms and axiomatic concepts are not founded independently of each other.

Question 5. My last question is about the issue of validation. Jim holds that Aristotle's elenctic demonstration of PNC and generally any argument from "reaffirmation through denial" is not a genuine form of non-deductive validation. Why not? Is the idea that a genuine form of validation is either a priori and deductive or empirical and inductive and, since the elenctic proof is neither, it does not constitute a genuine sort of validation at all? But does Aristotle have to be impaled on either horn of this dilemma? Why not think that his procedure in *Metaphysics* Γ is a hybrid of both modes of justification? For instance, as he claims, the PNC-denier denies and reaffirms specific instances of PNC pertaining to specific types of object and feature, and so in a way the elenctic proof is deductive as it presupposes (on the part of the PNC-denier) PNC, the foundation of deductive inference. Further, the PNC-defender extracts responses from the PNC-denier, formulates corresponding premises, and infers from them conclusions in the relevant dialectical syllogisms—again a deductive procedure. At the same time, however, if my suggestions about the role of essence and existence in the principle of determinate signification are plausible, our invoking claims about the essence of specific types of object and/or feature is neither a priori nor deductive. This is so, regardless of whether our conception of essence is innocuous (e.g., based on the signification of terms) or more demanding (e.g., relying on Aristotle's theory of scientific essences as set out in *Posterior Analytics* II). Further, the existential condition codified in the principle of determinate signification (whether anything should exist that is, e.g., a human) cannot be tested or ascertained in a purely a priori manner. If part of the elenctic validation of PNC or the other axioms consists in considering many such particular cases of the essence and existence of specific types of item and inferring conclusions from them, this sort of validation seems also to be non-a-priori or in some sense inductive. Why not conclude that Aristotle's elenctic defense incorporates both deductive and inductive aspects in this fashion and that it constitutes a robust form of underpinning the axioms by refuting any attempt to deny them?

3
Aristotle and Rand on "Being," "Existence," and the Primacy of Substances

JASON G. RHEINS

In his very fine paper, with which I concur too consistently for these to be comments in the critical sense, Jim Lennox has made several important contributions to the study of Ayn Rand's metaphysics and our understanding of her relationship to Aristotle. His discussion of her theory of axiomatic concepts is particularly welcome, as this theory has received relatively little treatment in the secondary literature despite its fundamental significance to her metaphysics.[1] By situating his interpretation of Aristotle's treatment of ontology and fundamental axioms alongside Rand's, Jim also enriches our understanding of the former. Students of ancient philosophy will recognize in his treatment of Aristotle's *Metaphysics* Γ a strong endorsement of the approach of Code (1986, 1987, 1997) and Bolton (1994), who reject the idea that in his science of being qua being Aristotle has abandoned the theory of first principles and demonstrative knowledge that he developed in the *Posterior Analytics*. Here, too, I am in strong agreement.

Rather than caviling over whatever minor disagreements there may be between us, either about *Metaphysics* Γ or Ayn Rand's metaphysics, I

---

1. I count myself an offender in this regard. For reasons of time and space I could not address time measurements in my chapter on Ayn Rand's metaphysics (Rheins 2016) in Gotthelf and Salmieri 2016, 245–71.

would like to build upon what Jim has offered us by exploring an interesting difference between Aristotle and Rand in their treatment of that most fundamental of all axiomatic concepts, "being" or "existence." This should be understood as further analysis of the similarities and differences between Aristotle and Rand with respect to the science of axioms and being qua being and especially germane to Aristotle's account of the unity of the science of being in *Metaphysics* Γ.

One of the two key puzzles for modern scholars about the relationship between the account of science in the *Posterior Analytics* and the science of being qua being in *Metaphysics* Γ is this: Aristotle denies that "being" is a univocal genus; he treats the various meanings of the term in different categories as distinct but "focally related" senses.[2] This has the important upshot that the science of being qua being cannot have "being" (*to on, to einai*) as its generic subject. Rather it is "substance" (*ousia*), the primary sense of "being"—that is, the genus of ontology. The other modes of being are studied in the same science per their subordinate relations to substance. While Rand enthusiastically agrees with Aristotle that all other categories are dependent upon primary substances or what she calls "entities," she treats "existence" as a univocal term such that "to exist" refers to the same fundamental fact whether one says an entity exists, an attribute exists, an action exists, and so on. Reflecting on this difference highlights what is fundamentally the same about Aristotle's ontology and Rand's with respect to the theory of categories—an agreement that Rand once called "the deepest thing Objectivism has in common with Aristotle (*AON* 28)"—but it also raises several questions.

The "Genus Puzzle" of the Science of Being qua Being

As Jim points out, some of the first puzzles about first philosophy and being/substance raised in *Metaphysics* B are whether there can be one science of substance (and if so, will it also encompass the attributes of substance) and whether it will be the same science that investigates the common axioms and substance (*ousia*).[3] In *Metaphysics* Γ Aristotle an-

---

2. The other puzzle relates to the so-called elenchtic demonstration of PNC and whether Aristotle intends it as a justification or proof of PNC. If he did, it would be a demonstration of a first principle, indeed of the first of the common axioms—the first of first principles, as it were.

3. *Met*. B.1 995b6–13, 19–27. The axiom question is discussed further at B.2 996b26ff., the question of whether there is one science of substances at 997a15ff., and the question of whether the science of substance will also be the science of the attributes of substance is elaborated upon at 997a25–34.

swers these questions in the affirmative. In its first sentence, he asserts that "There is a science that contemplates being qua being and the things that are in themselves."[4] In due course, he identifies the common axioms as subjects of this same science and discusses them as such for the remainder of *Metaphysics* Γ (Γ.3 1005a19*ff*). Why are these significant and perhaps even surprising findings?

According to Aristotle's theory of scientific knowledge (*epistēmē*) in the *Posterior Analytics*, every proper science is of a single, univocal genus (*APo.* I.1 76b11–13; *Met.* Γ.2 1003a19–22). "Being," however, is not a univocal term; it is "said in many ways"—that is, it has different meanings (*Phys*, I.3 186a23ff.; *Met.* Γ.2 1003a33). It means something different as potentiality and as actuality. For example, the acorn and the venerable tree both *"are* oak," but in different senses. "Being" also has distinct senses for each of the so-called categories. What it means "to be" in "Socrates *is*" or "Socrates *is* human" is different from its meanings in "Socrates *is* educated" (quality), "Socrates *is* so many feet tall" (quantity), "Socrates *is* speaking" (action), "Socrates *is* in the agora" (place), and so on. Each of these is a kind of being distinct from the others, but they are not species of a single univocal genus ("being"), because in that case "being" would mean the same for each of them. But "being" is something different for each. Rather, the categories themselves are the broadest genera of beings.[5] Thus the puzzle: if "being" is not a single, univocal genus, how could there be a science of being qua being?[6] Let us call this the "genus puzzle" of ontology.

"Substance" as the Focal (pros hen) Meaning of "Being"

Aristotle's solution to the genus puzzle is his identification of a relationship of logical and metaphysical subordination and dependence distinct from the genus-species relationship. In *Metaphysics* Γ, after claiming that there is a science of being qua being, Aristotle identifies its subject as sub-

---

4. "Ἔστιν ἐπιστήμη τις ἣ θεωρεῖ τὸ ὂν ᾗ ὂν καὶ τὰ τούτῳ ὑπάρχοντα καθ' αὑτό" (*Met.* Γ.1 1003a21–22).

5. See Frede 1987.

6. The problem of scientific genera with "transcategorical" (i.e., cross-category) scope is not restricted to ontology: many other terms that are central to various arts and sciences are meaningful in different ways and qua different ontological categories. A favorite of Aristotle's is "health." For example, some bodies are *healthy,* some foods are *healthy,* some occasions are *healthy,* some activities are *healthy,* and so on. Medicine is the art of producing health, and it is part of the healer's art to know what a healthy human body looks like, what foods are healthy for a person to eat, which activities are conducive to health and when, and so on (*Met.* Γ.2 1003a35ff.).

stance (*ousia*). Now, whatever "*ousia*" means (form, or matter, or both in combination; individual substances or essences; etc.), it is clear that the term does not indicate a generic sense of "being" of which all other senses of "being" are subtypes or species.[7]

Quality, quantity, relationship, action, and so on are neither subtypes of entities nor entity kinds—nor, conversely, are individual entities (substances) or specific entity kinds (essences) qualities, magnitudes, and so on. For the sake of convenience, I will sometimes refer to the non-substantial genera of being as "modes." Although the "modes" are not species of the genus substance, they are subordinate to it as its dependents: substance(s) relate to the modes by being the kind of being(s) upon which all modes depend, in which they inhere, and to which they all ultimately pertain (*Cat.* 5 a34–b7). Hence, the other meanings of "being" have "substance" as their "focal meaning"; they stand to it *pros hen*—literally "(in relation) to one" (*Met.* Γ.2 1003a33ff.).[8]

Although ontology will not study the other categories of being as species of substance, it will study the modes focally (*pros hen*) as the dependencies of substance. Thus, the inclusion of these modes as topics in the science of being is the epistemological corollary of the fact that substance is the focal meaning of "being." Because of this focal unity, the science of substance includes the study of its modes and what holds good qua being

---

7. In the *Categories*, "substance" (*ousia*) is presented as having two main senses. Its primary sense is "substance" or particular beings (*tode ti*) that are neither generic predicates "said-of" other subjects nor accidents/dependents "said (to be) in" other subjects, but capable of taking on contraries in the other categories (*Cat.* 5 2a34ff., 3a7ff., 3b10ff., 4a10ff. Its secondary sense is the species and genera of those things that are generically "said-of" individual substances, but that are not modes or accidents (said to be) *in* their subjects (*Cat.* 5 2a14ff., 3a7ff.). Thus, Aristotle makes the universal ontologically subordinate to and in some sense dependent upon the individual. However, while a genus or a species is a qualification of an individual substance, it is no mere quality. An individual substance cannot take on contraries with respect to its species and genera—for example, when Socrates ceases to be a man or an animal, he ceases to be Socrates. Thus secondary *ousia* is related in some way to essence, the "what it is to be" something (*to ti ēn einai, to ti esti*). In the central books of the *Metaphysics*, Aristotle explores several different senses of being and of substance: in Z and H he explores how *ousia* is variously spoken of as matter or underlying subject (*hupokeimenon*), as form/species (*eidos*), and as the combination of form and matter; in Book Θ he discusses being as potentiality and as actuality. He draws further distinctions between first and second potentiality and first and second actuality in *De Anima* 2.1. Aristotelian scholarship has long been divided over which, if any, of these senses of *ousia* is ultimately the primary one. *Ousia* as form and its relation to universals is an especially contentious matter. For the investigation of the senses of *ousia* as contributing to Aristotle's metaphysics as a science of principles, see Code 1997, 357–58.

8. On focal meaning, see Owen 1960, Shields 1999. For a critical assessment of Owen, see Code 1996, 1997.

about the modes of being, even though these modes are not species of the genus "substance."

What about the common axioms? The science of substance (and of the other senses of "being" *pros hen*) studies what holds good of being qua being. Thus, it is the science that identifies and makes demonstrations about those determinations that are always predicable of being (and unity) in the case of substance and the other categories *pros hen*—for example, "same" and "other" in their various senses.[9] This, Aristotle argues, is also the science in which the common axioms are to be treated. This is because the axioms are principles about being and not-being that hold good of being qua being in the primary sense of substance and for all the other senses of "being." Aristotle's specific formulation of PNC is thus apropos of the immediately prior discussions—in as much as it makes clear how the axiom is about substance as such and how it is related to all the other senses of being.[10]

It is significant that PNC is formulated in terms of the impossibility of the same thing "being *present* (*huparchein*) and *not present* in a substance" at the same time and in the same respect, as against "*being* and *not being*" at the same time and in the same respect. The latter formulation either would be speaking of "being" homonymously, if it were meant to apply to all the categories, or else, if it meant "being" in only one sense, it would leave open the possibility of contradictions in the other senses.[11] Neither option would be tenable. Still, one might worry that Aristotle's actual formulation applies non-contradiction to all the dependent senses of "being" that obtain or do not obtain with respect to one and the same substance (at the same time, in the same respect), but that it does not apply non-contradiction to the being and not being of (a) substance as such.

If it were not otherwise clear, Aristotle does not think that very same primary substance can both be and not be at the same time and in the same respect. That is not how he would put it. In terms he might prefer,

9. *Met.* Γ.2 1003b22ff.

10. The rather different formulation of PNC as 'an affirmation and its denial cannot both be true' at Γ.6 1011b13–15 is similarly apropos of its immediate context: Aristotle is discussing those who maintain that both a statement and its negation can be simultaneously true.

11. One might argue that X potentially is Y and potentially is not Y, where Y has the modality Aristotle calls "possibility"—that is, something that can be so and at actual times is so, and that can be not so and at actual times is not so. Yet, even here, the Law of the Excluded Middle mandates that at any given time it is either Y or it is not Y, in which case X is not potentially Y and potentially not Y in the same way, for it is *actually* one of these and not the other, though it may be possible for X to cease to be the one and to become the other.

he does not think that the same form can be present and not present in the same particular matter at the same time and in the same respect. He also does not think that the same secondary substance can truly be said of and not said of the same primary substance at the same time and in the same respect. On the contrary, we saw earlier that a change with respect to essence or secondary substance ipso facto is the generation or destruction of a primary substance. I raise this issue, though, because it begins to show us how Aristotle's rejection of a univocal sense of being constrains his formulation of PNC. By contrast, when Rand speaks of PNC she gives it the simpler gloss that nothing "can be and not be at the same time, and in the same respect" (PWNI 20).

Focal meaning goes a considerable way toward integrating the different senses of "being," but it cannot make the central term and its satellite usages synonymous. Yet despite the restrictions that Aristotle's theory of univocity and multivocity places on his ability to capture a fully transcategorical sense of the concept of "being," he does at times use the term "being" in a way that might seem to reject such limitations. Most notably, he will use the term "beings" (*ta onta*) simply to refer to things that are, in a manner rather close to Rand's use of "existents." Aristotle also has various terms for the universe, and of these *to pan* ("the all" or "everything") seems to come closest to Rand's use of "existence." Such features of his thought mitigate the limitations to his overall worldview, which might otherwise be the result of lacking a unitary sense of "being." At the same time, they point to the very real need to have an account of a transcategorical but univocal meaning of "being" or "existence."

Rand's Agreement with Aristotle regarding Individual Entities and Abstractions

Where Aristotle speaks of *ousia* in the primary sense (per the *Categories*) or *ousia* as form and matter combined, Rand has the ontological category of "entity." It comes very close to Aristotle's usage of "primary substance"—at least sensible substances—but with the following caveats:

1. Rand does not consider naturally formed entities as more fully exemplifying the category of "entity" than artificially made or even accidentally assembled entities, but the contrary view has sometimes been attributed to Aristotle, and there is at least some ambiguity about his view on this point.

2. In addition to sensible primary substances, Aristotle argues for and endorses the existence of intelligible, immaterial primary substances—for example, god(s). For Aristotle, such substances are metaphysical primaries, but they are epistemologically posterior to sensible primary substances. They are better known "according to nature" but less well known "to us," as he would say—that is, they are more causally and explanatorily fundamental, but they are not known as immediately or as easily. For Rand, entities in the most basic sense are objects of sense perception.[12]

3. Rand refuses to mandate a priori that the familiar ontological categories of the human-perceptual scale will be applicable at every physical scale. Subquantum phenomena might not be describable as actions rather than attributes or vice versa. However, whatever such phenomena are, they will remain ontological primaries with respect to their "concreteness" and their "identity," or what the scholastics would have called their *haecceity* and *quiddity*, respectively. That is, subquantum phenomena will not be universals, but particulars (though not necessarily discrete countables), and they will be what they are, subject entirely to the law of identity.[13]

Rand is in deep agreement with Aristotle with respect to the priority of the category of primary substance or entity. Rand takes entities as primaries. Metaphysically, all the other basic categories could not exist without entities. Epistemologically, entities are the primitive objects of sense perception, our first and firmest form of awareness. The other categories can only be isolated and grasped through a process of abstraction:

> I was speaking here in the context of entity as against attribute or action. Actually, I was speaking here in the Aristotelian sense of the primary "substance"—which is a very misleading term, but what he meant was that the primary existent is an entity. And then aspects of an entity can be identified mentally, but only in relation to the entity. There are no attributes without entities, there are no actions without entities. Entity is that which you perceive and which can exist by itself. So that characteristics, qualities, attributes, actions, relationships do not exist by themselves. An entity is anything that can exist by itself. Character-

---

12. Rand is also prepared to speak of entities more loosely, though, so that they can include complex systems that cannot be directly perceived (*ITOE* 268–73; corresponding to *Workshops* 355–62). See Rheins 2016, 255.

13. *ITOE* 291–95 (cf. *Workshops* 345–49). See Rheins 2016, 254.

istics, qualities, attributes, actions, relationships do not exist by themselves" (*ITOE* 264).¹⁴

This illuminates Rand's meaning in the passage where she says that her agreement with Aristotle on the metaphysical and epistemological priority of entities is "The deepest thing Objectivism has in common" with his philosophy.

> Now the deepest thing Objectivism has in common with Aristotle—and it has many things in common—is this: Aristotle was the first to grasp what most people still do not, namely, that everything that exists is a specific, concrete entity, or an aspect of one, such as an action of an entity, an attribute of an entity, a relationship it bears, etc. But the base of everything is an entity—not an idea or abstraction. An abstraction is the form in which we organize these entities in order to understand them. To be an Aristotelian all the way down, you must grasp that only *concrete* events, *concrete* relationships, *concrete* problems exist. (*AON* 28)

Here, Rand is contrasting entities with their aspects (attributes, actions, relations), and she is contrasting them with abstractions. This might be puzzling, as the particular quality of a particular entity, such as the shade of green of this blade of grass, is not a type or a concept. Rand's point is that to cognitively isolate and identify a quality apart from the rest of an entity—or to grasp a concept of a quality, such as "green"—requires abstraction.

The priority of entities with respect to all other categories in Rand's philosophy accords very closely with Aristotle's discussion in the *Categories*, where the metaphysical primaries, "primary *ousia*," are individual, independent (not "in" another, per se) substances. The species and genera which are said of primary substances are *ousia* in a secondary sense (*Cat.* 2a14–19).¹⁵

The comparison becomes more complex when we try to make sense of Aristotle's conceptions of *ousia* as form and essence, especially in the *Metaphysics*. Rand herself endorsed the traditional interpretation of Aristotle as the "ancestor (unfortunately)" of "moderate realists" who

---

14. This corresponds to material from *Workshops* 51. See also *ITOE* 251 (cf. *Workshops* 191) and "The Stolen Concept" (*TON* 2[1] 2).

15. Greg Salmieri has suggested to me that the penultimate line of Rand's quote is especially apt for Aristotle's position in the *Categories*, given that a primary substance is a particular or a "this" (*tode ti*) while a secondary *ousia* signifies a sort (*poion*)—that is, it qualifies the many this-es that it is said of (*Cat.* 3b10–24).

"hold that abstractions exist in reality, but they exist only in concretes, in the form of metaphysical essences, and that our concepts refer to these essences" (*ITOE* 2). Thus, in her view, Aristotle did not think that abstractions are only "the form in which we organize these entities in order to understand them." They are intrinsic metaphysical forms.

> Let us note, at this point, the radical difference between Aristotle's view of concepts and the Objectivist view, particularly in regard to the issue of essential characteristics. It is Aristotle who first formulated the principles of correct definition. It is Aristotle who identified the fact that only concretes exist. But Aristotle held that definitions refer to metaphysical essences, which exist in concretes as a special element or formative power, and he held that the process of concept-formation depends on a kind of direct intuition by which man's mind grasps these essences and forms concepts accordingly. Aristotle regarded "essence" as metaphysical; Objectivism regards it as epistemological. (*ITOE* 52)

Rand still regarded her fundamental philosophy as Aristotelian in spirit—more consistently Aristotelian than Aristotle unfortunately was himself. She seems to think that her own view is the proper spirit of Aristotle's in as much as she sees him as having (1) correctly developed a rational, senses-based epistemology, (2) identified the laws of logic including the structure of definitions, and (3) as having moved in a positive direction away from Plato's other-worldly primacy of consciousness approach and "extreme realism" wherein entities depend on independently existing abstractions, the Platonic Ideas.[16]

Similar to Aristotle, Rand both relates all the other categories back to entities and takes these ontological categories to be incommensurable with one another. She was asked during the workshops about the formation of concepts of metaphysical categories such as "attribute" or "action." Specifically, she was asked if there must be a commensurable characteristic between, for example, attributes and other kinds of existents. Her

---

16. She may have thought he was able to accomplish these feats despite being a moderate realist because of an underlying and anti-Platonic commitment to this world or the "Primacy of Existence," on which see below. Or she may have thought that he was an incipient or inchoate proto-moderate realist, but was a far less "intrinsicist," sclerotic kind of moderate realist than his Thomistic epigones—a "very moderate realist," as it were. More recent scholarship on Aristotle's view of concepts (some of it by scholars influenced by Rand), suggest that Aristotle was not a moderate realist, and that his view may have been closer to Rand's than she realized though still distinct from it. On this issue, see Allan Gotthelf's Chapter 4 in this volume and the sources cited therein.

answer is that we do not form "attribute" in contrast to actions or "action" in contrast to relations or the like. Rather, the concepts of the subordinate categories are all formed in distinction from "entity" by grasping them as indivisible aspects of the entities to which they belong. So, each distinct subordinate category is irreducible—in the sense that it has no "conceptual common denominator"—that is, commensurable characteristic that it shares with the other subordinate categories (*ITOE* 274, *Workshops* 81). There is no common axis on which quality is one value and quantity or action is another. Rather, each category concept is grasped separately by uniting specific qualities, specific actions, and so forth, in contradistinction from "entity."[17] Here, too, she is in agreement with Aristotle about the other senses of "being" are understood by reference to substance/entity and are not species of a common genus.

Rand and the Univocity of "Existence," "Existents," "Exists"

There is, however, an important difference between Rand and Aristotle in their thought concerning the primary sense and scope of the concept "being" or "existence." Aristotle rejects the unqualified univocity of being; and the primary sense of "being," *ousia* as (primary) substance does not refer to all beings (*onta*). For Rand, on the other hand, the fundamental ontological fact is existence, the fundamental concept is "exists"/"existence," and she endorses a univocal sense of "existence," "exists," and "existent."

The terms "existence" and "existent," as Rand uses them, have transcategorical meanings—that is, there is a non-homonymous and irreducible sense in which Rand would say that a given quality, entity, relationship, and such, all "exist" or "are." By "existence" she means all that there is, "all that which exists." By "existent(s)" she means any individuated part(s) or aspect(s) of existence.[18] Does "all that which exists" mean only entities? Or does it include all actions, all relations, and so on, as well? We can answer this if we can determine whether only entities count as "existents" or if attributes, actions, and so forth are also "existents." It is the latter. "The units of the concepts 'existence' and 'identity' are every entity, attribute, action, event or phenomenon (including consciousness) that exists, ever existed or will ever exist" (*ITOE* 56).

While discussing the subtle differences between the concepts of "fact" and "existent" in the workshops, Rand explains that the term "ex-

---

17. *ITOE* 276–77, corresponding to material from *Workshops* 105–9.
18. *ITOE* 241 (cf. *Workshops* 212).

istent" is used to indicate a particular thing that exists—be it an entity, an attribute, a relation, or any such.[19] Particular relationships, actions, attributes, and such all count as existents. Again, while explaining that "existence" is wider than the concept of "external world," she makes it clear that the "exist–" concepts apply to all categories: "The axiom 'existence exists' is wider than the concept of the external world. It includes everything, as I indicated, including your mental states, mental processes, and such phenomena as ideas or feelings, which are not in the same category as physical reality, but they exist" (*ITOE* 242–43; see also *Workshops* 236).

Attributes, relations, actions, and so on do exist, they are properly referred to as "existents," and they are parts of "existence." The fact that they do not exist by themselves apart from entities and that they must be grasped through a process of abstraction does not mean they do not exist. "Length does exist in reality, only it doesn't exist by itself. It is not separable from an entity, but it certainly exists in reality. If it didn't, what would we be doing with our concepts of attributes? They would be pure fantasy then. The only thing that is epistemological and not metaphysical in the concept of 'length' is the act of mental separation, of considering this attribute separately as if it were a separate thing" (*ITOE* 279; see also *Workshops* 112). Thus the "exist–" concepts are univocal, whether speaking of an entity an action, an attribute, or a relation; something physical or mental; a single thing or a sum of things; and so on. For whether one speaks of particular existents or of existence as a whole, for Rand the common meaning is the fundamental, irreducible fact that it exists.

Does This Difference Make a Difference?

To fully assess the significance of the differences I am presenting, we would need to do at least three things: First, we would need to situate Aristotle's theory of meaning in the context of his theory of universals, both in itself and as it differs from Rand's theory of concepts. Second, we would need to assess the way that the concept of "being" encompasses both "existence" and "identity" without necessarily marking the subtle distinction Rand draws between them. Such a discussion would likely need to draw considerably upon the abundant literature on the Greek

---

19. *ITOE* 249 (cf. *Workshops* 213–14). The term "fact," in her view, can refer to a particular existent or to a complex of them (for example, an event or series of events), but it adds an epistemological emphasis: to call something a "fact" emphasizes that the putative existent(s) really exist(s)—that is, the concept of "fact" is a perspective on what truly does exist in light of the human capacity for error.

verb "to be" and the much debated relationship between its predicative and existential usages.[20] Third, to assess the overall impact on their respective systems of metaphysics (and their epistemologies), we would need to compare the most fundamental views of each philosopher with respect to reality as such. For Rand, such a view is the product of a philosopher's acceptance or rejection of the axioms. Thoroughgoing acceptance results in an overall orientation to existence and consciousness that Rand calls the "Primacy of Existence" (PoE). She takes Aristotle to be the father and first champion of PoE; she sees her own philosophy as a more consistent, refined form of the PoE, free of Aristotle's deviations from it. Its opposite, the Primacy of Consciousness, she attributes to Plato and sees culminated in Kant. In the next section I will present a sketch of how Aristotle's worldview is fundamentally in the PoE camp, albeit with some important divergences, but first I will suggest a few upshots of the univocity of the "exist-" concepts for Rand's philosophy.

Rand's account of "existence" as an axiomatic concept could not have been what it was had she not understood existence as transcategorically univocal and universal. Rand holds that perception is necessary for the infant to form the implicit concept of "entity," but all the material of the implicit concept of "existence" is furnished in the first act of awareness of any conscious organism, even if its consciousness is capable only of the simplest, unintegrated sensations.[21] In that sense then, the fundamental fact of existence is a fact available from any contact with *any aspect* of reality. Sensations alone would be inadequate to form categories such as "entity," "quality," and "quantity" or to distinguish between subject and object, but even one sensation suffices to make manifest the fundamental fact that there is something (*ITOE* 5–6).

Moreover, the fundamental facts that are grasped in axiomatic concepts and made explicit in the axioms are primitive. Existence, according to Rand, is unanalyzable (*ITOE* 55ff.; Rheins 2016, 248–49). The concept of "primary substance," on the other hand, is analyzed by Aristotle as a combination of form and matter, neither (said) in nor said of any other kind of being, capable of taking on contraries in the other categories without immediate destruction.

20. See Kahn 2004, 381–405; reprinted in Kahn 2009.
21. "Existence, identity, and consciousness . . . are implicit in every state of awareness from the first sensation to the first percept to the sum of all concepts. After the first discriminated sensation (or percept) man's subsequent knowledge adds nothing to the basic facts designated by the terms 'existence,' 'identity,' 'consciousness'—these facts are contained in any single state of awareness" (*ITOE* 55–56).

Rand agrees with Aristotle that actions, attributes, and so forth could not exist except as the actions and attributes of the entities that perform or possess them, but they are no less real than entities. They are dependent, but they exist, and the fundamental fact of existence does not come in degrees or varieties; that is, it is the same fundamental fact—being in reality—whether we are speaking of the existence of an entity, an action, an attribute, and so on. Rand frequently emphasizes the dependence of the other categories on entities. Nevertheless, to emphasize the inseparability of entities and attributes, she goes so far as to say that "an entity *is* its attributes" (*Workshops* 62). It would be impossible to say this without a univocal sense of existence that applies to attributes as well as entities. What this means, then, is that a univocal sense of "existence" is necessary in order to fully grasp and retain the perspective that existence and identity are one and inseparable.

Aristotle formulated PNC, so one can hardly say that he failed to respect the fact that "A is A."[22] And yet, he does divide the identity of a substance into two metaphysically distinct varieties: essences and accidents. For Aristotle, there is a much stronger tie between a substance and its essence than between the substance and its qualities or discrete actions or relationships. For a substance to lose its essence is for it to cease to be, whereas it can persist through taking on contraries with respect to qualities, relationships, and so on. Essences are said of but not (said to be) "in" substances, whereas individual qualities are (said to be) in a substance and universals of qualities are also said of substances (*Cat.* 5 3b13–21). So for Aristotle, essences are an ontological category distinct from qualities, whereas Rand would only draw a distinction between epistemically fundamental and nonfundamental attributes of an entity (or anything else). No doubt this difference owes much to the two philosophers' different approaches to the problem of universals, but I would conjecture that a significant factor is also the fact that Rand has a univocal sense of existence and Aristotle only has distinct senses of "being" focally related to substance.

Some Parting Thoughts on Aristotle and the Primacy of Existence

To close, I wish to suggest a further way to compare Aristotle and Rand

---

22. Rand seemingly accepts Professor E's claim that it was Aristotle who made the concept of "identity" explicit. *ITOE* 263 (cf. *Workshops* 218). Plato introduces a kind of proto-PNC principle in *Republic* IV. "It is clear that the same thing will never be able to do or undergo opposites in the same way, in relation to the same thing, at the same time" (436b8–9).

with respect to axioms. For Rand, the integration of the axioms and their corollaries gives the overall metaphysical orientation of the Primacy of Existence. To the extent that a philosopher evades the axioms, their philosophy has the opposite orientation, the Primacy of Consciousness. Even if a philosopher has not identified all the axioms explicitly, the extent to which they consistently advance the Primacy of Existence becomes a proxy for their implicit acceptance of them.

Rand's celebration of Aristotle as the founding father of the Primacy of Existence is worth quoting at length:

> Even though the influence of the Witch Doctor's views permeated the works of the early philosophers, reason, for the first time, was identified and acknowledged as man's ruling faculty, a recognition it had never been granted before. Plato's system was a monument to the Witch Doctor's metaphysics—with its two realities, with the physical world as a semi-illusory, imperfect, inferior realm, subordinated to a realm of *abstractions* (which means, in fact, though not in Plato's statement: subordinated to man's consciousness), with reason in the position of an inferior but necessary servant that paves the way for the ultimate burst of mystic revelation which discloses a "superior" truth. But Aristotle's philosophy was the intellect's Declaration of Independence. Aristotle, the father of logic, should be given the title of the world's first *intellectual,* in the purest and noblest sense of that word. No matter what remnants of Platonism did exist in Aristotle's system, his incomparable achievement lay in the fact that he defined the *basic* principles of a rational view of existence and of man's consciousness: that there is only *one* reality, the one which man perceives—that it exists as an *objective* absolute (which means: independently of the consciousness, the wishes or the feelings of any perceiver)—that the task of man's consciousness is to *perceive,* not to create, reality—that abstractions are man's method of integrating his sensory material—that man's mind is his only tool of knowledge—that A is A. (FTNI 22)[23]

What Rand refers to here as "the *basic* principles of a rational view of existence and of man's consciousness" is what she elsewhere calls the "Primacy of Existence." Almost all the principles she identifies with the PoE here or elsewhere are held and argued for by Aristotle.[24]

---

23. See also Peikoff, "America's Philosophical Origin" (*ARL* 270–71).
24. See *PWNI* 2–3, 24–26, from "Philosophy Who Needs It" and "The Metaphysical and the Man-Made," respectively. See also Peikoff 1991, 17–23; Rheins 2016, 246, 258–60.

Rejecting Plato's nativism and otherworldly rationalism, Aristotle takes the objects of sense perception to be (self-evidently) real. He holds that all human knowledge must begin from looking out at the sensible world rather than by turning our attention inward or to another, higher world.

Aristotle is the arch defender of eternalism. He rejects any possibility that the universe could come to be or pass away, and he specifically rejects Plato's views that the world came to be because of god(s) and that nature (*phusis*) is dependent upon the designs of divine mind(s) (*De Caelo* I.10–12).[25]

Aristotle holds that perceptible objects are what they are prior to and independent of the act of perception (*Met.* Γ.5 1010b30–1011a2). In fact, it is in his discussion of PNC in *Metaphysics* Γ.4–6 that Aristotle gives his most extensive discussion and refutations of relativism and subjectivism. PNC is itself the cornerstone of this refutation; as the firmest of principles, it must be known by anyone who knows anything at all, and no one can meaningfully deny or disbelieve it. The very attempt to deny it must reaffirm it.

The most obvious way that Aristotle diverges from the PoE is in positing the existence of a consciousness conscious of nothing but itself. "Thought thinking of thought" is how Aristotle famously describes god, the unmoved mover in *Metaphysics* Λ, an immutable, self-referential activity of immaterial intellect (*Met.* Λ.9 1074b34–35). But although the unmoved mover is (a) god, it does not create the world, it does not give the world or its parts their identity, and it does not even act in any direct way to sustain the world; it is the spark of pure, unchanging activity upon which the perpetuation of motion depends, not by being the first moving mover, but by inspiring the first of these movers to move in perpetual emulation of its own unmoving activity. In this respect at least, Aristotle's god is even less an abandonment of the PoE than that of Spinoza or the Deists.

This is only a sketch. More can be said on this topic, and I believe it would be quite edifying to do so, but much more needs to be said before we can capture a full crisp picture of Aristotle's philosophy through the lens of Rand's concepts of "PoE" and "PoC." Of this I am personally and palpably aware. When I first met Jim some twenty years ago, I was giv-

---

25. Aristotle rejects the idea that there is no teleology without deliberation See *Phys.* II.8 199b26–33. For Plato's views, see *Timaeus* 28a4–29d3, 29d7–30a7, 48a3–5, 53b2–7; *Laws* X 892a2*ff.*, and XII 966d8–67e2.

ing a presentation based on my undergraduate honors thesis on Aristotle and PNC. In that presentation, I took the bold step of suggesting ways in which Aristotle was enunciating a fundamentally PoE approach to reality and thought or language in his refutations of relativism in *Met.* Γ. Jim rightly pressed me to further develop my claims and to furnish them with the careful analysis and argument they required. Regrettably, this is not that, but I hope not to keep him waiting another twenty years to see it done.

Section II
UNIVERSALS AND CONCEPTS

4
Concepts and Essences in Aristotle and Ayn Rand

ALLAN GOTTHELF

Ayn Rand thought one could ask whether her theory of concepts was Aristotelian. She thought that Aristotle had a theory of concepts, at least in outline and that her own theory, while working from an essentially similar philosophic base and with similar aims, was essentially different from his. And she thought that in some sense her work completes his.[1] In this paper I want, essentially, to agree with this assessment of her relationship to Aristotle—except to suggest that there are directions in Aristotle's thinking, particular about *sameness* and *unity*, that may bring their thinking on the nature and basis of concepts closer than she thought.

Rand's Theory of Concepts and Essence

Rand, as Jim Lennox notes in his paper, viewed concepts as "philosophy's central issue" (*ITOE* 1). She held that one's view of the nature, basis, for-

---

1. We can see this in an important passage that Jim Lennox discusses in his chapter above: "Centuries ago, the man who was—no matter what his errors—the greatest of your philosophers, has stated the formula defining the concept of existence and the rule of all knowledge: *A is A*. A thing is itself. You have never grasped the meaning of his statement. I am here to complete it: Existence is Identity, Consciousness is Identification" (*Atlas* 1016). Rand's theory of concepts is part of her account of the nature of the identification that proper conscious activity is. In that sense this passage may be taken to endorse the proposition that her theory of concepts completes Aristotle's, as we shall see.

mation, and validity of concepts shapes one's views across philosophy—from metaphysics and epistemology to ethics and esthetics. At stake, she said, is no less than "the cognitive efficacy of man's mind" (*ITOE* 3; *VOR* 6) and with it, our image of ourselves as beings in the world, including our self-esteem and our moral stature.

Rand's epistemology is founded on her axioms (on which see Lennox's chapter in this volume, "Axioms and Their Validation in Aristotle and Ayn Rand") and on their corollary: the primacy of existence—the thesis that things exist and are what they are independent of consciousness, and that consciousness is essentially directed on a reality independent of itself. She holds that our basic cognitive contact with mind-independent reality is *perception*, which is a direct awareness of entities, of things, discriminated from each other and from their backgrounds. Concepts are not required for perceptual awareness as such (though once acquired on the basis of prior perception, they may of course facilitate perceptual recognition).

Human beings, Rand observes, are not able to survive by perceptual awareness alone. We need to *integrate perceptual data into concepts*, and these concepts into a vast body of hierarchically structured, higher-order concepts.

To understand concepts, Rand holds, we have to understand this integration—the cognitive *integration*—involved in moving from multiple grasps of a small number of units to a single unitary grasp of indefinitely many such units (e.g., from the perception of a number of tables to the concept of *table*, encompassing in a single awareness all tables, past, present, and future; and, later, from the concepts of *table, chair, bed,* etc., to the concepts of *furniture* and *end table*; and so forth). That is, we have to understand the process of *concept-formation*, at all its levels. We will focus on the earliest levels, to see the heart of the process.[2]

Our ability to form concepts and to build our knowledge on them, Rand holds, depends in part on certain facts about the world and in part in certain facts about the nature of a conceptual consciousness. These facts about the world include, among others, the existence of a certain

---

2. Since, beyond the earliest concepts, according to Rand, this process is volitional, and subject to error, as measured by the goal of acquiring and using the knowledge we need in order to live successfully, there will be norms for the formation and application of concepts. And there are relationships between the norms that Rand has identified and ideas in Aristotle. In the space we have here, we will have to focus on the process itself—what one might call the mechanics of concept-formation—including the role of definitions and the nature of essence.

type of similarity—a type based in the fact of commensurability. The key fact about a conceptual consciousness is that it integrates by way of a process Rand calls "measurement-omission" (*Workshops* 199, *ITOE* 144).

Traditional realists claimed that the basis in reality of our conceptual groupings is some sort of mind-independent, identical form or essence or property found in (or intimately connected with) each of the individuals of a group. Rand rejects this view. In so doing, she means to reject both the view that the individuals share a numerically identical element and the view that each of the individuals has a form or essence of its own, which forms or essences, though numerically distinct are qualitatively identical. She also rejects the common thread she finds in traditional nominalism and conceptualism, viz. that conceptual groupings are ultimately arbitrary, are based on subjective, irreducible resemblances, and are selected at most for pragmatic reasons.

Similarity, for Rand, is neither identity underlying difference nor subjective unanalyzable resemblance. Similarity is objective, and analyzable—in terms, as I've said, of commensurability. To take some simple examples, when a child first experiences two tables as similar to each other and different from some chairs, or two colored objects of different shades of red as similar to each other against an object of some shade of blue, the experience of similarity is a matter, not of noticing, intuitively, underlying identity, but of noticing, perceptually, lesser difference along some quantitative or, as Aristotle would put it, more-and-less, axis. The similar items, as Rand puts it, share with the contrasting items a commensurable characteristic "such as shape in the case of tables, or hue in the case of colors" (*ITOE* 13). Later, similarity must be detected conceptually; but the requirement of an underlying commensurability will remain.

The grasp of similarity is a matter of implicit measurement, of relating particulars to each other, along some quantitative axis. "The element of *similarity* is crucially involved in the formation of every concept; similarity, in this context, is the relationship between two or more existents which possess the same characteristic(s), but in different measure or degree" (*ITOE* 13).[3]

---

3. Tables are differentiated from chairs and other types of furniture by possession of a range of shape and use and vary themselves along numerous quantitative axes, including that range of shape, their size, number of supports, materials, the disposition of the bodies (living or not) that use them, and so forth. This analysis of similarity applies as well, Ayn Rand argues, to the similarity that is the basis of higher-order concepts, although there the similarity must be grasped conceptually. To take the simplest case, tables, chairs, beds, and so forth—*furniture*—will not be experienced as similar, prior to the formation of the con-

This reference to "the same characteristic(s)" is not an endorsement of realism. Characteristics exist only in some measure or degree. Different lengths (of a stick, a ruler, a hallway, for example) each exist in some determinate amount. But they are all quantitatively relatable to a unit length. That relational fact about them, I believe Rand intended, is what their being of the same characteristic consists in.

By isolating particulars based on perceived similarity relationships (e.g., the tables against the background of chairs, or the shades of red against the background of blue), a human consciousness is in position (as an animal consciousness is not) to retain the relevant attribute and omit the measurements. The model is the algebraic variable. The stick, ruler, and hallway are all x inches long. Rand writes: "Bear firmly in mind that the term 'measurements omitted' does not mean, in this context, that measurements are regarded as nonexistent; it means that *measurements exist, but are not specified*. . . . The principle is: the relevant measurements must exist in *some* quantity, but may exist in *any* quantity" (*ITOE* 12).

As Harry Binswanger (1989) has explained, measurement-omission is not an insight into a universal element. It is rather an interrelating of the commensurable determinate particulars. Measurement-omission, as he puts it, is measurement inclusion. In retaining the attribute—length, or table-shape—the child retains not some "universal" but a range within an axis of measurement. That is, the child recognizes implicitly that the commensurability of the various lengths or table-shapes allows for many more particular lengths or table-shapes, indefinitely many along that axis of measurement. It is precisely this grasp of the relevant range within the axis of measurement, with all its available points or slots, that open-ends the awareness to include all lengths (or table-shapes), past, present, and future, and creates the concept.

Based on this account of concept-formation, Rand offers the follow-

---

cepts of *table, chair, bed*; they are too different for their similarity, against the background say of walls, floors, and windows, to be noticed perceptually. One would need first to form the lower-level concepts. But once one is positioned to notice the similarity of types of furniture, one can do so only against the background of other parts of a human habitation, which vary in quantity or degree from them along one or more commensurable characteristics, one or more axes (e.g., shape, size, type of moveability, type of use, including disposition of the body, and so forth), such that the pieces of furniture are less different from each other than they are from the contrasting items. Once one has formed concepts of consciousness, the units of these concepts come to be distinguished by use for which they are generally intended and eventually their function; but conscious phenomena vary "in measure or degree" too, as Rand explains in *ITOE*, ch. 4, though the type of measurement is very different. (For further discussion, see Gotthelf 2013; Salmieri 2013 and 2016d.)

ing definition of a concept: "*A concept is a mental integration of two or more units possessing the same distinguishing characteristic(s), with their particular measurements omitted*" (*ITOE* 13; italics in original).

In her monograph, Rand applies this theory to a full range of concepts (including higher-level abstractions, concepts pertaining to consciousness, and axiomatic concepts) and discusses at some length both the objectivity of concepts and the norms for their formation and use. She also gives over an extended chapter to the nature, purpose, and rules of definition, the nature of an essential characteristic, and the difference between her theory of concepts and essence and those of the traditional schools I mentioned earlier, in the context of which she discusses Aristotle.

The purpose of a definition, she says, "is to distinguish a concept from all other concepts and thus to keep its units differentiated from all other existents" (*ITOE* 40). It does this in part by specifying the distinguishing characteristics.[4] But, as one's knowledge of the distinguishing characteristics of the particulars grasped by a concept expands, one can't specify them all in a definition: no one can hold all those characteristics in mind, as a single unit, clearly grasped. What's needed is a single distinguishing characteristic, or a very small number of them, that will bring readily to mind all the other distinguishing characteristics.[5] It's here that Rand introduces her conception of *essence*.

She observes that the only distinguishing characteristic of a concept's referents that readily bring to mind all of the referents' other distinguishing characteristics—and thereby defines the concept—is the one on which those others, or the greatest number of them, depend—the causally fundamental one. The causally fundamental characteristic is thus essential to the concept's referents: without that characteristic (and the others that depend on it), the referents would no longer fall under the concept and no longer be the kind of things they are.[6] The essential characteristic, then, is the *fundamental distinguishing characteristic*—the one that is *responsible for* (and thus explains) the greatest number of other distinguishing characteristics—*in a given context of knowledge* (*ITOE* 42–46).

---

4. "A definition . . . specifies the distinguishing characteristic(s) of the units, and indicates the category of existents from which they were differentiated" (*ITOE* 41).

5. Although Rand recognizes that in certain cases the definition will specify more than one distinguishing characteristic, I will in what follows, for simplicity of formulation, talk as if there is always only one.

6. "A definition must identify the nature of the units [of a concept], i.e., the essential characteristics without which the units would not be the kind of existents they are" (*ITOE* 42, cf. 45–46).

Now, should one come to discover a more fundamental distinguishing characteristic—on this understanding of the role of a definition—then the definition would have to change to reflect that new knowledge. The earlier essential characteristic, though still true of the kind, is no longer essential to it. (A historical example is the process by which the definition of atoms in terms of atomic weight came to be replaced by the definition in terms of atomic number.)

So, essences, for Rand, are contextual. They are also, as she puts it, "*epistemological.*" An essential characteristic, she writes, "is factual, in the sense that it does exist, does determine other characteristics and does distinguish a group of existents from all others" (*ITOE* 52). And in a given context of knowledge, which characteristic is the essential one is fixed by those facts. But its designation as "essential," under those conditions, reflects its performance of a necessary epistemological function.[7]

Rand on Aristotle

Having completed the presentation of her views on definition and essence, Rand continues:

> Let us note, at this point, the radical difference between Aristotle's view of concepts and the Objectivist view, particularly in regard to the issue of essential characteristics.
>
> It is Aristotle who first formulated the principles of correct definition. It is Aristotle who identified the fact that only concretes exist. But Aristotle held that definitions refer to metaphysical *essences*, which exist *in* concretes as a special element or formative power, and he held that the process of concept-formation depends on a kind of direct intuition by which man's mind grasps these essences and forms concepts accordingly.
>
> Aristotle regarded "essence" as metaphysical; Objectivism regards it as *epistemological*. (*ITOE* 52–53)

So, for Rand, Aristotle is a kind of moderate realist on concepts, and she views the difference between his view of concepts and her own as significant, even fundamental.

Nonetheless, in certain other contexts, when she is distinguishing

---

7. It is not often discussed why Rand chooses to call characteristics that perform this epistemological function *essential*, when that term, and especially its corresponding noun, has a long history of designating a certain metaphysical status. There are clues to the reason in the previous note, and in the text to which it is attached, but there is much more to be said, for which I regrettably do not have time.

Aristotle's metaphysics and epistemology from Plato's and insisting that the distinction between their two philosophies is fundamental, she identifies with Aristotle's approach to abstractions—that is, concepts. In one place she says that part of Aristotle's "incomparable achievement" lay in his identification "that abstractions are man's method of integrating his sensory material" (*ITOE* 54).[8] In another, informal context, she identifies with Aristotle's grasp that "the base of everything is an entity—not an idea or abstraction. An abstraction is the form in which we organize these entities in order to understand them," describing this as "the deepest thing Objectivism has in common with Aristotle."[9]

In both passages, Rand ascribes to Aristotle the view that abstractions—that is, concepts—are the result of processes of integration of sensory-perceptual data. Though it is clearly Plato from whom she is differentiating Aristotle, her discussions of Kant in the title essay of *For the New Intellectual* and elsewhere make it clear that Aristotle is also being differentiated from Kant and others who hold that perception of entities is the result of the bringing to the world of preexistent concepts, and that our perception of "objects" or entities is itself the product of an application of concepts. (It is interesting that by page 7 of his extremely influential *Mind and World*, contemporary Kantian John McDowell [1994] has already appealed to Peter Geach's [1957, §§6–11] "trenchant criticism" of

---

8. "No matter what remnants of Platonism did exist in Aristotle's system, his incomparable achievement lay in the fact that he defined the *basic* principles of a rational view of existence and of man's consciousness: that there is only *one* reality, the one which man perceives—that it exists as an *objective* absolute (which means: independently of the consciousness, the wishes or the feelings of any perceiver)—that the task of man's consciousness is to *perceive*, not to create, reality—that abstractions are man's method of integrating his sensory material—that man's mind is his only tool of knowledge—that A is A" (*FTNI* 17–18).

9. "I have often said that the whole history of philosophy is a duel between Plato and Aristotle, and that this conflict is present in every issue. If you think principles, and therefore philosophy, exist apart from concretes, then you are a Platonist. Plato believed abstractions are archetypes or universals that exist in some other realm, in the form of nonmaterial, supernatural entities. Now the deepest thing Objectivism has in common with Aristotle—and it has many things in common—is this: Aristotle was the first to grasp what most people still do not, namely, that everything that exists is a specific, concrete entity, or an aspect of one, such as an action of an entity, an attribute of an entity, a relationship it bears, etc. But the base of everything is an entity—not an idea or abstraction. An abstraction is the form in which we organize these entities in order to understand them.

To be an Aristotelian all the way down, you must grasp that only *concrete* events, *concrete* relationships, *concrete* problems exist. (If you are not Aristotelian all the way down, it is no moral crime; but it will cause problems, so train yourself to be one.)" (*AOF* 28, cf. *Letters* 394, 517)

"the abstractionist picture of the role of the Given in the formation of concepts.") Aristotle's contrasting approach to concepts, and the entire broad metaphysical and epistemological approach of which it is a part, is for Rand (as one might put it) "world-historical"—and profoundly true—and in relation to it, she thinks of herself, as she once implied, as "Aristotelian all the way down" (*AOF* 28; see also *Letters* 394, 517).

Aristotle on Concepts and Essences

Let us take a look at Aristotle ourselves and then return to an evaluation of Ayn Rand's assessment of her relationship to him. Does he, to start, even have a concept of *concept*? We can begin to answer this question by looking at a well-known passage from the first chapter of *On Interpretation*:

> Now spoken sounds are symbols of affections (*pathemata*) in the soul, and written marks symbols of spoken sounds. And just as written marks are not the same for all men neither are spoken sounds. But what these are in the first place signs of—affections of the soul—are the same for all; and what these affections are likenesses (*homoiomata*) of—actual things (*pragmata*)—are also the same. These matters have been discussed in the work on the soul and do not belong to the present subject. Just as some thoughts (*noema*) in the soul are neither true nor false while some others are necessarily one or the other, so also with spoken sounds. For falsity and truth have to do with combination and separation. Thus names and verbs by themselves—for instance 'man' and 'white' when nothing further is added—are like the thoughts (*noemata*) that are without combination and separation; for so far as they are they are neither true nor false. (*Int.* 1 16a3–13)[10]

Here we have "affections" in (or of) the soul, each associated with a word, that are persisting units of thought without truth value, which join to make thoughts that are true or false, each "of actual things" (*pragmata*). Since there are other passages in his works in which Aristotle speaks in a similar vein (e.g., in *DA* III.6–8), and no passages I am aware of that deny that there are such uncompounded units of thought, I am prepared to say that Aristotle has a grasp of what a concept is, and for our purposes might be said to have a concept of *concept*, even though he does not here, or perhaps anywhere, have a fixed term for it. He has at least what Rand (*ITOE* 5–6, 159–62) would call an "implicit concept" of *concept*.

---

10. All translations from Barnes 1984, unless indicated otherwise.

We can ask, then, how Aristotle thinks that these concepts are formed, and to what they refer (in Rand's sense of "refer")—what are they directly *of*? Since Aristotle was not focused on the issue of concept-formation in the way Rand was, his views on the subject need to be extracted delicately from a series of difficult texts on related subjects. For reasons of space, I will not attempt to do this here, though we will touch on some of these texts below.[11]

Turning then to the question of what a concept refers to, we can ask whether the "actual things" mentioned in the *On Interpretation* passage are *universals* or *particulars*? (Is there, directly, one thing per "affection," or many?)

Metaphysics B is a presentation and review of central and difficult questions that Aristotle's lectures on first philosophy will have to answer. At the opening of chapter 4, he introduces "the hardest of all [difficulties] and the most necessary to examine" (*Met.* B.4 999a24–25): "If, on the one hand, there is nothing apart from individual things, and the individuals are infinite in number, how is it possible to get knowledge of the infinite individuals? *For all the things that we know, we know insofar as they are somehow one and the same (*hen ti kai tauton*), and insofar as something belongs (*huparchei*) to them universally*" (999a26–29; emphasis added).[12] But if not (to paraphrase the continuation of the passage), then kinds will exist apart from the individuals, and we will run into all the problems the Platonists do.[13]

Now, the word I have translated as "belongs" (*huparchei*) is a standard verb in Aristotle's logical works to signal a predication. So, what we need, if knowledge is to be possible, according to this passage, is not yet

---

11. See Salmieri 2008 (esp. ch. 4), for the fullest treatment I know of Aristotle's view of concept-formation.

12. Here and in the continuation (in the next note), I have made some modifications to Ross's translation in Barnes 1984. Ross translates *hei katholou ti huparchei* as "insofar as some attribute belongs to them universally." It could be translated as "insofar as some(thing) universal belongs to them" or "...is present in them."

13. The passage continues: "But if this is necessary, and there must be something apart from the individuals, it will be necessary that kinds exist apart from the individuals,—either the lowest or highest kinds; but we found by discussion just now that this is impossible.— Further, if we admit in the fullest sense that something exists apart from the concrete thing, whenever something is predicated of the matter, must there, if there is something apart, be something corresponding to each set of individuals, or to some and not others, or to none? If there is nothing apart from individuals, there will be no object of thought (*noeton*), but all things will be objects of sense, and there will be no knowledge of anything, unless we say that sensation is knowledge." (*Met.* B.4 999a29–b3; trans. W. D. Ross)

some metaphysical essence but, rather, something that can be truly predicated universally of the indefinitely many subjects—they have to all be that; where in so being they are in some way the same, and one.

The same point is made in the *Posterior Analytics* in I.11 and I.22, two places where Aristotle rejects the Platonic thesis that *epistēmē*, or knowledge proper, requires the existence of separate Forms: "For there to be *forms* or some one thing apart from the many is not necessary if there are to be demonstrations; ... There must, therefore, be some one and the same thing, non-homonymous, holding of several cases" (*APo.* I.11 77a5–9). (Scholars will recognize that Aristotle does not say *synonymous*—having the same definable essence—but *non-homonymous*.)

The harsher criticism of the Forms in *APo.* I.22 offers, as what's needed for knowledge, true subjects and true predicates, "one thing said of one thing" (83a21). But there too, the kind of unity or sameness required is not specified. This is important, because for Aristotle, there are different types of unity and sameness, for both general subjects and predicates, and some of them do not support a moderate realist interpretation of the concepts for those subjects and predicates, and those cases are surprisingly widespread, as we will see shortly.

The two chapters that are perhaps most frequently quoted in support of the moderate realist reading of Aristotle are *De Anima* III.4 and *Posterior Analytics* II.19. In *De Anima* Aristotle speaks of "the thinking part of the soul" as "capable of receiving the *form* of an object" (*DA* III.4 429b16; emphasis added), and he says that, while sense-perception "discriminates" the (material) thing, it's the thinking part of the soul that "discriminates" its essence (literally, "what it is to be" the thing). For example: "a magnitude and what it is to be a magnitude, and ... water and what it is to be water" (429b10–11). This opens the question as to what an Aristotelian essence is, and how we come to know it.

Posterior Analytics II.19 is concerned with the nature and source of our knowledge of first principles of demonstrative knowledge, *epistēmē*. The chapter is notoriously obscure. But among other things, Aristotle says that from memory and experience "the whole universal ... [comes] to rest in the soul (the one apart from the many, whatever is one and the same in all those things)" (*APo.* II.19 100a4–7).

Note that in this passage the universal is in the soul, but it corresponds to "whatever is one and the same in [the particulars]."[14] We must, then,

---

14. There are also passages, even one in the vicinity of the passage I've just quoted, in

turn to Aristotle's account of the different types of sameness and unity. I'll focus on sameness. Aristotle distinguishes, in various texts, same *in number*, same *in form*, same *in kind*, same *by analogy*.[15] I'd like to focus on same in kind. But first some examples. A human being's nose is the same in number with itself, as is the human being with himself.[16] The noses of any two human beings are the same in form, as are the human beings themselves. A *human* nose and a *horse's* nose are the same in kind, which Aristotle glosses in *Historia animalium* as "they *are* the same, but they differ in more-and-less" (*HA* I.1 486a21–23; emphasis added). In an important passage in *Parts of Animals*, he elaborates: "[T]hose animals that differ by degree and the more and the less have been brought together under one kind . . . I mean for example, that bird differs from bird by the more or by degree (for one has long feathers, another short feathers)" (*PA* I.4 644a16–18, 19–21; trans. Lennox 2001a). But, we may say, they all have feathers.

What's important here I think is this. Although the fact of the quantitative or dimensional variation possible to eagle feathers or to human noses is no part of their being the same in form (since whatever the variation, they make the same contribution to eagle life or to human life), this is not so for sameness in kind. For eagle and sparrow feathers to be the same in kind, they not only have to both contribute to a life in which flight is crucial, but they have to have quantitative difference that makes a functional difference to their flying and in general living.

The quantitative specification is central to what it is to be an eagle or a sparrow. The kind (bird), and therefore the concept *bird*, are thus quite different from what moderate realism calls for. For, at times Aristotle says that the kinds are potentialities: bird, then, is not so much a class unified by a logically complete essence, but a generic potentiality that exists in all birds for being specified across many quantitative dimensions. In passages in *Metaphysics* I.8, he explains: the "Animal" itself is different in the human and the horse case. Kinds, then, don't exist as such, but only as differentiated, as specified into forms. And that points to a clear difference between sameness in kind and the sort of abstract identity across the instances of a concept called for by moderate realism. (And to a similarity

---

which Aristotle appears to speak as if the universal is in the particulars. In a fuller treatment than is possible here, these would, of course, have to be addressed.

15. These include, among others, *Top.* I.7, *Met.* Δ.9 (with 6), several chapters in *Met.* I, and various passages in the biology, especially *PA* I.4–5 and *HA* I.1 (and with these, *APo.* II.14).

16. As Aristotle might say: Socrates' nose and that snub nose over there (when I'm pointing at Socrates) are one, and the same, in number.

between genus-concepts in Aristotle and concepts in general in Rand, but we'll come back to that.)[17]

That leaves sameness in form, which is precisely the cases where, according to Aristotle, we have a definable essence in the primary sense. I will now just say this. The notion—characteristic of the position I called "moderate realism"—that the definition that states the essence describes some mind-independent identity shared by different individuals of an indivisible form of a kind—and that this identity (whether numerical or qualitative) is (i) the form(s) of the particulars, and (ii) is grasped intuitively in cognition, has become increasingly uncertain with the continued study of both Aristotle's *Posterior Analytics* and his biological works. At least in *Generation of Animals* IV.3, it seems clear that the form of an individual reaches down to heritable features that do not define the "species," such as facial shape, as important work by David Balme (1987) and John Cooper (2004), among others has shown; indeed Balme suggests that form reaches all the way down to the unique particulars. And serious questions about the traditional view of sameness in form have been raised by Jim Lennox (1985, 1987) in two valuable papers and explored further by Gregory Salmieri (2008, 56–122; 2012).

It is not entirely clear to me what the implications of this understanding of form are for our understanding of Aristotle's view of concepts and their objects. But it suggests to me that Aristotle may have been less of a moderate realist, even in regard to his first-level *infimae species*, his indivisible forms of a kind, and more of (if I may say) an "Aristotelian" than Rand and other scholars of the tradition have thought. I acknowledge the issue is open.

However, even if it turns out that Aristotle does hold that our concepts of *infimae species* group things together because of a shared metaphysical essence (the metaphysical side of moderate realism), it is doubt-

---

17. There are yet other cases where Aristotle implicitly rejects the moderate realist notion that instances of a concept share some identical feature or definable mind-independent essence—some readers will know his thesis that the unity (or sameness) of beings—of things that are said to be—is a "focal" or *pros hen* unity, and there is the cumulative unity that underwrites the concept of soul, where there is no significant universal feature that all levels of souls share as souls. Cases of sameness by analogy are tricky ones, because there typically won't, and shouldn't usually, be a common name, though under some description (see "namelike phrase" [*APo*. II.10 93b30–31]), features that are the same by analogy can, and should, be treated as a unit for scientific investigation, and this unit then counts as a universal predicate. (*APo*. II.14 98a20–23 [with 13–19]; *PA* I.4–5; see Gotthelf 1997 and Lennox 2001a on these passages). Aristotle has to understand all concepts of things united by these various samenesses differently from what a moderate realist would think about these concepts.

ful that he was an intuitionist about how essences are grasped. The last several decades of scholarship on *Posterior Analytics* II and on Aristotle's practice, especially in his biological works, make it clear that he thinks the grasp of essence is the result of a complex process of explanatory reasoning based in perceptual data.[18]

Moreover, as I argue in "Aristotle as Scientist: A Proper Verdict" (Gotthelf 2012, 371–98), this process proceeds in stages, with earlier definitions being supplanted when they are explained by more fundamental ones, culminating in the definition that will take its place as a first principle of a completed Aristotelian science. There is a sense, then, in which Aristotelian definitions (and perhaps, by extension, essences) can be said to be contextual—or relative to a context of knowledge, but this is not how Aristotle himself would have put the point, and it is not the whole of what Rand meant when she said that essences are epistemological rather than metaphysical.[19]

The reservations we have found about Rand's understanding of Aristotle as a moderate realist who believed that essences were grasped by some form of intuition only strengthen our picture of Rand as Aristotelian, by revising our picture of Aristotle, and thus of the extent to which she agrees with him in metaphysical and epistemological fundamentals.

Still, I would be prepared to say that Rand's metaphysics and epistemology of concepts is indeed Aristotelian, even if it were to turn out that Aristotle is fully a moderate realist, believing that (i) all concepts are grouped via metaphysical essences and that (ii) these essences are grasped intuitively. For, even such a moderate-realist-Aristotle, as Rand points out, endorses the primacy of the mind-independent concrete entity and the basing of concepts in perception and, in so doing, rejects the heart of Platonic (and, in advance, Kantian) metaphysics and epistemology. And that endorsement—with Aristotle's aim of developing fully worked out integrated theories to support that endorsement—initiates and defines a philosophical tradition, a tradition of which Ayn Rand is a proud member, and which she profoundly advances. I have tried to make a case that

18. Charles 2000 is especially important for its interpretation of the *Posterior Analytics*. On Aristotle's biological practice and its connection to the *Analytics*, see especially the papers collected in Part I of Lennox 2001b and sections II, IV, and V of Gotthelf 2012.

19. I regret that I have been unable to discuss the relationship between Rand and Aristotle on essences. This is a very complex matter, on which I hope I have provided at least some leads.

Rand and Aristotle are, in their respective theories, even closer than that. Either way, Rand's theory of concepts shares a fundamental aim with Aristotle's, and, insofar as it is, as I think, a substantially developed theory, and true, it may be said, as she thought, to complete Aristotle's project.[20]

As for the details of their theories, I've also alluded to the striking similarity between Aristotle's view of the relation, in reality and in concept, between (e.g.) eagle and bird and Rand's view of the relation between individual eagles and eagle. This aspect of Aristotle's thought and many other aspects that I've touched on warrant more attention from Aristotle scholars than they've yet gotten. Likewise, in my view, Rand's own rich metaphysics and epistemology of concepts deserves much closer study from a much wider range of philosophers than it has so far gotten.

Editors' Note

Allan Gotthelf presented a version of this paper at the December 29, 2005, meeting of the Ayn Rand Society, and it was distributed to members of that society shortly beforehand. In the years preceding his death in 2013, he made some minor modifications to the paper with an eye to its inclusion in this volume. The editors have made some further light revisions to prepare it for publication.

---

20. See n. 2 above. There will of course be many contexts in which one wants to stress the differences between Rand's theory and Aristotle's—focusing on the theory's advance over his, and its success as a theory of concepts. On certain narrower meanings of "Aristotelian," then, Rand's theory is, of course, not Aristotelian. That fact does not contradict the claim made here at the appropriate level of abstraction—and a profoundly important level of abstraction—her theory is indeed Aristotelian.

5
Comments on "Concepts and Essences in Aristotle and Ayn Rand," by Allan Gotthelf

ANDREA FALCON

> The deepest thing Objectivism has in common with Aristotle—and it has many things in common—is this: Aristotle was the first to grasp what most people still do not, namely, that everything that exists is a specific, concrete entity, or an aspect of one, such as an action of an entity, an attribute of an entity, a relationship it bears, etc. But the base of everything is an entity—not an idea or abstraction. An abstraction is the form in which we organize these entities in order to understand them.
>
> AYN RAND, *AOF*

There is a great deal of interest in this quote. Here I will concentrate on the claim that abstractions—namely, concepts—are the form in which we organize entities in order to understand them, and on the observation that this claim is the deepest thing that Objectivism has in common with Aristotle. To this end, I will offer some reflections on how Aristotle introduces, and indeed justifies, three key concepts that he employs in his study of the physical world: matter, form, and privation. For Aristotle, these concepts are so basic they have to be in place early on in order to study the physical world. In short, we cannot do science without them.

A close study of how these concepts are introduced is interesting for at least two reasons. First, we are not given these concepts and told that they are essential to our scientific project; rather, we are led to their discovery. Second, the concepts in question are true abstractions in the sense that they map the totality of the physical world. In light of the above, the most obvious questions are two: (1) How do we arrive at such abstractions? (2) How do these abstractions relate to the complexity of the physical world around us?

The points of contact between the Objectivist and the Aristotelian accounts of concept-formation are two, in my view. First, the Aristotelian concepts do not reduce, let alone eliminate, the complexity of the physical world. On the contrary, they are best understood as abstractions by which we organize, and thereby illuminate, that complexity. Second, these concepts are not grasped intuitively but, rather, they are reached by means of a rational analysis that starts from the data given by sense-perception. At least for Aristotle, this analysis does not become expendable once these concepts are reached. On the contrary, it is our best argument for the view that these concepts are objective in the sense that they possess the explanatory power that is required to make sense of the world around us. What is at stake can be highlighted with the help of another question: What is the method that allows us to reach concepts that are truly objective? Answering this question is at the heart not only of the Aristotelian project but also of the philosophy that Ayn Rand called "Objectivism."

In the pages to follow, I first introduce the method that Aristotle employs to reach these principles. It is outlined in the opening chapter of *Physics* I. Then, I look at how Aristotle applies this method in the rest of the book, with a concentration on the extended argument offered in *Physics* I.5–7. At that point, it still remains to be seen whether, and eventually to what extent, the method employed in *Physics* I can be extended beyond the narrow boundaries of the discovery and justification of highly theoretical concepts such as matter, form, and privation. In the final section, I offer a few remarks that begin to address this large question.

Physics I.1

In *Physics* I.1, Aristotle outlines what he describes as a natural road:

> It is natural, the road which is from what is better known and clearer to us to what is clearer and better known by nature: for it is not the case that the same things are known to us and also without qualification. So it is necessary to proceed in this way from what is unclear by nature but clearer to us to what is clearer by nature and better known. The things

that are confounded to a degree are at first evident and clear to us: it is only later, starting from these [confounded] things, that the elements and the principles come to be known to those who analyze them. (*Phys.* I.1 184a16–23)

Since this road is natural, it is presumably open to all of us. And yet, there may be no alternative to it. In other words, this road may be forced upon us by our (human) nature. Aristotle may be thinking that, as human beings who want to understand the world around us, we have no choice but to take this road. This would explain why Aristotle says that it is necessary to proceed in this way—namely, from what is better known and clearer to us to what is better known and clearer by nature. Note that what is better known and clearer to us is better known and clearer to perception. This equivalence is not explicitly made in our passage. It is, however, an equivalence that Aristotle accepts elsewhere.[1]

When we take to this road, we engage in an epistemic journey that Aristotle describes in terms of clarity. Aristotle elaborates on how he conceives of this journey in the second part of our passage by saying that we are required to start from the things that are confounded to a degree but initially clear and evident to us (to perception). The key words are "confounded to a degree" (*mallon sunkechumena*). What Aristotle has in mind can be illustrated with the help of a parallel passage from the *Historia animalium*. There, Aristotle recalls his well-known thesis that living bodies display up to three functional parts—namely, up/down, front/back, and left/right. These functional parts are most clearly articulated in the human body because of its erect posture. But the human body is the exception rather than the rule. The other animals either do not have all three dimensions or "they do have them but confounded to a degree" (*HA* I.15 494a32). Of course, Aristotle does not mean to say that these functional parts are not present in the second group of animals; rather, he means to say that they are found in the same animal. And yet, he can discriminate the front and the up in a living body, even if they are found in the same place, because he can trace these functional parts to different capacities of the living body. For Aristotle, the front is where the sense organs are implanted, whereas the up is the entry point of nourishment. This distinction may not be evident to perception but is always clear to reason. Put differently, and more generally, Aristotle has a biological the-

---

1. Aristotle identifies what is better known to us with what is closer to perception. See *APo.* I.2 72a1–5. See also *Top.* VI.4 141b5–14.

ory that enables him to bring to light the functional organization of the living body.

The *Historia animalium* passage suggests that the cognitive process outlined in *Physics* I.1 is understood by Aristotle as a process entailing the progressive articulation of what is initially confounded to a degree. We start our investigation from what is clear and evident to us. What is clear and evident to us is clear and evident to perception. It reveals its complexity and structure as we proceed in our analysis. Even if Aristotle does not elaborate on what he means by analysis (*diairēsis*), it is safe to assume that the relevant analysis involves the use of reason. It is only by means of reason that we move from what is clear and evident to us (to perception) to what is clear by nature. Analysis will reach its natural end when maximal clarity is reached. Relative to what we are trying to understand, the latter does not admit of further articulation and discrimination.

Physics I.5

The cognitive process outlined above can be made more concrete by looking at how the argument unfolds in the rest of *Physics* I. The ultimate goal of the book is the introduction of the concepts of matter, form, and privation. For Aristotle, the introduction of these concepts is the first step in the study of the physical world. To understand why, we should keep in mind that, for Aristotle, the physical world consists of things that are subject to change. It is therefore imperative for Aristotle to develop concepts that help us make sense of change. In the Aristotelian jargon, matter, form, and privation are *principles of change*. These principles are introduced in *Physics* I.7. But it would be a mistake to think that this is a self-standing chapter as if the argument that leads us to the analysis offered in this chapter were expendable.[2]

Let us begin, therefore, with a central thesis introduced in *Physics* I.1—namely, that we are required to start from what is better known and clearer to us. For Aristotle, we are required to proceed in this way by our (human) nature, or so I have argued. The pre-Socratic investigations are no exception to the rule. They too proceed from what is clear and evident to us. What distinguishes them from one another (and from Aristotle's investigations) was not their starting point but how they proceed in the analysis of the data available to them. This is a simple observation, but it is an observation that suffices to motivate Aristotle to review what was

---

2. For a recent attempt to rethink the place of chapter 7 in the whole argument, I refer the reader to Kelsey 2008, 180–208.

accomplished by his predecessors and contemporaries. What they have accomplished (or failed to accomplish) can teach him (and us) an important lesson.

A main lesson that Aristotle derives from this review is that his predecessors and contemporaries agreed in making the contraries the principles of change. Toward the end of the chapter, Aristotle gives us the following assessment of what they accomplished: "all identify the elements and what they call the principles with the contraries, as if they were forced by the truth itself, even though they posit their contraries without reason (*aneu logou*)" (*Phys.* I.5 188b27–30). Aristotle's assessment consists of two parts. On the one hand, he thinks that his predecessors and contemporaries identified the principles with the contraries forced, as it were, by the truth itself. The truth in question is *empirical*: the observation, for instance, that any change in temperature takes place between hot and cold, where hot and cold are to be regarded as the extremes of a process that can take place anywhere in between. On the other hand, he thinks that his predecessors and contemporaries posited their contraries without a reason (*aneu logou*). It is precisely because they did not possess a *logos* that enabled them to analyze what was forced upon them by the truth itself that they ended up making contraries to be their principles. More directly, their selection of the relevant contraries turned out to be arbitrary: whereas some identified the principles with what is better known to us, others made them identical with what is better known to reason.

We can illustrate what Aristotle has in mind with one example. Consider the physical theory that makes the dense and the rare to be the principles of change. Supporters of this theory did not simply select the dense and the rare over other pairs of contraries; they also tried to explain all the natural processes that there might be in terms of condensation and rarefaction. However, the prospects of explaining everything in terms of condensation and rarefactions are (to say the least) not very good. What is better known to perception (*kata aisthesin*) is always a particular thing. But, at least for Aristotle, advancement in science does not take place by reducing the complexity of the natural world to a particular thing.

There are, of course, physical theories that are better equipped than the one that tries to explain everything in terms of condensation and rarefaction. For Aristotle, these theories are more promising because they select contraries that are better known to reason (*kata logon*). For instance, the view that the great and the small are principles marks a clear improvement on the search for principles because it singles out contraries that are better known to reason. The view is to be attributed to Plato. The details of this theory do not concern us. What matters here is only this: Aristotle is not willing to grant that any one of his predecessors or contemporaries, including Plato, was successful in his search for the first principles.

To see why we have to recall that, at least for Aristotle, we are confronted with fundamentally different pairs of contraries, and that our task does not consist in finding out which pair should be privileged to the expense of the others; rather, our task consists in working out a rational and objective way to subsume all of them under a first pair of contraries. Aristotle gives two criteria that are central to any search for the primary pair of contraries. These contraries are primary because (1) all the other contraries are derived from them, and (2) they do not derive either from one another or from something else.[3]

Physics I.6–7

At the end of *Physics* I.5, Aristotle is able to establish that the contraries are the principles of change. Each of the two contraries is open to further analysis—the sort of analysis outlined in *Physics* I.1, where we are told that the things confounded to a degree are clear and obvious to us. This analysis is taken up in *Physics* I.6 and 7.

What Aristotle starts doing in *Physics* I.6 can be described as an exercise in the progressive articulation of what is initially confounded. *Physics* I.6 contains two objections to the claim that the contraries are changed. First, change is not just the replacement of one contrary with the other, but its explanation requires a third thing that undergoes change by being acted upon by the contraries. Second, the contraries are not themselves substances but are said of a substance. These objections point to the conclusion that change involves at least another (non-contrary) thing. And yet, they are not conclusive. Quite tellingly, Aristotle concludes *Physics* I.6 by saying that it is not yet clear whether the principles involved in change are two or three (189b26–29). *Physics* I.7 concentrates on this question by looking at the example of a man that becomes musical (189b32–90a31). By reflecting on this example, Aristotle is able to establish that change always entails something that undergoes change, and that this thing, even though it is one, can be analyzed into two elements: a subject of change (man) and a kind of contrary (unmusical). When a man becomes musical, the second element is replaced by the other contrary (musical). So it is only in *Physics*

---

3. I extract these criteria from *Phys.* I.5 188a27–30.

I.7 that Aristotle is able to establish *that* the principles are two *and* three and to explain *how* they are two *and* three. Briefly, the principles are two: the subject that undergoes change, which Aristotle calls *matter*, and the *form* that the subject takes up at the end of the process. Since the subject of change can be described as the thing that does not yet have the form, there is also a third principle—namely, *privation*. It is clear that there is a difference between this last principle and the other two. Aristotle tries to capture the difference by saying that privation is a principle only in a coincidental way.

A detailed study of *Physics* I.6–7 goes emphatically beyond the scope of these pages.[4] Here suffice it to say that both chapters are part of an extended argument that starts in *Physics* I.5. What is especially interesting about this argument is that we are led to their discovery of the principles by means of a procedure that has several points of contact with the one outlined in *Physics* I.1. In particular:

1. It starts from what is clear and evident to us.
2. It ends with what is better known by nature.
3. It entails an analysis of what is initially confounded to a degree.

The equivalence between clear and evident to us and clear and evident to perception brings to light another crucial element of the procedure outlined in *Physics* I.1:

4. It starts from what is clear and evident to perception.

In *Physics* I.7, Aristotle also makes it clear that there is no unified subject of change but, rather, different things that undergo change: for instance, bronze becomes a statue and wood becomes a bed. For Aristotle, what we call subject of change is "known by analogy" (I.7 191a8–12). It is precisely for this reason that the principles introduced in this chapter have little in common with those discovered by his predecessors and contemporaries. We have already seen that they ended up offering particular things as the principles of change (e.g., the dense and the rare, or the hot and the cold). By contrast, at least for Aristotle, advancement in science does not consist in reducing the complexity and variety of the physical world to a particular thing. Rather, it consists in providing a conceptual schema to deal optimally with that complexity and variety.

---

4. I have elaborated further on this front in Falcon 2017, 41–59, and 2021, 367–82.

Ordinary and Theoretical Concepts

I looked at the formation of three concepts that Aristotle considers central to his scientific enterprise. I argued that these concepts are abstractions reached at the end of a rational process. It remains to be seen whether this process can be extended beyond the narrow boundaries of the discovery and justification of highly theoretical concepts of the sort introduced in *Physics* I. This is indispensable if we would like to develop a theory that applies to ordinary concepts. The latter are at the heart of any theory of concepts. Rand's theory is no exception to the rule.

This is, no doubt, a huge task. Here I am content to make two initial points. Taken together, they suggest that, at least for Aristotle, there is a difference between ordinary and theoretical concepts, but there is also some continuity. Aristotle might have placed ordinary and scientific concepts respectively at the beginning and end of the same continuous cognitive process.[5] First, recall that Aristotle describes the procedure he adopts in *Physics* I as a natural road. Aristotle places great emphasis on the constraints that human nature places on how any search for the principles of nature should be conducted. But his language can be taken as evidence that the method he adopts has a more general significance: it is a procedure open to all of us.[6] Second, Aristotle adds two examples. Here I concentrate on the second, which draws attention to a mistake children commit at an early stage of their cognitive development: at first, they call all men fathers and all women mothers, and only later do they distinguish each of the two (I.1 184b12–14).[7] The choice of this example suggests that, at some level, there is continuity between the formation of ordinary concepts such as "mother" and "father" and the formation of highly theoretical concepts such as "matter," "form," and "privation." However, this continuity must be dealt with delicately. It is important to see that Aristotle is drawing attention to a mistake committed by reason. It would be surprising (to say the least) if Aristotle would try to undermine the power of perception by suggesting that children cannot perceptually discriminate their mother and father from all other women and men. He is assuming that the normal operations of our senses are sufficient to tell apart

---

5. This would be another point of contact between Aristotle and Objectivism. Ayn Rand did not consider the difference between ordinary concepts and theoretical concepts as a fundamental one. See, in particular, Gotthelf 2013, 27–28; contra Kelsey 2008, 180–208.

6. Cf. *Met.* Z.3 1029b3–5: "learning happens for all in this way: from things that are less known by nature to things that are more known."

7. I have elaborated on this example and its significance in Falcon 2021, 367–82.

the parents from one another and from all other women and men, and that what is missing, in the case of children, is the capacity to employ the relevant concepts "mother," "father," "man," and "woman." It is precisely for this reason that children commit false generalizations of the sort illustrated by Aristotle's example. It turns out that we too commit similar mistakes when we engage in a search for the principles of change. Recall that, according to Aristotle, his predecessors and contemporaries did not possess a *logos* that enabled them to analyze what was forced upon them by the truth itself, and for this reason ended up making some contraries their principles. Like children, they too committed false generalizations when they posited particular things such as the dense and the rare (or the hot and the cold) as their principles of change.

Section III
FOUNDATIONS OF VALUE THEORY

6
Ayn Rand and Aristotle on Value and Choice

FRED D. MILLER JR.

Is Ayn Rand's ethics "Aristotelian"?[1] This is a hard question to answer—as is suggested by her own words. Although she compares Aristotle to "a philosophical Atlas who carries the whole of Western civilization on his shoulders," she finds his greatest contributions in the fields of metaphysics and epistemology (*TON* 2:5 18).[2] She emphatically rejects John Herman Randall's "assertion that: 'Aristotle's ethics and politics are actually his supreme achievement'" (19). She elsewhere remarks that "the greatest of all philosophers, Aristotle, did not regard ethics as an exact science" (*VOS* 14).[3] Yet, because she acknowledges that "whatever intellectual progress

---

1. This essay is a revised version of a paper originally presented on the theme "Ayn Rand as Aristotelian" at a meeting of the Ayn Rand Society on December 29, 2005.

2. Rand, in a review of John Herman Randall, *Aristotle* (New York: Columbia University Press, 1960). She also credits Aristotle with defining "the *basic* principles of a rational view of existence and of man's consciousness: that there is only *one* reality, the one which man perceives—that it exists as an *objective* absolute (which means: independently of the consciousness, the wishes or the feelings of any perceiver)—that the task of man's consciousness is to *perceive*, not to create, reality—that abstractions are man's method of integrating his sensory material—that man's mind is his only tool of knowledge—that A is A" (*FTNI* 17–18). In quotations from Rand's works all emphasis is in her original text.

3. Rand is also critical of many of Aristotle's political views—including his claims that the *polis* is prior to the individual, his advocacy of coercive moral education by the state, and his defense of natural slavery. Nevertheless, she says, "Throughout history the influence of

men have achieved rests on [Aristotle's] achievements" (*TON* 2:5 19), it is reasonable to inquire into the extent to which her own moral philosophy may presuppose Aristotelian ideas. The question as to whether Rand's ethics is "Aristotelian" should not turn merely on whether Rand and Aristotle make similar moral pronouncements but, rather, on whether there are deeper parallels involving fundamental principles and methodology.[4] In this essay I will focus on a fundamental topic—their concepts of value—and I will consider where they agree on this topic and where they seem most opposed. (A comprehensive discussion of their ethical theories would require book-length treatment.)

Ayn Rand's Critique of Aristotle's Ethics

Rand maintains that Aristotle failed to discover a "rational, scientific, *objective* code of ethics." Instead, he "based his ethical system on observations of what the noble and wise men of his time chose to do, leaving unanswered the questions of: *why* they chose to do it and *why* he evaluated them as noble and wise." Aristotle was not alone. "No philosopher," according to Rand, "has given a rational, objectively demonstrable, scientific answer to the question of *why* man needs a code of values. So long as that question remained unanswered, no rational, scientific, *objective* code of ethics could be discovered or defined." What is needed, according to Ayn Rand, is the "metaphysical cause and objective validation" for morality (*VOS* 14–15).

Is Rand's criticism of Aristotle justified? Her phrase "the noble and wise men" presumably refers to individuals whom Aristotle would call "practically wise" (*phronimos*) or "excellent" (*spoudaios*). The point of Rand's objection may be illustrated by examining Aristotle's claim in *Nicomachean Ethics* that "virtue is a state of character . . . determined by a rational principle, and (*kai*) by that principle by which the man of

---

Aristotle's philosophy (particularly of his epistemology) has led in the direction of individual freedom, of man's liberation from the power of the state.... Aristotle (via John Locke) was the philosophical father of the Constitution of the United States and thus of capitalism" (*TON* 2:5 19).

4. Wheeler (1986) points out a number of similarities between Rand and Aristotle and criticizes Rand for claiming originality while "ignorantly criticizing" Aristotle. Although Wheeler makes some interesting comparisons, he tends to exaggerate the parallels between Rand and Aristotle and makes no attempt to explain why Rand was critical of Aristotle's method in ethics. Nor does he mention Rand's essay "Causality versus Duty," which was originally published in 1970 and republished in *PWNI* in 1982. As will be seen, this particular essay is of fundamental importance in comparing the moral philosophies of Rand and Aristotle.

practical wisdom would determine it" (*EN* II.6 1106b36–1107a2).[5] It is very natural to take Aristotle's point to be that virtues such as courage or temperance are defined by the rule that a practically wise person would give for performing a courageous or temperate act. Thus, virtue and vice are, in effect, simply what practically wise people say they are.[6] This may well be how Rand understood this passage, and she would by no means have been the only reader to do so. Aristotle's account of virtue, understood in this way, would seem vulnerable to Rand's objection, since there is no further explanation of why the virtuous man *is* practically wise. It cannot be because he is rational, because then the account would be circular.[7]

There is, however, another way of translating the passage under discussion: "virtue is a state of character determined by reason and (*kai*) that by which (*hōi*) the man of practical wisdom would determine it." Understood this way, the passage makes two points: that virtue is defined by reason—that is, the rational faculty—and that the practically wise person uses the rational faculty to define virtue.[8] On this understanding, "the practically wise person" is defined by reason rather than the reverse. This is consistent with the definition of practical wisdom (*phronēsis*) as "a true and reasoned disposition to act with regard to the things that are good or bad for man" (*EN* VI.5 1140b4–6, see also VI.1 1138a25, VI.13 1144b27–28). On this second reading Aristotle could escape Rand's objection, although he would still owe his readers an independent account of the nature of this rational capacity.

5. Translations of the *Nicomachean Ethics* are by W. D. Ross 1915, which is the version Rand probably consulted and will be cited in this essay. The "rational principle" mentioned is the one that defines virtue; Aristotle explicates this principle in his doctrine that virtue is a mean between deficiency and excess (e.g., courage is the mean between cowardice and foolhardiness). This account of virtue is not endorsed by Rand herself (see Smith 2006, 50). I am responsible for translations of Aristotle's works other than the *Nicomachean Ethics*.

6. On this understanding the word "and" (*kai*) is epexegetic, equivalent to "that is." On Ross's translation, therefore, the rational principle in ethics is defined as the rule the practically wise person would apply in choosing actions.

7. On the problem of whether Aristotle's definition of virtue is in fact circular, see Bostock 2000, 97–100.

8. On this understanding, the word "and" (*kai*) is a conjunction (in contrast to Ross's interpretation). An added complication is that the translation in the main text follows a modern editorial emendation followed by most translators. The words "by which" translate *hōi*. The Greek manuscripts have instead *hōs*, following which the passage would be translated "determined by reason *and as* (*kai hōs*) the practically wise person would define it" (emphasis added). The second interpretation is more natural if we follow the manuscripts. Moreover, the emendation seems unnecessary because the manuscript reading is perfectly intelligible as it stands.

Several commentators offer interpretations in keeping with the second reading, according to which human beings are able to theorize rationally on the nature of flourishing and thus reflect critically on conventional moral practices. According to John Cooper, for example, this is implied by Aristotle's statement that the rational part of the soul is able to control the nonrational part of the soul by giving rise to rational desires.[9] By "rational" Aristotle means value-judgments that rest upon reasons—that is, a "process of reasoning for the purpose of figuring out what one should do, i.e., what one has the best reasons for doing". By reasoning we can grasp that "all living things as such have a good, and the good of each member of a species consists in its living an active life fully according to its nature" (Cooper 1999b, 243, 244–45). The point of Aristotle's function argument in *Nicomachean Ethics* I.7 is that the human good consists in "functioning in some way that expresses our developed natural life-capacities. On Aristotle's own theory, the first and essential part of our good consists in how the rational parts of our souls are structured and disposed" (Cooper 1999a, 268; cf. 1975, 96–98.). Not all scholars accept this interpretation. John McDowell, for example, objects: "[W]herever someone who believes in this kind of external validation might expect Aristotle to appeal to it, in saying what determines the rightness of right action, or the propriety of proper deliberation, or whatever, he disappoints such expectations; rather than giving a criterion that works from outside the ethic that he takes for granted, he says that such things are as the virtuous person determines them" (1998, 35). According to McDowell, we never find Aristotle "stepping outside the standpoint constituted by an inherited mode of thought, so as to supply it . . . with an external validation" (36).[10] This interpretation of Aristotle's ethics seems closer to Rand's understanding of his position.

Rand's observation that Aristotle relies on "the noble and wise men of his time" was presumably prompted by the fact that he frequently refers with approval to the opinions of his predecessors, including Homer, Hesiod, and later poets, the Seven Sages (including Solon), and philosophers such as Socrates and Plato. Rand's interpretation may also seem to

---

9. Cooper suggests that Aristotle seeks "a criterion, discoverable perhaps by philosophical reflection on moral experience, by which the results of ordinary moral reasoning could, at least to some extent be defended" (1975, 115; cf. 1999b). Compare Irwin 1980 and Reeve 1992. Their interpretations differ on important points, but they agree on the whole in taking Aristotle to offer a philosophical validation of moral judgments.

10. Broadie also criticizes Cooper's interpretation, which she dubs "a Grand End" theory of practical wisdom (1991, 198–202).

be supported by a passage in the *Nicomachean Ethics* where Aristotle discusses how we should make use of opinions in resolving philosophical disagreements. He prescribes the following procedure: "We must, as in all other cases, set the observed facts before us and, after first discussing the difficulties, go on to prove, if possible, the truth of all the common opinions about these affections of the mind, or, failing this, of the greater number and the most authoritative; for if we both refute the objections and leave the common opinions undisturbed, we shall have proved the case sufficiently" (*EN* VII.1 1145b27). The phrase "common opinions" translates the Greek term *endoxa*, a term that Aristotle defines elsewhere as follows: "opinions accepted by everyone or by the majority or by the philosophers—i.e. by all, or by the majority, or by the most notable and reputable of them" (*Top.* I.1 100b21–23). Now, read superficially, the above passage might seem to advocate simply collecting all the opinions about some issue and then uncritically deferring to those opinions that are held by most people or the acknowledged experts. However, Aristotle presents a more nuanced account in his other work on ethics, the *Eudemian Ethics*: "A method must be obtained that will best explain the opinions held on these topics, and also put an end to difficulties and contradictions. And this will happen if the contrary views are seen to be held with some show of reason; such a view will be most in agreement with the phenomena; and both the contradictory statements will in the end stand, if what is said is true in one sense but untrue in another sense" (*EE* VII.2 1235b13–18). Aristotle here indicates that we should consider not only the conflicting opinions on a given issue but also the reasons that people hold these different views. This often enables us to discover that those on opposing sides are in fact not in total disagreement, because their respective beliefs each contain a grain of truth.

Aristotle often considers the opinions of his predecessors when he is dealing with philosophical issues over which his predecessors have disagreed, not only in ethics but in metaphysics and natural science. For example, in the *Metaphysics* and *De Anima* (*On the Soul*), he sets the stage for his own inquiry with detailed surveys of the doctrines of earlier thinkers. Aristotle also wraps up discussions of issues by acknowledging the opinions of others. In the *Nicomachean Ethics*, after giving his own account of the true nature of human happiness, he declares, "The opinions of the wise seem to harmonize with our arguments" (*EN* X.8 1179a16–17). Taken in isolation this seems to support Rand's interpretation that Aristotle bases his views on the views of the wise and noble men of his day.

Aristotle, however, immediately adds, "But while even such things carry some conviction, the truth in practical matters is discussed from the facts of life; for these are the decisive factor. We must therefore survey what we have already said, bringing it to the test of the facts of life; and if it harmonizes with the facts we must accept it, but if it clashes with them we must suppose it to be mere theory" (1179a17–22). For Aristotle, then, agreement with his predecessors carries some epistemic weight, but it is not the final verdict because there is a truth in ethics—in this instance, what is the true nature of happiness—that is independent of our beliefs and must be found by examining "the facts of life."

It is noteworthy that Aristotle explicitly treats ethics as a science or system of knowledge (*epistēmē*): it belongs to what he calls practical science as distinguished from the theoretical and productive sciences (see *Top.* VI.6 145a15–16; *Met.* E.1 1025b25, K.7 1064a16–19; *EN* VI.2 1139a27–31, b3–4, VI.5 1140b1–2). These sciences differ, however, in their subject matter, their aims, and the degree of precision that they can attain. For example, mathematics is a theoretical science concerned with abstract objects such as geometrical figures, aimed solely with arriving at true propositions about these objects, and is able to do so with certainty. Ethics as a practical science is concerned with action (*praxis*), specifically with noble and just actions that "admit of much variety and fluctuation," so that ethics cannot be expected to achieve the sort of precision found in geometry and other theoretical sciences (*EN* I.3 1094b14–16). In just what sense Aristotle views ethics as a science is a difficult matter of scholarly interpretation beyond the scope of our present discussion.[11]

Aristotle is emphatic about the superiority of knowledge to belief, going so far as to declare: "He who has opinions is, in comparison with the man who knows, not in a healthy state as far as the truth is concerned" (*Met.* Γ.4 1008b27–31). Although the immediate context concerns metaphysics, Aristotle would make a similar claim for ethics. For, as we have seen, he maintains that we must not merely accept the opinions of the wise but test our views by a study of the facts of life. But why then does Aristotle show such respect for the opinions of other people? This important question deserves a discussion of its own.[12] But the short answer is

---

11. Aristotle's most important text on this subject is the sixth book of the *Nicomachean Ethics*. The status of ethics as a science is touched on in many general treatments of Aristotle's ethics, but monographs devoted specifically to the topics include Reeve 1992 and 2013, and Karbowski 2019.

12. I discuss Aristotle's view of the relation of belief to knowledge in F. Miller 2013.

suggested by the first line of the *Metaphysics*: "All men by nature desire to know" (*Met.* A.1 980a21). Moreover, human beings grasp the truth and the approximate truth by means of the same capacity—namely, the faculty of reason. Aristotle in *Rhetoric* infers that anyone who is capable of aiming at knowledge is similarly capable of aiming at reputable opinions (see *Rhet.* I.1 1355a14–18). We should therefore pay heed to the beliefs of others—especially those of "noble and wise men"—though this is in the end no substitute for genuine knowledge.

The upshot of the foregoing remarks is that Aristotle was more in agreement with Rand on the nature of ethics than Rand herself realized. Her interpretation of Aristotle's ethics has some basis in the text, but, as a fuller understanding of his method indicates, he maintains that moral principles must be grasped as knowledge and not merely based on opinions, even those of "wise and noble men." Thus Cooper and like-minded interpreters may be correct that Aristotle attempts to offer an objective validation of the judgments of putatively virtuous agents in terms of his own theory of the human good. In that case, Rand and Aristotle are arguably engaged in a similar project: to offer an objective validation of moral value judgments.

Aristotle and Rand on Values and Flourishing

Ethics is, for Rand as for Aristotle, a practical science like medicine or engineering. While metaphysics and epistemology are the theoretical foundation of philosophy, ethics "may be regarded as its technology.... Ethics, or morality, defines a code of values to guide man's choices and values" ("Philosophy: Who Needs It?" *PWNI* 3–4). Rand undertakes to explain the "metaphysical cause and objective validation" for morality in the context of her wider philosophy ("Objectivist Ethics," *VOS* 14). By an "objective validation" she understands the derivation of a concept or judgment through a process of reasoning based, ultimately, in sense perception. This presupposes her theory of concepts. Concepts are formed by differentiating and integrating perceived entities and their characteristics. Concepts must be formed in a specific manner as demanded by the nature of consciousness and of its objects as revealed by perception. To validate a judgment, then, is to identify the place of its constituent concepts in a logically ordered hierarchical system of concepts ultimately based in perception. She states, "No philosopher has given a rational, objectively demonstrable, scientific answer to the question of *why* man needs a code of values. So long as that question remained unanswered, no rational, scientific, *objective* code of ethics could be discovered or defined" (*VOS* 14–15).

According to Rand, moral philosophy must begin with the question, "Does man need values at all—and why?" It must consider whether the concept of value, the concept of good and evil, is "based on a metaphysical fact"—that is, the nature of human beings as a specific type of living being whose mechanism of survival is reason, a form of consciousness that "has a limitless capacity for gaining knowledge," but which must be initiated and sustained by choice ("Objectivist Ethics," *VOS* 13–14, 20–21). She starts with a definition of value: "'Value' is that which one acts to gain and/or keep. The concept 'value' is not a primary; it presupposes an answer to the question: of value to whom and for what? It presupposes an entity capable of acting to achieve a goal in the face of an alternative. Where no alternative exists, no goals and no values are possible" (15). The "to whom?" question implies that there are no free-floating values. Something is of value only if it is a goal for an individual agent that must act in a particular way to bring it about or preserve it. The "for what?" question implies that it will matter to the agent whether the goal is realized. Moreover, this outcome will depend on whether the agent follows one course of action rather than another.

Every value involves an alternative: for example, a squirrel can either pick up an acorn or not. Rand argues that the squirrel faces a more basic alternative:

> There is only one fundamental alternative in the universe: existence or nonexistence—and it pertains to a single class of entities: to living organisms. The existence of inanimate matter is unconditional, the existence of life is not: it depends on a specific course of action. Matter is indestructible, it changes its forms, but it cannot cease to exist. It is only a living organism that faces a constant alternative: the issue of life or death. Life is a process of self-sustaining and self-generated action. If an organism fails in that action, it dies; its chemical elements remain, but its life goes out of existence. It is only the concept of "Life" that makes the concept of "Value" possible. It is only to a living entity that things can be good or evil. (*VOS* 15–16, quoting *Atlas*)

As remarked earlier, the validation of a concept involves locating it within the complex hierarchical system of concepts ultimately based on sense-perception. The objective validation of the concept of value thus involves demonstrating the way in which it depends on the more fundamental concept of life. Rand's point is not that being alive is merely a necessary condition for valuing. Rather, the self-sustaining, self-generating character of life explains why values exist. For example, a squirrel must act in a specific way—for example, seeking out acorns and burying some for later use—in order to survive. It must pursue particular values in a particular manner in order to stay alive.[13]

Rand argues further that all other values ultimately depend upon life as an ultimate value. "It is only an ultimate goal, and *end in itself*, that makes the existence of values possible. Metaphysically, *life* is the only phenomenon that is an end in itself: a value gained and kept by a constant process of action. Epistemologically, the concept of 'value' is genetically dependent upon and derived from the antecedent concept of 'life.'" An ultimate value "sets the standard by which all lesser goals are *evaluated*. An organism's life is its *standard of value*: that which furthers its life is the *good*, that which threatens it is the evil" ("Objectivist Ethics," *VOS* 17).

This provides the basis for the objective validation of values: "the fact that living entities exist and function necessitates the existence of values and of an ultimate value which for any given living entity is its own life. Thus the validation of value judgments is to be achieved by reference to the facts of reality. The fact that a living being *is*, determines what it *ought* to do" (*VOS* 17). A squirrel does not worry about the philosophical problem of the "is" and the "ought." It relies on its sense-perception and experience of pleasure and pain, and it "knows" unreflectively that it is good for it to pick up the acorn. In contrast, "man has no automatic code of survival" (19). In order to survive, even primitive human beings must use their reason, to discover how to plant and grow food or to make weapons for hunting. According to Rand, "Reason is the faculty that identifies and integrates the material provided by man's senses. It is a faculty that man has to exercise by choice" (20). Hence, a human being has to choose to use reason to form concepts and acquire the knowledge necessary to achieve life-sustaining values. "A code of values accepted by choice is a code of morality" (23, quoting *Atlas*). Ethics is the science which discovers what moral code is required for man's survival. The standard of value "is *man's life*, or: that which is required for man's survival *qua* man. Since reason is man's basic means of survival, that which is proper to the life of a rational being is the good; that which negates, opposes or destroys it is the evil"

13. For further discussion, see Gotthelf 2000, 81.

(23). Elsewhere, Rand explains a moral code and its standard in terms of teleological measurement: "A moral code is a system of teleological measurement which grades the choices and actions open to man, according to the degree to which they achieve or frustrate the code's standard of value. The standard is the end, to which man's actions are the means" (*ITOE* 42).[14]

This standard implies three cardinal values: reason, purpose, self-esteem. These values "together, are the means to and realization of one's ultimate value, one's own life." Because virtue is the act by which one gains and/or keeps what is of value, there are three cardinal virtues: rationality, productiveness, pride ("Objectivist Ethics," *VOS* 25). One exemplifies these virtues insofar as one acquires knowledge and pursues values in a consistently rational manner, one devotes one's conscious mind as fully as one can to productive work, and one maintains a sense of self-worth by means of acting in a consistently rational manner. These virtues are not merely self-regarding, implying integrity and self-reliance; they apply also to one's relations to other rational beings, so that they include honesty and justice.

Finally, individual human beings must realize their highest value in their own personal lives. That is why Ayn Rand "holds man's life as the *standard* of value—and *his own life* as the ethical *purpose* of every individual."[15] She explains the difference between standard and purpose as follows: "a 'standard' is an abstract principle that serves as a measurement or gauge to guide a man's choices in the achievement of a concrete, specific purpose." Furthermore, "the achievement of his own happiness is man's highest moral purpose." "'Happiness' can properly be the *purpose* of ethics, but not the *standard*. The task of ethics is to define man's proper code of values and thus to give him the means of achieving happiness." Happiness Rand understands as an emotional state that results from achieving one's values. Hence, it is closely related to the successful fulfillment of the ethical standard: "The maintenance of life and the pursuit of happiness

---

14. Rand (unlike Aristotle) restricts teleological explanation to conscious purpose. "Aristotelian final causation," on her view, "applies only to a conscious being" ("Causality versus Duty," *PWNI* 119). Her theory of value, which applies to all living organisms, presupposes only goal-directedness, which includes the automatic functions of living organisms, that is "actions whose nature is such that they *result* in the preservation of an organism's life" ("Objectivist Ethics," *VOS* 16n). See Binswanger (1990, 1992) for an account, inspired by Rand, of how the (arguably) teleological concepts at the foundation of this ethics are grounded in the nature of life.

15. The quotations in this paragraph are all from "Objectivist Ethics," *VOS* 25–29.

are not two separate issues. To hold one's own life as one's ultimate value, and one's own happiness as one's highest purpose are two aspects of the same achievement. Existentially, the activity of pursuing rational goals is the activity of maintaining one's life; psychologically, its result, reward and concomitant is an emotional state of happiness."

Aristotelian Parallels in Ayn Rand's Ethics

On the basis even of a comparatively brief overview, it is evident that Rand's discussion exhibits striking parallels with Aristotle's ethics. Her definition of value as that which one acts to gain and/or keep resembles Aristotle's definition of the good as "that at which all things aim" (*EN* I.1 1094a2–3). Again there is her aforementioned argument that there must be an ultimate standard of value: "Without an ultimate goal or end, there can be no lesser goals or means: a series of means going off into an infinite progression toward a nonexistent end is a metaphysical and epistemological impossibility" (*VOS* 17). Aristotle reasons similarly, "If, then, there is some end of the things we do, which we desire for its own sake (everything else being desired for the sake of this), and if we do not choose everything for the sake of something else (for at that rate the process would go on to infinity, so that our desire would be empty and vain), clearly this must be the good and the chief good" (*EN* I.2 1094a18–22).[16]

Rand differs from Aristotle over what the ultimate value is. For Aristotle it is *eudaimonia*, which is commonly translated as "happiness" but is rendered here as "flourishing" in order to avoid confusion with Rand's understanding of happiness as an emotional state supervening on successful living.[17] In contrast, Rand views survival as the ultimate value and happiness as the emotional state resulting from success in achieving the end. It is noteworthy that Rand credits Aristotle with a fundamental insight: "Life—and its highest form, man's life—is the central fact of Ar-

---

16. The conclusion of this argument is that there must be an ultimate end for the sake of which everything else is chosen, but not that there is only one ultimate end. The latter would not follow from Aristotle's premises, and Aristotle does not claim (as critics have charged) that he has here established a unique end. He leaves this open, as is evident from a later passage: "Therefore, if there is only one final [i.e., complete] end, this will be what we are seeking, and if there are more than one, the most final of these will be what we are seeking" (*EN* I.7 1097a28–30). Further argument is thus needed to establish that flourishing is the only thing we choose for its own sake and never for the sake of anything else.

17. A leading proponent of "flourishing" as a translation of *eudaimonia* is Cooper (1975, 89n1). In the following translations from the *Nicomachean Ethics* "flourishing" replaces "happiness," the word Ross used to render *eudaimonia*.

istotle's view of reality. The best way to describe it is to say that Aristotle's philosophy is '*biocentric*'" (*TON* [May 1963]: 18). Rand's understanding is confirmed by Aristotle's own suggestions that life is the source of value. For example, the fact that "existing (*einai*) is better than not existing, living (*zēn*) than not living," explains why animals have the bodily parts they do and why they procreate and produce other animals.[18] An analogical argument is applied to artistic production. Artists love their productions, Aristotle says, because "existence (*einai*) is to all men a thing to be chosen and loved, and we exist by virtue of activity (i.e., by living and acting), and the work (*ergon*) *is* in a way the producer in activity; he loves his work, therefore, because he loves existence" (*EN* IX.7 1168a5–8, cf. *EE* VII.12 1244b23–36).[19] But, as we have said, the highest end for Aristotle is living *well* or *eudaimonia*.

Finally, Ayn Rand holds that "man's rational faculty is his essential distinguishing and defining characteristic" (*ITOE* 46) and that "reason is the faculty that identifies and integrates the material provided by man's senses" ("Objectivist Ethics," *VOS* 20). This is in basic agreement with Aristotle when he claims that the distinguishing function of man is activity of the soul in accordance with reason (*EN* I.7 1097b34–98a8) and that "no one can learn or understand anything in the absence of sense perception" (*DA* III.8 432a7–8; see also *APo* I.18). As we have noted, Rand credits Aristotle with first discovering these facts. Whether these parallels are due to Rand's study of Aristotle or to her arriving independently at similar conclusions (or some combination of these explanations) cannot be decided here. But the similarities are deep and significant.

Furthermore, the interpretation of Aristotle may shed valuable light on certain of Rand's claims that some readers find difficult to understand. One issue concerns the relation between the ultimate value (man's life) and the three cardinal values (reason, purpose, self-esteem), which, according to Rand, "together, are the means to and realization of one's ul-

---

18. Cf. *Generation and Corruption* II.10 336b28–9, *Generation of Animals* II.1 731b27–30, and *Parts of Animals* I.1 640a33–b1. Allan Gotthelf remarks that "for Aristotle the goodness of something, at least in biological contexts, is regularly its capacity to contribute to the continued life (*zēn*) of the organism which has or performs or undergoes that something, where the notion of what it is to live does not itself rest on a prior notion of the good" (1988, 117).

19. Again, Aristotle's argument that the happy man needs friends proceeds from the premise that the happy man values his own life: "[L]ife itself is good and pleasant (which it seems to be from the very fact that all men desire it, and particular those who are good and blessed)" (*EN* IX.9 1170a25–27). In the *Politics*, also, he says that "the good for each thing is what preserves it" (II.2 1261b9–10).

timate value, one's own life" ("Objectivist Ethics," *VOS* 25). One might wonder how the same thing can be both "the means to and realization" of a higher end. If they cannot be the same, is Rand conflating productive activity, a mere means to human survival, with survival itself? A similar problem arises in connection with Aristotle's claim that virtuous acts are good for their own sakes and also the means to flourishing. Some commentators propose that Aristotle distinguishes between two sorts of means—an instrumental means, as medicine is a means to health, and a constitutive means, as wisdom is a constitutive means to flourishing: "being a part of virtue entire, by being possessed and by actualizing itself it [i.e., philosophic wisdom] makes a man flourish" (*EN* VI.12 1144a5–6).[20] Aristotle here speaks of theoretical activity as if it were a constitutive means to flourishing, and other scholars have argued that morally virtuous acts that are valuable for their own sakes are also constitutive means.[21] Ayn Rand evidently has a similar point in mind, which she justifies by explaining that life is a process of self-generating, self-sustaining action, so that life-promoting actions are constitutive of life as an end in itself.[22]

A related issue concerns Rand's characterization of the standard of moral value as "man's survival qua man" ("Objectivist Ethics," *VOS* 23). "Survival qua man" contrasts with "momentary or merely physical survival"—the way an animal survives, by acting on momentary urges that lead the animal to provide for long-term needs because they are programmed to do so by factors of which the animal is unaware. By "man's survival qua man" she means "the terms, methods, conditions and goals required for the survival of a rational being through the whole of his lifespan—in all those aspects of existence which are open to his choice" (26).[23] It involves adopting lifelong policies of acting in a consistently rational

20. For this interpretation, see Greenwood 1909, 46–47; see also Cooper 1975, 22.

21. For interpretations along this line, see Ackrill 1974, Cooper 1975, 1999a, and Keyt 1983.

22. Tara Smith makes this point concerning flourishing: "Flourishing is both end and means. By acting as life demands, a person attains the reward of flourishing—which consists simply of more living—of extending the very process of engaging in those activities. . . . Just as a person does not putt *in order* to play golf but as part of playing golf, so a person acts morally as a part of flourishing. The activity of flourishing is what the end of value consists of. Proper action is constitutive of flourishing" (2000, 128; original emphasis).

23. This invites comparison with Aristotle's *Nicomachean Ethics* (I.7 1098.18–19): After defining flourishing as the activity of the soul in accordance with reason and virtue, Aristotle adds: "in a complete life, for one swallow does not make a summer, nor does a single day. And so too one day, or a short time, does not make a man blessed and flourishing."

and productive manner, and adhering to the principle of trade in his relationships with other rational agents: "He deals with men by means of a free, voluntary, uncoerced exchange—an exchange which benefits both parties by their own independent judgment" (31).

This part of Rand's ethical theory has met with objections.[24] Critics contend that human beings can, and do, survive by becoming parasites, by relying on force or fraud in their relations with others. They object that Rand does not demonstrate that each and every individual in every particular situation would benefit from the lifelong policies she advocates. Hence, they also complain that she conflates survival, in the sense of continuing to exist, with a particular way of life: that of a producer and a trader. These critics also express puzzlement over Rand's use of the expression "man's survival qua man." One critic complains that "Rand's continual invocation of the generic 'man' and his generic 'survival' . . . draw[s] attention away from counterexamples to the claim that, for each human individual, conceptual awareness and productivity are provided for her survival" (Mack 2003, 34).

But to understand Rand's argument it is necessary to explain the Aristotelian "qua" locution. Aristotle employs this locution to underscore the fact that an entity has certain characteristics or that it acts or is affected in a certain way because it possesses a more fundamental characteristic. When Hippocrates cures a patient, he does so qua doctor, not qua Greek or qua man. The "qua" locution is used to indicate characteristics of a thing that explains why it exists or acts in a certain way regularly and not merely accidentally (cf. *Met.* Γ.1 1003a30–1).[25] It is also important to note that causal connections may hold only for the most part due to the complexity of material nature: "for example, that honey-water is useful for a patient in a fever is true for the most part" (*Met.* E.2 1027a22–26). Hence it may be true to say that a potion qua honey-water is a cure for fever even if Coriscus failed to recover when he drank honey-water on the day of the new moon.

Rand is clearly using "qua" in this Aristotelian sense in her argument

---

24. See, for example, Nozick 1971, Long 2000, and Mack 2003.

25. The following passage illustrates Aristotle's "qua" locution: "number qua number has peculiar attributes, such as oddness and evenness, commensurability and equality, excess and defect, and these belong to numbers either in themselves or in relation to one another. And similarly the solid and the motionless and that which is in motion and the weightless and that which has weight have other peculiar properties. So too certain properties are peculiar to being as such, and it is about these that the philosopher has to investigate the truth" (*Met.* Γ.2 1004b10–17).

concerning "man's survival qua man." It is possible for individuals to survive in the short term or by luck even though they ignore long-term rational policies, "just as [man's] body can exist for a while in the process of disintegration by disease" ("Objectivist Ethics," *VOS* 24). A medical doctor's prescriptions are based upon knowledge of the nature of the human body as well as the patient's particular circumstances. Based on medical science, the scientist advises us to stop smoking—although centenarians occasionally attribute their longevity to their daily cigars. Surely this does not mean the doctor's advice is mistaken. Rand's argument concerns general moral principles about human beings as rational beings. When she says that, "Since reason is man's basic means of survival, that which is proper to the life of a rational being is the good, that which negates, opposes or destroys it is the evil," she means by "proper to the life of a rational being" actions that qualify as objective values because they can be known to promote the end of man's life (23).[26] There is no need for her to deny that there are cases in which individuals may survive as parasites. Her argument is on the level of general principles and policies.[27]

Aristotle and Rand on the Role of Choice in Morality

We have so far considered important parallels between the ethical theories of Aristotle and Ayn Rand. There is an important issue, however, on which they seem to diverge—namely, the role of choice in morality. To be sure, they both evidently agree that the ultimate value on which morality depends is an object of choice. For Aristotle, as we have seen, this is flourishing: "Flourishing . . . we always choose because of itself and never because of something else. But honor, pleasure, understanding, and every virtue, though we do choose them because of themselves as well (since if they had no further consequences we would still take each of them), we

---

26. Mack objects that Rand uses "proper to" equivocally in the sense of "characteristic" and "right for" (2003, 39–40). Although space does not permit a full response to Mack, it must be noted that Rand's argument does not require the alleged equivocation; for it relies instead on a distinction between those actions that are known to result in successful survival over an entire lifespan and those that do so by chance, luck, or coincidence.

27. Cf. Gotthelf 2016, 77: "[Rand's] point, of course, is not that a single action that does not aim at life will necessarily (or even usually) result in death. However, by squandering time, energy, and other resources that may be needed for life-sustaining goals, any action that does not aim at life imperils it and lessens the range of circumstances in which the organism will be able to survive." Admittedly much more needs to be said on this issue—for example, why would it be irrational to adopt the long-term policies of a predator or parasite? See Den Uyl and Rasmussen 1978; Smith 2000, chs. 4–6; Wright 2019; and Salmieri 2019 for explorations of these issues.

also choose for the sake of flourishing, supposing that because of them we shall be flourishing. Flourishing, on the other hand, no one chooses for the sake of these things or because of anything else in general" (*EN* I.7 1097a34–b6). For Rand, the ultimate value and object of choice is life, as stated in John Galt's speech in *Atlas Shrugged*: "My morality, the morality of reason, is contained in a single axiom: existence exists—and in a single choice: to live. The rest proceeds from these" (*Atlas* 1018).

Beyond this, however, there is an important difference. The passage from Aristotle is preceded immediately by these remarks: "We say that what is in itself worthy of pursuit is more complete than what is worth pursuing because of something else, that what is never choiceworthy because of something else is more complete than things that are both choiceworthy for themselves and choiceworthy because of it, and that what is unconditionally complete, then, is what is always choiceworthy in itself and never choiceworthy because of something else. Flourishing seems to be most like this, since *it* we always choose because of itself and never because of something else" (*EN* I.7 1097a30–b1). Thus, Aristotle says that we choose something because we regard it as worthy of pursuit (*diōkton*) or choiceworthy (*haireton*). He assumes that we ought to choose flourishing because it is the highest good. This is evident from another passage where he describes how thought leads to action:

> "I ought to make a good, and a house is a good." Straightaway one makes a house. "I need a covering, and a coat is a covering. I need a coat. What I need I ought to make. I need a coat." I make a coat. And the conclusion, "I ought to make a coat," is an action. And one acts from a starting-point. If there will be a coat, this is first necessary, and if this then this. And one does this directly. It is evident, then, that the action is the conclusion. And the premises leading to action are of two kinds, through the good and through the possible. (*MA* 7 701a17–22)

The general form of practical reasoning proceeds from the premise that X is good to the conclusion that I ought to do Y (where Y is the means to X). It is because flourishing is the highest good and not the means to any other good that we ought always to choose it. This idea was made explicit later on by Thomas Aquinas (who was heavily influenced by Aristotle's ethics) as the first principle of practical reason: "Do good and avoid evil!" (*Summa Theologiae* IIII.Q.79a1) Thus the fact that an action is good entails a moral obligation to perform it.

Rand has a very different view. Rather than reasoning that we have a moral obligation to choose life because it is our fundamental good, she holds that what we morally ought to do rests on the basic choice to live. It is noteworthy, as Gregory Salmieri points out (2016a, 66), that Rand evidently held a view similar to Aristotle's in an earlier "aborted treatise" called *The Moral Basis for Individualism* in which she tried to ground morality on the axiom that "Man exists and must survive as man" (*Papers* 032_002_21/*Journals*, 255). This is in contrast with the passage quoted above from Galt's speech, in which he distinguishes "the single axiom: existence exists from the single choice: to live." As Salmieri remarks, "the *Moral Basis* treats it as a fundamental *fact* that one's survival as a human being is desirable, but Galt takes valuing one's life to be a *choice*. It is only insofar as a person chooses to live that any facts (or the sum of all facts) can make anything good for him or any choice of action right" (2016a, 66). The view expressed in the *Moral Basis* is very similar to that of Aristotle who bases his ethics on the fact that happiness is most choiceworthy. Salmieri here offers a clear and succinct summation of what we may call "the standard interpretation" of Rand's considered view concerning the choice to live.[28]

The strongest evidence for the standard interpretation is found in Rand's essay "Causality versus Duty," where she is arguing against the view of Immanuel Kant that morality must be grounded in duties that are based on what he calls the "categorical imperative." For example, Kant maintains that we have an unconditional duty to tell the truth no matter how dire the consequences for ourselves or others. Against this view Rand states;

> Life or death is man's only fundamental alternative. To live is his basic act of choice. If he chooses to live, a rational ethics will tell him what principles of action are required to implement his choice. If he does not choose to live, nature will take its course.
>
> Reality confronts man with a great many "musts," but all of them are conditional; the formula of realistic necessity is: "You must, if—" and the "if" stands for man's choice: "—if you want to achieve a certain goal." You must eat, if you want to survive. You must work, if you want to eat. You must think, if you want to work. You must look at reality, if you want to think—if you want to know what to do—if you want to know what goals to choose—if you want to know how to achieve them. (*PWNI* 133)

---

28. Discussions of this issue include Peikoff 1991, 241–49; Gotthelf 1990/2016; Smith 2000, 97–111; Smith 2006, 22–23; Wright 2011, 29–32.

Rand adds that these conditional "musts" are found by means of "Aristotelian final causation, ... i.e., the process of choosing a goal and finding the actions necessary to achieve it" (133). The reference to Aristotle is apt, as is evident from the passage from *Movement of Animals* quoted above. However, her view that morality derives from a basic choice to live rather than from the obligation to do good seems antithetical to Aristotle's.

Some critics of Rand object that she is lapsing into a kind of voluntarism here—that is, of asserting that "the value of [an] end is *conferred on it* by its being chosen," so there are no "ends whose value does not depend on their being desired or chosen" (Mack 2003, 61n15).[29] Other more sympathetic commentators have suggested that on the standard interpretation of Rand, morality rests on a fundamental "premoral" or "prerational" choice.[30] As evidence against such interpretations, one might cite Rand's emphatic statements: "I reject the evil idea that choosing ends by reason is impossible. It has destroyed ethics. Everything that I have written is devoted to proving the opposite." More positively, she states, "Ends are *not* chosen irrationally. We choose our ends by reason, or we perish" (*Q&A* 107).[31] This implies that the choice of life, which is our ultimate end, must have some sort of rational justification. If this is Rand's intention, there would seem to be some common ground between her position and Aristotle's.

A valuable source of insight concerning the comparison of Rand and Aristotle on the role of choice in ethics is an exchange at a meeting of the Ayn Rand Society in 1990 between Douglas B. Rasmussen, who challenged the standard interpretation in "Rand on Obligation and Value" and Allan Gotthelf, who offered a reply in "The Choice to Value" These influential essays were subsequently published with some revisions although the central theses remaining unchanged.[32] This is not the place to try to adjudicate this dispute, which raises many deep issues of interpretation. I will focus here on a few themes that bear most directly on Rand's relationship to Aristotle on the issue of the choice of the ultimate end.

---

29. Similarly, Rasmussen (2002) argues that Rand in "Causality versus Duty" implies a moral "voluntarism" that is at odds with the Aristotelian theory of value in "The Objectivist Ethics."

30. For "premoral," see Gotthelf 2000, 84 (Gotthelf provides a fuller explanation in 2011, 43–45). For "prerational," see Smith 2000, 107.

31. This was part of Ayn Rand's answer to a question following a 1969 lecture at the Ford Hall Forum. The passage serves as the epigraph of an essay by Darryl Wright that is an insightful discussion of Rand's views concerning the relation of choice and reason to moral ends. See Wright 2011.

32. Rasmussen 2002 and Gotthelf 2011.

Rasmussen's central argument is that, if Rand's moral system is truly objective, she cannot hold that all moral obligations are ultimately grounded on a choice to live. For if the choice to live is itself not morally obligatory, then there would be "no reason to be moral." The choice to live would be "optional" or "arbitrary," and morality would be "based on an irrational or *a*rational commitment" (Rasmussen 2002, 73). Since Rand emphatically rejects this implication, Rasmussen contends, she cannot accept the premise that all moral obligations are grounded on a fundamental choice to live. As Rasmussen indicates, the passage from "Causality versus Duty" does not say explicitly that rational ethics will provide guidance only if one has already chosen to live. He maintains that this passage must be understood within a wider context provided by Rand's essay "The Objectivist Ethics." He points to Rand's statement that life alone satisfies her definition of an ultimate value: "the final goal or end to which all lesser goals are the means—and it sets the standard by which all lesser goals are *evaluated*." For an ultimate goal is "an *end in itself*, that makes the existence of value possible." Only life fits this description because "metaphysically, *life* is the only phenomenon that is an end in itself: a value gained and kept by a constant process of action" (*VOS* 17–18). Rasmussen notes the parallel with Aristotle's argument that everything we choose must ultimately aim at the chief good (*EN* I.2 1094a18–22), and he points out that Rand makes no mention of "choice" in this context (2002, 76). By identifying life as the standard of value, this passage of Rand's by implication also identifies the standard for whether a choice is right or wrong. For an agent the right choice, according to Rand, is the action that will further its ultimate value, which is its own life. "Choices are judged in terms of the end and standard of man's life" (77). Rand's theory would be circular if she maintained that the basic choice of life is judged in terms of this standard. Rasmussen thus offers what might be called a "neo-Aristotelian" interpretation of Rand's moral theory.

Gotthelf in his reply to Rasmussen makes several observations that bear especially on the alleged parallels between Rand and Aristotle. First, although Aristotle's argument that there must be a chief good and Rand's argument that there must be an ultimate value are similar, they draw different conclusions. Rand does not conclude that we have an obligation to choose life. All her argument establishes is that *if* a human being chooses to act, then he must choose to live, to continue to exist, and "*if* a human being chooses to live, then, given the nature of life, his own life is—and only his own life can rationally be—his ultimate value" (Gotthelf 2016, 38). Rand accepts Aristotle's analysis of how human beings act to rationally pursue their goals, while maintaining that life as the ultimate human value depends on the choice to live.

Against Rasmussen's argument that if life is of value because it is chosen it cannot be the standard by which all our choices are judged, Gotthelf replies that life is the standard for "judging specific choices made in the pursuit of the value of life by those who have already chosen to live" (2016, 41). This point can be restated in terms familiar to Aristotle who used two different words for choice: the general term "choice" (*hairesis*) for our choices of ends as well as means (as at *EN* I.7 1097a34–b6 quoted above) and the narrower term "deliberate choice" (*prohairesis*) for choices of means identified through a process of rational deliberation. And since deliberation is the process of reason by which an agent finds the best means to a given end, deliberate choice is choice of the means—that is, the action under our control that will lead to the desired end (*EN* III.3 1113a2–3, III.5 1113b3–5). Restated in Aristotle's terminology, Rand's view is that all of our deliberate choices are to be judged by the ultimate value, but our choice to live is a basic choice of an ultimate end and not a deliberate choice. This does not rule out the possibility that the choice to live is rational in some other sense. The fact that Rand also asserts that "ends are *not* chosen irrationally" suggests that it is rational to choose to live and irrational to fail to do so.[33]

The final issue concerns how Rand and Aristotle understand the concept of good. As we have seen, Aristotle holds that it is rational to choose flourishing above all things because it is more choiceworthy than anything else. Aristotle supposes that flourishing has value or is good regardless of whether we choose it. But from Rand's standpoint, this is arguably an unacceptable way of understanding the good. She distinguishes three different theories of the good: the intrinsic, the subjective, and the objective. The intrinsic theory holds that "the good is inher-

---

33. The idea that the choice to live can be in some sense rational has been explored by some recent commentators. Wright suggests that when one acts and experiences one's life as a value "there are easily accessible grounds for making the choice to value one's life." Here Wright explains by "non-deliberative grounds" a cognitive input that occasions the choice, and to which the choice is an intelligible and rational response, but which does not have propositional content" (2011, 28–29, 29n21). Salmieri suggests that the choice to live is a commitment that is essential to rational agency. "Rand's position that one commits to certain moral norms by the very act that commits one to holding values at all invites comparison to neo-Kantian 'constitutivist' theories where a commitment to norms is partially constitutive of agency" (2016a, 71n28).

ent in certain things or actions as such, regardless of their context or consequences." It implies that "the good resides in some sort of reality, independent of man's consciousness." The subjective theory holds that "the good bears no relation to the facts of reality, that it is the product of a man's consciousness, created by his feelings, desires, 'intuitions,' or whims, and that it is merely an 'arbitrary postulate' or an 'emotional commitment.'" The objective theory holds that "the good is neither an attribute of 'things in themselves' nor of man's emotional states, but an evaluation of the facts of reality by man's consciousness according to a rational standard of value. (*Rational*, in this context, means: derived from the facts of reality and validated by a process of reasoning.)" Hence the objective theory holds that "the good is an aspect of reality in relation to man" (*CUI* 13–14). Rand regards life as an objective good because it is a value that is chosen by the agent.

Where is Aristotle's concept of the good to be found in Rand's threefold classification? Aristotle's moral paragon is the practically wise person (*phronimos*), who knows how to achieve the good by means of his actions. Aristotle consistently describes the good at which the virtuous person aims as "the noble" (*to kalon*, alternatively translated as "the fine") (*EN* III.7 1115b11–13, III.8 1116b30–31, 1117b14, IV.1 1120a24–25). Aristotle describes practical wisdom as involving cleverness, which is the ability to identify and perform the actions that will hit a proposed target. "If the target is a noble one, the capacity is praiseworthy, but if the target is a base one, the capacity is unscrupulous. That is why we call both practically wise people and unscrupulous ones clever" (*EN* VI.12 1144a23–28; see also VI.1 1138b21–25). A plausible interpretation is the following: We are to imagine a myriad of targets only one of which is the right target. The virtuous archer is able and disposed to take aim at and hit the correct target, while the unscrupulous archer is able and disposed to aim at and hit any and every target. Which target is the right one is settled before the individual archers enter the field. The problem is to discover which target is the choiceworthy one and succeed in hitting it. The virtuous person must discover what it is to live well by discovering what actions are noble, and nobility is a choiceworthy attribute that belongs to our actions prior to and independently of any choices that we make. The fact that the target is choiceworthy independently of the agent's valuing and must be found by the agent suggests that the noble is an intrinsic good rather than an objective good in Rand's sense.[34]

---

34. For arguments along these lines, see Wright 2011, 10, and Gotthelf 2011, 39.

Do Rand and Aristotle Agree on Value and Choice?

Ayn Rand criticized Aristotle for failing to provide an objective validation for morality. Recent scholars disagree over whether Aristotle tried to provide such a validation—but even if he did, Rand offers a distinctive method of validating value judgments based on her Objectivist epistemology. Yet she offers striking parallels to Aristotle's biocentric philosophy, his concept of final causation, and his account of the role of reason as man's essential attribute. Moreover, her theory of values and happiness is better understood when considered in the light of broadly Aristotelian concepts such as final causation and flourishing. Finally, where Rand does clearly disagree with Aristotle—on the fundamental role of choice of ends in morality—she is, arguably, working within a broadly Aristotelian framework.

7
"Man's Life" as the Standard of Value in the Ethics of Aristotle and Ayn Rand

GREGORY SALMIERI

> There *is* a morality of reason, a morality proper to man, and *Man's Life* is its standard of value.
> AYN RAND, *ATLAS SHRUGGED*

It is with this sentence from *Atlas Shrugged* that Ayn Rand began her first exposition of her mature moral philosophy.[1] The Aristotelian resonances are palpable. Aristotle was the first to conceive of life as an activity of which there are distinct forms corresponding to different species, such that there could be such a thing as "Man's Life"—a form of life specific to human beings.[2] Aristotle characterized this human form of life as a life of

---

1. Her two expositions of the moral philosophy as a systematic whole occur in John Galt's speech in *Atlas Shrugged* (starting with this sentence at *Atlas* 1014), and in her essay "The Objectivist Ethics" (*VOS*, ch. 1).

2. I will use the phrase "Man's Life" (with capitals) to refer to the specifically human form of life, when discussing Rand and Aristotle's respective views of it. The phrase itself comes from Rand, but (as I have indicated) captures an idea of Aristotle's. "Man" as Rand used the word in this and related locutions is (of course) intended to refer generically to all members of the human species. Such gender-neutral usages of the word "man" are now widely disfavored, because they treat adult males as the paradigms of the human species (see Miller and Swift 1976, Moulton 1981, and Warren 1986).

Aristotle himself certainly treated adult males as paradigms. His view of males as the paradigmatic members of a species stems from his view of male superiority (on which see note 12, below), and he views adults as paradigmatic because actuality is explanatorily prior to potentiality, so that children's distinctive features are to be understood in terms of their role in the developmental process that culminates in adulthood. Rand likely would have accepted this view of the paradigmatic status of adults (as I do). She differs sharply from Aristo-

reason, and he was the first to hold up such a life as a standard of value—a "target for living well"—with reference to which an individual could choose all of his goals and actions (*EE* I.2 1214b6–11). In these respects, Rand's ethics is deeply Aristotelian, but her conception of the rational, human form of life differs markedly from Aristotle's own, and there are related differences in the roles the standard of Man's Life plays in their respective moral philosophies.

According to Aristotle, the ideal of Man's Life is realized most fully by a philosopher engaged in contemplation of eternal verities—an activity that (in his view) is not meant to bear fruit in action. This same ideal is realized, though in a secondary way, by a political leader prudently deliberating for the sake of his city.[3] The contemplator and the statesman both live lives of *leisure*, in which their time is released from the activities needed to produce the goods needed for survival, and so they are able to focus on *living well* as distinct from merely living. Thus, for Aristotle, a life of moneymaking (*chrēmatistēs*) fails to realize the ideal of Man's Life, because it is something forced upon one by lack of resources (*EN* I.5 1096a5–6).[4] By contrast, Rand wrote that "the words 'to make money' hold

tle in holding that women are equal to men in all the distinctively human abilities, but I doubt she would have been sympathetic to the idea that treating men as paradigmatic is somehow unjust to women, for she subscribed to an asymmetric view of sexual psychology according to which femininity is to be understood in relation to masculinity. (On this aspect of Rands' thought, see "About a Woman President" [*VOR*], *Answers* 106. See also Lewis and Salmieri 2016, 372–73, 395n83, and the additional sources cited therein.) We can think of this as licensing a symbolic or aesthetic reason for preferring gender-neutral masculine language.

In any case, for most purposes, a gender-neutral alternative to "Man's Life" would be preferable, but the alternative formulations have their own problems: "the human form of life" is too wordy; "human life" is ambiguous between singular and plural; and "Human's Life" isn't idiomatic English. So, for the purposes of this paper, I use "Man's Life," capitalizing it to reflect the quote that serves as our epigraph and to indicate that the term is being used in a specialized sense.

3. The precise relation between these two best sorts of human life and the extent to which the activity that characterizes each is involved in the other are matters of some scholarly controversy. I am most persuaded by the accounts given in Lear 2004 and Cooper 2012.

4. The Greek noun *chrēma* can refer to a thing, to business, or specifically to money. The suffix *-istēs* designates a person involved with something, and *-istikē* designates the activity or discipline practiced by such a person. So a *chrēmatistēs* is someone involved with business or money—a businessman, tradesman, or moneymaker. (Note, however, that the word is not built from verbs for producing or exchanging.) And *chrematistikē*, which Aristotle discusses in *Pol.* I.8–11, would be the art or discipline of commerce (or trade, or moneymaking, etc.). In the present passage from *EN* I.5 Aristotle contrasts the life of the *chrēmatistēs* to three other lives that he thinks are "most favored" and from which people draw their conceptions of the good. These are the life of gratification (*apolaustikon*) and the lives of the statesman (*politikos*) and contemplator (*theorētikos*) (1095b14–19). He rejects the life of gratification as

the essence of human morality."⁵ It is "the Producer" whom she regarded as "the man of reason" or "the thinker" (*FTNI* 21), and she characterized production as "the application of reason to the problem of survival" (*CUI* 17). Although she writes of producers in all professions and at all levels of ability, her ideal is epitomized by "[t]he great creators—the thinkers, the artists, the scientists, the inventors" (*Fountainhead* 710).

In the first two sections of this paper, I elucidate the content of the human form of life as understood by Aristotle and Rand, respectively. In my third section, I show how the differences in their view of Man's Life reflect (and contribute to) different views of how a form of life can serve as an ethical standard. These differences, in turn, have implications for the extent to which their respective moral philosophies provide objective guidance rooted in knowledge of human nature, rather than merely systematizing existing mores or reading them into human nature. Accordingly, I close with a discussion of the objectivity of what each thinker regards as moral knowledge.

---

one "for grazing animals," and (eventually) concludes that the other two lives do embody the human good, though not equally so.

5. The quote is from a speech by Francisco d'Anconia. That he is speaking here for Rand is confirmed by her inclusion of this speech in her book *For the New Intellectual*, under the title "The Meaning of Money." Immediately before the quoted passage, Francisco credits Americans with coining the phrase "to make money": "No other language or nation had ever used these words before; men had always thought of wealth as a static quantity—to be seized, begged, inherited, shared, looted or obtained as a favor. Americans were the first to understand that wealth has to be created." Rand doesn't give a source for Francisco's claim about the origins of the phrase, and taken literally, the claim is untrue. The *Oxford English Dictionary*'s earliest attestation of the phrase "to make money" predates Columbus's 1492 voyage (see usage P.2.a.i. in the *OED*'s entry on "money"), and Cicero wrote of "making wealth" (*pecuniam facere*) (Cicero, *De Divinatione* 1.49.111, cited in this connection by Liberman 2006). However (an n-gram search on "make money" and related phrases in Google's English 2019 corpus reveals that) the phrase only started appearing regularly in print around the turn of the nineteenth century and was more prevalent in American than British publications. This reflects the unprecedented embrace of commerce in the early United States (on which see Wood 1991, 325–47) and so supports the spirit if not the letter of Francisco's claim.

The claim itself had enough currency in the nineteenth century that the author of a book on *Americanisms* found it necessary to refute it: "It is equally unjust to charge Americans with the invention of the phrase, to make money, much as they may be addicted to the practice. Dr. Johnson already rebuked Boswell sharply for using it, and said: 'Don't you see the impropriety of it? To make money is to coin it; you should say, to get money'" (de Vere 1871, 296; cited by Freeman 2011). Notice that Johnson's rebuke reflects the attitude that Francisco says Americans displaced. Interestingly, just prior to this passage, de Vare addresses the claim, also considered in *Atlas Shrugged* (683), that the dollar sign is based on the initials of the United States. It's unlikely that da Vare is Rand's source for these two philological claims (since he refutes the claim Franciso endorses), but it may be that he's responding to some earlier source that she also read.

Aristotle's Leisurely Ideal[6]

The subject of Aristotle's inquiry in ethics is "the human good"—that is, the ultimate end sought in and achievable by human action. By the end of *Nicomachean Ethics* I.7 (cf. *EE* II.1) he has identified this good with the excellent performance of the human function. For Aristotle, life is (in its fundamental sense) an activity (*DA* II.3), and what distinguishes human life from plant and animal life is that the activity centrally involves reason. Thus he thinks that the target at which we must aim to live well is *a complete life of reason-involving activity performed excellently*. To do something well or excellently is to do it in accordance with the appropriate virtues, and human virtues are those states from which reason functions well. Consequently, most of the rest of the *Nicomachean Ethics* (and *Eudemian Ethics*) is given over to examining virtue. Since Man's Life is political—that is, lived in city-states—the treatise ends (*EN* X.9) with a transition into the *Politics*, which work provides further details about Man's Life, taking care to distinguish its proper realization—"living well"—from mere "living" (*Pol.* 1257b41–8a1).

Aristotle's teaching in *Nicomachean Ethics* can be briefly summarized as follows. Virtue comes in two broad types corresponding to two broad roles that reason plays in our lives: *intellectual virtue* perfects our thinking itself, whereas *characterological virtue* perfects our desires (and consequently our decisions) so that they accord with excellent reasoning.[7]

Thinking can be subdivided into two broad types: *contemplation* of truths that cannot be changed and *deliberation* about things we can effect. Contemplation is perfected by the sciences (*epistēmai*)—chiefly by *sophia*, which is the science by which we contemplate being qua being in light of its fundamental and universal causes. Deliberation is divisible into deliberation about how to produce specific types of effects (such as health or buildings) and general deliberation about how to act (including whether and when to produce the aforementioned effects). The first

---

6. I borrow the phrase "leisurely ideal" from "Aristotelian Practical Wisdom as a Leisurely Ideal," a talk that Gabriel Richardson Lear presented at several conferences in the 2010s.

7. The word I'm translating as "characterological" is ēthikē. It is sometimes translated as "moral" or with the phrase "of character." I prefer "characterological" because it avoids some potentially misleading connotations of "moral" and preserves the link to the noun ēthos (character), while being a single adjective (rather than a propositional phrase).

sort of deliberation is perfected by the various arts (*technai*), and the second, by *phronēsis*.[8]

The characterological virtues are stable dispositions to have desires or feelings that accord with the dictates of *phronēsis*. Each characterological virtue corresponds to a type of desire or feeling—for example, temperance, to the desire for bodily pleasures; mildness, to anger; wit, to the desire to joke and laugh. The virtue is a disposition to have the relevant desire or feeling in the right amount along any of the dimensions along which it might be possible to have it excessively or deficiently. Anger, for example, may be too intense or not intense enough, it may be directed at too many people or too few, and it may come on and pass too quickly or too slowly. Along each of these dimensions, this is a way of being angry that is intermediate between the errors of excess and deficiency, and this is the way that accords with *phronēsis*. The characterological virtue of mildness (the subject of *EN* IV.5) consists of being disposed to be angry in this intermediate way. Since desires or feelings motivate action, each characterological virtue motivates its possessor to act in a characteristic way, and one acquires a characterological virtue by being habituated into its characteristic way of acting.

Phronēsis and the characterological virtues form a set, as neither is possible (in its fully developed form) without the other. The exercise of these virtues is an instance of the functioning that is a human being's chief good. Because of this, a life focused on exercising these abilities to their fullest qualifies as a happy or successful life. This is *the political life*—the life of a statesman. For it is in managing the affairs of a city that one has occasion to exercise one's deliberative abilities on the largest scale with regard to the most important practical problems, and in doing this one faces many decisions that call for the exercise of characterological virtue. However, there is a still better life: *the contemplative life*, which is devoted to the development and exercise of *sophia*.

---

8. I will leave *sophia* and *phronēsis* untranslated throughout. The traditional translations are "wisdom" and "prudence," respectively. This is somewhat unfortunate as "wisdom" in contemporary English is more naturally associated with what Aristotle means by *phronēsis* than what he means by *sophia*. Some translators have thus used wisdom for *phronēsis*, and found another word for *sophia*, but there's no obvious alternative, and the presence of "sophia" as a root in the word "philosophy," which is well-known to mean the "love of wisdom," makes translating it differently awkward. Sometimes the distinction between the two words is marked by translating them "theoretical wisdom" and "practical wisdom." This plausibly captures their meanings, but it creates the false impression that Aristotle regards them as two variants of a single thing, wisdom.

The contemplative life is better than the political because the activity on which it is focused is valuable only for its own sake, rather than being valued (even partially) for any contribution it makes to anything distinct from itself. By contrast, some of the value of a statesman's deliberation derives from the fact that it enables contemplation.[9] The productive activity that is perfected by the arts is primarily valued for its products, which are valuable (ultimately) because they enable activities of the other two types. Although there are indications (esp. *Met.* A.1) that Aristotle accords some intrinsic value to productive activity, and although there is a tradition inspired by Aristotle that extols the *technai* as virtues, it is clear from the *Politics* that Aristotle does not think that a life centered around productive work can be well lived. Indeed, he thinks that the performance of many of these activities is incompatible with living well (and so should disqualify one from citizenship).[10] For some people to live well—to fully realize the human form of life—these activities must be relegated to their inferiors, who then participate in living well only by enabling it in their superiors.

What, then, is the human form of life that serves as an ethical standard for Aristotle? Schematically, it is an ordered set of activities in which one activity (contemplation) is intrinsically valuable and performed entirely for its own sake, while all the others exist at least in part to serve it. This subservience makes the subservient activities less valuable than the activity they serve. Some of the lesser activities may also have some intrinsic value (perhaps, as suggested by Lear [2004], due to their resemblance to the one best activity), but others are merely instrumental. The merely instrumental activities (at least many of them) diminish any life that includes them.

9. The contemplative life, too, will presumably include some exercise of *phronēsis* and the characterological virtues, since they're needed to arrange one's life to make contemplation possible. However, the contemplator will exercise these virtues primarily within the scope of his personal life and in the management of his own estate. He may exercise them also on a civic scale as a voter or in discharging some other temporary office, which he deems it prudent for him to accept, but this will not be his central occupation (or else he would be living the life of a statesman).

10. For the tradition that extolls the *technai* as virtues, see Nederman 2008, 25–26. Aristotle is particularly critical of the *banausoi* (or, "vulgar craftsmen") whose lives he sees as improperly focused on work for trade. For instance, see *Pol.* VIII.2 1337b5–15, where Aristotle writes that "any work, art, or learning should be considered *banauson* if it renders the body or mind of free people useless for the practices and activities of virtue. That is why the arts that put the body into a worse condition and work done for wages are called *banauson*, for they debase the mind and deprive it of leisure." Although the *banausoi* perform work that is necessary such as farming, building, weaving, and such, they are likened by Aristotle to slaves (*Pol.* I.12 1259b41, III.5 1278a13).

At best, such instrumental activities are an unwelcome distraction from the real business of human living; but Aristotle thinks that many of them also degrade the soul of anyone who performs these activities, and that this makes such people unfit for the leisurely activities of contemplation and statesmanlike deliberation.[11] Such productive activities can thus have no part in the lives of those individuals who most fully realize the human form of life, so on a societal scale Man's Life is characterized by a caste system in which some classes of people exist to serve others.[12]

This social hierarchy recapitulates an ontological hierarchy, at the top of which sits Aristotle's God—a self-sufficient, supernatural mind that engages only in contemplation of itself. The movements that make up the natural world can be characterized as a side effect of this divine self-contemplation. The natural world is no part of God's aim, but realizing something like the self-sufficiency of God's contemplative activity is the aim of the motions of the bodies within the natural world (from stars down to animals and plants). The human contemplator approximates this ideal most closely, becoming godlike in a way that makes it ambiguous whether he, in performing this activity, is part of the natural world at all.[13]

Thus, Aristotle suggests that the life of contemplation may be a divine form of life that is better than the human one. If so, then it may be that it is God's Life, rather than Man's, that is the standard of value—the target at which we should aim in all our actions. Aristotle raises this possibility in *Nicomachean Ethics* X.7, where he rejects the advice to "think human, since you are human" (1177b33) and urges readers to pursue the divine life of contemplation, which seems superior to human life. However, the conclusion of that chapter makes clear that he doesn't accept the premise behind the advice that pursuing the life of contemplation (insofar as this is possible to a human being) amounts to directing one's aim away from Man's Life. Since a man's mind is his best and most controlling element, it is what he is most of all. Thus, in aiming away from contemplation (which most gratifies the mind), a man would be aiming away from his own life.

---

11. See *Pol.* III.4 1277b3, III.5 1277b34–36, 1278a7, VII.9 1328b39, VIII.2 1337b8–13.

12. Aristotle's devaluing of production is also a motivation for his view of women as inferior to men. Reproduction is a plantlike function, and animals are divided into sexes in order to concentrate as much as is possible of this lower activity in the inferior members of the species, thereby freeing their superiors for the higher activities that are distinctive to the species. On this view, females are nature's equivalent of factory seconds, which have been segregated early in the reproductive process and adapted to perform a lower function.

13. On Aristotle's God, see especially *Met.* Λ.6–10.

Still, even if Aristotle can resolve the tension between a human being's aiming at the divine and at the human, the role of divinity in Aristotle's philosophy complicates the idea that Man's Life is the standard of value in his ethics. For the very notion of the divine creates a standard that is distinct from Man's Life. It is in accordance with this divine standard that Man's Life is better than that of other animals and that, among human lives, a contemplator's life is better than a statesman's or a producer's. To fully realize the standard of Man's Life, as the best contemplators do, is to realize as fully as mortality permits this supernatural standard.

Rand's Productive Ideal

For Rand, the activity that epitomizes reasoning is not a contemplation detached from meeting material needs; it is *production*: "the application of reason to the problem of survival" (*CUI* 17). By (almost all) contemporary lights, this view has an obvious advantage over Aristotle's: if producing things required by human survival is an essential part of Man's Life, rather than a distraction from it (or worse), then the ability of some of us to lead fully human lives needn't depend on some exploited underclass's doing this (intrinsically worthless, but instrumentally valuable) work for us. However, some might worry that, in centering human life on productive work, Rand is overfocusing on material needs and neglecting the higher values in life that make it worth living. In Aristotle's terms, we might worry that by centering human life on "the problem of survival," Rand is showing that what she prizes is merely *living*, rather than *living well* (*Pol.* I.9 1257b40). This is Aristotle's criticism of those who overvalue moneymaking (*chrematistikē*). By his lights, such an attitude is slavish, and one might even imagine Aristotle viewing contemporary society as one from which freedom rather than slavery has been eliminated.[14]

This notion of universal slavery looms large in criticisms of capitalism (Rand's ideal form of society) from all quarters.[15] Critics of Rand have often pointed out the limitations of (what they see as) an ethics that makes all value merely instrumental on prolonging one's life.[16] Some

---

14. Gross 2018 is a fanciful interview in which "Aristotle's ghost" makes this point.

15. See Øversveen 2022 for a summary of the revival of Marx's critique on the basis of alienation. See Deci 1995, 135, 204, for a critique of the way in which society imposes an instrumental motivation on us through capitalism. Other critiques come from egalitarian (e.g., Sandel 2013), feminist (Fraser 2013), and black studies (Robinson 2019) perspectives. For a recent, related defense of the ideal of the contemplative life, see Hitz 2020.

16. See Huemer 1996, §5; 2002; 2019.

readers have tried to avoid these implications by interpreting Rand along more Aristotelian lines.[17] In explicating her view of Man's Life as one of production, we should be mindful of how she might respond to such criticism. Toward this end, it will be helpful to consider how she developed her mature view (which is the target of such criticism) starting from a position that is closer to Aristotle's.

In early notes and in her first novel, Rand draws a distinction that might be compared to Aristotle's distinction between living well and merely living. It is the distinction between *living* (as Rand's protagonists do) and merely *existing* (as she thought most people did).[18] Distinctions along these lines can be found in other literary authors, and considering a few quotes will help us see what is and is not distinctive to Rand:

- A contemporaneous English translation of an essay by Victor Hugo (1864a), whom Rand considered the "greatest novelist in world literature" (*RM* 147), reads: "It is by the real that we exist, it is by the ideal that we live. Now, do you wish to realize the difference? Animals exist, man lives. To live, is to understand. To live, is to smile at the present, to look toward posterity over the wall. To live, is to have in one's self a balance, and to weigh in it the good and evil. To live, is to have justice, truth, reason, devotion, probity, sincerity, commonsense, right, and duty nailed to the heart. To live, is to know what one is worth, what one can do and should do. Life is conscience." (Hugo 1864b, 256)[19]

- Leo Tolstoy (2000, 239) wrote of people who exhibit "a lack of life

17. For example, Rasmussen (2002, 2006, 2007a, 2007b) interprets Rand as holding what amounts to the eudaimonist position. Mack (1984, 2003), Badhwar (1999), and Long (2000, 2010, 2016, 2020) interpret her view as ambiguous between a survival-focused consequentialism (which they find implausible) and a value-infused eudaimonism (which they regard as preferable). For reasons that these interpretations are untenable, see Gotthelf 2016, 78–79; Salmieri 2016b, 134–36, and 2019, 168–76.

18. On this distinction in Rand's early work, see Wright 2005 and Salmieri 2016a, 49–53.

19. The translation is misleading, however. The passage in Hugo's (1864a) French begins "*C'est par le réel qu'on vit; c'est par l'idéal qu'on existe*" (397). Throughout the translator used "live" for Hugo's "*existe*" and "exist" for Hugo's "*vit*," effectively reversing his terminology. A second nineteenth-century translator who made the same curious choice adds: "Perhaps it should be noted that, in the original, existence is made the higher, more absolute mode of being; *e.g.*, '*Les animaux vivent, l'homme existe*'" (Hugo 1887, 295). That similar distinctions could be made in opposite language shows that there is terminological optionality here (as is generally the case when distinctions are drawn), but the fact that two early English translators chose to reverse Hugo's words suggests that it was more natural in English to use "living" for (what the latter translator calls) "the higher, more absolute mode of being." This is the English usage we see in the (later) passages by Wilde, Burnett, and Lewis.

force, of what is known as heart, of that yearning which makes a man choose one out of all the countless paths in life presented to him and desire that one alone."

- Oscar Wilde (1891, 17), in extolling the individualism he thought would be possible only under socialism, wrote, "To live is the rarest thing in the world. Most people exist, that is all. It is a question whether we have ever seen the full expression of a personality, except in the imaginative place of art. In action, we never have."

- Jack London (2015, 6493) described many people as "unburied dead" and is reported to have declared: "The proper function of man is to live, not to exist. I shall not waste my days in trying to prolong them. I shall use my time."[20]

- Francis Hodgson Burnet (1907) described the protagonist of her novel *The Shuttle* as having "a genius for living, for being vital": "Many

---

20. These sentences come from what is sometimes called London's Credo: "I would rather be ashes than dust. I would rather that my spark should burn out in a brilliant blaze than that it should be stifled by dry-rot. I would rather be a superb meteor, every atom of me in magnificent glow, than a sleepy and permanent planet. The proper function of man is to LIVE, not to exist. I shall not waste my days in trying to prolong them. I shall use my time."

The Credo seems to have first been published by Ernest J. Hopkins in the *San Francisco Bulletin* on December 2, 1916. Hopkins describes it as a "striking summary of his personal philosophy" that London enunciated "not two months before his death, to a group of friends," by whom it was "recalled with emotion" when London died. Hopkins may himself have been among those friends. In an article in the November 23 issue of the same paper, he describes how he had visited London at the Glen Ellen Ranch a week earlier and mentions a prior visit during which London discussed "his view of life."

Hopkins published London's Credo as a quotation in a prefatory blurb for the *Bulletin*'s reprinting of London's 1905 essay "What Life Means to Me." In the essay, London writes that many in the upper classes are "not *alive*" but "merely the unburied dead," and that, of those who were alive, most were "alive with rottenness, quick with unclean life" (London 2015, 6492). He looks forward to a day when a worker's revolution will "topple over" the current order "with all its rotten life and unburied dead" and build a "new habitation for mankind" in which "the air that is breathed will be clean, noble, and alive." In this future society, "man shall progress upon something worthier and higher than his stomach, when there will be a finer incentive to impel men to action than the incentive of today, which is the incentive of the stomach" (6493).

The Credo later appeared as an epigraph to Irving Shepard's introduction to *Jack London's Tales of Adventure*, where it is followed by the sentence "Only the brilliant, restless personality who was Jack London could have conceived of such a dynamic and challenging credo as this" (London 1956, vii). Shepard was the son of London's stepsister and was raised on Glen Ellen Ranch, so he may have had firsthand knowledge of the occasion on which Hopkins reports that London spoke the Credo. However, apart from its opening sentence, no copy of the Credo survives in London's published work or in his handwriting, so scholars are skeptical about whether and in what form he authored it (cf. Stasz 1999).

people merely exist, are kept alive by others, or continue to vegetate because the persistent action of normal functions will allow of their doing no less" (112, cf. 60). "She's Life itself! . . . What a thing it is for a man or woman to be Life—instead of a mass of tissue and muscle and nerve, dragged about by the mere mechanism of living!" (274).

- Sinclair Lewis (1920, 265), who was Rand's favorite contemporary writer in the 1930s (cf. Mayhew 2007b, 219–20), wrote of people who exhibit "the contentment of the quiet dead, who are scornful of the living for their restless walking."

There are differences between the views expressed in these passages, but in all of them "living" (or being "alive") is associated with a spiritual quality that many (perhaps most) people lack. The people who aren't alive engage in metabolism and move about in the world eating and working to satisfy their physiological needs, but their existence lacks purpose and is devoid of passion.

In contrast to such people, consider what Kira Argounova, the heroine of Rand's *We the Living*, says about being alive: "What do you think is living in me? Why do you think I'm alive? Because I have a stomach and eat and digest food? Because I breathe and work and produce more food to digest? Or because I know what I want and that something which knows how to want—isn't that life itself?" (*WTL36* 496, cf. *WTL* 385).[21] What Kira has wanted since childhood was to build aluminum bridges (*WTL36* 43, *WTL* 35). What she seeks out of life is a specific productive career, but in Rand's descriptions of this ambition, we read nothing about the purpose the bridges are to serve or why she thinks building them out of aluminum will serve this purpose; much less do we hear about any money she hopes to make from the bridges. What attracts Kira to building is not any survival need that she thinks her bridges will serve (for herself or for others), nor is it a protestant (or proletarian) ethic that valorizes work as such. We're told that Kira "had chosen a future of the hardest work," despite her "aristocratic . . . conviction that labor and effort were ignoble" (*WTL36* 42–43, cf. *WTL* 34). What attracts her is a spiritual quality in her chosen work. It is the *audacity* of shaping the physical world on a grand scale—of bending it to her will. What Kira admires and seeks to realize in her own life is the self-assertiveness of a unique individual's cre-

---

21. I quote (here and below) from the first edition of the novel, published in 1936, and provide references to the corresponding text in the revised 1959 edition. On the nature of Rand's revisions, see Mayhew 2004.

ating something on a grand scale. We can see this same attitude in Rand's admiring description of Petrograd: "Petrograd was not born; it was created. The will of a man raised it where men did not choose to settle. An inexorable emperor commanded into being the city and the ground under the city" (*WTL36* 285, cf. *WTL* 223).

Howard Roark, the hero of *The Fountainhead*, is also a builder. Here is what he says, early in the novel, about why he chose this career: "It's because I've never believed in God. . . . Because I love this earth. That's all I love. I don't like the shape of things on this earth. I want to change them" (*Fountainhead* 38–39). It is certainly not for the sake of the clients that Roark wants to build: he tells us early in the novel that he intends to have clients in order to build, rather than the reverse (14). He later describes "the meaning of life" as "the material the earth offers you and what you make of it," illustrating his point by bending a tree branch into an arc and saying, "Now I can make what I want of it: a bow, a spear, a cane, a railing" (577).

Although the careers that Rand extols in her early writing (through *The Fountainhead*) do meet survival needs, she focuses not on solving the problem of survival but on the spiritual-cum-physical achievement of imposing one's vision on the world. This, for the early Rand, is what Man's Life is about. To use a distinction employed by Eddie Willers in *Atlas Shrugged*, we might say that the early Rand saw Man's Life as a life of living up to "the best within us" rather than a life devoted to such mundane matters as "business and earning a living" (*Atlas* 6).[22] The mundane matters are for the sake of the higher, spiritual ones.

In *Atlas Shrugged*, however, this way of thinking is subverted. In the novel's denouement, Eddie comes to realize that "business and earning a living and that in man which makes it possible—*that* is the best within us" (1166). Rand's point here is not that Kira's and Roark's priorities in her earlier novels were inverted. Her point is, rather, that it is essential to the spiritual activity she extolled in those earlier works that this activity is the ultimate source of the material values on which human survival directly depends. Recognizing that the spiritual activity that Kira called "living" is self-sustaining enables us to live (and to love our lives) more fully and consistently.

We can see some germs of this perspective, in Rand's earlier work and in some of the other nineteenth- and twentieth-century authors

---

22. On the development in Rand's thinking on these issues, see Wright 2005 and 2009 and Salmieri 2016a.

quoted above. These authors often portray the spiritual qualities associated with living (as opposed to merely existing) as making characters *effective*, and this efficacy extends to such productive enterprises as the factory by which Jean Valjean reinvigorates the town of Montreuil-sur-Mer in Hugo's *Les Misérables*, Betty Vanderpole's rebuilding of the Stornham Court estate in Burnett's *The Shuttle*, and Martin Edin's literary career in London's eponymous novel. Burnett is explicit about the connection between Betty's "genius for living" and literal survival, for she writes of this genius keeping her alive and contrasts this with being "kept alive by others."

The revitalizations of Montreuil-sur-Mer and Stornham Court are instances of bourgeois or upwardly mobile newcomers supplanting the practices of an exhausted aristocracy, and so these episodes could be seen to represent a respect in which the emerging capitalist social system is more vital than the feudal system it was supplanting. Socialist authors, such as Wilde and London, looked forward to the greater material prosperity that they imagined would result once the abolition of private property (somehow) enabled more widespread vitality. We can see this same motivation in Andrei Tagonov and Stepan Timoshenko, the most admirable Communist characters in Rand's *We the Living*. These men are among the living, and they "made a revolution" in order "to raise men to our own level."[23] In time Tagonov and Timoshenko realize that the Soviet regime they have made possible sacrifices the living for the sake of those who merely exist and that the result is both spiritual desolation and grinding poverty. This point is made also in Rand's *Anthem* (published between *We the Living* and *The Fountainhead*), which depicts a collectivistic society of the future that, because of such sacrifices, has regressed to a pre-industrial state of existence in which hardly anyone lives past middle age.

Howard Roark articulates the point in his courtroom speech in *The Fountainhead*. He attributes the spiritual activity that is characteristic of Rand's heroes to the faculty of reason, and he emphasizes reason's role in both Man's "glory" and his survival:

His vision, his strength, his courage came from his own spirit. A man's

23. Timoshenko twice says that he and Tagonov "made a revolution" (*WTL*36 391, 455; *WTL* 304, 352). In both cases he speaks of their motivations in exalted spiritual terms and extols the will with which they acted but bemoans the sordid horror of the world that resulted. Tagonov tells Kira that his goal is "to bring [most men] up to my level" (*WTL*36, 94; *WTL* 74) and "to raise men to our own level" (*WTL*36, 408; *WTL*, 316).

spirit, however, is his self. That entity which is his consciousness. To think, to feel, to judge, to act are functions of the ego.

The creators were not selfless. It is the whole secret of their power—that it was self-sufficient, self-motivated, self-generated. A first cause, a fount of energy, a life force, a Prime Mover. The creator served nothing and no one. He lived for himself.

And only by living for himself was he able to achieve the things which are the glory of mankind. Such is the nature of achievement.

Man cannot survive except through his mind. He comes on earth unarmed. His brain is his only weapon. Animals obtain food by force. Man has no claws, no fangs, no horns, no great strength of muscle. He must plant his food or hunt it. To plant, he needs a process of thought. To hunt, he needs weapons, and to make weapons—a process of thought. From this simplest necessity to the highest religious abstraction, from the wheel to the skyscraper, everything we are and everything we have comes from a single attribute of man—the function of his reasoning mind. (*Fountainhead* 678–79)

The elevated way of life celebrated in Rand's early fiction is one that she views both as the proper human form of life and as quite different from how people typically lead their lives. In these respects, her view is like Aristotle's distinction between living well and merely living. But Rand's early conception of Man's Life differs from Aristotle's in two important respects. The first is that Rand emphasized individuality and personal values in a way that Aristotle did not (but nineteenth-century literary authors did). The second is that the life Rand idealized involves such paradigmatically productive activities as building bridges, skyscrapers, and (in *Anthem*) light bulbs.

From Rand's early conception of Man's Life, it is a comparatively small step (especially after the industrial revolution) to observe that the work of creative geniuses plays an outsized role in human survival. This takes us to *The Fountainhead*'s view of the great creators. It is a further step from here to grasp that the same spiritual activity (though in different forms and at different scales) makes possible all of the actions by which human beings produce the (spiritual and physical) values on which human survival depends. It is a still further step to grasp that this fact about the spiritual activity with which Kira identified living is essential to this activity. This last step, which is unique to Rand, marks a fundamental development in the understanding of Man's Life. Absent this step,

"Man's Life" is understood as a certain, elevated *lifestyle*—a specific way of spending one's time—to which human nature suits us. Rand's insight upgrades it into a genuine conception of a *life*.

Rand characterizes life as "a process of self-sustaining and self-generated action" (*VOS* 16, cf. Aristotle, *DA* 416b17 on the power of nutrition). For different living species to have different forms of life is for them to sustain themselves by different processes of self-generated action. The human process—the only process by which even a human being's crudest physiological needs can be met—is a rational process. Rational activity is not just a distinguishing feature of human life by dint of which we live well, as opposed to merely living; rather, reason (or "man's mind") is man's "basic tool of survival" (*Atlas* 1011).

This is true even in the most primitive hunter-gatherer conditions (which Roark alludes to in his speech). But, so long as human beings lived a primarily agricultural and low-tech form of existence, it would have been difficult to appreciate the full scope of reason's role in human survival. Aristotle, of course, acknowledges that reason (via the *technai*) plays a significant role in the process of human survival, but he thinks that all the relevant *technai* were discovered and perfected (or nearly perfected) long ago, and their continued exercise doesn't much impress him.[24]

The most intense and impressive activities of reason of which Aristotle was aware (such as those involved in axiomatizing geometry or in identifying causes of astronomical phenomena) played no obvious role in human survival, so it is not surprising that he regarded such exercises of rationality as ends-in-themselves that make no contribution to the business of living. From Rand's perspective, however, Aristotle's view represents an intense valuing of the mind coupled with an impoverished understanding of what she called "the role of the mind in man's existence" (*FTNI* 97, *RM* 72). This last is what she described as the theme of *Atlas Shrugged*.

Before delving deeper into *Atlas*, it's worth commenting on the allusion to Aristotle in the passage from Roark's speech. Roark describes the creator's mind as "a first cause, a fount of energy, a life force, a Prime Mover." Roark's creators are like the Aristotelian Prime Mover in at least two respects. First, they are first causes, as opposed to things that act only because they are moved by others. The primary contrast here is to the people Roark calls "second-handers" (*Fountainhead* 633–36)—those

---

24. This at least is the impression conveyed in *Metaphysics* A.1, and the passages from the *Politics* mentioned earlier.

whose lives are animated only as the aftereffects of the thinking of others. In the years after *The Fountainhead*, Rand would further articulate her view of human thought as a first cause into a theory of free will that is centered on a primary choice to engage or disengage one's mind.[25]

The second respect in which Roark's creators are like Aristotle's Prime Mover is that they engage in their activity for its own sake, rather than for the sake of an end beyond itself, and (at least many of) the positive effects of their activities on others form no part of their motivation. However, unlike the purely contemplative activity of the Aristotelian Prime Mover, the Roarkian Creators' activities are productive and so are deeply engaged with the natural (and, in some cases, social) world.[26]

The work Roark regards as an end-in-itself isn't limited to contemplating architectural principles, or even to designing buildings in his head or on paper. He loves to build. This love certainly includes the products of the building; for it is essential to the activity (and to Roark's love of it) that it produces buildings that serve a purpose.[27] Nevertheless, Roark doesn't build for the mere sake of the buildings' existing (or their purpose's getting served), but for the sake of *building* them. If he found that there were already plenty of buildings of the sort he liked in the world (apart from his action), rather than being fulfilled he would look for something else to create. What he wants isn't simply the world to *be* shaped a certain way; he wants to *shape* it.

As the example of Roark illustrates, valuing a productive activity stands in a subtle relation to valuing its product. For the activity to be productive it must be aimed at the product, and the activity's value depends on the product's actually serving a survival need. But what one values in valuing the product is not the (generic) fulfillment of that need,

---

25. On Rand's theory, see Ghate 2016, 107–14; Rheins 2016, 260–65; Binswanger 2014, 321–61; and Peikoff 1991, 55–72.

26. Rand evoked the same Aristotelian idea (in a different translation) by titling Part I, Chapter IV of *Atlas Shrugged* "The Immovable Movers." On the significance of that title, see Ghate 2009 7–9, and on the novel's use of the immovable mover imagery, see Salmieri 2007, Lecture 1 0:55:00–1:00:30.

27. In the scene where Roark first explains that he seeks clients in order to build, rather than the reverse, he explains that "nothing can be reasonable or beautiful" unless it's integrated around a single central idea and that the central idea for a building is the solution devised by the architect to a unique problem set by the building's purpose, site, and materials (*Fountainhead* 12). The purpose is determined by the client's needs. Thus Roark needs clients to build not only because he'd lack the material resources to build without them but because their needs create the context for the work itself. Thus he comments: "I need people to give me work. I'm not building mausoleums" (158). Later, explaining the difference between himself and a friend who is a sculptor, he observes: "He can work without clients. I can't" (399).

but the product itself. And part of valuing a product as such is regarding it as something *produced* (whether by oneself or by someone else). Loving a productive activity is not just loving either a need's getting met or the product by which it gets met; it is valuing the *activity* of meeting the need by creating the product. The need is an essential part of the context that gives rise to the activity, but the need's satisfaction is not that for the sake of which the activity is loved.

If Rand's ethics is correct, then all proper human activities play a role in fulfilling biological needs, and this is essential to these activities' being proper. Nevertheless, it is possible for someone to love such an activity without attending to the need that gives rise to it (as Kira does in the case of engineering), or without even being aware of this need. Hidden in the remains of a railroad tunnel from a collapsed and forgotten industrial civilization, the hero of *Anthem* begins conducting scientific experiments with no purpose in mind beyond satisfying his curiosity. It is only after he has reinvented the light bulb that he comes to realize that the scientific research he loves is life-sustaining as well as spiritually rewarding, and it is later still that he comes to see working to sustain one's life as noble.[28] Arguably, Aristotle was in a similar epistemic position when he regarded contemplation as an end-in-itself. Like the hero of *Anthem*, he loved seeking causes, which he saw as epitomizing the activity of reason, but he misunderstood the role of such reasoning in human life as a whole.

This brings us to *Atlas Shrugged*'s theme of the "role of reason in man's existence." As I've written elsewhere (Salmieri 2009b), this theme can be divided into two broad aspects: reason as the productive faculty and reason as the valuing faculty. As the productive faculty, reason is the source of material values on which human life depends. The novel illustrates reason's role (through technology) in the production of food, shelter, and other necessities of survival. It illustrates the grand scale of the reason-guided productive activity that makes possible the comparatively long, safe, and healthy lives that modern residents of first world countries take for granted. And it illustrates the intensity of the reasoning involved in the relevant productive achievements. Reason is also the valuing faculty, in that it is responsible for the spiritual activities that Rand extolled in her earlier writing. It is by reason that (as Kira put it) we "know how to

---

28. On the progression of this character's thoughts, see Salmieri 2005. It is true that early on, he thinks that great inventions (such as the candle) can come from "the science of things," but the goal of creating such inventions is no part of his motive when he begins his clandestine research.

want," and this knowing is the source of personal commitments to values and of the emotional intensity that the early Rand viewed as essential to living (as distinct from merely existing).

Atlas treats these two aspects of reason's functioning as a systematic whole. The activity that the heroes love and engage in as an end-in-itself is one of rationally conceiving life-supporting values and then bringing these values into existence through productive action. This activity is portrayed as the core activity of human life. The novel illustrates how values of many sorts (romantic love, sex, abstract science, philosophy, art, wealth, friendship) each play a role in this process, and it shows the corrupted and destructive form these values take when pursued in ways that drop this context. Thus, for the mature Rand to say that man is the "rational animal" (*ITOE* 44) is to say that the very process by which human beings live is essentially rational.

The components of this life stand in various means-end relations, as when one cooks a meal in order to eat it, but these relations are not all unidirectional (as the Aristotelian means-end relation seems to be), and so the value of a means is not always derived from and lesser than the value of the end. One cooks in order to eat, but one eats in order to have energy to perform activities of which cooking is one. Living, which is the ultimate end, is not some atomic activity to which all one's other activities are mere means. Rather the end—one's life—is a complex, self-sustaining activity, composed of many parts (some more central, others peripheral).

Rand's conception of one's life as one's ultimate value should not be confused with the idea of an "inclusive end" that figures in the secondary literature on Aristotle's ethics.[29] An inclusive end is one that subsumes (some of) the other values that are pursued for its sake rather than merely resulting causally from them. In some versions of this view, the other values are made more valuable by being constituents of the inclusive end, but as the idea is usually understood, each of the values subsumed in the inclusive end has some intrinsic value apart from its effects and from its participation in a larger whole. The inclusive end is valuable because it combines things that are valuable in themselves, and (perhaps) because the combination enhances its constituents in such a manner as to make the whole more valuable than the sum of its parts.

---

29. Hardie (1965) introduced this idea into the literature. See Ackrill 1974 and Kenny 1977 for some of the early debate about whether Aristotle regards *eudaimonia* as an "inclusive" end. And see Lear 2004, 2–3 (esp. 3n2) for a useful summary of the positions taken in this literature.

For Rand, by contrast, there are no intrinsic values, and the value of each component of a life depends entirely on its effects and on its relation to the whole life.[30] This is true for life in general (e.g., for a plant's life or an animal's). In the human case, there's an added component. Since it is reason that integrates the pursuit of these many values into a self-sustaining life, each value's status as a value depends on the valuer's knowing how to achieve and utilize the value in a way that serves his life as a whole. Of course, this knowledge can be more or less extensive and more or less explicit. We will see in the next two sections how Rand thinks moral philosophy gives us explicit abstract knowledge of how to integrate values into a human life, and how Aristotle's ethics relates to hers on this count.

Abstract Standards and Personal Purposes

Because Aristotle's conception of Man's Life includes practicing one of two specific occupations (that of a philosopher or that of a statesman), it strikes contemporary readers as unduly narrow and insensitive to the deeply personal factors that incline different people to different careers. We now take it for granted that there is a wide range of possible and equally valuable careers, and that a person's choice between them will depend on personal preferences or other individuating factors.

Aristotle isn't blind to the fact that ethical principles need to be applied to individuals in a way that is tailored to their differing features and circumstances—indeed this is something he stresses. But there is a difference between tailoring the same suit differently for different individuals and designing a different suit for each. This point should be familiar from *The Fountainhead*: Keating adapts old designs to new sites (which requires a modicum of intelligence), whereas Roark creates a new design for each building (always following the same abstract architectural principles). There is an emphasis on the value of creativity, individuality, and the personal in Rand's work (and in modernity generally) that is missing (or at least muted) in Aristotle. We can see this in the somewhat differing

---

30. On whether even the ultimate value of life is "intrinsic," see *Letters* 561, where Rand (writing in 1961) comments to John Hospers on the distinction between instrumental and intrinsic values. Provisionally accepting the distinction as Hospers (1961, 104–38) draws it, she says that only life is an intrinsic value. But she calls doubt on the distinction. In "What Is Capitalism" (*CUI* 13–15) from 1965, she rejects the idea of "intrinsic" goods altogether. The sense in which she uses the term here is broader than that in which intrinsic goods (or values) are generally contrasted with instrumental ones, but it includes this sense (though she doesn't say so in as many words). On this issue, see Salmieri 2016b, 135–36.

roles that (what amounts to) the idea of a standard of value plays in the work of the two philosophers.

Although I suggest Aristotle and Rand both treat Man's Life as a standard of moral value, the terms "standard of value" and "morality" are not found in Aristotle, so it is worth saying a bit about how Rand uses them and about the corresponding terminology in Aristotle. Rand defines morality as "a code of values to guide man's choices and actions—the choices and actions that determine the purpose and the course of his life" (*VOS* 13). And she defines a "standard" as "an abstract principle that serves as a measurement or gauge to guide a man's choices in the achievement of a concrete, specific purpose" (27). So, when she speaks of the standard of value of a morality, she means an abstract principle by which one can guide one's life as a whole by selecting specific goals and specific means to them.

Aristotle formulates what amounts to this same idea of a comprehensive guiding principle for life via the metaphor of a target: "Everyone who is able to live according to his own choice should set up some target for living well (whether it's honor or reputation or wealth or education) looking to which he will take all of his actions; since not having one's life arranged toward some end is a sign of great folly. So, first of all, we must define for ourselves without haste or carelessness (i) those things in which living well consists and (ii) those things without which living well is impossible for human beings" (Aristotle, *EE* I.2 1214b6–14).[31] The idea of a "target for living well" is explained by the comment that it is something the person can "look to" in taking all of his actions and, thereby, arrange his life toward an end. Aristotle's advice isn't simply that everyone who can should erect *some* such target; for the context makes clear that he thinks there is a *correct* target, which we can identify by attending to two questions: (i) In what things does living well consist? (ii) What (other) things are prerequisites for a human being's living well? The four possible targets Aristotle suggests ("honor, reputation, wealth, or education") are candidate answers (which Aristotle goes on to reject) for the first of these questions.[32] The candidates' function in the passage is to concretize the

---

31. Notice that Aristotle's advice is directed specifically to those "who are able to live by their own choice." This category clearly excludes young children, whose reason is not yet developed, and enslaved persons, who aren't at liberty to live by their own choice. Aristotle likely also means it to exclude people without enough wealth to live leisured lives, and those people (such as women and "natural slaves") whom he thought were congenitally incapable of directing their lives by their own reasoning.

32. Reputation and wealth are rejected as the constituents of "living well" a few Bekker pages later (1215a20–33). Honor and reputation approximate to virtue and contemplation, respectively, but these are only valuable assuming those conferring honor and reputation them-

idea of a target around which a life could be organized. Each target is abstract enough to serve as a standard of value (in Rand's sense)—a guide by which a person could select his more specific goals and values. And each leads to a distinctive and recognizable type of life. Having introduced the idea of a target (or standard of value), Aristotle immediately shifts to the task of identifying the correct target.

The passage we have been discussing comes from Aristotle's *Eudemian Ethics*, but we find the target metaphor also in the *Nicomachean Ethics*. There it is introduced after Aristotle discusses the goods of various endeavors and the respects in which one good can be subordinate to another. This suggests to him the idea of a "chief good," which is desired for its own sake and for the sake of which we do everything we do. If there is such a good, Aristotle writes, knowledge of it will make us "like archers with a target to aim at, more likely to hit on what is right" (*EN* 1094a22–24). Later, he recapitulates that "there is a target to which the man who has reason looks and heightens or relaxes his activity accordingly" (1138b22–23).

I take it that, for Aristotle, the target and the ultimate good are the same in one respect but distinct in another. To use an Aristotelian turn of phrase, they are the same in number, but their being is not the same. There is a certain item—a certain activity (as we'll see)—that is the chief good for human beings, and this item is the human good, whether or not anyone recognizes it as such. Moreover, this activity is the good of each particular human being, whether or not that human being recognizes this. But it is only when I recognize this item as my good that it becomes a *target* for me—something I can use to consciously *guide* my action. And the good's status as a target makes it easier for me to attain it.

Does Rand share this view of the relation between the ultimate value and the target? She writes: "An *ultimate* value is that final goal or end to which all lesser goals are the means—and it sets the standard by which all lesser goals are *evaluated*. An organism's life is its *standard of value:* that which furthers its life is the *good*, that which threatens it is the *evil*" (*VOS* 17).

Here the ultimate value is said to *set* the standard of value rather than to *be* that standard, but the same thing—an organism's life—is placed in both roles. We saw earlier that Rand distinguishes between a standard and a purpose; the former is an abstraction that serves as a guide to the

---

selves have virtue and practical wisdom; since otherwise the human good is not up to oneself and can easily be taken away by another (1095b28–37).

achievement of the latter, which is a concrete. She applies this point to the human case as follows: "Man must choose his actions, values and goals by the standard of that which is proper to man—in order to achieve, maintain, fulfill and enjoy that ultimate value, that end in itself, which is his own life" (*VOS* 27).

The point that a standard is abstract—whereas a purpose is concrete—presumably applies in the case of nonhuman organisms as well. Lassie's life will be her ultimate value; and because Lassie is a dog, Dog's Life will be the standard with reference to which it can be determined what furthers or threatens Lassie's life.[33] Of course, Lassie herself will not consciously appeal to this abstract standard when evaluating things, but her owner or veterinarian may make decisions for her with this standard in view. Moreover, an account of the reason Lassie pursues the various items she does would appeal to the standard of Dog's Life. For example, an explanation of why she's so protective of Timmy would appeal to the fact that a dog is a domesticated pack animal that lives by serving its human master. Unbeknownst to Lassie, this fact about Dog's Life (when combined with facts about Lassie's circumstances) explains her valuing of Timmy. This distinction between standard and purpose is more important in the case of human beings precisely because, unlike dogs, we can have an abstract understanding of our form of life and use this understanding to select our personal values. Moreover, the process of applying the abstract standard to one's own concrete case is an important instance of the reasoning that is the distinguishing feature of human life.

The target Aristotle speaks of in the first books of the *Eudemian* and *Nicomachean Ethics* is presumably meant to be the relatively abstract account he's providing in those works. This account is the same for a beginner in gymnastics and for Milo the wrestler (to repurpose Aristotle's example from *EN* 1106a33), even though the specific actions that each one will need to take to hit this target will be different. Central to Aristotle's conception of practical virtue is the ability to reason well about particular cases. This reasoning involves a nuanced recognition of how relevant abstract considerations pertaining to the standard apply to an individual case, in light of the many factors that differentiate the individual and his circumstances from those of others.

For Rand, there is an additional respect in which the distinction between the abstract standard and the concrete purpose matters: part of reason's role in life is choosing one's purposes—including one's overarch-

33. Or, perhaps, Rough Collie's Life, if what is good for dogs varies with their breed.

ing purpose in life. This is not simply a matter of recognizing how some predetermined, universal end can best be achieved given one's distinctive features and circumstances. Rather, it is a matter of conceiving of a new, distinctive end for oneself. "You set the goal and the meaning; the field of choice and possibilities is immense; the only necessity involved is that you use the material as it is and your tool (reason) as it is—that you understand them for what they are before you choose or achieve a purpose" (*Papers* 032_11B_002_060 / *Journals* 294).

Once one recognizes all the pertinent facts, including those that give rise to the need for a moral standard and all the particular facts about oneself and one's circumstances, there are inexhaustibly many possible lives one can choose as one's purpose. Each of these purposes constitutes a concrete instance of the human form of life that must be conceived with reference both to the abstract standard (and the facts that give rise to it) and to the differentiating features of oneself and one's circumstances. This *conceiving* is not merely a matter of *adapting* an existing form to a new concrete situation, it's a new creative act.

An analogy may be instructive here. Think of a poet composing a sonnet for the wedding of two friends. In doing so, he makes reference both to the abstract form of a sonnet and to the many specific details of the couple and the occasion. But there are many possible poems that are instances of the sonnet form and that would be suitable to recite at this wedding. The poet's task is not to pick out the most suitable poem from this infinite set (as if the infinity of potential poems already existed somewhere to be selected from).[34] Rather, his task is to *compose* a sonnet for the occasion. The sonnet is a new creation of the poet. And, even though a sonnet is a fairly rigid form, think of how different the poet's activity is from simply plugging concretes about the couple into some preset formula—like filling out a Mad Lib. Most notably, the poem will need to have a theme and a central idea for how to express this theme in the sonnet form.[35] But neither the theme nor the central idea is established by the sonnet form, by the occasion of the wedding, or by any facts about the couple. All of these factors will be relevant to the poet's choice of theme

---

34. In a discussion of nonfiction writing (*AON* 48, 163), Rand discusses how authors are sometimes stultified by a "Platonic" view of writing along the lines of the view from which I've differentiated our poet's task.

35. On the concept of a "central idea" or "core combination" in art and Rand's concept of "plot-theme" (which is the version of this idea specific to literature), see *Fountainhead* 12–13; "Basic Principles of Literature" (*RM* 84); *AOF* 17; Boeckmann (2007a, 123–24; 2008; 2016, 438–40); and Salmieri 2016a, 55–59.

and central idea—and to all the other choices involved in executing the central idea—but the choices themselves involve new acts of *creative reasoning* on the poet's part. Composition consists largely in such acts of creative reasoning. And it is in the nature of such acts that, no matter how well the poet does his job, it would be possible for someone to do it equally well by composing a wholly different sonnet (perhaps with a wholly different theme). It is this sort of creative reasoning that, in Rand's view, is involved in setting the core purposes that shape one's life and thereby composing an ultimate value (or purpose) for oneself. In this process moral principles (including the standard of Man's Life) play something like the role of principles of literary composition.

I don't know that Aristotle would disagree with this point. Even within the contemplative life, there must be many choices about which things to study in which ways. How does one divide one's time between studying mathematics and the natural world? In one's study of nature, does one focus more on animals (as Aristotle did) or on plants (as did Theophrastus)? Even if different options may be better for different people with different talents or circumstances, it's doubtful that such considerations would mandate a single best syllabus for any individual's contemplative career. Likewise, there are presumably different roles a statesman could play in his city, and it may be that, even given a particular set of facts about his talents and circumstances, there are multiple political careers for him to choose among. However, although Aristotle's view is consistent with there being such scope for personal choice and may even imply it, this is not something he calls attention to, and he does not valorize the making of such choices as an exercise of reason.

To return to the example of the wedding sonnet, if we value the sonnet, we do not value it simply as a functional item that serves its purpose in the wedding ceremony (to whatever extent it does). Rather, we also value it as the work of a specific artist, bearing the mark of his specific personality and sensibility. Likewise, when Dagny Taggart in *Atlas Shrugged* loves Taggart Transcontinental and John Galt (the two concrete values that are central to her life), she loves them not merely as values that can constitute and sustain *a* human life, but as *her* specific chosen ends. There is an individualistic element here that we might call *Romantic*, insofar as it stems from an emphasis on the *choices* of individuals reflecting the details of their souls.

This individualistic, Romantic perspective is largely absent from Aristotle. He comes nearest to it when he points out that poets love their own works (and parents, their own children) more than they do other people's, because they are *their own* creations.³⁶ But there is something impersonal—and unromantic—in his accounts of love and of literary creation. Although, as Robert Mayhew argues in chapter 13 of this volume, Aristotle's theory of literary creation stresses some of the methods of literary integration that would later be essential to the Romantic movement in literature, it lacks the emphasis on the author's distinctive personal values that is also characteristic of this school.³⁷ Likewise Aristotle's account of love (discussed by Allan Gotthelf in chapter 14 of this volume) stresses the importance of character and virtue to the highest forms of love, but he says comparatively little about the sorts of individualizing features that make one person love a particular other person as distinct from others who may share his virtues—the sorts of features that Rand captures in her concept of a "sense of life."³⁸

Rand's distinction between a standard and a purpose brings out the abstractness of the former and the concreteness of the latter. The relation of the abstract standard to the concrete purpose isn't one of tailoring the former to the latter but, rather, of using the former as a guide in one's creation of the latter. This distinction helps us think in a new way about what we might call paradigmatic instances of the standard—individuals that fulfill it perfectly and dramatically. Aristotle's God and the people whom Rand (borrowing Aristotelian language) calls "Prime Movers" are examples of such paradigmatic instances of Aristotle's and Rand's respective moral standards—of Man's Life.³⁹

The more we think of contemplation (or whatever one holds as the highest activity) as a single concrete activity that admits of some variation (such that it can be tailored to individual cases), the more natural it is to identify this standard with an individual who embodies it most fully. If one does this, one's standard becomes in effect *likeness to this individual*. Aristotle's cosmology and ethics are both plausibly interpreted along these lines. The stars revolve in order to be like God, and the philosopher contemplates for the same reason. We can describe this as seeking to be like God—or as seeking to realize in oneself the abstraction of which God

---

36. Indeed, even in the *Rhetoric* and *Poetics*, which are about literary composition, there is less emphasis on individual creativity than one might expect.

37. On the relation between Romantism's method of literary integration and its projection of personal values, see Boeckman 2016, 440–47.

38. See "Philosophy and Sense of Life" and "Art and Sense of Life" (both in *RM*). Rand describes art and romantic love as the "two aspects of man's existence which are the special province and expression of his sense of life" (*RM* 21).

39. God's life qualifies as a paradigm instance of Man's Life insofar as a man is most of all his reason and God's life is just the life of reason.

is the fullest embodiment. But insofar as the standard is such that there is a single way to embody it most fully, these two descriptions amount to the same thing. By contrast, when a standard is understood as an abstract principle that exists for the sake of guiding us in the achievement of different concrete purposes, there cannot be any single, unique paradigm instance of the standard with which it can be identified in the way that the activity of contemplation can be identified with Aristotle's God.

John Galt is Rand's fullest literary embodiment of her moral standard, and there is a sense in which anyone attempting to live up to this standard is striving to be like Galt. Indeed, Galt serves as an inspiration to the other heroes in *Atlas Shrugged*, and Rand writes of the ways in which literary heroes can serve such a role.[40] However, it is in the nature of Rand's standard that Galt's life is just one of a potentially infinite number of different lives that could fulfill the standard perfectly—lives that involve wholly different careers, interests, friends, priorities, and so on, all falling equally under such abstractions as "rationality," "productiveness," and "pride." Such lives are not variations on any single theme, any more than are all Romantic piano concertos or all buildings designed in accordance with Roark's principles. It is essential to a building's perfectly realizing these principles that it is not just numerically unique but is integrated around a distinct idea conceived to fulfill its individual purpose in its individual setting. In the same way, Galt's individuality is essential to his realizing Rand's ideal. One seeks to be like Galt (or to build like Roark or to compose like Tchaikovsky) not by seeking to be concretely like him but by realizing *in a new and distinctive way* the same abstractions that he epitomizes.[41]

For Rand, paradigmatic concretes play a heuristic role in helping one to hold and implement a standard, rather than themselves serving as standards to which other things approximate. We can see this in her brief discussion of the "psycho-epistemological function of a personified (concretized) human ideal":

40. In *Atlas* (517, 633–37, 640–41, 812), Francisco and Dagny sometimes describe their dedication to ideals in terms of their "serving" Galt. Francisco does this thinking of Galt concretely; Dagny initially thinks of an idealized image of a man at the end of the railroad tracks, and then of the inventor of the motor she discovers, but she comes to identify both figures with Galt. Rand's early notes on what Galt represents for several other characters (*Journals* 505) also connect him to their ultimate motivations.

41. Thus, at the beginning of Roark's career, his mentor, Henry Cameron, praises him as follows: "What you're doing—it's yours, not mine, I can only teach you to do it better. I can give you the means, but the aim—the aim's your own. You won't be a little disciple putting up anemic little things in early Jacobean or late Cameron" (*Fountainhead* 68).

Observe that every religion has a mythology—a dramatized concretization of its moral code embodied in the figures of men who are its ultimate product.... This does not mean that art is a substitute for philosophical thought: without a conceptual theory of ethics, an artist would not be able successfully to concretize an image of the ideal. But without the assistance of art, ethics remains in the position of theoretical engineering: *art is the model-builder.*

Many readers of *The Fountainhead* have told me that the character of Howard Roark helped them to make a decision when they faced a moral dilemma. They asked themselves: "What would Roark do in this situation?"—and, faster than their mind could identify the proper application of all the complex principles involved, the image of Roark gave them the answer. They sensed, almost instantly, what he would or would not do—and *this helped them to isolate and to identify the reasons, the moral principles that would have guided him.* ("Psycho-Epistemology of Art," *RM* 10, emphasis added)

The concretized ideal is a model created by the artist to dramatically embody abstract principles. And its proper function is to help us to isolate and identify these principles, rather than to serve as a standard directly. We live well, not to the extent that we approximate to being Roark but to the extent that we, like Roark, act with such virtues as independence and integrity.[42]

The Objectivity of the Moral Code

Part of the appeal of the idea of a distinctively human form of life as a standard for ethics is that it purports to provide an objective standard for morality. We are a certain species with a certain nature that fits us to live in a certain way. Moral principles can be derived from an understanding of this nature and its implications, rather than being mere systematizations of our (personal or societal) preferences or prejudices. I take it that the promise of some sort of objective grounding for ethics accounts for much of the appeal of works such as Philippa Foot's *Natural Goodness*,

---

42. Importantly, for Rand, each of these virtues is a principle—that is, a recognition of a fact that can be formulated abstractly, rather than a characterological disposition that can only be elucidated by reference to how paradigmatically virtuous individuals would behave in various situations. The respective facts recognized by independence and integrity are (1) that "nothing can help you escape" "the responsibility of judgment" and (2) that "you cannot fake your own consciousness" (*Atlas* 1019, cf. *VOS* 28). For elaboration, see Peikoff 1991, 251–67; Gotthelf 2016, 92–94; and Smith 2006, 106–13, 176–83.

with its suggestion that moral goodness and badness are akin to features that make members of other species fit or unfit to carry on the ways of life of their species.[43]

I indicated earlier how the most abhorrent features of Aristotle's ethics—his endorsement of slavery and attitude toward productive work—stem from his distinction between instrumental and intrinsic values, and I showed how Rand's alternative view of value underwrites a view in which a nonexploitative harmony of interests is possible between people (and within each individual). Now I want to raise a related, methodological question. Is there anything in Aristotle's approach to ethics that provides a ground on which he could and should have rejected the exploitative features of the classical Greek way of life that we now regard as evil? More generally, does an Aristotelian approach to ethics put us in a position to reflect critically on the way of life into which we have been acculturated?

Of course, we cannot expect that Aristotle could have seen everything that we now recognize as wrong with every classical Greek practice or institution. Nor should we expect it to be easy for us to identify any immoral aspects of current mores that may be obvious to future generations. However, part of the job of moral philosophy is to equip us to differentiate the good from the parochial—to determine what is wrong as well as what is right about the ways of life to which we're accustomed and to evaluate challenges to this way of life once they've been suggested. The idea of a human function or form of life that can serve as a moral standard brings with it a promise of objectivity. It suggests that the way of life the Aristotelian advocates is grounded in *nature* rather than in the customs or prejudices of an individual or a society. If the human form of life is our standard of value, then, once we encounter radical suggestions such as that slavery may be wrong or that moneylending may not be, we should be able to use the standard to settle the matter. No doubt, it may take skill or nuance to apply the standard correctly, but it ought to be possible to do it, and it ought to be possible to recognize cases in which it has been done. Otherwise, the standard is nothing more than a codification of our preexisting moral attitudes—including any relevant prejudices we may have.

The abhorrent and parochial features of Aristotle's own view of Man's Life should make us sensitive to the possibility of simply reading into na-

---

43. See de Liège 2023 for an argument that Foot's framework cannot realize this promise.

ture our own prejudices, whatever they may be. The connection between Man's Life and survival in Rand's ethics is meant to give us a means to ensure that no mere prejudices get included as elements of Man's Life.

When Rand describes "Man's Life" as the standard of value, this phrase is not meant to name some preferred lifestyle that she counts as "living well" for a man and that she venerates over other ways in which men might equally well sustain themselves. Rather, she means "man's survival *qua* man"—that is, "the terms, methods, conditions and goals required for the survival of a rational being through the whole of his lifespan—in all those aspects of existence which are open to his choice" (*VOS* 26). Each of the moral values and virtues that she identifies as components of "Man's Life" are supposed to play a causal role in the process by which a human being survives across a human lifespan. This is not to say that a person would necessarily (or even probably) die young without it. There are all sorts of ways in which organisms can subsist despite dysfunctions. But a trait is not a dysfunction at all unless it drains or distracts from the process by which the organism survives. Likewise, any alleged immorality is not genuinely immoral unless it is a drain or distraction from the process by which a human being survives, and conversely nothing is genuinely moral unless it makes some contribution to this process. Rand's morality is meant to identify in abstract and essentialized terms the portions of that process that are subject to choice. (Dysfunctions that aren't due to choice are unhealthy—or otherwise bad—without being immoral.)

The idea of an ethical standard based on Man's Life cannot provide objectivity if our conception of that form of life derives the whole of its content from the habits and mores that happen to be dominant in our milieu. This is, in effect, how Rand viewed Aristotle's standard: "The greatest of all philosophers, Aristotle, did not regard ethics as an exact science; he based his ethical system on observations of what the noble and wise men of his time chose to do, leaving unanswered the questions of: *why* they chose to do it and *why* he evaluated them as noble and wise" (*VOS* 14). Aristotle did consider—at least to a certain extent—why a *phronimos* acts as he does. The chapters on the characterological virtues, for example, describe some of the considerations relevant to particular virtues. But Rand is right that Aristotle didn't think these questions admit of exact and abstract answers.

In any case, the neo-Aristotelian virtue ethicists who extol *phronēsis* do not prize any of the specific considerations from which Aristotle says the *phronimos* reasons. What these ethicists stress (and often exaggerate) is the quasi-perceptual character of *phronēsis* itself.[44] Thus they reference the *phronimos* as the standard of what to do, and the standard (such as it is) to which Aristotle himself appeals is neglected. Some interpreters and revivers of Aristotelian ethics go so far as to deny that there is any abstract standard there.[45]

If the idea of a human form of life as a standard of value is to do any real work, it needs to derive at least some of its content from a broadly biological understanding of what a form-of-life is, in general, and what the human form is, in particular. However, it would also be a mistake to read off ethics in too facile a manner from an antecedent understanding of biology. Some worry that the attempt to ground morality in biological functions opens up the possibility that traits such as violence and deception could turn out to be virtues.[46] And we should not forget that forms of nonprocreative sex have often been deemed vicious on the grounds that they involve uses of our sexual organs that are counter to what are supposed to be their natural biological purposes. If we think such conclusions are unwarranted, we must be on guard against the possibility of erring in our attempts to derive ethical content from our understanding of human biology.

If we are concerned about objectivity, we can neither prejudicially valorize as parts of Man's Life whatever moral views we happen to hold, nor can we blithely infer moral content from biology while remaining (as Aristotle puts it) "inexperienced in the actions of life" (*EN* 1095a3). There is a third alternative. If there is a human form of life, if moral goodness consists in realizing it (or approximating to it), and if we are decent people who know some significant moral truths on the basis of our inarticulate experience (or because of our upbringing), then we ought to be able to draw on an independent understanding of our natures as members of the human species to understand why the actions or traits that we correctly regard as morally good form part of the human form of life (whereas their contraries do not).

The fact that the human form of life is essentially rational is a rudi-

---

44. In this, these ethicists are following an interpretation advanced most influentially by John McDowell (1980 and 1998).

45. For instance, Broadie (1991, 212) argues that it is a mistake to think the *phronimos* model offers us an "explicit, comprehensive, substantial vision" of the human good. Moss (2011) argues that characterological virtues are wholly nonintellectual.

46. Moosavi (2019) voices this concern. To foreclose it, she suggests that we adopt an irreducibly normative understanding of human biological functioning, which conception would include much of what we antecedently suppose to be the content of ethics.

mentary biological fact graspable without specialized study—analogous to the fact that falcons and other birds of prey live lives of predation, whereas deer lead lives of grazing and fleeing. Rand's ethics, which is intended as an articulation the contents of Man's Life, traces out the consequences of this and related facts. These consequences are not meant to be deduced from biological facts ab initio. Just as, in an Aristotelian science, many of the facts to be demonstrated are already known on the basis of experience, so too in ethics, decent and experienced people may already possess and live by moral knowledge, before they come to understand the basis of this knowledge in the requirements of Man's Life. Thus, one of the minor heroes of *Atlas Shrugged* says that the character who taught him this moral code has "merely named what I had lived by, what every man lives by—at and to the extent of such time as he doesn't spend destroying himself" (*Atlas* 447).

The moral code (or explicit moral theory) formulates the relevant truths explicitly and identifies them as parts of the human survival process. In this way it helps an individual who already knew and lived by some of these truths in an inarticulate manner to integrate his pursuits into a self-sustaining whole (a life). The process of integration is error-correcting in that conflicts among one's values (including between one's concrete values and one's moral code) are evidence that some of the values (or moral beliefs) are mistaken and must be revised.[47]

What are these ethical facts that form part of Rand's moral theory but can initially be grasped and applied experientially? One is the value of the spiritual qualities (such as passion, independence, and creativity) that the early Rand extolled. Another is the recognition that the values on which one's life depends need to be produced by reason-directed human effort so that (if one is not to be a parasite, which is self-defeating in innumerable ways) one must live productively. Other parts of Rand's code include the virtue of honesty (which she conceptualizes as the recognition that the unreal is unreal and can have no value), the virtue of independence (the recognition that thinking is not an activity one person can perform for another), the virtue of justice (the recognition that one must be objective in assessing the characters of others and that one must treat them accordingly), and the "trader principle" (which states that one must

---

47. In *Atlas Shrugged*, Francisco D'Anconia tells Dagny Taggart: "Contradictions do not exist. Whenever you think that you are facing a contradiction, check your premises. You will find that one of them is wrong" (199). Rand's advice to "check one's premises" was a recurring appeal to epistemic integration that she would offer in discussions with friends and students.

deal with others only voluntarily, to mutual benefit by mutual consent, rather than treating people as prey or as objects of charity). The validation of these virtues is too large a topic to take up here.[48] I mention them just to give a sense of the sort of content included in the moral code and to indicate the role Rand thinks it plays in human life.

Notice that these virtues are more abstract and more absolute than the content of Aristotelian ethics. Earlier I noted that, for Rand, an individual must compose his life using the standard of Man's Life as an abstract guide in the process; the content of Rand's ethics can be seen as principles of composition for a life analogous to principles of literary composition. The moral principles specify the broad values that a human life requires, and the broad sorts of actions by which those values can be pursued in a coherent and self-sustaining manner.

The putatively biological fact about human beings that neo-Aristotelian ethicists most often appeal to is that man is a social animal. I take it that the point of describing man as a social animal and of comparing human beings in this respect to bees, ants, and herd animals (rather than simply just pointing out that human beings live in societies) is to draw on biology in something like the way I recommended earlier. We don't simply catalogue the ways people conduct their lives and claim that this constitutes a human way of life, which is our function. Instead, we recognize our form of life as one that is rooted in our nature and that can be illuminated by comparisons to the lives of animals with relevantly similar natures.

But such comparisons with other animals that live in groups cannot be illuminating unless they are drawn with due attention to the characteristics that differentiate us from *all* other animals. The essence of humanity—our fundamental distinguishing characteristic—is rationality, and rationality makes a profound difference in every aspect of life that we engage in consciously (as opposed to the physiological activities of what Aristotle calls the nutritive soul). We should, therefore, expect it to make a profound difference in the nature of our sociality. This is Rand's view, at any rate. "Man," one of her protagonists says, "is a social being, but not in the way the looters preach" (*Atlas* 747). The "looters" in question are those who think that we should live in a collectivistic, rather than an individualistic, society. In a later essay, she elaborates on how the faculty of reason (here described as "a conceptual consciousness") requires a distinctive form of social existence:

---

48. For discussion of them, see Gotthelf 2016, 81–96; Smith 2006; and Peikoff 1991, 1998.

> Individual rights is the only proper principle of human coexistence, because it rests on man's nature, i.e., the nature and requirements of a conceptual consciousness. Man gains enormous values from dealing with other men; living in a human society is his proper way of life—but only on certain conditions. Man is not a lone wolf and he is not a social animal. He is a *contractual* animal. He has to plan his life long-range, make his own choices, and deal with other men by voluntary agreement (and he has to be able to rely on their observance of the agreements they entered). ("A Nation's Unity," *ARL* 2:2, 127)

The idea that rationality makes human beings very different from other animals, even with respect to functions or faculties that we share with them at a generic level, brings me to a point mentioned earlier in connection with the worry about inferring ethical conclusions from (putatively) biological knowledge about a human function. Sexuality is one area in which many such inferences have been drawn that may strike us as misguided. It is obvious that reproduction is the—or at least *a*—"natural" function of our sex organs, and this has sometimes been thought to justify condemnations of various nonreproductive forms of sex as unnatural and (therefore) improper. But human beings are essentially rational animals, and part of reason's role in human life is to enable each human being to compose for himself an individual life made up of specific values and practices that cohere into a self-sustaining whole. As the faculty that directs and organizes human life, reason replaces (or supersedes) the physiological or psychological mechanisms by which the activities of other organisms are organized into self-sustaining lives. Reason is free to find new uses for any of our faculties—uses for which they may not have evolved and for which they may not be employed in other species. Reason is likewise free to discover ways to alter these faculties (e.g., via birth control pills, vasectomies, or abortions) to better suit them to these chosen purposes.

In the process of natural selection organs often come to serve purposes other than those for which they initially evolved. There is nothing to prevent reason from similarly repurposing faculties within the span of any individual's life. New, life-sustaining uses for faculties can be discovered and promulgated through the culture. This is what has happened with the many nonprocreative uses of our sexual faculties by which we pursue pleasure and celebrate spiritual values. Likewise, reason is free to find new ways to achieve the values played by reproduction in individual human lives. Reproduction serves such material values as ensuring that there are young people to assist in one's dotage, and it serves spiritual values such as having progeny to whom to pass on one's way of life (which, for a human being, crucially includes one's ideas and values). All the ways discovered thus far to achieve these values require that some people reproduce; but a given individual needn't have offspring himself to share in these values. In some social animals (e.g., bees), a small subset of the community specializes in reproduction, and the rest of the community is sterile. So, we cannot infer that every human being should seek to reproduce from the facts that everyone has reproductive organs and that reproduction is a part of life. Fundamentally, what ethics has to say about sex is simply that one should be *rational* about it; this rationality includes creativity in the formation of values that can meet our physiological and psychological needs and can be achieved through the use of our faculties.

There are many more detailed questions, of course, about what sorts of sex lives can be good for us. Some of these questions (e.g., those involving issues of consent) are straightforwardly ethical and come under some of the moral principles alluded to earlier. But others lie near the border that separates ethics from psychology and they require the empirical research methods of that field. There are many such questions concerning sexual practices that have been derided (by various parties) as "unnatural": homosexuality, polyamory, polygamy, monogamy, masturbation, incest, relationships between (consenting) people distant in age, fantasizing about abusive forms of sex. Most of us think that at least some of these practices are bad for us, and few of us think that all are. If any one of these practices is bad for us, it must be because it runs contrary to human nature in some way other than its merely being atypical or different from the function that our sexual capacity evolved to serve. This could be because the practice stems from and reinforces a psychological state, such as low self-esteem, which saps our ability and motivation to engage in other vital activities. Or it could be because the sexual practice is incompatible with our using our sexual faculties to satisfy some crucial (physiological or psychological need) that we cannot otherwise meet.

Rand thought that promiscuity and homosexuality were immoral for reasons of the two sorts indicated above.[49] I think she was wrong about homosexuality and right about promiscuity. Settling either question would take us beyond the scope of this paper; I mention them here to

---

49. On promiscuity, see Rand *Atlas* 489–91. On homosexuality, see Lewis and Salmieri 2016, 396n87 and the sources cited therein.

indicate how Rand's conception of Man's Life sets up a standard by which such practices could be established as moral or immoral. The application of this standard will require identifying the actual causal relations in which these practices stand to the essential activities by which human beings sustain ourselves.

This takes us back to the general issue of the objectivity of the moral standard and of how we can differentiate between ways of living that are second nature to us simply because we're accustomed to them and those that are grounded in our biological nature. A given practice or norm could turn out to be required by the standard of Man's Life, or to represent one possible way (among others) of satisfying this standard, or to be contrary to this standard (and, therefore, immoral). Aristotelian ethics is not objective, because it lacks the means to distinguish among these three categories; and it is the integration with biological fact that enables Rand's ethics to do so.

In some cases, the data we need to establish the relevant biological facts are available in ordinary experience. I have in mind facts such as that reason is our means of survival. This fact is biological in the broad sense that it is a fact about living things and how they live. But our knowledge of it doesn't depend on the *science* of biology. For it doesn't require the specialized methods of collecting and analyzing data that distinguish natural science from ordinary rational thinking and from philosophy. Indeed, it is only on the basis of a great deal of such nonspecialized knowledge about various types of living things that a science of biology could get off the ground.

But to settle the sorts of questions of sexual ethics we were just discussing, we need additional knowledge about human nature—and especially about the nature of the human mind. The same is true for a host of other questions pertaining to whether and when one should or can change or resist various desires or emotions—for example, questions concerning addiction (or putative addiction) or concerning states that may be mental illnesses. Most of our moral opinions on issues of these sorts reflect assumptions about these psychological questions. These assumptions are generally informed by our experience, which we can (and sometimes should) critically evaluate and work to enlarge. But they are assumptions of the sort that could be (and, in some cases, have been) confirmed, refuted, or modified by empirical research in psychology and allied fields.

The straightforwardly moral questions—the ones belonging to philosophy—are those that can be answered well without reliance on this specialized research. I think of questions that require research as involving distinguishable philosophical and scientific components. But even if this perspective on these issues is correct, the interplay of philosophical and scientific matters is complex and there are many borderline cases. Much of the subject matter of Aristotelian ethics—or at least of many of the characterological virtues—falls in this complex area at the border of philosophy and psychology. Rand had things to say about such questions as well. Indeed, as a novelist, she couldn't have avoided issues of psychology (as well as issues on the borderline between it and philosophy), since novel-writing requires projecting characters with complete personalities. But the issues she emphasizes when writing as a moral philosopher are more abstract and structural, and I can find few parallels to them in Aristotle's ethics.

When she writes about virtues, for example, she focuses not on characterological states but on abstract principles that she argues one must recognize in order to live as a human being—for example, the principle that the unreal is unreal and can be of no value. Of course, to recognize such principles in one's thinking and conduct, one must apply them contextually, and they must factor centrally into one's motivation. For this to happen over time, recognition of the principles must be automatized into a perspective on the world and a characteristic form of motivation that we can think of as a characterological virtue. But, for Rand, the concept "virtue" primarily refers to the abstract principle rather than to the form it takes in an individual's psychology. There is much to explore about how such principles are realized psychologically. Rand addresses some of these in various contexts, and comparison to Aristotle's accounts of characterological virtue and *phronēsis* might be illuminating in exploring her views.[50] But I see such comparisons as matters of detail when relating Rand's ethics to Aristotle's.

The central point of comparison is that each philosopher is recommending to us a certain way of living on the grounds that it is the one for which we are naturally suited as human beings—as rational animals. Each urges us to take Man's Life as our standard of value, but they differ in their understanding of this life and of how it can serve as a standard. For Aristotle, Man's Life is the distinctive manner of functioning that is characteristic of human beings and enabled by human nature. Rand adds that it is the process by which human beings *survive*. This means that,

---

50. Some of these issues concerning character are explored by Neera Badhwar and Ben Bayer in their chapters in this volume.

on Rand's view, to qualify as part of Man's Life, something must make a vital contribution to that process by which a human being sustains his existence across a human life span.

The moral content that follows from Rand's conception of Man's Life is more abstract than the subject matter of the Aristotelian virtues, and because of this, the moral guidance she offers can be objective and precise. For, as Aristotle noted, "the universal is honorable because it reveals the cause" (*APo.* 88a5–6). Because Rand's ethics identifies Man's Life at the right level of abstraction, this ethics can reveal to an individual the causal role played in his own life by each of his chosen values. Thus it enables him to harmonize these values into a life by which he can sustain himself without compromise and experience the profound, "non-contradictory joy" (*Atlas* 1022) that is the concomitant of living rationally, "in accordance with virtue" (*EN* 1098a17).

8
Comments on "'Man's Life' as the Standard of Value in the Ethics of Aristotle and Ayn Rand," by Gregory Salmieri

JOSEPH KARBOWSKI

I would like to thank Gregory Salmieri for giving us such a rich, clear, and stimulating paper comparing and contrasting Aristotle's and Ayn Rand's views on the normative standard of ethical value. He shows us that both philosophers agree that there is such a standard, that it is the human form of life, and that rationality is crucial to that form of life. However, Greg also points out that Aristotle and Rand differ in their conceptions of the human life form and in their corresponding views of reason and its role in a human being's life.

Briefly, Aristotle views the human form of life as, to quote Greg's excellent summary, "an ordered set of activities, in which only one activity (contemplation) is intrinsically valuable and performed entirely for its own sake, while all the others exist at least in part to serve it" (116). As such, Aristotle's conception of the best human life is generally inflexible and elitist. It is a picture according to which one or two specific ways of life (modulo some contingent differences between individuals) that are open to only a select few privileged members of society count as forms of human flourishing. By contrast, Rand's picture of the human form of life is more abstract and leaves greater room for diversity. In her view, the human form of life involves "rationally conceiving life-supporting values and then bringing these values into existence through productive action" (128). It is an inherently creative and productive mode of life, not only in the sense that it recognizes the intrinsic value of productive activity (unlike Aristotle's picture) but also in the sense that it leaves it up to the agent to craft his or her own concrete value system. This rational creative process is norm-governed: the values embodied in the scheme must be life-supporting. However, this constraint still leaves room for an indefinite number of realizations and so allows a far greater range of lifestyles to count as flourishing. These contrasts are interesting in themselves. But Greg's purpose in his paper isn't merely to contrast Aristotle and Rand for contrast's sake; it is to raise philosophical questions about the notion of a form of life and its role as a standard of ethical value. Greg's paper is a gem because deep philosophical insights are peppered throughout it. For example, I think his diagnosis of the problems in the Aristotelian conception of the human form of life are spot on, and I found his discussion of how the Randian framework tackles controversial questions about sex very illuminating. The issue, however, that intrigues me most is the methodological question he raises about Aristotelian ethics. The question, as he puts it, is whether there is "anything in Aristotle's approach to ethics that provides a ground on which he could and should have rejected the exploitative features of the classical Greek way of life that we now regard as evil?" (138)

Greg's answer, in brief, is "no." He doesn't think that anything in Aristotle's approach to ethics would in principle provide him with a reason to abandon the more unsavory views he held. Rand's approach fares much better on this score, Greg thinks. She adopts a biological approach which does not simply try to "infer moral content from biology" (140). Her approach is biological insofar as it appeals to objective facts about our nature as human beings, but as Greg points out, these are rudimentary facts that are "graspable without specialized study—analogous to the fact that falcons and other birds of prey live lives of predation, whereas deer live lives of grazing and fleeing" (141). These are the sorts of considerations that Rand thinks we can appeal to in order to adjudicate controversial ethical debates and to assess seemingly counterintuitive ideas in potentially profitable ways (though they might sometimes need to be supplemented with results from biology and/or psychology).

I don't take issue with Greg's point about the virtues of the Randian method as he describes it. I agree that it is clearly superior to the alternatives he sketches. What I wonder, however, is whether Aristotle's approach to ethics is all that different from Rand's. Greg doesn't actually say much about Aristotle's ethical method in his paper. He talks almost exclusively about Aristotle's conception of the human form of life. When he does get to talking about Aristotle's method, he cites Rand's take on the matter, which presents Aristotle as effectively systematizing the views of his time—but that's about it.

In the spirit of giving Aristotle a fair shake, I'd like to ask Greg if he would be willing to say more about what he takes Aristotle's method to be and how it compares to (is similar to and different from) Rand's. To make it easy, he could simply focus upon the function argument. What sort of considerations is Aristotle appealing to there, for example, when he argues that rationality is characteristic (*idion*) of humans? Is he appealing to commonly accepted opinions (*endoxa*)? Is he appealing to principles of his antecedently established psychological and biological theories (as Terence Irwin would have it)? Or do the relevant considerations have a different status?

The main motivation for the view that Aristotle's ethical starting points are *endoxa*, the views of the many and the wise, is a well-known methodological remark toward the end of *Nicomachean Ethics* VII.1, where he describes a three-stage procedure that involves first setting out the *endoxa* about a topic, then raising puzzles about them, and finally, solving the puzzles in a way that salvages as many of the initial *endoxa* as possible. Scholars find a beautiful application of this method in the inquiry into *akrasia* in *EN* VII.1–10; and, noting some similarities with how Aristotle proceeds elsewhere, they conclude that it is his general philosophical method.

The second approach alluded to above—the one according to which Aristotle is appealing to antecedently established principles of his psychology and/or biology in the function argument, which has been defended by Terence Irwin (1988a)—takes for granted that his ethical starting points are *endoxa*, on the strength of the methodological remarks in *EN* VII.1. But the second approach is motivated on philosophical grounds not to rest content with that claim. The problem as Irwin sees it is that *endoxa*, the views of the many and the wise, are not guaranteed to be true. Consequently, they are not capable of justifying belief in objective ethical principles all on their own. Irwin claims that Aristotle knew this and accordingly expanded the set of his ethical starting points to include antecedently established principles from his psychology and biology. These are things known to be true—and so they can shoulder the burden of vindicating belief in objective principles when they work together with ethical *endoxa*.

These two interpretations bear striking similarities to the alternatives Greg has sketched in his paper: the Scylla of deferential appeal to parochial beliefs and the Charybdis of "scientizing" ethics. And I believe that they fail as interpretations of Aristotle. Greg himself has powerfully argued that the so-called endoxic method of *EN* VII.1 is not Aristotle's general ethical method (Salmieri 2009a). Now, it cannot be denied that the inquiry into *akrasia* observes that method. But even a superficial glance at the structures of the other inquiries in the treatise reveals that they do not have that exact structure. Not all of them rely upon *endoxa* or puzzles; and even when they do, they do not necessarily play the same role they play in the so-called endoxic method described in *EN* VII.1.

Irwin's interpretation, by contrast, fails to do justice to Aristotle's own descriptions of his ethical starting points. Twice he describes his starting points, claiming that they are "facts" acquired on the basis of a good upbringing (*EN* I.4 095b6, I.7 1098b2). This is easy to overlook, but it is of central importance. For facts are articulate claims of the form *S is P* the truth of which has been vindicated by reliable (truth-establishing) mechanisms: perception, induction, experience, and so forth. A good moral upbringing is on that list, and so Aristotle's own characterization of his ethical starting points belies the motivation for Irwin's interpretation. Aristotle doesn't need to wheel in the antecedently established principles of his biology or psychology because he believes that the starting points to which he is appealing are true.

That he is not appealing to principles of his psychology or biology is further confirmed by his claim to be relying upon a popular division of soul and the correlated denial of the need for expertise in psychology (*EN* I.13). The political scientist, Aristotle believes, needs *some* knowledge of the soul. However, he does not need robust scientific knowledge of it. The degree of knowledge needed is that which someone who has been well brought up and has political ambitions can acquire on the basis of ordinary experience or reasoning from their ordinary experience.

This interpretation seems to capture very nicely the status of the claims that Aristotle actually appeals to in the function argument. For example, while it is true that an expert biologist will know that humans have a function, the claim that living things (in addition to tools and body parts) have functions was a commonplace among ancient philosophers (compare the argument at the end of Plato's *Republic* I). Similarly, even though an expert psychologist will know, among other things, that reason is distinctive of humans, that information is not something that only they could know. It is something that someone with ample life experience, living among people and interacting with the environment around them, can discover through induction.

More can be said on all of these matters. But I take it that this is enough to motivate my central question to Greg: How different, after all, is Aristotle's method from Rand's? I may, of course, be wrong. But if Aristotle's view is as I described above, the gap between them does not seem all that wide. Hence, even if we find fault with where the method led Aristotle, that is more a fault of his application of the method than of the method itself.

9
Thoughts on Ethical Methodology
In Response to Joseph Karbowski
GREGORY SALMIERI

In his gracious comments on my chapter, Joseph Karbowski points out that I neglected a topic of mutual interest: Aristotle's ethical methodology. I didn't address it in the paper because I thought that bringing it in would distract from the comparison I was drawing between Aristotle's and Rand's respective conceptions of Man's Life as a standard of value. But I'm pleased to take this opportunity to comment on method in response to the questions Joe raises. It may help to first say a word about the context in which Joe and I come at these issues.

At the end of the twentieth century, when the two of us started studying Aristotle, the scholarly literature was dominated by the view (endorsed by G. E. L. Owen, Terence Irwin, and others) that Aristotle's method in ethics (and perhaps, everywhere) consisted in working to render coherent a set of received opinions (*endoxa*). We've each worked to displace this orthodoxy. Joe references my (barbarously named) paper "Aristotle's Non-'Dialectical' Method in the *Nicomachean Ethics*" (2009a) in which I show that Aristotle's "cognitive goal" in the treatise is not to render coherent a set of opinions but, rather, to establish definitions of key ethical kinds (making clear, when relevant, how derivative features of those kinds follow from the essential features specified in the definitions). In the 2009 paper I also showed how the treatise's arguments "are premised on discriminations and evaluations that issue from experience and good character and do not qualify as *endoxa*" (2009a, 315, 312).

Joe develops and defends these same points (in greater detail and engaging more deeply with the scholarly literature) in his 2019 book *Aristotle's Method in Ethics: Philosophy in Practice*. In the book he also addresses a number of other topics that I haven't written on (or, in some cases, even thought about). One of them, which he also raises in his comments on my paper, is whether (and in what ways) ethics is autonomous as opposed to depending on other disciplines to justify or explain its principles (Karbowski 2019, 217–45).

Terence Irwin (1988a), who was a defender of the endoxa-coherentizing interpretation of Aristotle, thought that some of Aristotle's ethical arguments draw on scientific conclusions from other disciplines, rather than on endoxa, and that these conclusions are themselves demonstrated from principles that are established by (a version of) the method of endoxa-coherentizing.[1] In particular, Irwin thinks Aristotle's ethics rests on his psychology, which in turn rests on his metaphysics, the principles of which are established by what Irwin calls "strong dialectic." Contra Irwin, Joe argues that Aristotelian ethics is *justificatorily autonomous*—that is, not reliant on other disciplines to justify its principles. Joe further argues (contra Dominic Scott [2015] and others) that Aristotelian ethics is *explanatorily autonomous*: that its truths are not explained by other disciplines.

Thus Joe contrasts Aristotle's ethical method both to the endoxa-coherentizing method and to methods that would make ethics dependent on other disciplines. He sees Rand's approach (as I describe it) as doing the same—as navigating a channel between "the Scylla of deferential appeal to parochial beliefs and the Charybdis of 'scientizing' ethics." Thus he wonders whether Aristotle's method is really is as different from Rand's as I suggest, and whether I can be right to deny there is "anything in Aristotle's approach to ethics that provides a ground on which he could and should have rejected the exploitative features of the classical Greek way of life that we now regard as evil." Aren't Aristotle and Rand both justifying their ethical principles on the grounds of rudimentary

---

1. Irwin and others call this endoxa-coherentizing method "dialectic," and Irwin (1988a) distinguishes what he calls "strong dialectic" from other forms. I'm avoiding this terminology here, because, as I have argued (2009a, 312–13), I do not think this is what Aristotle himself meant by "dialectic."

biological facts about human beings that can be grasped without specialized study? And, if so, then how could it be that Rand's ethics has the resources to validate or reject inherited cultural mores, whereas Aristotle's does not?

In short, my answers to these two questions are that the philosophers' methods are the similar in the use they make of biological knowledge that one doesn't need to be a biologist to have, but that there are other differences in their methods that give Rand's ethics a sort of objectivity that Aristotle's lacks. Before elaborating on their respective methods, I should say a bit about the errors Joe characterizes as Scylla and Charybdis.

Joe and I agree about why an ethicist must steer clear of Scylla: ethics aims at moral knowledge, and rendering a set of prejudices coherent does not make it any sort of knowledge. We also agree that Aristotle is attempting to do something other than systematize endoxa, but I think Aristotle gets devoured by Scylla nonetheless. In due course, I'll explain why he meets this doom. First, we need to consider Charybdis.

If I understand Joe's view correctly, the Charybdis of "scientism" he's concerned about is ethics losing its autonomy, as he thinks would happen if its principles need to be justified or explained by some other branch of knowledge. This isn't an issue that I've given much thought to. As a matter of Aristotle scholarship, I think Joe is right that Aristotle doesn't think his ethical principles need to be justified by any demonstrations from his *De Anima* or *Metaphysics*. I incline toward Scott's view that Aristotle thinks material from the disciplines pursued in these treaties can *explain* some ethical content. But even if such explanation is possible (and desirable), I don't believe Aristotle thinks this content stands in any need of explanation for the purposes of ethics.

Although I didn't bring this point out in my paper, Rand's ethics is meant to depend on her epistemology and metaphysics, for she views all three as parts of the single hierarchically structured science of philosophy. The most obvious example of this dependence is that the fundamental virtue in her ethics, rationality, is practiced by recognizing the axiom at the root of her metaphysics—that existence exists.[2] Her ethics is not, however, supposed to rest on any knowledge from the science of biology; for in her view, philosophy is prior to the special sciences.

2. See Gotthelf 2016, 81–81, and Rheins 2016, 245–49, on the moral dimensions of this axiom. On the axiom more generally, see Peikoff 1991, 1–36; Rheins 2016; and chapters 1–3 of this volume.

I'm worried about a somewhat different Charybdis. It is twofold. My first worry is that attempts to ground ethics on facts about human biology (or psychology) often conflate vice with natural defect and virtue with natural ability. They do this by failing to take account of the distinctive normative character of ethics (and ethical concepts). Ethics is normative not only in the sense of this term that applies to everything biological, but in the specific sense of *prescribing* norms that we must adhere to *by choice*. Second, I am worried about too facile and fixed a view of what our biological needs or abilities are. A human life is fundamentally a rational life, and reason is capable of repurposing many of our faculties and of finding radically new ways to meet our needs. Reason also gives rise to spiritual needs (such as the needs for art and love) that biologically minded thinkers sometimes overlook or mistake for animalistic urges.

Such thinkers (e.g., those who style themselves "evolutionary psychologists") too often treat us as just another organism, ignoring the most important biological fact about us—that we're rational animals. They either ignore the wealth of knowledge we have by experience of the specifically human way of life or they try to assimilate this knowledge in too facile a way to something that's vaguely analogous in other organisms. (Consider, for example, the talk of "hierarchy" in other species that is sometimes used to justify pecking orders among human beings; or, in popular culture, consider those who fret over whether they're "alphas.")

Like Aristotle, I think we need to take seriously that ethical reasoning develops out of our experience living human lives. And this brings me back to Joe's question of how different Aristotle's ethical method is from the one I both endorse and attribute to Rand. Here I think we need to distinguish between different levels of abstraction at which we might describe a philosopher's method. Described abstractly, Aristotle's method is to induce universal and causally deep principles from more superficial knowledge readily formed on the basis of experience and then to demonstrate other truths (including the earlier-known facts) from these principles, thereby explaining this earlier knowledge and (often) elevating its epistemic status. This broad method is shared by Rand, and it is sufficient to generate knowledge and to correct prejudices.

But, as Joe observed (Karbowski 2019, 100–105; see also Lennox 2021, 64), applying this method in any specific discipline involves discovering and following *local norms*, which are specific to the relevant domain. Local norms are based on the sorts of access we have to the objects in the relevant domain that we seek to know and on the causal relationships that obtain among these objects.

As Joe notes in his book, Aristotle takes certain things to have "intrinsic value"—value that "cannot be captured by teleological demonstrations because it does not depend upon an item's relation to some other valued end" (Karbowski 2019, 181–82). This then influences the sorts of demonstrations that are to be sought in ethics and the sorts of principles that can serve as premises of these demonstrations. Rand, by contrast, doesn't think that anything is intrinsically valuable in this sense. Every value other than an individual's life as a whole is valuable to him in part due to the causal contribution it makes to his life, and his life considered as a whole is a (causal) means to its own continuance.

Thus, for Rand, demonstrating something to be a value (or virtue) will always involve showing how it helps to sustain a human life, whereas for Aristotle, it need not do this. Indeed, for him, showing that something helps to sustain human life would establish that its value is (at least partially) instrumental rather than intrinsic. It is precisely Rand's teleological, causal approach that I argued gives her ethics the means to differentiate genuine moral values and virtues from prejudices. Aristotle's intrinsic conception of values and the local methods attendant on such a conception prevent him from being able to make such differentiations. This is what I think dooms his ethics to being infected with prejudice.

Rand is right to see Aristotle's ethics as a systematization of what the people he deems wise do, without much insight into why they do it or why he deems them wise. But this shortcoming is not caused by his following a method of systematizing endoxa. His arguments start not from endoxa but from the value judgments of people whom he considers well-bred and experienced. And, rather than seeking to remove inconsistencies among these judgments, he seeks to derive the judgments from a principle of goodness. He thinks such a principle would have to be something that is intrinsically good and that causes the goodness of anything that instantiates, resembles, or causally enables it. This view of values leads to local norms for ethical inquiry that devalue production, and these norms (at least when practiced by someone in Aristotle's cultural milieu) point toward the conclusion that the human good is a life of contemplation supported by slave labor.

If I'm right, an Aristotelian can avoid this error only by correcting his conception of ultimate value and discovering the ethical methodology that is attendant on Rand's alternative understanding of value. Checking one's premises, reconceptualizing value, and discovering the proper local methods for ethics are in accordance with the broader Aristotelian philosophical method described earlier. And I think that Rand was following this when, armed with millennia of historical knowledge that Aristotle lacked, she identified the correct foundations and method for ethics. So there's a sense in which we can say that he did have the methodological resources to correct the errors. But these are *general* philosophical resources rather than parts of his approach to ethics as such. So I stand by my statement that Rand's ethics is objective in a way that Aristotle's is not—that her ethics has resources that his ethics lacks for assessing one's own preconceived moral judgements.

All this said, I agree entirely with Joe's take on the function argument in *EN* I.7, which he asked me to comment on. I think that it is based on widely available experiential knowledge; this knowledge is biological in the sense of being about living things, but it is not a product of the science of biology. On the contrary, it's the sort of knowledge that would be needed to get that science off the ground: knowledge that there are different kinds of living things that live in characteristic ways and have characteristic needs. However, although this is an important argument in Aristotle's ethics, I think it is a somewhat misleading example to use when thinking about what he regards as the *starting-points* of ethical argument.

The premises of this argument are things that can be known even by people who are inexperienced and have poor characters. Of course, they could not be known by someone who had *no* experience. All discursive learning presupposes some experience, but Aristotle distinguishes fields of knowledge (such as mathematics) in which young people can excel from fields (such as *sophia* and *phusikē*) which require an experienced student (*EN* VI.8 1142a12–21). The function argument could probably be understood by anyone experienced and intelligent enough to learn mathematical proofs. It doesn't require the wealth of experiential knowledge necessary to evaluate the account of animal reproduction in the *Generation of Animals* or the argument in *EN* III.6 that bravery (the characterological state from which certain people are willing to place their lives on the line in a noble cause) is distinct from a number of other states that motivate some people to do various frightening things.

To accept this last argument, one needs not only to be experienced but also to have formed a certain sort of character by having internalized a certain (noble) way of acting. Not all arguments in Aristotle's ethics presuppose such premises; but many do, and such premises are necessary to develop his account of the good beyond the barest outline. The function argument just establishes that there's a specific human way of life involving reason that is our function and that the human good is living this life fully in a way that is perfected by virtue. But, for all this one argument says, this human good could turn out to be a Thrasymachean life—or a Stoic or Epicurean or ascetic life. To grasp and evaluate the specific way of life Aristotle is advocating, one must notice and appreciate the differences between the brave and the reckless and between the prudish and the temperate; one must be able to grasp that there's a distinct state intermediate between easily taking offence at jokes and being willing to joke about everything. One also needs to know that the competencies by which one makes good decisions for one's family and one's city are not the same as those by which one understands the motions of the heavens, and one needs to know about the ways in which each of these competencies can and cannot serve the other. All of this requires experience and character.

The same applies to Rand's ethics. To follow her reasoning beyond its barest outline, one needs to be in a position to appreciate what's admirable about characters like Howard Roark and Dagny Taggart and what's vicious about Lillian Rearden and James Taggart, and one needs to be able to see such characters as embodying traits that one encounters in different forms in the people around one.[3] Here too the ability to follow the argument relies on one's experience and character.

To reason to moral principles, one must make use of experience-based discriminatory abilities and habits of evaluation. But these judgments and habits will be deeply colored by the practices we've been raised in and the standards we've imbibed from our culture. It's likely that these standards and practices will include some aspects that are morally good and necessary for living as a human being. But they will also likely include elements that are morally optional, and some that are morally wrong—that contradict and undermine the requirements of human life. In order to reach *true* moral principles, we need to *differentiate* the actual moral norms (required by human nature) both from norms that merely represent one viable way for people to live and from norms that actually hinder human life.

How do we do this? One way is by expanding our experience, by getting to know other cultures. If the Egyptians do something differently from how it's done here in Athens, and yet they seem to be getting on

---

3. I discuss this issue in the case of *Atlas Shrugged* in Salmieri 2009c.

just as well with respect to whatever (partial) measures we've identified of well-being, that's a reason to think that the Athenian practice isn't something required by human nature (though it may be one fine way to instantiate a broader natural requirement). If we observe that nineteenth-century England and the Northern Untied States of America were socially organized along radically different lines than any earlier countries had been, and we further observe that this reorganization brought about a doubling of life expectancy and an unprecedented expansion in knowledge, art, and almost everything else we recognize as good, then these observations constitute evidence that the new social system meets a need inherent in human nature that was unmet by previous social systems. This evidence then reveals a way in which the earlier social systems were incompatible with living well.[4] If we notice that abstract knowledge that is initially valued only for intellectual edification often ends up having unexpected practical applications and that some of these applications give us godlike powers, such as the ability to navigate across oceans, then this may lead us to reconsider our earlier view of the causal and axiological relations between different sorts of knowledge. In these ways, growing experience is a major driver of moral knowledge—and moral progress.

But this progress is not just a matter of increased experience. There is intellectual work to do conceptualizing that experience and reevaluating existing norms on the basis of it. This is the work of philosophers. Thus Francis Bacon, having observed some of the facts I noted above, reconceptualized the value of abstract, theoretical knowledge. He grasped that causally deep, theoretical knowledge empowers us, that this empowerment is a sign that putative knowledge of deep causes is genuine, that it is part of what makes the knowledge valuable, and that this fact about its value does not make it servile. Rand's philosophical innovations are of this same sort. They're made possible by the new (historical) experience of the Industrial Revolution, but this experience isn't sufficient for the innovations. They represent new intellectual work. Part of this work is the establishment of a distinct approach to ethics as a discipline—an approach that makes the field objective for the first time.

Aristotle (and later Bacon and others) had given us more general principles of method that enable objectivity. Examples of such principles include that knowledge must be grounded in experience, that facts must

---

4. This, of course, is Rand's understanding of why capitalism is the only moral social system. See "What Is Capitalism" (*CUI*); Peikoff 1990, 378–405; Salmieri 2016b, 294–95; and Salmieri 2023.

first be established before they're explained, and that different fields have different principles and admit of different sorts of precision. What Rand gives us is a specifically ethical methodology—a method for validating values by the standard of Man's Life (understood as the distinctive activity by which human beings sustain ourselves).

This standard enables us to determine whether a given practice is part of the human way of life. Rather than simply considering whether human beings (or the noblest and wisest of them) engage in the practice, or whether the practice coheres with the other things they do, we can now inquire into whether the practice is a per se component of the system by which human beings live. This means inquiring into whether the practice is such that every human being must engage in it (in some form) to the extent that he is sustaining his life. We can answer this question affirmatively in the case of the moral principles Rand identified—most notably, the virtues of rationality, independence, integrity, honesty, productiveness, and pride, the practice of interacting with other human beings by trade (to mutual advantage by mutual consent) rather than by seeking or making sacrifices, the principle of individual rights (which defines and endorses this way of interacting) and the social system of capitalism (which is based on this principle).

A practice that is not a per se component of the system by which human beings live may yet be an important component of the system by which a particular person lives, by being a specification in his case of something that is part of Man's Life generally. This will be the case with most of a person's specific values: his specific career, relationships, hobbies, and so forth. But there are some practices that are contrary to Man's Life, such that they constitute a drain on the lives of any person or society that engages in them. This is the case with the practice of slavery, with regarding woman as inferior to men, with the moral code of altruism, with belief in God, or with living under a monarchy, a dictatorship, or a government that places controls on speech or on the economy.

As my last examples illustrate, questions about what is per se part of our method of survival and what is contrary to it are contentious. But if Rand's ethical methodology is correct, there is a standard in accordance with which such claims can be adjudicated. It is just such a standard that I think Aristotle lacks.

Section IV
VIRTUE AND CHARACTER

10
Aristotle and Ayn Rand on the Unity of Virtue

NEERA K. BADHWAR

In Plato's *Laches* and *Protagoras*, Socrates argues that virtue consists of knowledge of good and evil, and that if you have knowledge of one form of good and evil, you have knowledge of every form of good and evil.[1] Thus knowledge is one and undivided, and the virtues are inseparable, if not identical. Aristotle agrees with Socrates that virtue requires knowledge of good and evil and that someone who has one virtue must have all virtues. But he holds that there really are different virtues, and that they require more than knowledge of good and evil. They require practical wisdom, which is an intellectual virtue of practical reason made possible only by properly habituated emotions and appetites—that is, by "virtues of character."[2] Someone with knowledge of good and evil but without virtues of character will have wayward emotions or appetites and, thus, either fail to act rightly or act rightly with difficulty. In the former case, he is *akratic* or weak-willed, and in the latter *enkratic* or strong-willed, but not virtuous. Full-fledged moral virtues thus require the practical wisdom that incorporates both knowledge of good and evil and properly ha-

---

1. Plato, *Laches* 196e–97c; *Protagoras* 350c, 352b–c.
2. All references to Aristotle are to the translation in Irwin 1999, unless otherwise specified.

bituated emotions and appetites. These virtues are individuated by these emotions and appetites as well as by their ends or goals.

Some scholars reserve the term "unity of virtue" for the Socratic thesis that all the virtues reduce to one and the term "reciprocity of the virtues" for the Aristotelian thesis, but I will follow the more usual convention of calling the latter also the unity of the virtues (see, for example, Irwin 1988b). Insofar as Ayn Rand holds that all the virtues are forms of rationality applied to different aspects of human life, and that our emotions are governed entirely by our conscious value judgments, her view of virtue and of the unity of virtue is similar to that of Socrates. But her depiction of her heroes in her novels and some of her later statements about emotions and character suggest a view closer to Aristotle's.

It is often assumed that the unity of virtue must be global—that is, it must extend across every domain of an individual's life. But this globalist thesis does not follow from the thesis of the unity of virtue, because it is possible for the virtues to be restricted to only some domains of an individual's character. This entails that, if the unity of the virtues thesis is true, it is true only within some domains of an individual's character. I will start by discussing Aristotle's conception of virtue, his view of the unity and scope of the virtues, and then move on to Rand's views on these matters. I will also briefly address each philosopher's conception of vice and its scope.

Aristotle's Conception of Virtue

A virtue is an excellence, and a moral virtue is an excellence of character. Aristotle argues that moral virtue requires both the intellectual virtue of *phronesis*, and virtue of character—that is, habituated emotions, appetites, and actions in favor of the good and against the bad. As he puts it: "we cannot be fully good without prudence (*phronesis*, practical wisdom), or prudent without virtue of character" (*EN* VI.13 1144b31–32). Further, "one has all the virtues if and only if one has prudence, which is a single state" (1145a2). In other words, phronesis cannot be compartmentalized, so if you have phronesis, you have all the moral virtues, and if you have all the moral virtues, you have phronesis. A wholly virtuous person, in Aristotle's view, is a person who is disposed to think, feel, choose, and act "at the right [appropriate] times, about the right things, towards the right people, for the right end, and in the right way" (*EN* II.6 1106b2ff.). Just as in the case of a well-made product, nothing can be added or subtracted without detracting from its excellence, so in the case of a moral virtue (hereafter simply "virtue"), nothing can be added or subtracted without detracting from its excellence (1106b11–16). A virtuous person must have the practical wisdom—the phronesis—to know what is good or bad for human beings in general (*EN* VI.5 1140b5ff.). But phronesis itself is made possible only by virtue of character, such that the virtuous individual characteristically does the right thing with pleasure (*EN* VI.12 1144a8–10, VI.13 1145a5, I.8 1099a18ff., III.9 1117b1–2) or at least without pain (II.3 1104b7ff.).

Aristotle uses two independent criteria to individuate the virtues: they are means in different passions and actions (*EN* II.6 1106b24–27), and they belong in different spheres. For example, bravery is a mean in fear and confidence, exercised in standing up to threats to something that is worth protecting, temperance is primarily a mean in our appetites and secondarily in our emotions, generosity is a mean in giving and taking, and so on. But—and this is Aristotle's doctrine of the spheres—bravery is shown only on the battlefield, not in other threatening situations, temperance only in our desires for food, drink, and sex (or in our emotions), not all physical desires (for example, not in desires for massages or aromas), generosity only in matters of money, not how or how much we give of our time or how we judge other people, and so on.

Aristotle's reasons for his doctrine of the spheres, however, are not very convincing. For example, his reason for confining bravery to the battlefield is that bravery should be defined with reference to the "greatest and finest danger," and only war is such a danger because it threatens death, is fought for a good cause (*EN* III.6 1115a30–32), and allows the brave to use their strength (1115b4–6). But fighting a mob in order to protect yourself or your friend also meets these criteria (indeed, many of us would hold, meets them better than most wars). And standing up for your principles in the face of, say, a threat of execution by an unjust state meets two of the criteria. Thus, Aristotle's notion of the proper sphere of bravery is too narrow even by his own criteria. But even if he includes these activities in the sphere of bravery, we are left with the question of which virtue of character we exercise in other fearful situations that threaten important values short of life. Interestingly, at *EN* III.6 1115a20–22, Aristotle seems to recognize that bravery is required in other spheres also, when he remarks that some people who are cowards in war nevertheless face the prospect of monetary loss with confidence, as required by bravery. But hamstrung by his own doctrine of the spheres of the virtues, he goes on to say that such people are courageous only "by similarity" with the brave in war. Given the problems with the doctrine of the spheres of the virtues, I will ignore it in favor of the doctrine of the virtues as means in various emotions and actions. Those who are persuaded by the doctrine of the spheres can follow Aristotle in thinking of virtue V in the "wrong" sphere as a V only "by similarity" with V in the proper sphere.

Aristotle's list of virtues includes traits that most people would regard as virtues—justice, generosity, courage, temperance, and honesty with and about oneself—as well as at least one they might find dubious: magnanimity or pride. Magnanimity, according to Aristotle, is the crown of the virtues, a virtue an individual can possess only if he possesses all the other virtues (*EN* IV.3). So focusing on the magnanimous person is the best way for us to understand Aristotle's notion of ideal virtue.

The magnanimous man "thinks himself worthy of great things and is worthy of them" (*EN* IV.3 1123b29–30). He performs great acts because he knows he is worthy of them. He expects to be honored for his virtue but doesn't crave it, and he disdains honor from the wrong people as well as dishonor from anyone, since he knows that it is unearned. He is kind, being eager to help (1124b18) and to avoid giving people unnecessary pain.[3] He is also modest about his achievements with those who are inferior to him. He despises the truly despicable but is forgiving of slight infractions. He doesn't hold grudges, doesn't gossip or complain about small setbacks, and is open, not devious. He values truth above people's opinion and is independent in that he doesn't let others, except friends, "determine his life," because doing otherwise "would be slavish" (IV.3).

Rand would find Aristotle's portrait of the magnanimous man as someone who performs great acts because he knows he is worthy of them, who doesn't crave honor, and who is independent, honest with and about himself, and above the pettiness of gossip or resentment especially congenial. Not, however, those elements of the portrait that are obviously influenced by Aristotle's class-conscious culture and its wrongheaded view of what counts as ignoble. The most important of these elements is that the magnanimous man's "possessions are fine and unproductive rather than productive and advantageous"—as though using one's possessions to make something useful to exchange with others for money were beneath his dignity.[4] This, as I will argue below, stands in sharp contrast to

---

3. This feature is mentioned in IV.6, where it is said to be part of the virtue of friendliness in social intercourse (1126bff.). But since the magnanimous man has all the virtues, and since kindness fits the portrait Aristotle has drawn of him, he must also have this one.

4. Aristotle also attributes other features to the magnanimous man that seem to be taken from a common picture of the male hero—a picture that, interestingly, persists in the

Rand's view of productivity as a virtue. But first I need to discuss Aristotle's doctrine of the unity of virtue.

Aristotle's View of the Unity and Scope of Virtue

Phronesis is "concerned with action about what is good or bad for a human being" (*EN* VI.5 1140b5–6) "in general" (1140a28)—that is, phronesis is not specialized knowledge of a field of inquiry or a craft. It is knowledge about how to live as a human being. As we have seen, Aristotle holds that phronesis entails all the virtues, and because phronesis is "single" or global, someone who has one virtue has all the virtues, and someone who lacks even one virtue lacks all of them. In other words, the virtues are united. Further, because phronesis is undivided, concerning the entire range of human life, someone who has the virtues in one domain of his life must have them in every domain. In contemporary terminology, the virtues are cross-situationally consistent, or global.

It is easy to see that being virtuous in Aristotle's conception of virtue is no easy task. One must not only characteristically do the right thing for the right reason in every sort of situation, one must do it with the right emotions. If you typically find it hard to stand up to your boss when he treats you or others unfairly, but you still manage to do it, you are strong-willed (and praiseworthy for being strong-willed). But you are not brave. And if you are brave (or brave by similarity) in the situation just described, you must also be brave (or brave by similarity) in other fearful situations that call for bravery. If Aristotle is a virtuous philosopher, he must also be a virtuous father, son, friend, brother, citizen, and so on. The lack of even one virtue in one area of his life implies that he has no virtues at all. (This implication of his theory falls hard on its author, given his attitudes and actions toward slaves and women.)

But why must phronesis be all or nothing? According to Terence Irwin (1988b), Aristotle believes this because he believes that the human good is interconnected, so that being wrong about one part of it leads us to be wrong about the other parts. Yet as a claim about the way phronesis is instantiated in real people, it seems obviously false. For surely it is possible for someone to, say, choose her career wisely—that is, with due regard to its objective worth and its fit with her abilities, interests, and other important values—without choosing her friends or lovers wisely. Or to be a good statesman without being a good father. Moreover, even Aristo-

---

figure of the heroes of many Westerns: "slow movements, a deep voice, and calm speech" (IV.3).

tle would have no trouble accepting that, even though all truths are connected, it is possible for someone to be, say, a good biologist without being a good historian or cosmologist.[5] So there is no good reason to make a special case of phronesis. Indeed, a consideration of the demanding nature of Aristotelian virtue, in conjunction with everyday observation of human life and the experimental evidence from psychology, suggests, as I argue now, that global practical wisdom and, thus, the global unity of virtue are psychologically impossible.

Aristotelian virtue requires the right principles, emotional dispositions in tune with these principles, and the ready ability to characteristically apply these principles to every sort of situation we might encounter (VI.8). But someone who is naturally timorous is unlikely to ever succeed in having an emotional disposition in tune with the requirements of courage across the board, even if she succeeds in reasoning and acting as courage requires across the board. Similarly, someone with a naturally angry or impatient constitution is unlikely to ever acquire the virtue of justice or kindness across the board, even if he succeeds in always *reasoning and acting* as justice and kindness require. And so on. A poor or mixed moral education also contributes to blind spots that lead us, without our awareness, to compartmentalize our habitual evaluations, emotional responses, and actions—in short, to compartmentalize our character traits. But even someone born with a perfect emotional temperament and excellent early moral education faces an insuperable obstacle to global virtue: the epistemic requirement of Aristotelian virtue.

Virtue requires self-knowledge, but self-knowledge can be as hard to acquire as knowledge of human beings in general (on which it partially depends) or of the natural world.[6] Like knowledge of the natural world, knowledge of human beings in general and of oneself in particular is a work in progress. Cognitive psychology has made us aware, or more clearly aware, of the biases we are all subject to, biases that prevent us from achieving global virtue. These include confirmation bias, the in-group bias, and the "implicit egoism" that leads us to see our achievements as more important than other people's achievements and our

---

5. Here and below I borrow these arguments against global virtue from Badhwar 1996 and 2014b, ch. 6.

6. Rand's belief that all we need for self-knowledge is honest introspection is, unfortunately, contradicted by research as well as careful everyday observation. The way other people respond to us (including but not limited to what they tell us about ourselves) constitutes crucial data for learning about ourselves. So does observation of our actual behavior, which can contradict what we introspectively believe about ourselves. See Wilson 2002.

failures as less important than other people's failures.[7] For obvious reasons, these biases play an important part in our failure to be just to other people, yet they are part of the structure of our cognitive and affective machinery.[8]

Global virtue also requires an understanding of society and social institutions, since how we act in the public sphere, what we support or deplore, depends on such understanding. But the social sciences themselves are far from attaining a complete understanding of psychology, economics, politics, or society. Hence we all hold many morally significant mistaken empirical generalizations about many matters—generalizations that have played a role in the existence or persistence of slavery, racism, sexism, condemnation of homosexuality, the American Drug War, and other injustices great and small. Indeed, Aristotle himself states that phronesis is difficult because it "may be in error about either the universal or the particular," where the universal is an empirical generalization and the particular is an instance of it (*EN* VI.8 1142a22–24).

It might be thought that, since Aristotle's ethics is committed to basing its requirements on human nature, all it can ask of us with respect to our cognitive and emotional limitations is that we acquire the dispositions necessary for being alert to them and dealing with them as best we can. But this amounts to the admission that we cannot be virtuous across the board. For dealing with our limitations "as best we can" is not the same thing as succeeding in being virtuous or acting in accord with virtue. Further, those who are unaware, or only dimly aware, of these cognitive and emotional limitations—that is, the vast majority of human beings—are not in a position to even try to deal with them. So the best human beings can be and do is even further from what is in fact right. To take a mundane example, someone who is only dimly aware of confirmation bias may not realize that his political commitments seem to be confirmed by the evidence only because he is disposed to dismiss contrary evidence, and that he can "refute" arguments that challenge his commitments only because he never seriously considers them. Consequently, even though he values being fair and objective and does his best to be fair and objective, he fails in this regard with respect to his political commitments.

It seems that globally virtuous people exist only in fiction and in its close cousin hagiography. Fortunately, Aristotle seems to be aware of

---

7. See Merritt et al. 2010 and Alfano 2013.
8. Not all the alarm these experiments have occasioned is justified, however. See Badhwar 2014a.

this. For alongside his portrait of the ideally virtuous person, he gives us a portrait of the imperfectly virtuous person.[9] This comes out most clearly in his discussion of "character friendship"—that is, the friendship that is based on virtue rather than expedience or mere pleasure.[10] One of the main benefits of such a friendship, he argues, is that it enables the friends to help improve each other's character (*EN* VIII.8 1159b5–7, IX.12 1172a11–13), something that would be impossible if virtuous friends were perfectly virtuous. Aristotle also claims that character friends can be unequal in their virtue (1162a34–b1) or can become unequal when one friend improves her character more than the other (*EN* IX.3 1165b26–36), or one friend becomes steadily less virtuous than the other (1165b19–21). What this discussion shows is that Aristotle recognizes that virtuous people need not be perfectly virtuous. Indeed, the fact that he mentions by name only one virtuous person, Pericles (*EN* VI.5), suggests that he can't think of anyone else with perfect virtue. And since global virtue entails perfect virtue, it follows that he thought practically no virtuous person was globally virtuous.

Another realistic feature of Aristotle's view is his recognition that certain situations "overstrain human nature," so that even a globally virtuous person can act contrary to virtue. In *Politics* III.15 (1286b27), Aristotle excuses a virtuous king who puts his unfit son on the throne because it's asking too much of a human being to deny one's son the throne. We needn't agree with Aristotle's claim here in order to appreciate the fact that he recognizes how some situations stretch our ability to act virtuously to the breaking point. Along the same lines, he argues that if a corrupting situation lasts too long, virtue can be lost. One example of such a situation is political power unconstrained by the rule of law, "for desire is a wild beast, and passion perverts the minds of rulers, even when they are the best of men."[11] So although virtue is enduring, it is not immune to the influence of situational factors and the passions they evoke even in "the best of men."

It is important to note, however, that the rejection of globalism and perfection is compatible with the view that anyone who has a virtue in one domain of her life must have others in that domain. This is because any pursuit important enough to call for virtue is complex enough to call

---

9. Russell (2009) and Drefcinski (1996) both argue that Aristotle gives us both an ideal of moral virtue to aspire to and a realistic picture of the imperfectly virtuous person.
10. See Badhwar and Jones 2024 for a detailed discussion of this.
11. Aristotle, *Politics* III.16 1287a31–32, in Barnes 1984.

for several virtues. So someone who has one virtue in a given area of her life must have all the virtues relevant to it. In short, the unity of virtue thesis is true within particular areas of a person's life but not globally. The following example illustrates and explains why such a limited unity is inescapable.

Imagine that your boss has started demanding that his employees deceive their customers by giving them misleading information. You refuse to do so, as you have refused wrong orders before, even though you fully appreciate the possible negative consequences for yourself, such as getting fired in a tight labor market. What enables you to refuse is that you appreciate even more highly the importance of not betraying your (correct) principles and not harming your customers. In doing so, you exercise not only courage and integrity, but also honesty and a sense of justice.[12] Substitute a vice for any one of these virtues, and your actions cease to be expressive of the other virtues as well. For example, if you are a coward vis-à-vis your boss, you will obey his orders to deceive the customers because you "know" that sensible people obey orders when their job is on the line. You might not think of deceiving customers when left to yourself, but you are perfectly willing to deceive them in order to keep your job. Your lack of integrity is shown not so much in a betrayal of your principles as in an absence of principles in this realm—other than the "principle" of expediency. The same is true if you are dishonest or unjust in your professional life. If you have one of these vices, you cannot have any of the virtues in your professional life. As we shall see, however, this does not mean that if you have one vice, you must have all the other (relevant) vices.

Aristotle on Vice and the Disunity of Vice

One reason the vices are disunited is that, in Aristotle's view, every virtue, except perhaps justice, is opposed by two contrary vices. For example, courage is opposed by both cowardice and recklessness, generosity by both stinginess and prodigality, magnanimity by both vanity and pusillanimity (humility), and so on. But no one can be both cowardly and reckless, or both stingy and prodigal, or both vain and pusillanimous, in the

---

12. Aristotle does not include integrity in his list of virtues, but integrity is implicit in his account of a virtuous person, since it is of the essence of a virtuous person to live virtuously even when the going gets tough. Aristotle's virtue of honesty consists of truthfulness about oneself, both in speech and in manner of living (*EN* IV.7). In particular, an honest person is straightforward, neither a boaster nor a self-depracator, motivated as he is by a love of the truth. Again, Rand's heroes fit this conception of honesty.

same sorts of situations. So if he has one vice in a certain area of his life, he can, at most, have only some of the other relevant vices in that area.

It is also important to remember that lack of a virtue does not entail the possession of a vice. As noted earlier, on Aristotle's taxonomy of character traits, there are two other states between virtue and vice: *enkrateia* (strength of will) and *akrasia* (weakness of will). So even if you lack the virtues relevant to standing up to your boss and disobeying his wrong orders, you can be strong-willed (*enkratic*) and do the right thing for the right reason with an effort. But if you are weak willed (*akratic*), you will fail to do the thing you know to be right and be filled with regret. You are then, in Aristotle's colorful figure of speech, like a city that flouts its own good laws (*EN* VII.10). If you are vicious, you have bad principles as well as bad emotions—you take pleasure in doing the wrong thing or, at least, experience no regret about it, because (according to Aristotle) as a vicious person, you are unconscious of your vice. You are, in another colorful figure of speech, like a city that obeys its bad laws without recognizing them as bad (VII.10).

In *EN* VII.10, Aristotle suggests that a vicious person's unawareness of his own bad principles is due to ignorance rather than self-deception or evasion. In *EN* IX.4, however, he offers a different portrait of a vicious man. The vicious man here is depicted as filled with conflict and regret and self-hatred, a self-hatred that leads him to shun his own company. The vicious man, he says, has many friends but leads a life of great loneliness, because he is afraid to reveal himself to others—or even to himself. And out of "cowardice or laziness," he shrinks from doing what he regards as best for himself.

These are, of course, "pure types" of the strong, the weak, and the vicious. But if our character traits are not global, a person can be strong, weak, or vicious in different areas of his life. So even someone who is more weak than vicious can shrink from doing what he regards as best for himself. Readers of *The Fountainhead* will be reminded here of the hypersocial but lonely Peter Keating, who jilts the woman he loves for the sake of contracting a loveless but more prestigious marriage to Dominique Francon.

I turn now to Rand's conception of virtue and the unity of virtue, and see where it resembles or differs from Aristotle's or Socrates' conceptions.

Ayn Rand's Conception of Virtue

According to Rand, we need virtue in order to sustain our lives and achieve happiness.[13] Different virtues express a recognition of different basic facts of human nature and the nature of the world we live in and aim at different basic values, all of which play an essential role in the ultimate value of a happy life. Thus, "[v]alue is that which one acts to gain and/or keep—virtue is the act by which one gains and/or keeps it."[14] By this definition, virtues are actions, not character traits. This comes as a surprise, because the word "virtue" means goodness or excellence, and goodness is a property, and thus not an act. There are virtuous acts, of course, just as there are beautiful acts, but neither virtue nor beauty are themselves acts. Rand does not explain why she is departing from standard usage in both everyday discourse and the long history of philosophy in defining a virtue as an act. Be that as it may, she departs from this definition of virtue later in the same essay and defines it as a character trait of a certain sort:

> The virtue of Rationality means the recognition and acceptance of reason as one's only source of knowledge, one's only judge of values and one's only guide to action.... It means a commitment to the fullest perception of reality within one's power and to the constant, active expansion of one's perception, i.e., of one's knowledge. It means a commitment to the reality of one's own existence, i.e., to the principle that all of one's goals, values and actions take place in reality and, therefore, that one must never place any value or consideration whatsoever above one's perception of reality. It means a commitment to the principle that all of one's convictions, values, goals, desires and actions must be based on, derived from, chosen and validated by a process of thought.... It means one's acceptance of the responsibility of forming one's own judgments and of living by the work of one's own mind (which is the virtue of Independence). It means that one must never sacrifice one's convictions to the opinions or wishes of others (which is the virtue of Integrity)—that one must never attempt to fake reality in any manner (which is the virtue of Honesty)—that one must never seek or grant the unearned and undeserved, neither

---

13. Rand often states that the ultimate value is survival qua human being, but she just as often states that it is happiness. For example, "My philosophy in essence is the concept of man as a heroic being, with his own happiness as the moral purpose of his life, with productive achievement as his noblest activity and reason as his only absolute" (*Atlas* 1170), and "Life is the reward of virtue and happiness is the goal and reward of life" (1020). The claim that happiness is the ultimate value is far more plausible than the claim that survival is the ultimate value, as the latter implies that a long miserable life is more desirable than a somewhat shorter but happy life. If survival were the ultimate value, it wouldn't matter whether one survived happily or unhappily. See Badhwar 2001 for discussion.

14. "Objectivist Ethics," *VOS* 25, *For The New Intellectual* 121.

in matter nor in spirit (which is the virtue of Justice). It means that one must never desire effects without causes, and that one must never enact a cause without assuming full responsibility for its effects—that one must never act like a zombie, i.e., without knowing one's own purposes and motives. (*VOS* 28)

In this passage, a virtue is presented as a commitment to its corresponding value, and a commitment is something long-term, something that involves certain evaluative dispositions or tendencies and certain patterns of action. By this definition, a virtue is a type of character trait, not an action.

In a comment on an earlier version of this paper, Gregory Salmieri suggests that the definition of virtue as an act that gains or keeps a value can be reconciled with the definition of virtue in terms of a long-term commitment if the former "essentially involves long-range commitments." In other words, we can interpret a virtuous act as an act that expresses a long-range commitment. To be sure, a virtuous act expresses a certain kind of long-term commitment. But this is just another way of saying that a virtuous act expresses a virtue or virtues, which is different from saying that virtue itself is an act. The latter amounts to holding that a virtuous act expresses a virtuous act. Further, if virtue is an act, then someone who is not acting at any given moment cannot have virtue. But a virtue is not something that disappears when a person is not acting either physically or mentally. Thus, for example, someone with the virtue of rationality is someone who characteristically or habitually focuses her mind "to a full, active, purposefully directed awareness of reality" (*VOS* 21), a trait that continues to exist even when she is asleep, or too tired to act on her commitments, or even too tired to think.[15]

Rand's conception of virtue as a rational commitment is, like Socrates's conception, entirely cognitive or intellectual. Of course, both Rand and Socrates believe that the virtuous individual's emotions will be integrated with his reason, and that they will be different from the vicious individual's emotions. But both regard the emotions as determined entirely by the individual's cognitive faculty. In Rand's words: "emotions are the automatic results of man's value judgments integrated by his sub-

---

15. There are also actions that come from the right motives—say, honesty—at the moment of action but not from the virtue of honesty. I don't know if Rand discusses such actions explicitly, but she does show her unvirtuous characters, such as Peter Keating and Gail Wynand, sometimes doing the right thing from the right motives.

conscious; emotions are estimates of that which furthers man's values or threatens them, that which is for him or against him—lightning calculators giving him the sum of his profit or loss" (*VOS* 27). And again, "[m]an's emotional mechanism is like an electronic computer, which his mind has to program—and the programming consists of the values his mind chooses" (27).[16] If he chooses not to think, not to focus, he will adopt values through "social osmosis or blind imitation" (27).

Given this view of the emotions as totally dependent on a person's value judgments, there is no reason for Rand to give them equal billing with the individual's rational commitments in her conception of character. In "Philosophy and Sense of Life," however, Rand does just this when she argues that an individual's "sense of life" is his "implicit metaphysical value judgments of man and of existence . . . [that] sets the nature of a man's emotional responses and *the essence of his character*" (*RM* 14, italics mine). An individual's choices and implicit value judgments of himself and other human beings and the world around him and of his ability to deal with the world are integrated "into an emotional sum that establishes a habitual pattern and becomes his automatic response to the world around him" (15). A sense of life reflects a person's "deepest values" (21).

Surprisingly, these statements make a person's emotional, automatic responses to the world as central to his character and actions as his reason and conscious convictions, if not more so ("the essence of his character" [*RM* 14]). How should we understand this? Rand is probably thinking here of someone whose sense of life is in harmony with his convictions, whether right or wrong. In such a person, his automatic responses are as deep set, and thus as central to his identity and character, as his convictions, whether virtuous or vicious. By contrast, someone who acts on his conscious rational values, in spite of a sense of life that expresses irrational values, obviously endorses and values the former and rejects and disvalues the latter. His emotional appraisal of life is at odds with his rational convictions and is no longer as important to his identify and character as his rational convictions. Such a person is what Aristotle calls *enkratic*, or strong-willed.

Rand's novels support the claim that a virtuous person's character is a harmonious integration of their sense of life (their emotional appraisal of life) and their conscious values and that their actions are characteristically an expression of their character. Her virtuous characters are

---

16. Rand often uses "mind" to mean the rational faculty and typically conceives of the rational faculty as entirely conscious.

individuals who not only think and act in recognition of the facts but who also love and desire the virtues in themselves and others, who take pleasure in doing the right thing and in seeing others do the right thing, who admire good people and deplore bad ones, and so on.[17] Dagny Taggart, vice president of Taggart Transcontinental, is an excellent example of such a person. When Dagny learns of the "moratorium on brains," the legislation meant to benefit the friends of the legislators (including her brother, James Taggart, the president of Taggart Transcontinental, and thus Taggart Transcontinental) and hurt their competitors through strict wage and price controls, input and output quotas, and so on, she reacts with an anger that, we are told, is "her love of rectitude, the only love to which all the years of her life had been given" (*Atlas* 552). Her rectitude is at once a commitment to the right and a wholehearted love of it, a commitment and love that give her an immediate grasp of the situation and the motivation to do the right thing for the right reason. She throws her resignation in James Taggart's face, because she "will not work as a slave or as a slavedriver" (552). In her novels, Rand depicts virtue the way Aristotle conceives of it: as an integrated intellectual-emotional-action disposition.

By contrast, a vicious individual like Jim Taggart resents good people—people with integrity and honesty—and takes pleasure in plotting their downfall. Rand introduces him to the reader with a brilliant stroke of characterization: "Don't bother me, don't bother me, don't bother me," he snaps at Eddie Willers, when Willers arrives to inform him about yet another accident on the Rio Norte line (*Atlas* 7). We see the essence of Taggart's character in these three words repeated three times, and subsequent events confirm this first impression of Taggart as someone who spends his energy irritably pushing back against people because he is incapable of acknowledging his responsibilities, or handling any problems on his own, or admitting his shortcomings.

Thus, both Rand's heroes and her villains reveal who they are not only in what they say or do but also in the way they do it, in the emotions with which they do it, and in what they find pleasurable or aversive and salient or obscure. In Rand's own words, they reveal who they are in their "widest goals or smallest gestures," in their style of being in the world (*RM* 22).[18]

17. See Hursthouse 1999 on this point.
18. Cf. Henry James: "What is character but the determination of incident? What is incident but the illustration of character?" "The Art of Fiction," https://public.archive.wsu.edu/campbelld/public_html/amlit/artfiction.html

Rand argues that, in the event of a conflict between reason and emotions, one must always side with the former, because emotions are not tools of cognition (*VOS* 37). But what if a person's sense of life is closer to a correct perception of reality than his conscious convictions, a possibility that Rand acknowledges (*RM* 19)? More generally, what if a person's emotions are better than his convictions? To take an extreme example, think of those Nazis who, though committed to their evil ideology, could not always silence their humane impulses. When Heinrich Himmler, head of the SS, found that his men could not always go through with the killings they were ordered to carry out, he acknowledged that it was important for them to retain their human sympathies, their ability to "treasure life," but insisted that they needed to be "strong" and overcome their sympathies in order to do the "right" thing.[19] It is clear that Himmler should have allowed his feelings to challenge his convictions and counseled his men to do the same. Or take Andrei (in *We the Living*), the young communist who falls in love with Kira and learns through his love that his convictions are evil. His love for Kira, his admiration for her character, teaches him something that probably no argument could have done, leading to a change in both his convictions and his emotional dispositions.

Rand's fiction sometimes depicts the emotions of virtuous people also as tools of cognition—indeed, more trustworthy tools than their reason in certain situations. For her heroes sometimes justifiably accept the evidence of their emotions without quite understanding why. In an early scene in *Atlas Shrugged*, Dagny is depicted as being convinced that Francisco has become a worthless playboy who deserves no personal recognition. But when during a conversation she realizes that she still desires him, we are told that she neither fights it nor regrets it (*Atlas* 126). In *The Fountainhead* (499–500), Dominique tells Gail Wynand, a man whose principles she despises, that it will take her "years to understand" why she has started feeling loyal to him, for it "contradicts everything" she's done and thought—but she knows she owes it to him to warn him against Ellsworth Toohey. In contrast to Dagny, Dominique is not exactly depicted as virtuous for the greater part of the novel, but what she feels and says here is clearly presented as right.

Things get more complicated when there is a conflict not only between a person's sense of life and his principles but within his sense of life and his principles. Consider Gail Wynand. On the one hand, he spends his life pandering to the lowest common denominator and trying to prove

---

19. Quoted in Bennett 1974.

that no one has any integrity. On the other hand, Wynand falls for both Howard Roark and Dominique, the two individuals who would never compromise their integrity and who recognize the evil of Wynand's actions and desires. In spite of himself, Wynand has wanted to find people of integrity whom he couldn't break. So he admires and loves Roark and Dominique. There is no conflict here between his principles and his feelings as far as they are concerned. The conflict is between his principles and feelings vis-à-vis those two and his principles and feelings vis-à-vis others. Roark and Dominique are the great exceptions in his life. In the end, however, he doesn't—or cannot—change. When he has to choose between keeping his power over people and keeping his friendship with Roark, he chooses the former—and knows almost immediately that he has betrayed everything he truly loves and doomed himself to a lonely existence. Had he met Roark and Dominique earlier, he might have become a better person. But he didn't, and his character dooms him.[20] As Aristotle quips in discussing the possibility of rescuing your character after you have destroyed it: once you've thrown away a stone, you can't get it back (*EN* III.5 1114a19–21).

Another thesis about virtue is worth commenting on before turning to the issue of the unity of virtue. This is the thesis that virtue is a means to value—value being "that which one acts to gain and/or keep" (*VOS* 18, *Atlas* 1012). As I've already argued (Badhwar 2001), the ultimate value for Rand, as for Aristotle, is happiness, understood as a positive long-term disposition of thought and emotion that is both the result of and partly constituted by a life of virtuous activity. But Rand also identifies three cardinal values as the aims or ends of her three cardinal virtues. The three cardinal values are Reason, Purpose, and Self-esteem, and the virtues that aim at them are Rationality, Productiveness, and Pride, respectively (*VOS* 31). Rand does not stick to this framework, however. For she proceeds to state that these three values "imply and require all of man's virtues, and all his virtues pertain to the relation of existence and consciousness: rationality, independence, integrity, honesty, justice, productiveness, pride" (*Atlas* 1018).[21] Rand also identifies rationality as the

---

20. However, Wynand remains a puzzling character. Is it really possible for someone *so* evil to be attracted to the ideal human being Roark? Even more puzzling, is it really possible for the ideal human being to form a close friendship with someone *so* evil? Rand's art makes it all seem plausible, but intellectually it remains hard to understand.

21. According to Peikoff (1991, 251), Rand "did not regard this list as necessarily exhaustive," but he does not say which other traits she might have thought of as virtues. Perhaps they are the "virtues of benevolence," such as kindness and generosity, which I discuss later.

basic virtue, "the source of all ... [our] other virtues" (*VOS* 31).[22] This last statement contains an implicit argument for the unity of virtue: if all the virtues depend on rationality, then it follows that if you have one virtue, you must have rationality, and if you have rationality, you must have all the virtues. In short, one virtue entails all the virtues.

Ayn Rand on the Unity and Scope of Virtue

The pride of place that Rand gives to rationality suggests its kinship with Aristotle's virtue of practical wisdom—that is, phronesis. Unlike phronesis, however, rationality is not a success term. A moral virtue entails a grasp of the important aspects of human life and one's own life, and the disposition—the standing motivation—to act in a way that expresses that grasp. Virtue in Rand's novels refers not just to a commitment but to an achievement. It is a success term, a term that refers to a trait that characteristically leads to the right actions. But rationality does not entail such a grasp or such a disposition, because "a commitment to the fullest perception of reality within one's power and to the constant, active expansion of one's perception, i.e., of one's knowledge" (*VOS* 32) is compatible with a failure to perceive reality in one or another respect. A commitment, or even an intellectual-emotional disposition, to track reality, to never evade the facts, does not guarantee that one will characteristically succeed in grasping it.[23] A rational person may be systematically mistaken about many of his own needs or obligations or another's character. And to the extent that he is systematically mistaken in these ways, he cannot be wholly virtuous (which doesn't mean that he must be vicious). In other words, if rationality is defined simply in terms of a commitment to track reality, it is only a commitment to be morally virtuous and not a moral virtue itself. A commitment to track reality is, of course, itself praiseworthy because it is an excellence of the mind, an excellence that is necessary for moral virtue. For this reason, I regard it as an epistemic and deliberative virtue.

Hank Rearden in *Atlas Shrugged* illustrates my point that rationality is not a moral virtue. Rearden is rational in every area of his life, yet badly mistaken in many ways in his views of sex, of his wife's character, and of

---

22. Rand endorses Peikoff's (1976, cf. 1991) treatment of rationality as the most fundamental virtue.

23. Of course, someone who is committed to tracking reality will have more of a grasp of reality and sense of logic than someone like Peter Keating. For a general discussion of this issue, see Badhwar 2014b, ch. 4.

his obligations to her. He repeatedly attributes to his wife, Lilian, a nobility she doesn't possess, and to himself vices he doesn't possess. His mistaken view of sex leads him to insult Dagny and cheat himself of the happiness he could have had if he had left Lilian and pursued his relationship with Dagny openly. His rationality does enable him to learn from Dagny and, over time, to correct these mistakes. But this doesn't wipe out the fact that until he does, he is unjust to both Dagny and himself—without being irrational. A more dramatic example is Andrei Taganov in *We the Living*. In Rand's sympathetic portrayal of him, Andrei becomes a communist not because he is irrational but because he mistakenly believes that communism offers a remedy for the injustices of the tsarist regime that sent his father to his death in Siberia. Like Rearden, Andrei learns and changes for the better, in his case thanks to Kira and his love for her.

History also provides ample examples of the fact that a commitment to rationality doesn't guarantee success in grasping the truth. When slavery was the norm, few people could see that it was wrong. The same was true of attitudes toward women when women were regarded as the inferior sex and toward homosexuality when it was regarded as immoral. But there's no reason to think that all these misguided people simply lacked a commitment to see things as they are. More likely, some of them were scrupulously rational but simply saw no reason to challenge their culture's beliefs. The claim is not that no rational person in such societies could possibly see the light—that would make progress inexplicable—but that it is hard for even rational people in such societies to see it, and so it's not surprising that most fail.[24]

Rationality as a commitment to tracking reality is compatible with mistaken moral or political principles, or the misapplication of the correct principles in certain sorts of situations. In short, it is compatible with non-virtuous and contrary-to-virtue traits and actions. Rationality in this sense is, as I've already noted, a deliberative and epistemic virtue, a virtue that is necessary for a full-fledged moral virtue. But it is not a moral virtue in its own right. A moral virtue requires not only a commitment to tracking reality and emotions and desires in accord with it but also success in grasping the relevant principles and acting on them. For example, someone who is just in his professional life grasps the principle that he has a right to claim from others only what he has earned and owes others

---

24. Rand herself declared, on the basis of nothing but her "disgust," that homosexuality was immoral. Of course, consistently with her advocacy of the minimal state, she did not think that the government had any right to prohibit homosexuality.

only what they have earned; he understands how to apply this principle to various aspects of his professional life and characteristically acts justly wholeheartedly. Someone who is honest in her personal life grasps the principle that she should be truthful with herself and others, understands how to apply this principle to various aspects of her personal life, and characteristically acts honestly wholeheartedly. To the extent that someone is virtuous, he cannot have mistaken moral principles or emotions that conflict with them. Thus, Rand's heroes don't just commit themselves to being just or honest, they succeed in (characteristically) acting justly and honestly wholeheartedly. Should they fail to act virtuously on some occasion, it is not because their moral principles are mistaken, or because they don't know how to apply these principles to the situation but, typically, because they are ignorant of the particulars of the situation. A good example is Dagny's judgment that Francisco has become a worthless bum. Her judgment fails to do him justice only because Francisco refuses to tell her why he is behaving like a worthless bum, and not because her principles are mistaken, or because she doesn't know how to apply the principle of justice to the situation, or because her motives for making this judgment are unjust. Within the context of her knowledge of the facts, Dagny's judgment is perfectly rational.

In short, Rand depicts the virtues of her heroes not just as commitments but as achievements. She uses virtue as a success term. Hence I will call the trait of grasping reality through a commitment to rationality "realism," and in what follows, I will speak of realism rather than rationality as a virtue.

To illustrate the unity of virtue in Rand's writings, I will focus on what Rand calls "the central purpose of a rational man's life": productive work (*VOS* 31). Productive work is the central purpose because it is "the central value that integrates and determines the hierarchy of all his other values" (*VOS* 31).[25] There is no pride without productiveness and no pro-

25. Rand continues: "Reason is the source, the precondition of his productive work—pride is the result" (*VOS* 31). This is an example of what I pointed out earlier—namely, that with the exception of the ultimate virtue, a rational grasp of the facts (realism), and the ultimate value, happiness, Rand does not stick to her virtue-value framework. Nor is her distinction between values and virtues a hard and fast one. Thus reason, which is supposed to be the value that the virtue of rationality aims at, is now said to be the source and precondition of productive work and, presumably, of the virtue of productiveness. And pride, which is supposed to be the virtue of moral ambitiousness, is now the result of the virtue of productiveness. Whatever Rand's reasons for this, there are good reasons to not make any hard-and-fast distinction between specific virtues and values. For a virtue can itself be the value that someone who wants to become virtuous strives for. For example, if A wants to acquire the trait

ductiveness without rationality. But what is productiveness? And how is it connected to the other major virtues?

Productiveness consists of working to create something that you know to be objectively valuable—that is, something that protects or promotes your own or others' life and happiness. Productiveness is not a matter of working long hours or even creating something original. For example, devising an original method for stealing a popular writer's ideas without getting caught is not productivity but parasitism. Productive work is "the process by which man's consciousness controls his existence, a constant process of acquiring knowledge and shaping matter to fit one's purpose, of translating an idea into physical form, of remaking the earth in the image of one's values" (*Atlas* 1020).

The last two clauses highlight the fact that merely having a good idea is not enough for productiveness. The idea must take physical form—exist out there—to be valuable, whether the idea concerns quantum mechanics or choreography for a dance.[26] This does not mean, as some have thought, that the person who has the idea in question *must* write it down or give it a solid, material shape in order to count as having done something productive.[27] This would imply that, to the extent that jazz musicians, or Indian classical musicians, or standup comics improvise, they don't do productive work. It would imply that the poet or poets known as Homer, who created poetry before writing was invented, didn't do any productive work—yet Homer's poetry miraculously became productive work after other people wrote it down. But the playing of good music, the telling of good jokes, the recitation of good poetry—all these give physical form to the mental activity of the musician, comic, and poet, respectively, just as much as writing them down or recording them does.

Productiveness requires independence of mind—that is, the disposition to form one's own judgments instead of accepting others' judgments on faith—because creating value, big or small, requires that we think for ourselves. Productiveness also requires integrity, "the policy of acting in accordance with one's [correct] values, of expressing, upholding and translating them into practical reality," especially in the face of social

of productiveness, A recognizes productiveness as a value to her, and in doing worthwhile work, she expresses the value she places on being productive. The same is true if B wants to maintain her virtue of productiveness: she sees it as a value worth maintaining by being productive.

26. See Peikoff 1991, 292–303, for extended discussion.

27. Contra Smith's (2006, 199) claim that a "composer has not created a material value until he commits the melody he constructs in his mind to paper or a recording of some type."

pressure to surrender them ("The Ethics of Emergencies," *VOS* 59). Howard Roark is an exemplar of productiveness and integrity in the face of such social pressure.

A person with independence of mind and integrity is also honest with herself and others, since someone who is unafraid to translate her values "into practical reality" has no reason to hide her values from herself or others. Just as integrity is a matter of refusing to fake one's consciousness, honesty is a matter of refusing to fake existence (*Atlas* 1019)—that is, refusing to deceive oneself or others about the facts. And presumably, someone who is honest with herself and others must also be just in her evaluation and treatment of others, since justice is a "recognition of the fact that you cannot fake the character of men as you cannot fake the character of nature ... that every man must be judged for what he is and treated accordingly" (*Atlas* 1019). In productive work, honesty and justice translate into seeking a reward only for what you have produced without cheating anyone, giving credit to others for what you have learned from them, honoring your word, and so on. Finally, although Rand states that pride in the sense of self-esteem is the proper result of productive work, we can see that pride as she defines it elsewhere—moral ambitiousness (*VOS* 33)—is also a prerequisite of productiveness and the other virtues. For only someone who is morally ambitious can have acquired the virtues.[28]

It is in arguing for productivity as a virtue that Rand departs most strikingly from Aristotle and, indeed, from most philosophers. To be sure, Aristotle thinks highly of intellectual work, which, at its best, exhibits the intellectual virtue of *sophia* or theoretical wisdom. But he deplores the lives of laborers, artisans, or tradesmen as "ignoble and inimical to excellence," and thus incompatible with *eudaimonia*.[29] For activities that are done for the sake of the product (such as buildings, tables, or money) lack worth in themselves, deriving all their worth from the worth of the product. Productive activities (*poesis*) stand in contrast to activities done for their own sake (*praxis*), which alone can exhibit moral virtue (*arete*) and practical wisdom (*phronesis*). Productive activities debase the minds

28. Rand's concept of pride overlaps but is not identical with Aristotle's concept. For Rand, pride is what you need in order to aim for moral perfection, whereas for Aristotle it is what you have when you achieve moral perfection. For both, however, pride is related to self-esteem—that is, to a justified sense of one's own worth. And for both philosophers, this sense leads the proud individual to undertake great actions. In *Atlas Shrugged*, all the heroic individuals do so.

29. Aristotle, trans. B. Jowett, *Politics* VII.9 1328b32–29a2, in Barnes 1984.

and bodies of those who engage in them, rendering them incapable of achieving virtue or phronesis much less *sophia* (*Politics* VIII.2 1337b1–14).[30] Hence such activities should not be taught to children of citizens. And Aristotle thinks these things even as he also thinks, apparently inconsistently, that there is a virtue of thought—not of body but of thought—displayed in these activities when they are done well: *technē*.

By contrast, Rand holds that a person can acquire and display the virtue of productivity in any honest line of work (except perhaps, she once remarked, in operating an elevator). "Whether it's a symphony or a coal mine," she writes, "all work is an act of creating and comes from the same source: from an inviolate capacity to see through one's own eyes" (*Atlas* 783).[31] Indeed, as we've seen, to do one's work well, whether it's commerce, carpentry, or construction, one must have an independent mind, integrity, honesty, and justice. So it is not surprising that both *The Fountainhead* and *Atlas Shrugged* have heroes and admirable minor characters who work with their handsor otherwise engage in *poesis*. In the former, a construction worker, Mike Donnigan, is Howard Roark's only friend till he meets Gail Wynand. Howard Roark himself is an architect, and Dagny Taggart, the central character in *Atlas*, is a business woman.[32] And Atlantis is populated by businesspeople and workers (including a brakeman on Taggart Transcontinental, and several of Hank Rearden's workers), in addition to scientists and philosophers. This "egalitarianism" of virtue—the conviction that virtue does not require high intellectual ability or talent—is fundamental to Rand's outlook.

A controversial strand in Rand's portrayal of her villains, which include most of the business people in *Atlas,* is their incompetence. Not only do they lack the virtues, they lack basic competence. James Taggart, president of Taggart Transcontinental, is the most obvious example in *Atlas,* but there are others, such as Paul Larkin, Orren Boyle, Eugene Lawson, and Lee Hunsacker. These modern aristocrats, as Rand calls them, are like the aristocrats of old in not earning their wealth. They differ only in one respect: the aristocrats of old inherited their wealth, the new aristocrats get it through political connections, or pull. Given their incompetence, aristocrats of pull would never succeed in their businesses without

---

30. Thanks to Gregory Salmieri for clarification of this issue.
31. Of course, she means all honest work for a worthwhile goal.
32. Some would say that the central character is John Galt. But the story of John Galt and the other major characters in the novel is largely the story of their relationship to Dagny and is told from Dagny's perspective.

political connections. So, although Rand never claims that competence is a virtue, she does seem to think that only the virtuous are competent.

However, the idea that people who use the government to harm their competitors and benefit themselves are also incompetent at their work is contradicted by experience. If it were true, practically every large business in America would have to be deemed incompetent, for practically every large business gets subsidies or tax breaks from the government or tries to kill the competition by clamoring for regulations that smaller businesses cannot afford to implement. The same is true of many small businesses. For example, established florists and coffin sellers in Louisiana tried to kill the competition by lobbying state or local governments for expensive occupational licensing that newcomers could ill afford.[33] Yet if all such businesses were incompetent, it would be a mystery how the country became so rich and awash in so many great products.

Rand would have been right if she'd held that an enterprise that is *thoroughly* incompetent cannot make it without pull. But the vast majority of businesses that seek special favors are not thoroughly incompetent—they seek favors in order to make *bigger* profits, not to make profits, period.[34] Nor are the owners or CEOs of these companies thoroughly dishonest or lacking in integrity or independence of mind. The very same individuals who try to kill the competition might be scrupulously honest with their customers, just with their suppliers, and independent-minded in shaping their businesses. People's character traits are rarely global (cross-situationally consistent).

But would Rand agree with this? Or does she think that a virtuous person must be virtuous in every aspect of her life? Rand's novels depict both globally virtuous and compartmentalized characters. Her heroes—Kira Argounova, Howard Roark, Dagny Taggart, Franciso D'Anconia, and John Galt—are all depicted as virtuous across the board.[35] There are also passages in which Rand talks as though what I have dubbed real-

---

33. Florists were exempted from the licensing requirement after the Institute for Justice took the state government to court. See https://ij.org/ll/liberty-law-december-2012/l-l-12-12-federal-appeals-court-victory/. Altogether, in 2017, 102 occupations required a license in some or most states: https://ij.org/report/license-work-2/report/ranking-the-occupations/. Shampooing a customer's hair was licensed in thirty-seven states.

34. A complicating fact is that every individual business enters a market already contaminated by pull. Businesses that are harmed by this have an excuse, if not justification, for seeking favors that will "level the playing field."

35. We must remember, however, that with one or two exceptions, it is not clear that she regarded anyone in the real world as measuring up to her heroes.

ism (a rational grasp of reality) must be all or nothing—that is, global. Consider, for example, this passage from Galt's speech: "Whenever you committed the evil of refusing to think and to see, of exempting from the absolute of reality some one small wish of yours, whenever you chose to say: Let me withdraw from the judgment of reason the cookies I stole, or the existence of God, let me have my one irrational whim and I will be a man of reason about all else—that was the act of subverting your consciousness, the act of corrupting your mind" (*Atlas* 1037). Again, in "The Missing Link" (*PWNI* 53), Rand describes a successful, hardworking business man who "exercised a great deal of initiative and ingenuity within the limits set by his particular city district," but who seemed to have no interest in or ability for thinking in terms of philosophical principles, especially moral principles. He had, she states, an anticonceptual mentality, and because "the rational is the moral . . . the anticonceptual is the profoundly antimoral" (*PWNI* 55). This at least suggests that Rand thought he had no virtues in any domain of his life. The vice of being anticonceptual infected his entire character.

In her novels, however, Rand also depicts characters who are virtuous in some areas of their lives but not others. I've already discussed Hank Rearden and Andrei Taganov. Another good example of such a person is Howard Roark's mentor and employer for three years, Henry Cameron, who has a great deal of integrity, productivity, and independence in his architectural work, refusing to compromise for the sake of getting commissions. He is also honest with himself about his shortcomings as an architect, and he is just in never seeking the unearned. But he has never known "how to face people" (*Fountainhead* 45), and is often rude and brutally unjust to his clients, calling them "unprintable names" and behaving like "a feudal lord and a longshoreman" (44). Even in his heyday, when he was considered the best architect in the country, Cameron managed to get work only because his business manager knew how to mollify his clients. When times change, businesses and governments want skyscrapers that look like Roman palaces, and his business manager dies, Cameron is left without work and takes to drink. His virtues are confined to just one area of his life: the art and craft (but not the business) of architecture.[36] Less extreme forms of virtue-compartmentalization are also true of many other sympathetic figures in Rand's novels. So although Rand believes that virtue *can* be global, she also recognizes in many of

---

36. Cf. Peikoff 1991, 297: "a man may be better in his work than in the rest of his life," and although "this diminishes his character and his creative potential," he is still admirable.

her fictional portrayals that it need not be global, that virtue can be limited to certain areas of a person's life. On both points, there is agreement between Rand and Aristotle.

Insofar as Rand believes that the virtues can be global, what is the explanation for this belief? The explanation, in Peikoff's words, is that "everything in reality is interconnected."[37] So if we had a realistic grasp of all important matters and were motivated by this grasp, we would have all the virtues.

It is important to note that a lack of virtue in some domains of our lives doesn't have to stem from evasion. As I argue in my discussion of Aristotle's view, it can be due to blind spots resulting from a person's inborn temperament, early moral education, lack of self-knowledge or knowledge of the world, and mistakes in reasoning. This is another reason that even someone who is thoroughly rational may not be virtuous in every domain of his life. Such, as we've seen, is the case with Hank Rearden.

The Virtues of Benevolence

A major little-discussed question about Rand's view of the interrelationship of the virtues concerns what are sometimes called the "virtues of benevolence" in the virtue ethics literature, and "imperfect duties" in the deontological literature. These virtues—charity, kindness, and generosity—are recognized by the major ethical theories as being beyond the demands of justice but nevertheless extremely important. How are they related to each other or to the major virtues in Rand's ethics? Rand says little about charity and next to nothing about the other virtues in her essays. Yet kindness and generosity play an important role in her novels.[38] But let me begin with charity.

Charity comes into play with needy strangers or acquaintances. In "The Ethics of Emergencies" (*VOS* 59), Rand argues that helping those we love when they deserve help is not an act of charity but, rather, an act of love and integrity. Like other major ethical theorists, Rand holds that charity is not a moral obligation, hence not something anyone can claim from another. She also states that charity is a minor virtue (59). What she

---

37. Peikoff (1991, 225) is actually trying to explain why one evasion would lead to wholesale evasion if we "tried consistently to protect only ... [our] single starting evasion, turning aside methodically from everything that might threaten it." For Irwin's explanation of Aristotle's view that phronesis is global, see the section "Aristotle's View of the Unity and Scope of Virtue" above.

38. I discuss this in Badhwar 1993b.

is referring to here, however, is not the character trait of being charitable but, rather, acts of charity such as the huge sums of money donated by the Fords or the Rockefellers.[39] And she is surely right that such acts in themselves count for little compared to being a just, honest, productive person.

Rand does not say anything about the disposition to be charitable—that is, about charitableness as a character trait. But what she does say about helping strangers shows that she regards the complete absence of a charitable disposition as deplorable. Her most extensive discussion of the issue is in "The Ethics of Emergencies" where she first argues that people who are "totally indifferent to anything living and would not lift a finger to help a man or a dog left mangled by a hit-and-run driver" are "psychopaths" and then argues that it is appropriate to help a stranger only in an emergency and only when the risk to your own life or well-being is minimal (*VOS* 55–56). An emergency is "an unchosen, unexpected event, limited in time, that creates conditions under which human survival is impossible—such as a flood, an earthquake, a fire, a shipwreck" (61). But the principle of helping strangers in an emergency cannot be extended to other situations that leave people needy, such as illness, poverty, or ignorance, because these are not "metaphysical emergencies" (62). With a neighbor going through a hard time, however, we may offer help if we can afford to and if we have no reason to think that he is undeserving—but again, only till he can get back on his own feet. What makes charity a virtue under all these circumstances is that it is an expression of the generalized goodwill and respect that all normal people have toward others as beings who share with them the capacity to value (61–62). Such respect and goodwill are, in Nathaniel Branden's words, "profoundly egoistic," because they stem from the recognition that others have value because they are of the same species as ourselves ("Benevolence versus Altruism," *TON* 1:27 27, cited in *VOS* 60). In revering others, people "are revering their own life" (*VOS* 60). By being and acting charitably, people actualize this sense of kinship, without sacrificing their own well-being.

This is eminently plausible: we feel a sense of kinship with other human beings because they are like us, so in revering them we revere our

---

39. Strictly speaking, such acts of charity can't be said to be either virtuous or nonvirtuous in the absence of any information about the reasons for the acts. All we can say is that, if the givers acted from goodwill and a desire to help the recipients rather than, say, vanity, and they did so in the belief that the recipients would use the money well, then they acted from a virtuous motive.

own lives. There is a self-regard inherent in our natural goodwill toward others. But it's odd to call helping others out of respect and goodwill "profoundly egoistic" without also calling it what it obviously is: profoundly other-regarding. After all, it is in response to the other's need that we extend charity, not to our own desire to experience a sense of kinship. (There are far easier ways to experience a sense of kinship, e.g., by identifying with charitable characters in books or movies.) Helping others *expresses and actualizes* our sense of kinship with others; it is not the *goal* of the helpful act. The desire to show that everything decent in human life is wholly—or even primarily—egoistic does violence to common human experience. But I will return to the self-other issue in Objectivism later. For now, I just want to note that the same argument from a sense of kinship can be used to justify charity toward strangers in nonemergency situations—for example, toward those who are permanently disabled and unable to care for themselves. And although neither Rand nor Branden make this argument, Rand does implicitly justify charity toward strangers in a later essay, "What Is Capitalism" (*CUI* 19), where she argues that people who are unable to work have to rely on voluntary charity. Since, for Rand, taking is appropriate only when giving is appropriate, her reply implies that it is proper for us to support strangers through charity on a long-term basis if we can afford to, not only in an emergency.

Rand's view actually allows us to go further than she herself does on the general issue of helping strangers out of a general respect and concern for them as human beings: it allows us to argue that it is sometimes virtuous (and thus non-self-sacrificial) to help strangers over an extended period of time even at serious risk to our own lives. During the Holocaust, the villagers of Le Chambon and others in occupied Europe helped thousands of Jews escape at great risk to themselves and their families. For many this meant harboring Jews for years in their own homes. According to researchers who interviewed hundreds of rescuers in the 1980s and 1990s, when they asked rescuers why they took such great risks, practically all of them gave as explanation that they had no choice because not helping would have been unconscionable.[40] Practically all of them said

---

40. For references and detailed discussion, see Badhwar 1993a. As I explain there, I use "altruism" the way it is used by most social scientists and philosophers: "caring for others for their sake." On this conception, caring for others for their own sake is compatible with simultaneously caring for oneself for one's own sake. Unfortunately, Tara Smith (2006, 254n29) ignores my definition of altruism, insists that "altruistic" *has* to mean "self-sacrificial" (because

that had they refused to help, they would not have been able to live with themselves, that anyone in their situation would have done what they did, and that their help was no sacrifice. For rescuers, helping the victims of a monstrous injustice was an actualization of their sense of oneness with them as human beings and thus an affirmation of their own identity as human beings. According to some researchers, none of the rescuers they interviewed expressed any regret over their rescue activity, and most of them stated that they wish they could have done more. One rescuer was discovered harboring Jews by a major in a German army camp and had to become his mistress in exchange for his silence. Yet she told her interviewers, "[T]he older I get, the more I feel I am very rich. . . . I would not change anything. It's a wonderful feeling to know that today many people are alive and some of them married and have their children, and that their children will have children because I did have the courage and . . . the strength" (Badhwar 1993a, 106n28). By their actions, rescuers satisfied a fundamental human interest, the interest in shaping the world in light of their values and affirming their identity. In benefiting others for their sake, they also benefited themselves for their own sake: neither others nor they were mere means to each other's ends. Indeed, it is because rescuers saw saving these Jews as a part of their own overall good rather than in conflict with it, or as a mere means to it, that their concern for them was so wholehearted, and so virtuous.

This example shows that even when our goal is another's benefit, it needn't come at the price of our own benefit. Indeed, as the self expands to include the interests of others, benefiting them becomes a part of our own benefit. Just as working for the success of an intellectual or artistic project with which we identify is a central part of our own good, so working for the well-being of people with whom we identify is a central part of our own good. Hence it's not possible, either logically or psychologically, to see our own well-being as the ultimate goal of all our actions, and another's well-being as only an instrumental means to it. This is why it rings false to many readers when Rand's heroes proclaim—rather self-consciously—that what they are doing is for their own sake, and not another's. For example, when Dagny says to Hank Rearden, "You're saving Taggart Transcontinental a second time," he replies, "Why should I give a damn about saving Taggart Transcontinental? Don't you know that

that is how Rand defined it), and claims that it is "obvious" that an act can't be simultaneously both altruistic and self-interested.

I want to have a bridge of Rearden Metal to show the country?" (*Atlas* 169).[41] But there's plenty of reason that he should care about both for their own sake. If he thinks that Taggart Transcontinental is worth saving, and he bears goodwill toward the people it serves, and he loves Dagny (who loves Taggart Transcontinental), he has more than one reason to care about Taggart Transcontinental even if its success is irrelevant to his own work.[42]

The assumption that promoting our own rational interests has to be the *only* fundamental motive in every virtuous action, and promoting another's interests must be justified as an instrumental means to it, is the mirror image of the more common mistaken assumption that promoting another's rational interests has to be the *only* fundamental motive in every virtuous action, and promoting our own interests must be justified as an instrumental means to this. There is no reason to think that either alternative is true. Human psychology and human good are far more complex than either alternative allows, and both our good and our goodness depend on recognizing this and living accordingly.

In "Man's Rights," Rand argues that to respect others' rights is to act on the recognition that individuals are ends in themselves—not mere means to others' ends. This recognition of others as ends is the recognition that, like us, they have the capacity to value themselves and set their own ends, to live their own lives. To respect their rights is to respect them as autonomous beings. But we do not fully see and treat others as ends without recognizing that they are often in need of others' help or friendship. It is this recognition of others as both autonomous and vulnerable that is the shared foundation of all the other-regarding virtues: justice and honesty in our dealings with others, as well as charity, kindness, and generosity. For reasons I give below, all these traits express our recognition of the fact that people are ends in themselves. This suggests that these virtues are united, and in what follows, I'll argue for this claim. But first I will describe kindness and generosity as they are commonly understood,

---

41. Actually, Rearden precedes this statement with: "You used to be a better psychologist than that" (*Atlas* 169). I leave this in a footnote because Rand explicitly repudiates psychological egoism in her later writings.

42. Again, Roark claims in his defense that he builds only to give concrete form to "his own truth," that his motive was "[t]he creation, not the benefits others derived from it" (*Fountainhead* 710–11). But his own truth—his vision of how buildings should be built—is determined, in part, by the physical and mental needs of the human beings who are going to inhabit his buildings. He surely wouldn't be happy building structures that did no one any good—even if he was independently wealthy and didn't need their money.

discuss why Rand does not regard them as important in her essays, and then argue that they are as important as the other virtues we exercise toward others, supporting this with examples from Rand's novels.

Kindness is the direct opposite of cruelty. A kind person seeks to spare others unnecessary hurt or injury and offers them comfort when appropriate—that is, appropriate in terms of her own rational concerns as well as those of the recipients. Thus, kindness is the intellectual-emotional-action disposition to help or comfort others for the right reason, in the right manner, at the right time, and to the right extent. Unlike charity, kindness can be exercised toward friends as well as strangers and acquaintances. The same is true of generosity, the disposition to give gratuitously, with pleasure, from a desire to share one's abundance with another for the right reason, at the right time, in the right manner, to the right extent. Aristotle thinks that generosity is best exercised with friends, and Rand agrees, arguing that "the time, money or effort one gives or the risk one takes should be proportionate to the value of the person in relation to one's own happiness" (*VOS* 58).

Rand does not discuss kindness or generosity, thereby indicating that, like charity, she doesn't regard them as important. Is this because she thinks that the conditions under which they are properly exercised are only sometimes met? This, surely, is not true. Kindness can be shown in myriad ways in our daily lives, from helping someone pick up the papers she has dropped on the floor, to ignoring someone's faux pas in order to spare him embarrassment, to holding the door open for someone who seems to have trouble opening it himself. Generosity, too, is called upon not only when it's time to buy a birthday present but in our daily lives: saving the last peach of the season for your spouse because, although you both love peaches, she loves them more, spending extra time helping out a student who is having trouble keeping up with the class, and so on. Life might not be shorter without such small acts of kindness or generosity, but it is surely nastier.

Why, then, does Rand implicitly delegate kindness, generosity, and charity to the status of minor virtues? The reason might be a certain view of human life and of these virtues.[43] She argues that success and happiness are metaphysically more important than loss and unhappiness because it is proper for human beings to succeed and be happy, and because we *can* succeed and be happy: existence isn't inherently inimical to success and happiness. Those who see life in these positive terms live on what

---

43. An earlier version of my argument here appears in Badhwar 1993a.

she calls the "benevolent universe premise" ("The Inexplicable Personal Alchemy," *ROTP* 122)—the premise that "[s]uccess and happiness are the metaphysically to-be-expected" (Peikoff 1976, Lecture 8), and that suffering and calamity are "the abnormal exception[s] in human life" (*Atlas* 759). Moreover, regardless of our circumstances, it is success and happiness that we value and seek.

These considerations make our agency more important than our "patiency," since agency is what we exercise to avoid loss, overcome suffering, and achieve success and happiness. Rand's cursory treatment of charity, kindness, and generosity suggests that she thinks of these virtues as responses only or primarily to our patiency, our vulnerability to loss and unhappiness. From this it follows that they are not as important as the virtues that are responses to our status as agents.

Rand is undeniably right that existence isn't inherently inimical to our aspiration to succeed and be happy, that it is proper for us to succeed and be happy, and that in this sense happiness and agency are more important than suffering and patiency. But these are what she calls "metaphysical value-judgements" (*RM* 17). By contrast, a descriptive account of human nature must recognize that as human beings, our vulnerability to unhappiness and loss, our patiency, are as much a part of our nature as our agency. Whereas our agency distinguishes us from animals, our patiency distinguishes us from Superhumans and gods. Even under the best of circumstances, we are vulnerable to injury, loss, death, grief, and disease, and the kindness and generosity of others is often crucial to our ability to overcome our unhappiness and recover the full power of our agency. Agency and patiency are two sides of the same human coin, a coin that is loaded in favor of agency for the greater part of our adult lives but in favor of patiency at the beginning and (often) the end of our lives. We all start our lives as patients dependent on others' kindness and generosity (and sometimes even charity). Not only our survival but even our characters and our very capacity for happiness are heavily influenced by our caretakers' kindness and generosity in our childhood. Most importantly, our very ability for agency is dependent on how we are treated as patients. Children brought up on a strict diet of harsh discipline and unquestioning obedience are often impaired in their ability to trust their own judgment as adults. Most of us also end our lives as patients dependent on others' kindness and generosity (and sometimes even charity). And how we fare at the end of our lives plays a big role in our evaluation of, and feelings about, our lives overall.

It might be argued that if our early caretakers are parents who love us, then what I'm calling kindness and generosity are actually, for Rand, just exercises of love and integrity (*VOS* 59). But the fact that kindness and generosity are required by love and integrity doesn't imply that they are not really kindness and generosity. Justice and honesty are also required by love and integrity without ceasing to be justice and honesty.

In short, as beneficiaries of the virtues of kindness and generosity, these virtues are as important as justice, honesty, and so on, because (i) our vulnerability to pain and loss is an important part of our nature as human beings, especially at the beginning and end of our lives, (ii) the kindness and generosity of others is often crucial to our ability to overcome our unhappiness and recover the full power of our agency, and (iii) our very agency and capacity for happiness depend to a large extent on the love, kindness, and generosity our caretakers extend to us as children. Insofar as these virtues are responses to others' pain and loss, or to sheer need in infancy, they are responses whose ultimate aim is to enable their beneficiaries to achieve happiness and success.

It's important to note, however, that it is not only as beneficiaries of other people's kindness and generosity that these virtues are good for us. They are also good for us to *exercise* toward others. David Kelley (2014, 20) argues that, as forms of benevolence, these virtues are necessary "in order to achieve the values derivable from other human beings," whether material or spiritual. In his words, "*Benevolence is a commitment to achieving the values derivable from life with other people in society, by treating them as potential trading partners, recognizing their humanity, independence, and individuality, and the harmony between their interests and ours*" (28). Without this fundamental respect for, and trust in, others, we can have no reason to trade, and thus no reason to love or befriend anyone. Just as productiveness requires "the imaginative projection of new ways to exploit the potential of what exists and thus to create things that will serve our purposes," benevolence requires the imaginative projection of "ways to exploit the potential represented by other people, to create opportunities for trade, to remake our social environment in the image of our values" (30).

This is an insightful argument. The importance of these traits goes beyond their usefulness to us in our social lives, however. The recognition of others' humanity and individuality is none other than recognition of their status as ends in themselves, not mere means to our own ends ("Man's Rights," *VOS*). This recognition is inherent in all the other-regarding virtues, not only in respect for rights or only in benevolence, suggesting that there is a unity in all the other-regarding virtues. If this is right, then without the virtues of benevolence, we cannot even have the cardinal virtues of honesty or justice. The unity of the virtues extends further than Rand recognizes. Consider, for example, honesty, which involves a commitment to never fake reality, either with ourselves or with others, either about ourselves or about others. An honest person doesn't try to escape uncomfortable facts through evasion or fantasy. Nor does she present herself to others as someone other than who she is (see also Aristotle *EN* IV.6 1126b33ff.). An honest person also doesn't deceive others for the sake of some short-term gain or, for that matter, for the fun of it. Where truthfulness with others is concerned, she is truthful (as common sense and Aristotle would say), at the right time, for the right reason, in the right manner, and to the right extent. Simply blurting out irrelevant and hurtful truths is not honesty but tactlessness or cruelty, and only someone who is kind will succeed in discerning the right occasion for, and manner of, revealing the truth. The same is true of justice, the virtue of never seeking or granting "the unearned and undeserved... [either] in matter ... [or] in spirit" (*VOS* 32). This implies, among other things, judging people and actions as they are by an objective standard of evaluation. But only a kind person will do so in an appropriate manner and, as James Wallace (1978, 1937) argues, only a generous-minded person will see another person's moral or technical merit even when it's hard to see.[44] This idea should be especially welcome to Rand, given her view that admiring people for their virtue or other achievements is more important an aspect of justice than condemning them for their vices.[45]

Even though Rand relegates the virtues of benevolence to a secondary place in her nonfiction, her novels show that she recognizes their importance.[46] For her heroes are often extraordinarily kind and generous, not

44. See also Badhwar 1996.
45. See Peikoff 1991, 284–85.
46. Even though, as I argue in "Virtues of Benevolence," Rand sometimes seems ambivalent about them in *The Fountainhead*. Smith (2006, 265, 270–74, 282, 283) also provides a detailed discussion of these virtues but ends by concluding that they are not really virtues, because it is not always in one's rational interest to exercise them. But the real question is whether it's rational to have the traits of kindness and generosity, not whether being helpful, giving, and so forth to everyone all the time is rational. (No major philosopher, whether egoist or not, holds that being indiscriminately helpful or giving etc. is virtuous.) And surely it is rational to have these traits when we include the conditions under which it is proper to exercise them in their definition, as Aristotle does: Virtue V is an intellectual-emotional disposition to help others for the right reason, at the right time, in the right amount, and so

only to those they love but also to mere acquaintances, and sometimes even to adversaries. Striking examples include, from *The Fountainhead*, Howard Roark's unsought-for attempt to give hope and courage to Steven Mallory, the gifted young sculptor who is on the verge of a spiritual and physical collapse thanks to his failure to get work; Roark's visits to Henry Cameron in the last months of Cameron's life; and his unreproachful help to his erstwhile adversary, Peter Keating, when Keating falls on hard times. Perhaps most strikingly, Roark refuses to condemn or abandon his friend Gail Wynand, even when Wynand betrays him in the worst way possible. Roark refuses to condemn him not because he doesn't care about justice but because he still loves Wynand and continues to hope that he will redeem himself. In *Atlas Shrugged* (887–92), Dagny tries to help her heartbroken and despairing sister-in-law, Cheryl Taggart, when Cheryl apologizes for having treated Dagny with scorn in the past. More remarkably, Dagny never judges or reproaches Hank Rearden for his unjust and insulting treatment of her in the early part of their relationship. She lets him realize his mistake on his own. In turn, in order to be just toward his wife, mother, and brother, Rearden tries to interpret their actions and attitudes as generously as possible. Unfortunately, he fails to understand their motives and attitudes and ends up giving them far more than they deserve before he realizes their exploitative natures.

It is sometimes thought that kindness and generosity are the virtues of the weak, and on some conceptions of these traits they might be. But on the conceptions I have defended and that Rand's characters exemplify, they are virtues of the strong and self-sufficient. Readers who still doubt their importance should do this thought experiment: imagine Rand's heroes lacking these virtues, and then ask yourself if you would still find them (as) attractive and admirable. If the answer is "No," then you have good reason to give these virtues as much importance as Rand's cardinal virtues.

In the next section, a skeptical reader will see another reason for doing so. It is Rand's villains who lack these virtues, and they lack them for

---

on. This, as shown above, is also true of honesty (not all truths are worth relating), of courage (not all dangers are worth confronting—the expected gain is too small), of realism (not all facts are worth focusing on, some are trivial), of integrity (not all values are worth sticking up for all the time, some are marginal and sticking up for them might endanger the more important values), productivity (not all things are worth producing and not every moment should be dedicated to producing those that are), and so on. Smith's statement that these traits are not virtues for Rand is also at odds with the evidence of the novels, something she doesn't take into account.

the same reason that they lack justice and honesty—namely, they have a warped view of their own interests and of the value of others, and they lack the ability to see others as ends in themselves. They are wholeheartedly committed to, and love, the bad in every respect.

Rand's View of Vice and Its (Dis-)unity and Scope

We have seen that, for Rand, rationality in the sense of a commitment to the fullest perception of reality is a moral virtue, and that all the virtues are expressions of this virtue in different aspects of human life. I have argued that rationality is an epistemic and deliberative virtue, not a moral virtue. The moral virtue that does the work Rand wants rationality to do is what I have dubbed "realism": a rational grasp of reality. Rand also holds that irrationality (my antirealism), "the act of unfocusing... [one's] mind, the suspension of... [one's] consciousness, which is not blindness, but the refusal to see, not ignorance, but the refusal to know" ("Objectivist Ethics," *VOS* 25) is the basic vice, the source of every other vice: injustice, unproductivity, lack of integrity, dishonesty, lack of independence, and lack of pride.

Peter Keating (in *The Fountainhead*) and James Taggart (in *Atlas Shrugged*) provide good illustrations of this refusal to know, of "the suspension of... [one's] consciousness" (*VOS* 25). They are both evaders who are attracted to other evaders, and who resent or fear or simply feel uncomfortable with honest people. Their evasiveness is an ingrained habit of which they are typically unaware.

However, evil can be done consciously too: "a breach of morality is the conscious choice of an action you know to be evil, or a willful evasion of knowledge, a suspension of sight and of thought" (*Atlas* 1059). And indeed, two of Rand's most evil characters—Ellsworth Toohey (*Fountainhead*), and Dr. Floyd Ferris (*Atlas*)—consciously choose what they know to be evil. Gail Wynand of *The Fountainhead* also often does evil in full knowledge of its evil. As he confesses to Dominique, his desire to break people who show any integrity is "a kind of lust," a "sex urge," for the sake of a sense of power over them (*Fountainhead* 497).

An evil act, then, can, but needn't, involve a suspension of consciousness. It can be done in full awareness of its evil. What makes evil irrational is that it is contrary to what really matters in human life, and thus to the evil individual's own rational self-interest. This is the case not only with Wynand, but also with Toohey and Dr. Ferris, the top coordinator of the State Science Institute. Toohey's ambition is to rule people by breaking their wills, by making them feel small, mean, and insignificant. Dr. Ferris uses his scientific resources as a tool for political power. His proudest achievements are the torture machine called the Ferris Persuader, and Project X, a machine that can destroy buildings and all living things within a hundred-mile radius with ultrasound rays. Toohey and Ferris are worthy successors to John Milton's Satan, who calls on Evil to be his Good. Needless to say, Toohey and Ferris are both completely lacking in the virtues, in kindness and generosity as much as in Rand's cardinal virtues. Their characters illustrate, once again, the connections among these virtues and their lack.

Aristotle conceives of the virtues as habituated dispositions to deliberate, feel, and act in certain ways and argues that you can be fully virtuous if and only if you have the virtue of phronesis or practical wisdom. If you have even one virtue, you must have phronesis, and if you have phronesis, you must have all the virtues. Hence one virtue entails all. Rand's heroes dramatically and colorfully exemplify virtue and the unity of virtue understood thus. Insofar as Rand regards all the virtues as forms of a grasp of, and response to, reality, her conception of the virtues and of their interdependence is Socratic rather than Aristotelian. But in "Philosophy and Sense of Life," Rand recognizes that a person's sense of life is "the essence of his character" (*RM* 14), and both her heroes and her villains reveal who they are not only in what they say or do but also in the way they do it, in the emotions with which they do it, and in what they find pleasurable or aversive and salient or obscure. In short, they reveal who they are in their style of being in the world.

Aristotle presents us with two portraits of virtue and the virtuous person: an ideal, in which the virtuous person is maximally virtuous in every domain of his life, and a nonideal, in which the virtuous person is neither maximally virtuous nor virtuous in every domain of his life. Similarly, in some of her writings Rand assumes that the virtues are global, but in her novels she presents two portraits: an ideal, in which the virtuous person is fully virtuous in every domain of her life, and a nonideal, in which the virtuous person is neither fully virtuous nor virtuous in every domain of her life. All her heroes, except for Hank Rearden in the first two-thirds of *Atlas*, illustrate ideal virtue, whereas Henry Cameron in *The Fountainhead* illustrates nonideal virtue. A major difference between Rand and Aristotle lies in Rand's recognition of productivity as a virtue that a person can have in any line of worthwhile work, and Aristotle's dismissal of all but intellectual and political work as incompatible with virtue. Another difference between the two philosophers lies in the importance that Aristotle attaches to generosity and kindness, virtues that Rand excludes from her list of cardinal virtues, although, again, this difference shrinks if we take Rand's novels into account. The most important lesson of the thesis that the virtues are interdependent or united within certain areas of a person's life is that, if we want to live worthwhile and happy lives, we cannot afford to ignore any of the virtues. The most important lesson of the thesis that the virtues can be compartmentalized is that we cannot take the absence of virtue in a certain area of a person's life to signify the absence of all virtue in every area.

Author's Note

Thanks to Gregory Salmieri for his thoughtful comments on an earlier draft.

11
Comments on "Aristotle and Ayn Rand on the Unity of Virtue," by Neera K. Badhwar
Ayn Rand on Moral Virtue and Moral Character
BEN BAYER

One of the peculiarities of modern moral philosophy, especially as expressed by many representatives of the consequentialist and deontological traditions, is its exclusive focus on the study of right and wrong actions. This view often leaves questions about moral character (including, for instance, the value perspective of the agent) as something of an afterthought.[1] Against this backdrop, the newfound interest in moral character among neo-Aristotelian virtue ethicists is refreshing. This has led many of them to define ethical concepts by reference to supposedly more basic concepts related to character. For instance, Rosalind Hursthouse (1999, 28) proposes that an action is right if and only if it is what a virtuous agent would characteristically do in the circumstances. This in turn is to be un-

---

1. An exemplar is J. S. Mill, who claims in *Utilitarianism* that "He who saves a fellow creature from drowning does what is morally right, whether his motive be duty, or the hope of being paid for his trouble" (Mill 1871, 26). What matters to Mill is the consequences of the action, not the motives from which it springs. Even as deontologists express a concern for the maxim motivating actions, it's still actions that they're most concerned with evaluating ("Act only according to that maxim by which you can at the same time will that it should become a universal law" [Kant Ak. 4:421; translation, Gregor 1996, 73]). It's no surprise, then that thought experiments like the trolley problem became the twentieth-century battleground between consequentialists and deontologists.

derstood in terms of certain character traits, which are conceptualized as virtues embodying certain emotional dispositions and sensitivities to certain types of reasons.

As a representative of the virtue ethics tradition herself, Neera Badhwar has insight into what makes the tradition distinctive and powerful, and she wants to examine how Ayn Rand's moral philosophy might be understood using a virtue-ethical framework. On the one hand, Rand defines "virtue" as "the action by which one gains and keeps" values, which is in contrast to the virtue ethicists' focus on virtues as character traits (*Atlas* 1012). On the other hand, Rand's fiction often portrays her heroes and villains in a way that makes clear that their motives and other emotional dispositions are connected to their moral worth. Badhwar suggests there is some tension in Rand's view, tension that has implications for how to think about the validity of Rand's identification of the major virtues. The suggestion seems to be that, if Rand were to resolve this tension in favor of a virtue-ethical perspective and see virtues as enduring character traits, she would add new virtues such as benevolence to her existing list of major virtues.

I think Badhwar is right to notice that Rand's fiction (as well as her work on aesthetics) does spotlight the issue of character. However, I don't think there's any tension between this fact and Rand's identification of the virtues as actions. If we examine Rand's view of the virtues in the context of her broader metaethical perspective, there's a fundamental reason that basic ethical concepts like these need to denote actions. Still, Rand does not fall into the modern trap of seeing ethics as concerned with defining right action at the expense of understanding virtuous character. In her view, virtues are the actions prescribed by moral philosophy that are needed for the achievement of the values crucial to life, including central values of character. In this paper I'll first explore the metaethical perspective that leads to this view of the virtues, but then I attempt to explain how it integrates with Rand's focus on character. I'll finish by discussing the sense in which the virtues form a unity, and the implications of this view for the standards by which actions are judged to be virtues.

Why Rand Sees Virtue Primarily as a Type of Action

Scholars of Rand's moral philosophy often turn first to "The Objectivist Ethics" as the definitive statement of her metaethical outlook, but her first systematic presentation of both her metaethics and her virtue theory was in fact in Galt's speech in *Atlas Shrugged*. The argument for a new code of morality is the centerpiece of the speech, taking up roughly the first quarter of its length. It's worth noting some of the points emphasized early in this argument that bring out the reasons for her view of virtue as a type of action.

Even before Galt's discussion of the connection between the concept of "life" and the concept of "value," we are presented with the fact that the human mind is the basic tool of survival, and that reason is a volitional form of consciousness. For this reason, it's argued that a volitional being needs a code of values to guide his actions. It's in this immediate context that we get the canonical statement, "'Value' is that which one acts to gain and keep, 'virtue' is the action by which one gains and keeps it" (*Atlas* 1012). Galt then explores the roots of the concept "value" in facts about the nature of living organisms. But he quickly returns to the point that, unlike other living organisms, man has no automatic code of survival, that rationality is a matter of choice. For this reason: "Man has to be man—by choice; he has to hold his life as a value—by choice: he has to learn to sustain it—by choice; he has to discover the values it requires and practice his virtues—by choice. A code of values accepted by choice is a code of morality" (1013). Galt goes on to argue that the purpose of a moral code is self-preservation, even though one does not need to choose to live, to live as a man, or to think as a rational being. Each of these choices is either a "basic act of choice" or a "basic act of moral choice" that makes the prescriptions of morality meaningful: "if you choose to live, you must live as a man—by the work and the judgment of your mind" (1015). That you must live by the judgment of your mind is the essence of the moral norm Rand goes on to defend, so here she is describing her fundamental moral norm as a hypothetical imperative conditioned by the choice to live. Because one "cannot live as anything else," no other choice can ground these imperatives (1015). This suggests that moral norms are fundamentally hypothetical imperatives, a perspective she elaborates in greater detail in her essay "Causality versus Duty" (*PWNI*).

Galt then outlines the basic axioms of metaphysics and an associated epistemology of reason. He does this not as an academic exercise but, rather, to state the cause of his strike, to recognize these axioms that the rest of the world chooses to escape: "All the disasters that have wrecked your world, came from your leaders' attempt to evade the fact that A is A" (*Atlas* 1016). This epistemological norm integrates with and informs the moral norm, that one must live by one's own judgment. As Galt goes on to say, "man's reason is his moral faculty" (1017). Both reason and morality are concerned with the question "True or False?—Right or Wrong?" According to Galt, our only free will is the freedom "to think or not": this is the choice that controls all of our other choices and determines our life and character. As such *thinking* is our "only basic virtue, from which all the others proceed," and the refusal to think is our "basic vice" (1017). Galt punctuates his discussion of our basic choice and how it bears on moral norms by rejecting the commandments of religious morality on the grounds that they ignore the fundamental role of choice: "If I were to speak your kind of language, I would say that man's only moral commandment is: Thou shalt think. But a 'moral commandment' is a contradiction in terms. *The moral is the chosen*, not the forced; the understood, not the obeyed. The moral is the rational, and reason accepts no commandments" (1018, emphasis added).

Having established this context, Galt begins to define the norms of a morality of reason, which he says "is contained in a single axiom: existence exists-and *in a single choice*: to live" (*Atlas* 1018, my emphasis). The rest of his morality "proceeds from these" (1018). It's only *if* one chooses to live that one must pursue the cardinal moral values of reason, purpose, and self-esteem. Virtues are the chosen actions needed to achieve these chosen values. Galt lays out virtues of rationality, independence, integrity, honesty, justice, productiveness, and pride. After developing these, giving content to the goal of the happiness they aim to achieve and the implied social norms that follow from this ethics, Galt takes aim at the "morality of death" that represents the rejection of a morality of reason (1024). As an expression of this morality he names the doctrine of original sin, which he claims is a "monstrous absurdity" precisely because it, like the idea of moral commandments, denies the relevance of human choice: "A sin without volition is a slap at morality and an insolent contradiction in terms: that which is outside the possibility of choice is outside the province of morality. If man is evil by birth, he has no will, no power to change it; if he has no will, he can be neither good nor evil; a robot is amoral. To hold, as man's sin, a fact not open to his choice is a mockery of morality" (1025).

Clearly Rand's ethics, as expressed by Galt, is shot through with reference to the centrality of choice. Moral norms fundamentally guide our choices and presuppose the basic choice to live and to think. That's a lot of emphasis on the central role of choice in the foundation of an ethical system.

What then is the basic object of choice? Actions. Central ethical concepts such as virtues should then pertain most obviously to the actions we directly choose. Indeed, in light of Rand's distinctive theory of free will, the basic action we choose is to think or not, and everything else that we control volitionally we control in virtue of its relationship to that primary choice. Rand's major virtue is rationality, and each of her major derivative virtues (independence, integrity, honesty, justice, productiveness, and pride) is described first as a certain recognition of a fact about human nature. And recognition is a basic mental action. This makes all of the derivative virtues aspects of the virtue of rationality, the virtue of choosing to think and recognize the facts.

So even though, as we'll see, Rand thinks that the virtues achieve values that include values of character, she does not think ethical *advice* is primarily applicable to character. This is for the simple reason that we cannot change our character by any direct act of volition. Our character is (roughly) the set of automatized premises and associated emotional dispositions embodied in our subconscious mind. "It is not man's subconscious," Rand writes, "but his conscious mind that is subject to his direct control—and to moral judgment. It is a specific individual's conscious mind that one judges (on the basis of objective evidence) in order to judge his moral character" ("The Psychology of Psychologizing," *VOR* 29.) We do exercise indirect control over our character but only by means of more basic choices. This means that character is subject to a form of evaluation, but not the basic form in which we evaluate actions.

Nevertheless, Badhwar raises at least four different concerns about understanding virtue as a type of action. I take it that these concerns are meant to encourage us to consider the alternative that virtue is a type of character trait. One concern is that Rand "is departing from standard usage in both everyday discourse and the long history of philosophy." She doubtless departs from the way contemporary virtue ethicists use the concept of "virtue," and likely from Aristotle's canonical use of that concept as well. Admittedly, she is no stranger to repurposing language—sometimes to the dismay of her critics (as when she advocates a virtue of selfishness). But it's still not obvious that her view of virtue is a departure from common usage. The first definition of "virtue" that Google's dictionary returns is "behavior showing high moral standards." That sounds more like virtue as an act. Or consider a prominent figure who gave a famous list of virtues, Benjamin Franklin. They, too, are rules about action: "Temperance: Eat not to dullness; drink not to elevation; Silence: Speak not but what may benefit others or yourself; avoid trifling conversation."[2] And so on. Google's second definition is more characterological, "a quality considered morally good or desirable in a person." But the first one is also pretty common. If virtue ethicists focus exclusively on the second, one wonders whether it is they and not Rand whose use is a departure from common usage. That doesn't mean they're wrong either. There are surely distinct but equally valid senses of the term. But even if no one used "virtues" to refer to certain courses of action, it's clear that there's a need for some kind of moral concept to name the actions required for the achievement of values, especially because ethics is centrally concerned with guiding action. We could make up a word other than "virtue" to do the job, but since in fact a common use of the term does seem to fit the bill, it's not yet clear why we shouldn't use it.

Second, Badhwar argues that "the word 'virtue' means goodness or excellence, and goodness is a property, and thus not an act." To see why this doesn't yield an argument against identifying virtues with actions, we need to think about how to avoid equivocation with terms like "the good." In Rand's view, value concepts like "good" and "bad" are used to denote what might be called properties of entities. Now in her view, the entities in question aren't primarily agents, but the objects of their actions: "That which furthers [an organism's] life is the good, that which threatens it is the evil" (VOS 17). The really basic things that have goodness are the good things agents pursue. But note that a term for a characteristic ("good," or "valuable") is easily and often transmuted into a term for things that have the characteristic (the "goods" or the "values" we pursue). Words get used in different senses that cross metaphysical categories, especially when the word for one category derives from the word for a more basic category. If we don't keep this in mind, it's easy to slip into pre-Socratic errors such as the one about the impossibility of change—that is, to think that because hotness is not coldness, the hot cannot become the cold, and so change is impossible.

That's a fallacy because "the hot" can refer to the characteristic of hotness or to the entities that have the characteristic. Likewise "the good" can mean a property of things or the things that have the property. And of course "goodness" can get used in even more ways for even

2. Franklin 1996, 64.

more metaphysical categories than this, even as it derives from a property of certain objects of action.³ We can say actions are good if they help us get good things, and that good people are ones who characteristically undertake good actions, and so forth. And just as allowing that "the good" can mean a property of things or things that have the property, we can allow that "the good" can mean a property of actions *or the actions that have that property.* This happens in English all the time for other properties. Truth or truthfulness can refer to a property of the things we say or to the things we say themselves ("He speaks many truths!"). We can talk about the challenging nature of a hike, but we can also describe the hike itself as a challenge. When we say these things, there's no implication that actions are indeed properties of actions, or properties of anything else, unless we equivocate across different senses of the same word.⁴ All of this means that the fact that "virtue" is a kind of goodness doesn't mean that "virtue" can't refer to action. Language can be flexible without being equivocal. Goodness or the good can refer to a property of a person or a property of action, *or* to the action itself, provided that we understand these are all different (though related) senses of the word. Ordinary people speak of the good or virtue as action all the time. "Think of all the good you can do" is perfectly good English. So is "it's a virtue to identify wrongdoing."⁵

That's even though one can, of course, also use "goodness" or "virtue" to refer to the property of a person who characteristically does a lot of good or identifies a lot of wrongdoing. The question isn't whether one use of "virtue" is right or wrong; the question is which sense is the most relevant to moral philosophy. In Rand's view, the most basic use of "virtue" for ethics is as an action, because it is actions that are directly chosen for which we need guidance. Understanding a particular virtue as a character trait, like the virtue of justice, requires understanding the

---

3. Aristotle famously described the *pros hen* homonymy between different uses of "healthy": different kinds of food, exercises, and conditions can all be described as "healthy," even though these come from different categories of being and "healthy" as applied to each is used in a different sense. Foods are entities, exercises are actions, conditions are properties, and to equate the healthiness of each would be equivocal. But these different senses still have a focal meaning: the health of the organism that eats the food, engages in the exercise, or has the condition.

4. There's certainly no implication that properties themselves act: even if properties are actions, this doesn't imply that actions are things that act.

5. A Google search of "it's a virtue to" turns up 158,000 results, many of which end in infinitive phrases that clearly refer to actions.

more basic sense of virtue as an action: to possess the virtue of justice is to regularly and as a matter of disposition act justly. What's more, to acquire that disposition in the first place one must also act justly to habituate the disposition.

Badhwar's third worry is more concerning because it takes Rand to task for what appears to be an inconsistency with Rand's own view of the content of virtue. The fundamental virtue of rationality includes "the recognition and acceptance of reason as one's only source of knowledge" and "a commitment to the fullest perception of reality" within one's power, among other commitments (*VOS* 28). Badhwar notes that a commitment is "something long-term, something that involves certain evaluative dispositions or tendencies and certain patterns of action," which she suggests is a character trait, not an action. She acknowledges that Gregory Salmieri has observed that an act of virtue can itself essentially involve "long-range commitments." Badhwar responds that this would exclude commitments not presently being acted upon, which are real things. It surely would, and they are. But again, one can see "virtue" in moral philosophy as primarily about actions and acknowledge other senses of "virtue" that do involve commitments not being acted upon (that is, unless the argument above from the difference between property and action goes through). One sense can denote commitments only as they are occurrent to consciousness, while the other can include dispositions that are not. The only question is which of the two is basic and which is derivative.

A final worry occurs later in Badhwar's paper under the discussion of the unity of the virtues. She argues that because rationality as an action of committing oneself to the truth is not a "success term" in the sense of guaranteeing knowledge, it does not count as a real virtue. Badhwar's paper does not make entirely clear which kind of success rationality *should* have for it to be a real moral virtue. At times it seems that a moral virtue should guarantee success in some important aspect of human life—for example, the acquisition of knowledge. At other times it seems it should guarantee success in the performance of other moral virtues. The acquisition of knowledge and success in being morally virtuous are, of course, related because moral virtue requires knowledge. With regard to the first type of success, it's true that choosing to think, in any given case, doesn't by itself guarantee that one achieves knowledge.

This is a basic assumption of Rand's whole approach to epistemology: the reason we need epistemology is that we are neither omniscient nor infallible, and as such we need the guidance of epistemic norms.[6] Even if we follow these norms, there can be cases in which people who choose to think make systematic errors; following norms doesn't magically erase our fallibility. But any plausible examples of systematic error of this sort one could cite would be confined to a particular domain of knowledge. When someone who characteristically chooses to think makes such domain-specific systematic errors, they'll otherwise be gaining new knowledge outside of this domain when they choose to think.

The character of Hank Rearden in *Atlas Shrugged*, for instance, is characteristically rational in spite of some honest but erroneous assumptions about what morality requires of him. This leads to systematic errors in his approach to others, but as Badhwar notes, it's compatible with constantly learning things not only in domains outside of morality but even within it. It's because he's regularly rational that he's able to identify the contradictions in his approach and (especially with the help of Francisco) eliminate them.[7] With regard to the second type of success, it's important that it's plausible that Rearden's rationality is compatible with making honest mistakes about what morality requires. He can make and act on these mistakes and do the wrong thing in one sense but still be doing his best in another and so be acting virtuously. Although there's a longer argument to be made for this point, I think this is the way to understand many of the mistakes Rearden makes with regard to his relationship with Dagny.

6. "Man is neither infallible nor omniscient; if he were, a discipline such as epistemology—the theory of knowledge—would not be necessary nor possible: his knowledge would be automatic, unquestionable and total. But such is not man's nature. Man is a being of volitional consciousness: beyond the level of percepts—a level inadequate to the cognitive requirements of his survival—man has to acquire knowledge by his own effort, which he may exercise or not, and by a process of reason, which he may apply correctly or not. Nature gives him no automatic guarantee of his mental efficacy; he is capable of error, of evasion, of psychological distortion. He needs a method of cognition" (*ITOE* 78).

7. The fact that acting in a particular way doesn't always bring with it an expected effect is a consequence of what Objectivism calls the contextual nature of absolutes: we can succeed in isolating a causal factor that brings about an effect in one context and be mistaken about the scope of that context. But it doesn't mean there is no causal connection between an action type and the relevant effect type. If there weren't such a connection, the action recommended by the relevant virtue wouldn't be a virtue: "'Value' is that which one acts to gain and keep, 'virtue' is the action by which one gains and keeps it" (*Atlas* 1012). So even though a given case of choosing to think doesn't yield knowledge because of the interference of some accidental factor, choosing to think is the basic cause of knowledge. If people who characteristically enact this cause characteristically get this effect, it's because of the act/effect connection, not because of some new magic that is injected by the fact that choosing to think can become habitual (in a sense we'll later explore).

In the above, I've outlined Rand's reasons for regarding virtues as actions. But I've also emphasized that this position doesn't exclude the possibility of derivative senses of the concept "virtue." There's no problem with acknowledging that someone who regularly acts according to the virtue of rationality possesses a character trait of rationality, or that someone who regularly engages in productive acts has a character trait of productiveness. And possessing a character trait is not simply choosing separately many individual virtuous acts: there is something over and above these acts that virtues as character traits denote.

The Connection between Virtue and Character

While Rand thinks "virtue" is primarily a term denoting actions necessary for the achievement of values, character is far from an afterthought in her philosophy. The point here is not simply that she would allow that there is a secondary sense of "virtue" that denotes character traits associated with the regular engagement in virtuous action. *It's that some of the most important values that virtues help us achieve are values of character.* In this respect, Rand differs sharply from the modern approach that focuses exclusively on defining right and wrong action without respect to its origin in or consequences for our character.

But what *is* character over and above a set of actions? Rand never gave a formal definition of "moral character" as far as I know, but there's a good clue in a passage about Rand's concept of "sense of life" from which Badhwar quotes. Here is that passage in full:

> A sense of life is a preconceptual equivalent of metaphysics, an emotional, subconsciously integrated appraisal of man's relationship to existence. It sets the nature of a man's emotional responses and the essence of his character.
>
> Long before he is old enough to grasp such a concept as metaphysics, man makes choices, forms value-judgments, experiences emotions and acquires a certain implicit view of life. Every choice and value-judgment implies some estimate of himself and of the world around him—most particularly, of his capacity to deal with the world. He may draw conscious conclusions, which may be true or false; or he may remain mentally passive and merely react to events (i.e., merely feel). Whatever the case may be, his subconscious mechanism sums up his psychological activities, integrating his conclusions, reactions or evasions into an emo-

> tional sum that establishes a habitual pattern and becomes his automatic response to the world around him. What began as a series of single, discrete conclusions (or evasions) about his own particular problems, becomes a generalized feeling about existence, an implicit metaphysics with the compelling motivational power of a constant, basic emotion—an emotion which is part of all his other emotions and underlies all his experiences. This is a sense of life. ("Philosophy and Sense of Life," *RM* 14–15)

While sense of life is not all there is to character, Rand's idea is that this "preconceptual equivalent of metaphysics" is the essence of one's character, and so it's a good case study of how she understood the concept of "character." In the description above, several traits are important: sense of life as an aspect of character is derived from choices that lead to a certain implicit view, which is summed up by a subconscious mechanism that manifests emotionally, which leads to habitual, automatized responses. These latter aspects of character illustrate how it is something that exists and endures over and above the choices that help create it.

Badhwar notes that according to Rand, emotions themselves are products of the value judgments that result from one's choice to think (or not) and suggests that for Rand emotions should *not* be given "equal billing with the individual's rational commitments in her conception of character." But Badhwar argues that Rand does give equal billing, given that she understands sense of life itself as an "emotional, subconsciously integrated appraisal," which forms the *"essence of his character."* It's true that, for Rand, emotions are not equal to rational commitments in controllability, if we understand these as actions: the products of actions are not as directly controllable as actions themselves are. But here it's crucial to clarify what kind of "rational commitments" are integrated with emotions in the form of sense of life. Here's an example of the form that sense of life takes in someone's mind according to Rand:

> It is only those values which he regards or grows to regard as "important," those which represent his implicit view of reality, that remain in a man's subconscious and form his sense of life.
>
> "It is important to understand things"—"It is important to obey my parents"—"It is important to act on my own"—"It is important to please other people"—"It is important to fight for what I want"—"It is important

not to make enemies"—"My life is important"—"Who am I to stick my neck out?" Man is a being of self-made soul—and it is of such conclusions that the stuff of his soul is made. By "soul" I mean "consciousness."

The integrated sum of a man's basic values is his sense of life. (*RM* 18)

So, although it's true that Rand conceives of sense of life as "an emotional, subconsciously integrated appraisal," it's fundamentally a set of implicit "metaphysical value judgments" of the sort enumerated above. It's a set of value judgments that are integrated with emotions. And importantly, in Rand's view, value judgments are not identical to acts of rationality: they are themselves the products of rational action.[8] No value judgment—or any kind of considered judgment—is directly chosen. We can choose to assess the evidence that supports a given judgment, but we cannot directly choose to form a judgment independent of that assessment. Someone might choose to act as if he believes in the greatness of the Flying Spaghetti Monster to receive a reward from the Church of the Flying Spaghetti Monster. But no amount of money can help one choose directly to believe in the greatness of this entity in the absence of any evidence of its existence (see Salmieri and Bayer 2014).

So the fact that we directly control the choice to engage in rational activity is quite consistent with the fact that premises (one product of rational activity) are integrated with emotions (a further product of those premises). Both premises and emotions may then get "equal billing" in that both are enduring aspects of one's character and as such not directly controllable. Insofar as sense of life is essential to character, it's these enduring, subconsciously stored value judgments (which may themselves be rational or irrational) that are essential to character. All value judgments have emotional products, and in the case of the metaphysical value judgments involved in sense of life, they lead to an enduring "emotional sum."[9] Emotional dispositions do form a crucial component

---

8. This is implied by her statement in "Philosophy and Sense of Life" (*RM* 15) that "man makes choices, forms value-judgments, experiences emotions and acquires a certain implicit view of life." I understand this to be an ordered causal sequence: choices lead to emotions, which lead to a certain overall view. This is also the perspective she takes in "The Objectivist Ethics": "But since the work of man's mind is not automatic, his values, like all his premises, are the product either of his thinking or of his evasions: man chooses his values by a conscious process of thought—or accepts them by default, by subconscious associations, on faith, on someone's authority, by some form of social osmosis or blind imitation" (*VOS* 31).

9. Rand gives two stark examples of how sense of life influences one's emotional reactions: the emotional responses involved in both love and art. A person with one kind of sense

of moral character, but they are the product of value judgments that are the other component.

But Badhwar suggests that not everyone's value judgments are integrated with their emotions. There are some whose conscious convictions are at odds with their sense of life: she mentions Nazis who feel guilty about acting in accordance with their own ideology. Badhwar raises this to question Rand's argument that, in any conflict between reason and emotion, one should always side with reason against emotion. It's important that, for Rand, conflicts between sense of life and conscious convictions are *not* to be understood as conflicts between emotion and reason. For Rand, reason and emotion are not two independent faculties that issue their own independent, competing content, which is the view Badhwar would have to rely on to characterize the split in the soul of the person whose conscious convictions are at odds with his sense of life.

Rather, for Rand there is just one faculty, the rational mind. Following the guidance of reason means actively operating it, while following the "guidance" of emotions means letting the integrating mechanism of one's mind operate passively (or actively subverting it). The idea that there is a literal conflict of reason and emotion is denied by Nathaniel Branden in an essay Rand edited and approved: "Reason and emotion are not antagonists; what may seem like a struggle between them is only a struggle between two opposing ideas, one of which is not conscious and manifests itself only in the form of a feeling" ("Emotions and Values," *TO* 72).[10] Sense of life is itself a complex of judgments and resulting emotions,

---

of life (and character) tends to fall in love with people of a certain sort and responds favorably to a certain sort of art; a person of different sense of life (and character) may not share these responses. And this can habituate certain actions. Certain types of actions feel right to people of a certain type of character, which makes those actions more pleasant to choose, more painful not to choose (which doesn't mean that habituated actions aren't chosen).

Some of what Rand means by sense of life as an "emotional, subconsciously integrated appraisal," may be related to how she thinks sense of life is formed, which likely plays a role in the resulting emotional sum. She thinks one forms a sense of what is important in life through a process of "emotional abstraction" in which one "classifies things according to the emotions they evoke.... For instance: a new neighborhood, a discovery, adventure, struggle, triumph—or: the folks next door, a memorized recitation, a family picnic, a known routine, comfort.... For a man of self-esteem, the emotion uniting the things in the first part of these examples is admiration, exaltation, a sense of challenge: the emotion uniting the things in the second part is disgust or boredom" ("Philosophy and Sense of Life," RM 16).

10. Badhwar cites "The Objectivist Ethics" (VOS 37) in support of her claim that Rand thinks there are real conflicts between reason and emotion. Presumably she has this passage in mind:

while one's more explicit, conscious judgments have their own emotional products. A conflict between conscious convictions and sense of life is fundamentally a conflict between one's implicit and explicit judgments, which also results in a further conflict among one's emotional reactions. In such a case, there's not one set of emotional reactions that's central to a person's character: his emotional profile is characteristically fractious.[11] Rearden, for example, at times wonders at his lack of guilt for not wanting to please his family (as in the scene before his anniversary party) but, at other times, seems to feel intense guilt about his betrayal of Lillian while sleeping with Dagny.[12] The akratic or enkratic person's emotions are still central to his or her character, it's just that the essence of that character is conflict (a conflict between convictions and a corresponding conflict between emotions).

When a person's sense of life conflicts with his conscious convictions, it is possible that the sense of life is healthier and better connected

> If you achieve what is good by a rational standard of value, it will necessarily make you happy; but that which makes you happy, by some undefined emotional standard, is not necessarily the good. To take 'whatever makes one happy' as a guide to action means: to be guided by nothing but one's emotional whims. Emotions are not tools of cognition; to be guided by whims—by desires whose source, nature and meaning one does not know—is to turn oneself into a blind robot, operated by unknowable demons (by one's stale evasions), a robot knocking its stagnant brains out against the walls of reality which it refuses to see. (VOS 32)

Here Rand is certainly describing a conflict between being guided by reason and being guided by emotions. If there were no such conflict there would be no point to the virtue of rationality, which recommends siding with guidance by reason. But this is not the kind of conflict I mean to rule out. Rather, what Rand denies is that reason and emotions are separate faculties that issue their own independent content. Even in the passage Badhwar quotes it's clear that being guided by emotions really means being ruled by "stale evasions," which are (poor) choices about how to manage one's rational mind.

11. At one point in her essay "The Age of Envy" (*ROTP* 132), Rand says, "Since very few men have fully consistent characters, it is often hard to tell, in a specific instance, whether a given man is hated for his virtues or for his actual flaws." The fact that someone's character is inconsistent doesn't mean it's not a character.

12. From the party scene: "He had accepted the tenet that it was his duty to give his wife some form of existence unrelated to business. But he had never found the capacity to do it or even to experience a sense of guilt. He could neither force himself to change nor blame her if she chose to condemn him" (Atlas 123). And: "What was happening to him?—he wondered. The impossible conflict of feeling reluctance to do that which was right—wasn't it the basic formula of moral corruption? To recognize one's guilt, yet feel nothing but the coldest, most profound indifference—wasn't it a betrayal of that which had been the motor of his life-course and of his pride?" (126). But later, after he sleeps with Dagny for the first time, he says he feels contempt for Dagny and for himself, and that he loathes his desire for her. Dagny responds by saying, "I am much more depraved than you are: you hold it as your guilt, and I—as my pride" (239).

to reality. This, indeed, is Rearden's problem in *Atlas Shrugged*. He doesn't feel fundamental guilt about his lack of attention to his family, though he does feel guilt occasionally when he brings to bear his conviction that he owes them a duty. In Rand's view his belief in this duty is mistaken, and so his preconceptual judgments are more accurate. But this doesn't transform his sense of life or its associated emotions into tools of cognition. It remains true that his emotions are responses to his cognition, and in his case, none of his emotions will tell him which of his conflicting emotions or conflicting judgments are correct. He has to ask himself which of his conflicting judgments is actually true (that he owes a duty to his wife or that he has a right to be happy). In the scene when he confesses his contempt for himself and Dagny after sleeping with her, it's not true that he's going with his emotions over his reason. He's aware of a conflict between his convictions (and between the resulting emotions), and he's choosing one over the other. He simultaneously feels contempt for himself, loathes to name his desire, but also desperately wants Dagny. He makes his choice, saying he'll accept the consequences. One consequence is a lengthy process of self-discovery about whether his guilt is based on a valid judgment that he owes a duty to Lillian. Other apparent reason/emotion conflicts between Rand's characters can be understood along similar lines.[13]

The fact that there can be such conflicts between implicit and explicit convictions—and resulting conflicts of emotions—is part of the reason we need moral guidance. A conflict in our character is an impediment to acting morally. If we are of mixed emotions about a given action, we are not 100 percent motivated to do it. We can enkratically choose to do it, but this can be painful. So morality bids us to work to eliminate the conflict, so that we can free ourselves to act with unqualified motivation. In

---

13. For instance, Badhwar mentions Dagny's feeling that she still desires Francisco, even though she is convinced he is a worthless playboy. But Dagny's feeling here is based on other convictions: she is meeting him in his hotel room and he talks and acts like the same Francisco she has always known. While it's true that she doesn't regret this feeling, it's noteworthy she also doesn't act on it (say, by resuming her affair with Francisco). Like Rearden, she also faces a conflict between convictions, and she chooses one rather than the other and to accept the consequences (ongoing loneliness). Likewise, Badhwar mentions the scene between Dominique and Wynand, in which Dominique confesses feeling loyalty to Wynand which she doesn't understand. But here again, it doesn't contradict everything she knows. Notably, she knows Wynand has changed his behavior, largely under the influence of Roark. And like Rearden, in making this choice she is committing to a path of trying to understand her feelings (they lead her back to Roark).

Rand's view, the moral virtue that comes into play here is *pride*. One gloss on the virtue of pride can be found in "The Objectivist Ethics":

> The virtue of Pride can best be described by the term: "moral ambitiousness." It means that one must earn the right to hold oneself as one's own highest value by achieving one's own moral perfection—which one achieves by never accepting any code of irrational virtues impossible to practice and by never failing to practice the virtues one knows to be rational—by never accepting an unearned guilt and never earning any, or, if one has earned it, never leaving it uncorrected—by never resigning oneself passively to any flaws in one's character—by never placing any concern, wish, fear or mood of the moment above the reality of one's own self-esteem. And, above all, it means one's rejection of the role of a sacrificial animal, the rejection of any doctrine that preaches self-immolation as a moral virtue or duty. (VOS 29–30)

While there is a feeling of pride, the *virtue* of pride is not a feeling but, rather, like all the others a certain course of action aimed at the achievement of a value. Understanding what pride is in Rand's view helps underscore why she thought it was important to think of virtue as a kind of action. Pride for Rand is a kind of taking pride rather than simply feeling pride. The initial focus in the passage above describes this as "moral ambitiousness" or the pursuit of moral perfection. Importantly, acting according to the virtue of pride is not simply being moral all the time. This would not add much substance and would duplicate some of the territory already covered by the virtue of integrity. What's substantive is the way in which practicing pride allows one to pursue one's moral perfection: it involves rooting out false moral theories that lead to unearned guilt and to refusing to resign oneself to other character flaws.

An even richer gloss on pride, which brings out in greater detail the aspects of character it concerns itself with, is in the original passage from Galt's speech on the virtue:

> Pride is the recognition of the fact that you are your own highest value and, like all of man's values, it has to be earned—that of any achievements open to you, the one that makes all others possible is the creation of your own character—that your character, your actions, your desires, your emotions are the products of the premises held by your mind—that as man must produce the physical values he needs to sustain his life, so he must acquire the values of character that make his life worth sus-

taining—that as man is a being of self-made wealth, so he is a being of self-made soul—that to live requires a sense of self-value, but man, who has no automatic values, has no automatic sense of self-esteem and must earn it by shaping his soul in the image of his moral ideal, in the image of Man, the rational being he is born able to create, but must create by choice—that the first precondition of self-esteem is that radiant selfishness of soul which desires the best in all things, in values of matter and spirit, a soul that seeks above all else to achieve its own moral perfection, valuing nothing higher than itself—and that the proof of an achieved self-esteem is your soul's shudder of contempt and rebellion against the role of a sacrificial animal, against the vile impertinence of any creed that proposes to immolate the irreplaceable value which is your consciousness and the incomparable glory which is your existence to the blind evasions and the stagnant decay of others. (*Atlas* 1020–21)

Here, in particular, we get the idea that there are "values of *character* that [make] life worth sustaining" (emphasis mine). Because Galt goes on to describe "a sense of self-value" as both a requirement of life and self-esteem as a kind of reward that has to be earned, it's evident that self-esteem is one of the central values of character that the virtue of pride aims to achieve. What makes it a value of character is also described: it means cultivating a soul that values itself (a fundamental conviction) and desires moral perfection and issues a "shudder of contempt and rebellion against the role of a sacrificial animal" (an emotional disposition). To achieve these convictions and resulting emotions is not simply to have the capacity to do the right thing but, rather, to have the enduring dispositions to be motivated to do it, which makes the right thing easier to choose and the wrong thing harder to choose.

Pride is the virtue that encourages us to act so as to develop a character in which our enduring emotional dispositions motivate us to act virtuously and avoid vice. To practice the "moral ambitiousness" described in "The Objectivist Ethics" is to will the "selfishness of soul" of the person who introspects conflicts in his soul and is not content to live with them (*VOS* 29; *Atlas* 1020). This is a virtue that someone like Rearden desperately needs: mere enkratic action, choosing what happens to be a rational action in the face of guilt is not sustainable in the long term. Rearden needs to understand why his pursuit of happiness in business and in love is moral, and why he should not offer himself as a sacrificial animal to his wife, his family, his society. The fact that he chooses one side of his conflict with his eyes open—looking to learn more about why he's chosen it, especially with the assistance of Dagny and Francisco—is a sign that, in spite of whatever other errors he's making, he is indeed practicing the virtue of pride.

There are other aspects of character besides self-esteem that pride can help cultivate. As Onkar Ghate (2016, 10529) discusses in his essay "A Being of Self-Made Soul," sense-of-life and psycho-epistemology are two other major aspects of character that one's more basic choices redound upon. Whereas self-esteem is one's implicit evaluation of one's self (according to implicit ethical standards), sense of life is one's implicit metaphysics and psycho-epistemology is one's implicit epistemology. Each of these represent subconsciously integrated cognitive perspectives that result in emotional dispositions that habituate action. How do these perspectives and dispositions relate to values of character? In Objectivist philosophy, "self-esteem" is already defined in normative terms: it's the implicit perspective on the self that is valuable to have (the conviction that one is able to live and worthy of living). Sense of life and psycho-epistemology, by contrast, are defined in value-neutral terms: there can be positive and negative versions of both.[14] We should consider briefly how sense of life and psycho-epistemology, properly developed, can contribute to values of character such as self-esteem, but also to the other two cardinal moral values Rand mentions in conjunction with self-esteem—reason and purpose. A practitioner of the virtue of pride, being truly selfish about his soul, will actively seek to perfect it in all possible respects.

Consider sense of life, which we have already discussed as an implicit view that Rand sees as the essence of one's character. Whether one has the positive or the negative "metaphysical value judgments" on the previously quoted list from Rand, whether one has the conviction that the universe is open to value achievement or sees it as forever undercutting one's ability to pursue happiness, makes an enormous difference to self-esteem. However worthy of happiness one regards oneself, if one thinks the universe is a malevolent barrier to achievement, one cannot see oneself as efficacious in it. The only happiness available is the "happiness" of the Stoic, a detachment from things in the world and an absence of pain.

14. There are negative perspectives on the self as well—"pseudo-self-esteem," for example—that a broader, neutral concept of "self-perspective" would cover.

As with all subconsciously integrated perspectives, sense of life is not something one can control directly, and so one can't judge as good or evil the mere fact that one has a sense-of-life reaction. But the art one chooses to consume and the people one chooses relationships with (the two major expressions of sense of life) can make a difference in one's life, for better or worse. This is especially clear with regard to love: the right husband or wife can be an abundant source of happiness; the wrong one can kill you. Someone practicing the virtue of pride who recognizes that he or she has a sense of life that draws him or her to destructive people realizes this is something to be aware of—and (when possible) something to try to change for the better, through cognitive therapy, through deliberate changes to one's practices in dating and in the consumption of art, and so forth. None of this is simple or easy or likely to have immediate effects, but someone who strives to desire the best in all things will strive for what positive changes they can. Some sorts of sense of life are simply better to have than others, and they want the better ones. But to achieve a positive sense of life, one needs a moral principle recommending that one actively practice the kind of soul cultivation that pride involves.

The development of a proper psycho-epistemology influences one's achievement of other values of character. To use Leonard Peikoff's characterization, the term "psycho-epistemology" refers to man's "method of awareness, i.e., the method by which his mind *habitually* deals with its content" (my emphasis).[15] In Rand's view, there are, for instance, cognitively healthy and unhealthy ways of dealing with the relationship between abstractions and concretes, ways that strengthen or weaken one's grip on reality and hence strengthen or weaken one's confidence in the power of one's reason to serve as a tool for solving real problems, controlling nature, and improving one's life. Hence one's psycho-epistemology influences one's self-esteem: someone with a thoroughly stunted method can't think of oneself as thoroughly capable of living, even while regarding oneself as worthy. The character value most obviously at stake in the

---

15. Editor's footnote in "The Missing Link"(PWNI 293). Two prominent examples of deficient psycho-epistemology in the Objectivist literature are rationalism and empiricism. A rationalistic psycho-epistemology is a feeling of being at home in a world of abstractions detached from concrete reality, a preference for deducing conclusions from definitions rather than inducing one's knowledge from firsthand observations. Others have an empiricist psycho-epistemology that is averse to abstraction and to the generalization of principles, a preference for concrete data and approaching particular problems without relation to other problems.

health of one's psycho-epistemology is the cardinal value of reason.[16] Whether one achieves an enduring value of character, a well-developed faculty of reason that one is motivated to use, depends on a great many factors including, for instance, one's psycho-epistemology. As the history of philosophy bears witness, many important thinkers who verbally affirm the value of "reason" slip into mysticism or subjectivism.

As with self-esteem and sense of life, one's psycho-epistemology is not directly under one's control, and psycho-epistemological reactions are not evaluable as right or wrong. But here again, one who knows the crucial value of cognitive methodology to value achievement will seek to exercise psycho-epistemological pride and work to improve one's methodology. Striving to improve one's methodology requires a sophisticated philosophical perspective on the nature of knowledge. Objectivist philosophers have had a great deal to say about what it takes to do this, but Aristotle and Bacon among other practical logicians were striving to do the same. In striving to improve one's characteristic style of thinking, one is practicing a distinctively cognitive form of the virtue of pride.

The practice of psycho-epistemological pride is also relevant to achieving the cardinal character value of purpose. Achieving this value is not simply pursuing discrete goals. It's to have successfully put oneself on the premise of organizing one's life around a central purpose (typically a productive career). This means having become habituated to looking for ways to build a life out of the dizzying array of values it's possible to achieve, of seeking to make them mutually reinforcing, of working to constitute a life that is truly a self-sustaining process of activity. To have the value of purpose is to characteristically ask "What for?" as Francisco does, in the effort to understand how any of the concrete tasks and activities one might pursue could form a unity. At the same time, one's implicit views of one's self and the universe all play a role in whether one achieves this cardinal value.

I don't think there's any disconnect between Rand's nonfictional moral theory and the moral perspective found in her fiction. She surely shows that fully virtuous people such as Roark and Galt are ones whose characters motivate their virtuous action without significant internal

---

16. This value is not a simple recapitulation of the virtue of rationality. Rationality is the virtue of accepting reason as "one's only source of knowledge, one's only judge of values and one's only guide to action" ("Objectivist Ethics," VOS 28). In essence, to exercise this virtue means to choose to think. This does mean aiming to hold reason as a value. But to hold it as a value is not simply to politely affirm that reason is one's only means of knowledge.

conflict. Their conflicts are mostly with others who are not fully virtuous (and not just the villains). But when her positive characters like Dominique or Rearden are beset by internal conflicts, they are portrayed as acting virtuously (albeit often enkratically, *and often while making many mistakes about what virtue requires*), and some of their actions are aimed at eliminating these conflicts and acquiring a fully virtuous character.[17] In doing this, they are portrayed as taking pride in their character. But here again, it's important that there be basic moral principles denoting the actions needed for them to pursue these values of character.

The Unity of the Virtues

I believe Badhwar is correct that there is a clear statement of a form of the unity of the virtues in this passage from Galt's speech:

> My morality, the morality of reason, is contained in a single axiom: existence exists—and in a single choice: to live. The rest proceeds from these. To live, man must hold three things as the supreme and ruling values of his life: Reason—Purpose—Self-esteem. Reason, as his only tool of knowledge—Purpose, as his choice of the happiness which that tool must proceed to achieve—Self-esteem, as his inviolate certainty that his mind is competent to think and his person is worthy of happiness, which means: is worthy of living. *These three values imply and require all of man's virtues*, and all his virtues pertain to the relation of existence and consciousness: rationality, independence, integrity, honesty, justice, productiveness, pride. (*Atlas* 1018, emphasis mine)

But what does this view of the "unity of the virtues" actually mean? To get a grip on what Rand must mean, it's useful to discuss the question Badhwar raises about whether Rand thinks it's possible to be virtuous in some areas of one's life and not in others—that is, to be compartmentalized. I think it's fairly obvious that the answer is yes, and many of the examples

---

17. Rearden, for example, is torn about the virtue of his work in business and his sex life. His continuing conversations with Francisco represent his attempt to resolve this conflict and form a clear view of his work and therefore of his character. Rearden and Dagny are also both conflicted about the motives of others who stand in the way of their happiness. Judging them to be innocently mistaken leads them to pour time and resources into projects (such as the John Galt line) that they think can prove their opponent wrong; if their opponents are actually malicious, no persuasion is possible and these efforts are futile, leading to conflict over whether their ideals are achievable or unachievable. Both again are constantly making observations, asking questions, and making connections to reevaluate their initial judgment of "innocent," and their judgment of "guilty" leads them to go on strike, resolving the major conflict of the novel. I elaborate on these examples in Bayer 2022.

from Rand's fiction that Badhwar points to are relevant in seeing the reason. Yet Badhwar thinks this is in tension with certain things Rand says about the nature of rationality, that (as Badhwar puts it) it "must be all or nothing—that is, global." She cites, in particular, this passage from Galt's speech: "Whenever you committed the evil of refusing to think and to see, of exempting from the absolute of reality some one small wish of yours, whenever you chose to say: Let me withdraw from the judgment of reason the cookies I stole, or the existence of God, let me have my one irrational whim and I will be a man of reason about all else—that was the act of subverting your consciousness, the act of corrupting your mind" (*Atlas* 1037).

If, however, we recall that Rand's view is that virtues are actions, and rationality is one such virtuous mental action, whatever is "all or nothing" about this is "all or nothing" about particular actions, and I think this is pretty clear from the passage. Rand is saying *of the cases* one engages in the action of evasion, in those cases one is thereby acting to subvert one's consciousness.

Badhwar also references a point from Peikoff about how evasion cannot be localized because "everything in reality is interconnected" (Peikoff 1991, 224). But Peikoff's point here is that, to sustain an evasion, one would need to keep suppressing more and more evidence until one had "total nonperception" (225). He goes on to clarify that this line of thinking is a "pedagogical device," one which I take is to illustrate what's wrong with evasion (225). It's to answer someone who might ask, what would be wrong with evading just this one issue (e.g., the question of God's existence)? It's pedagogical because in reality, evaders are "not concerned with consistency" (225): they don't set for themselves explicit policies about when they'll permit themselves to evade, and they can't if they're to evade anything at all. They are able to evade what they evade and go on living because they don't identify the implications of their denial of some fact—that's part of what's being evaded. As a result, in reality they don't have to suppress awareness of the further facts that are inconsistent with the facts they know on some level they're evading. So they really do "localize" their evasion, just not as a matter of policy.

All of this is further to the point that what's "all or nothing" about rationality versus evasion is a fact about particular actions. Someone can evade in one moment and face the facts in another moment. That's part of what makes this an issue of choice. It's not the case that turning one's mind on in any given moment deterministically guarantees full awareness for the rest of one's life—or vice-versa. It was never part of Rand's idea that what gives the virtues some kind of unity was that by becoming virtuous in one moment of one's life one thereby becomes virtuous in every other moment. It is also not her view that being virtuous in any given moment leads one to correct the errors that would eliminate conflicts in one's convictions or emotions. Even someone who is rational across a great span of time does not necessarily eliminate these conflicts. But the absence of these conflicts and even the possession of virtues as more global character traits is not what the unity of virtue is about, for Rand.

It's worth revisiting the two statements Badhwar quotes to suggest that Rand maintains some kind of "unity of the virtues." First: "These three values [Reason, Purpose, and Self-Esteem] imply and require all of man's virtues, and all his virtues pertain to the relation of existence and consciousness." Second: "Rationality is man's basic virtue, the source of all his other virtues." I've now clarified why I think, in Rand's view, rationality is "all or nothing" with respect to particular actions. Earlier, I stressed her reasons for thinking that virtues are primarily actions, and only derivatively conceived of as states of character. All of this points to the idea that what's unified about the virtues is their causal character as actions.

To be rational means primarily to choose to think, to commit to knowing reality. But the fact that the virtue of rationality concerns a basic choice of mental action doesn't mean (as Badhwar suggests at one point) that virtue, in Rand's view, is "entirely cognitive or intellectual." In Rand's view, there is an underlying connection between the choice to think and the choice to live. At root they are the same, because both entail the choice to embrace reality. The choice to face reality entails recognizing the need to act in it. That's why, in Galt's speech, each of the derivative virtues involves the recognition of a basic fact about what human life requires. Independence recognizes "that yours is the responsibility of judgment and nothing can help you escape it." Integrity recognizes "that you cannot fake your consciousness." Honesty recognizes that "the unreal is unreal and can have no value." Justice recognizes that "you cannot fake the character of men." Productiveness recognizes that "you choose to live—that productive work is the process by which man's consciousness controls his existence, a constant process of acquiring knowledge and shaping matter to fit one's purpose." And pride recognizes that "you are your own highest value and, like all of man's values, it has to be earned—that of any achievements open to you, the one that makes all others possible is the creation of your own character" (*Atlas* 1019–20).

This is why rationality is thought of as the source of all the other virtues, each of which involves obvious commitments to act. This is most obvious with the virtue of productiveness, which Badhwar herself discusses: knowledge, to be valuable to human life, needs to be applied to create something in the physical world.[18] But it's true for all the others as well. Independence manifests itself not just in independence of thought but in one's relations with other people, in the commitment to exist by one's own means as a trader, not as a moocher. Integrity means not just having rational principles but having the commitment to act on them. Honesty means not just intellectual honesty but an unwillingness to fake reality in one's pursuit of values. Justice means not just objectively valuing the character of others but acting on that judgment by rewarding people of virtue and withdrawing sanction from and/or punishing those of vice. And pride means taking all of the actions necessary to perfect one's character so as to habituate virtuous actions in all the various ways we've now discussed.

The fact that all of the virtues are forms of rationality in action is the basic sense in which they form a unity. Badhwar herself does a fine job illustrating this for the virtue of productiveness, how it requires independence of mind, integrity, honesty, justice, and pride. To be rational in action causally requires productiveness, which requires all of these other virtues.[19] And the causality here is simultaneous: it's the nature of an action of one type to be an action of the other.

18. This doesn't mean it has to be written down or applied to some enduring concrete product; even speakers and performers are creating physical values through the medium of their voice, especially if they're being paid for it.

19. Interestingly, at one point Badhwar suggests that the first passage illustrating Rand's view of the unity of the virtues uses a different framework from the one Rand used later in "The Objectivist Ethics": "Value is that which one acts to gain and/or keep—virtue is the act by which one gains and/or keeps it. The three cardinal values of the Objectivist ethics—the three values which, together, are the means to and the realization of one's ultimate value, one's own life—are: Reason, Purpose, Self-Esteem, with their three corresponding virtues: Rationality, Productiveness, Pride" (VOS 31). I take it that Rand sees these as different frameworks because whereas in the latter passage, rationality is specifically paired with reason, productiveness with purpose, and pride with self-esteem, in the earlier passage the cardinal values are portrayed as requiring all of man's virtues. If we come to terms with what Rand actually means by the unity of virtues, there is no tension here. But if the virtues form a unity, the frameworks aren't really that different. Rationality, productiveness, and pride may all be especially salient with respect to the three cardinal values, but since all virtues are forms of rationality, all pertaining to seeking the right relationship between existence and consciousness, these three are only the most evident aspects of rationality needed to achieve the central values of character. All the rest matter as well.

To illustrate the point that the unity of the virtues is a point about the causal requirements of action, it's worth thinking about an example of someone who acts with virtue in some instances but not in others. Here Wynand is a good example. Arguably when he is fighting to save Roark from the mob he is engaging himself in fully virtuous action. And insofar as he is doing this, he is at this time drawing on all the virtues. He is rationally facing the fact that Roark, a great value of his, is under attack and is in need of defense. With great independence he is fighting against the overwhelming opinion of society and all of his usual allies and sponsors. He is not just contemplating an ideal in his art gallery but, with great integrity, acting to defend this ideal in reality. He is drawing on all of his productive virtues to keep his paper in business. His act is of course a supreme act of justice in defense of Roark. And above all it is an act of pride, an attempt to save his own character from the hideously malevolent sense of life that has been the leitmotif of his life ever since he wrote the editorial betraying the framed cop Pat Mulligan. But when Wynand betrays Roark and turns the paper against him, it is not through some innocent mistake of fact but through a willful act of self-destruction. When he does this, he stops acting virtuously in every respect and returns to vice. The character of Wynand changes, in various ways back and forth throughout the novel. But all of his virtues are unified at those times and to the extent that he is acting with virtue.

Which Action Types Rise to the Level of Virtue

Many of the considerations explored above are relevant to understanding why Rand identifies the virtues she does. The reason Rand identifies virtues as actions is because of the central role of choice in her moral philosophy. Ethics is a code of values for guiding choices, and it's only actions that are directly chosen. This has direct implications for understanding why kindness or generosity are not virtues in her view. As Badhwar understands it, kindness is "the intellectual-emotional-action disposition to help or comfort others for the right reason, in the right manner, at the right time, and to the right extent." Generosity is "the disposition to give gratuitously, with pleasure, from a desire to share one's abundance with another for the right reason, at the right time, in the right manner, to the right extent." But these complex dispositional traits are character traits, like sense of life or a healthy psycho-epistemology, and as such they cannot be directly willed.

Of course, one could reconceive kindness or generosity as action types as well. Why then does Rand not consider these to be virtues, or for that matter people who habitually engage in these action types to possess a moral virtue? It's important that in holding this, one isn't saying that the actions in question are vices. Giving gratuitously may be a good thing to do in certain circumstances—at the right time, in the right way, for the right reason, and so on.[20] But the need to add this Aristotelian qualification on when the action is appropriate is itself a reason this would not qualify as a virtue in Rand's sense. As I hope has become clear by now after the discussion of the unity of the virtues, what gives the virtues unity is that they are all perspectives on the virtue of rationality. And rationality is not something we engage in at the right time, in the right way, for the right reasons. Rationality is something we must always engage in if we choose to live—and to do it is to give the right reasons for everything else we do.[21]

The same is true for the derivative virtues. The virtues are the most universal principles of rational human action, the forms of recognizing basic philosophical facts about the requirements of human life that are applicable to everyone. Each virtue deals with a basic issue about the relationship between consciousness and existence. Independence says consciousness of existence is your responsibility. Integrity says you cannot fake your consciousness. Honesty says you cannot fake existence. Productiveness says you have to reshape existence in the shape of the ideals you project with your consciousness. Justice says you cannot fake the consciousness of others. Pride says you have to create the character of your own consciousness, and so forth. It's not at all obvious how kindness or generosity, even if conceived of as actions, are to be understood as the expression of a basic choice about the relationship between consciousness and existence. Kindness and generosity are of much too narrow a concern to be that. To think of them as virtues, we could just as easily think of eating as a virtue. Indeed, eating is more important to our lives than kindness. And yet it is something we have to do at the right time, in the right

---

20. I appreciate that kindness and generosity understood as character traits are not virtues that apply only at certain times, in certain ways, and so forth. Rather, the idea is that to have the virtue is to have an enduring character trait, which consists in the disposition to act in a certain way at certain times, but not at others. I am focusing here only on the proposal to identify those very actions with virtues as action types.

21. That's true even though these virtues obviously have contextual applications. Being productive doesn't require working for twenty-four hours seven days a week, and being honest doesn't require telling the truth to the murderer at the door. But that's because neither of these virtues as actions is identified with actions as concrete as work or as truth-telling.

way, for the right reasons. The need to qualify it like this is a sign that it's not a basic virtue. Virtues would multiply endlessly if they were subject to such qualified codifications. We'd no longer have a moral code but a moral laundry (or lunch) list.

None of the above is to suggest that individual acts of kindness or generosity can't be seen as virtuous. As Badhwar points out, in "Ethics of Emergencies" Rand argues that kindness and generosity *toward people we love* are expressions of the virtue of integrity: in this case they represent loyalty to our values, which is a type of action that is universally required to achieve values of character. Badhwar argues: "the fact that kindness and generosity are required by love and integrity doesn't imply that they are not really kindness and generosity." That's true, but it may explain why they are not equivalent with virtues of their own: appropriate acts of kindness or generosity may be virtuous not because kindness and generosity as such are virtues but because they are cases of integrity and integrity is a virtue. Even charity toward strangers could be virtuous in cases, for the sorts of reasons Badhwar stresses, without identifying charity as such as a virtue. In the specific circumstances when people are in trouble through no fault of their own, and when one can afford to help them, it is virtuous to help them because to do so expresses the kind of species solidarity that leads to a generalized goodwill. But the most salient virtue here is pride: the commitment to act in a way that cultivates positive character traits. Goodwill is preeminently the expression of a benevolent, positive sense of life.

It's noteworthy that it's not simply other-regarding virtues such as generosity and charity that are discounted as virtues by Rand's approach to the virtues. Classical virtues with a more self-regarding orientation such as courage, temperance, and wisdom all fail to make the cut as well. What's doing the work here is not her egoism per se, it's her identification of virtues as the most universal principles of rational action that involve recognitions of basic facts about the requirements of human survival in terms of the proper relationship between existence and consciousness.

Given that Rand acknowledged such a debt to Aristotle, it is worth reflecting on the reason she did not understand virtues primarily as character traits, but instead identified them as actions. I think there are two basic reasons. The first is that choice plays a central role in Rand's ethics in a way it could not for Aristotle. It's true that Aristotle thinks that the virtues are states of character that "are decisions of some kind, or [rather] require decision" (1106a3–5). But because of this "or" it's not clear that he regards them as directly chosen themselves (or that he has a view about what is directly chosen), and Aristotle does not seem to be as interested in offering ethical principles as a form of guiding choices as Rand is. In his view, the most relevant guidance we receive is in our upbringing, which gives us a character that is then either virtuous or not, and not much is said in his ethical works about what that upbringing is to consist in.

It's my view that this underemphasis on choice and on ethics as for guiding choices is a relic of the fact that free will versus determinism was not even on the philosophical radar screen in Western philosophy until after the Stoics. It's no wonder that modern philosophy, especially after Kant (for whom ethics as an expression of freedom is a central concern) is then so concerned with the evaluation of actions. In this respect modern philosophy is correct to be concerned with the evaluation of actions. But obviously, numerous additional errors (especially with regard to their understanding of what free will is) lead modern philosophers to detach their understanding of right action from that of morally worthy character, which is as regrettable as their other failures to understand right action.

The second reason I believe Rand identifies virtues as actions, unlike Aristotle, is because she is on the premise that ethics is a science. Aristotle famously thinks ethics is inexact, and we see this in his formulations of the virtues as involving vague dispositions to act at the right time, in the right way, for the right reasons, and so forth, as some kind of intermediate between different vices. Rand, by contrast, is aiming to formulate universal moral principles that identify the basic causal requirements of human life. She is arguably in the position to do this in a way Aristotle was not, having witnessed the practical power of theoretical reason in the wake of the industrial revolution. It's this power of reason that truly makes it the root of all virtues, including especially productiveness.

Morality, according to the first part of Ayn Rand's definition, is "a code of values to guide man's choices and actions" ("Objectivist Ethics," *VOS* 13). It's this part that speaks most directly to my argument for the reason virtues as major elements of this code have to denote actions: only actions can be chosen. But the second part of her definition speaks to the other major point I've argued in this paper. Morality is a code guiding choices and actions, but "the choices and actions that determine the purpose and the course of his life" (13). As I've argued, even though we are not in a position to make choices to change our character directly, the choices ethics helps guide us to make are still very much aimed at developing values of character such as reason, purpose, and self-esteem. It's insofar as our choices help develop these character values that they determine the course of our lives.

In this respect, the subject matter studied by ethics is very much the kind of life that's worth living, not the particular choices by which it's to be lived. It's this view of the subject matter of ethics that so much of modern ethics is missing out on, and that virtue ethics is rightly returning our focus to. Our aim is to live a certain kind of life, to be a certain kind of person. The principles that are to guide our chosen action need to reflect this overall purpose.

For the same reason, when Ayn Rand approached her task as an artist, she too aimed to project what it is to live the life of a certain kind of person: she described the goal of her writing as *"the projection of an ideal man"* ("The Goal of My Writing," *RM* 155). And to achieve this artistic goal, she thought she had to study ethics using a particular approach, one that identified value premises as fundamental to character:

> What kind of men do I want to see in real life—and why? What kind of events, that is, human actions, do I want to see taking place—and why? What kind of experience do I want to live through, that is, what are my goals—and why?
>
> It is obvious to what field of human knowledge all these questions belong: to the field of *ethics*. What is the good? What are the right actions for man to take? What are man's proper *values*?
>
> Since my purpose is the presentation of an ideal man, I had to define and present the conditions which make him possible and which his existence requires. Since man's character is the product of his premises, I had to define and present the kind of premises and values that create the character of an ideal man and motivate his actions; which means that I had to define and present a rational code of ethics. ("The Goal of My Writing," *RM* 156–57)

12
Reply to Ben Bayer
NEERA K. BADHWAR

Ben Bayer has gone to great lengths in commenting on my article. I will try to keep my reply short by concentrating on his main arguments.

Are Virtues Actions?

I make two objections to Rand's definition of virtues as actions that aim at certain values ("Objectivist Ethics").

(1) This definition is in tension with her portrayal of her heroes in her fiction, where their virtues are identified with their positive character traits. It also contradicts the definition she gives later in the same essay.

(2) The idea that virtues are actions reifies properties of actions and traits.

Ben Bayer argues that there is no tension between Rand's definition of virtue as an act of a certain kind and her identification of virtues with positive traits, because "virtues are the actions . . . that are needed for the achievement of . . . central values of character." But what are values of character? Are they virtues or something else? If they are something else, what are they? If they are virtues, then Bayer is saying that virtues are the actions needed for the achievement of central virtues of character. In other words, values of character are just character traits. But virtues understood as character traits are not actions, since actions and character traits are different things. What is true is that both actions and character traits can be *virtuous*—that is, have *the property of virtue*. But a property can't be identical with the thing it characterizes. Analogously, an act or an individual can be beautiful, but beauty is neither an act nor an individual.

Rand's definition of virtue as an act of a certain kind also contradicts her definition (in the very same essay) of virtue as a character trait of a certain kind. For example, she defines rationality as "a commitment to the fullest perception of reality within one's power and to the constant, active expansion of one's perception, i.e., of one's knowledge . . . a commitment to the principle that all of one's convictions, values, goals, desires and actions must be based on, derived from, chosen and validated by a process of thought" ("Objectivist Ethics," *VOS* 25–26). This implies that rationality is a character trait, not an act, because a commitment is something long-range, involving certain evaluative dispositions or tendencies, and certain patterns of action.

Ben answers that a commitment can be an act or a trait. However, although an act can express a commitment, it cannot be identical to a commitment. And again, if one defines virtue as an act of a certain sort, one cannot also define it as a trait of a certain sort, without implying that actions and traits are the same thing.

Bayer also states that, for Rand, thinking is our "only basic virtue, from which all the others proceed," and thinking is a mental action. But quoting another line in which Rand identifies virtue with an action doesn't dissolve the problem, it repeats it. Again, it makes perfect sense to say that thinking is the most basic virtuous action—but not that the most basic virtue is the act of thinking, or a type of behavior (Google's dictionary notwithstanding).

My second objection to Rand's definition of virtue as an act of a certain kind is that virtue is a property, and properties don't act. It's a metaphysical mistake to assert otherwise. Virtue is goodness or excellence, and goodness or excellence can be properties of actions as well as of character or motives. But they can't be actions. Consider another property: intelligence. It makes sense to say "That is an intelligent act" but not "Intelligence is an act of a certain kind."

Bayer does not try to show that my second objection is wrong, but instead gives several arguments to defend the claim that virtue is an act.

He argues that it's Rand's emphasis on choice, and the fact that we can choose only actions directly, that leads to her definition of virtue as a certain kind of action. However, these facts can be accommodated by highlighting the importance of virtuous actions without identifying virtues as acts. In any case, Rand is not the only philosopher to emphasize choice or hold that we can choose only actions directly. Most philosophers, including Aristotle and Kant, hold the same view, as does common sense.

Another argument Bayer gives is that, because we need ethics to guide our choices, virtue "should then pertain most obviously to the actions we directly choose." This doesn't follow. Moreover, if by "ethics" Ben means "ethical theory," then he is wrong about the best guide to choice. For the best guide is a virtuous character, not an ethical theory. The right ethical theory can help us examine our moral beliefs, correct the mistaken ones, and improve ourselves. But once we have a virtuous character, we don't need to keep referring to an ethical theory every time we want to do something. Rand's heroes, for example, don't think in terms of an ethical theory to make right choices. They think in terms of the right thing to do, the right principles, and it's their character that guides their thinking and decisions. So by Bayer's own argument, virtue should be defined in terms of character.

Bayer also argues that both actions and people can be good. True enough, but this is not relevant to our disagreement. What I deny is that the property of goodness (virtue) can itself be an action any more than the property of intelligence can be an action.

I find it puzzling that Bayer insists on defending virtue as an act because he agrees with me that virtue is goodness and that goodness is a property. Surely he doesn't think that properties act, except in children's books and myths and fantasies. You can personify properties, for example, by identifying the property of Evil with the Devil, or the property of Virtue with God. Then you can talk about Evil (Devil) or Virtue (God) acting. But unless you want to personify virtue or vice, it is a metaphysical error to assert that virtue or vice are acts.

Rationality Is Not a Moral Virtue

Leaving the act-trait issue aside, I argue that rationality, defined as a commitment to tracking reality, is not a moral virtue because a moral virtue entails a grasp of the important aspects of human life and one's own life, and the disposition—the standing motivation—to act in a way that expresses that grasp. But rationality does not entail such a grasp. A rational person may be systematically mistaken about many of his own needs or obligations or another's character or what morality requires and, thus, treat others unjustly and himself imprudently (think Hank Rearden or Andrei Taganov). In other words, an individual can *rationally* act unjustly or imprudently. This is why I argue that, unlike a moral virtue, rationality is not a success term. Rationality is an excellence of the mind—an epistemic and deliberative virtue—that is necessary for moral virtue. But it's not a moral virtue.

Bayer agrees that a rational person can be systematically mistaken in morally important ways, and that Rearden is an example of such a person. But he refuses to draw the conclusion that rationality is compatible with acting unjustly and imprudently.

Reason and Emotion

Rand's official position on the relation between reason and emotion is that "emotions are the automatic results of man's value judgments integrated by his subconscious.... Emotions are produced by man's premises, held consciously or subconsciously, explicitly or implicitly" ("Objectivist Ethics," VOS 27). So emotions don't get equal billing with the individual's rational commitments in Rand's conception of character.

In "Philosophy and Sense of Life," however, Rand argues that an individual's "sense of life" is his "emotional, subconsciously integrated appraisal of man and of existence . . . [that] sets the nature of a man's emotional responses and *the essence of his character*" ("Philosophy and Sense of Life," RM 14, emphasis added). A sense of life reflects a person's "deepest values" (RM 21). Surprisingly, these statements make a person's emotional, automatic responses to the world as central to his character and actions as his reason and conscious convictions, if not more so ("the essence of his character").

This view is in obvious tension with the view that the virtues are rational commitments to their corresponding values. Bayer tries to resolve this tension by arguing that a sense of life is "fundamentally a set of implicit *metaphysical value judgments*," and that it is these "subconsciously stored value judgments (which may themselves be rational or irrational)," and not their "emotional products," "that are essential to character."

But this will not do, because Rand identifies a person's sense of life with an "emotional, subconsciously integrated appraisal of man's relationship to existence" (RM 14) and makes it "the essence" of a person's character. She does not identify the essence of character with "implicit metaphysical value judgments" minus emotions (*RM* 25).

In a footnote, Bayer states that all he's denying is that reason and emotion are two separate faculties for Rand. According to Rand, our emotions depend entirely on our rational faculty, in particular, on our value judgments. I agree that this is Rand's view (and say so myself in my paper). But the view that our emotions depend on our rational faculty doesn't entail that emotion and reason are the same faculty. If they were, one could not be said to depend on the other, nor could they ever conflict. But they obviously do conflict, and Rand acknowledges that they do. Only in a perfectly virtuous individual are reason and emotion completely integrated, because a virtuous individual uses his mind (reason), and not his emotions, as his guide ("Playboy Interview").

The Unity of Virtue

Rand depicts many of her fictional characters as being virtuous in some areas of their lives and not others. So if there is a unity in their characters, it is not global, but restricted to some areas of their lives. Examples include Hank Rearden, Andrei Taganov, and Henry Cameron.

Rand's most important statement bearing on unity is her declaration that rationality is the basic virtue, "the source of all . . . [our] other virtues" (*VOS* 31). In other words, the virtue of rationality entails all the virtues. (Although I've argued that rationality is not a moral virtue, I'll ignore that in what follows.) If rationality has to be global, then rationality implies all the other virtues globally (i.e., in every domain of our lives). If, on the other hand, rationality can be domain specific, as illustrated by Rand's portrait of Cameron, then the other virtues can—indeed, must—also be domain specific.

Bayer argues, however, that rationality here should be understood as the rationality of particular actions. But a rational action can't be the *source* of all virtuous actions. It seems that what Bayer means is that, as I argue, a virtuous act, for example, an act of productivity, typically *exemplifies* many virtues. My reason for this claim is that situations are usually complex, calling on several virtues. Ben himself gives the excellent example of Gail Wynand fighting for Roark. Wynand's actions show integrity, justice, independence, productivity, and pride. However, I also argue that a virtuous action need not exemplify *all* the virtues. For example, if a situation that requires integrity has nothing to do with what we owe to others, or with issues of productivity, an act of integrity in that situation will not exemplify justice or productivity. So when Rand says that rationality is the source of all the virtues, she has to have character traits in mind, not particular actions.

I also give other evidence that Rand (sometimes) thinks that virtue is incompatible with vice in any domain, from which it follows that virtue is not only united (one virtue entails all) but also global (a virtue in any domain entails virtue in all domains).[1] For example, Rand discusses a businessman she knew who had great "initiative and ingenuity," but who was anticonceptual and thus "profoundly antimoral" (*PWNI* 53). For Rand, the vice of being anticonceptual infected his entire character such that he had no virtues in any domain of his life, in spite of the fact that he had great "initiative and ingenuity" as a businessman.

Bayer asserts that it was "never part of Rand's idea that what gives the virtues some kind of unity was that by becoming virtuous in one moment of one's life one thereby becomes virtuous in every other moment." True—this is not Rand's idea of the unity of virtue. Neither is it mine.

The Virtues of Benevolence

Rand's list of virtues is notable for what it contains as well as what it omits, viz., the virtues of benevolence, kindness and generosity. Yet kindness and generosity play an important role in her novels. Drawing on Aristotle's conception of the virtues, I define kindness as the intellectual-emotional-action disposition to respond to others' vulnerability for the right reason, in the right manner, at the right time, and to the right extent. In the same vein, I define generosity as the disposition to give gratuitously, with pleasure, from a desire to share one's abundance with another for the right reason, at the right time, in the right manner, to the right extent.

Bayer argues that it's because these traits have to be qualified with respect to reason, manner, time, and extent that Rand does not regard them as virtues. Rand's virtues, he says, do not need to be qualified. Rationality "is not something we engage in at the right time, in the right way, for the right reasons. Rationality is something we must always engage in if we choose to live—and to do it is to give the right reasons for everything else we do."

Bayer is right that we can and ought to act rationally all the time. But that is because rationality is a deliberative virtue, not a moral virtue. Since different circumstances call on different moral virtues, there is no

---

1. She could have held that virtue in one domain is compatible with *akrasia* and *enkrateia* in some other domain, but she never discusses these states.

moral virtue that we ought to act on all the time. For example, if you see someone fall down in front of you, unable to stand up by his own efforts, what is required of you is kindness, not honesty or justice. If you are in the grip of a dictator who has threatened to blow up the entire city unless you tell lies about his enemies, what is required of you is lies, not truthfulness. At such times, it is rationality in the sense of phronesis itself that tells you to obey the dictator. So kindness and generosity are not the only virtues that are not appropriate to act on all the time.

At the same time, although we ought to act rationally all the time, what rationality requires depends on the context. Rand's definition of rationality as "a commitment to the fullest perception of reality within one's power and to the constant, active expansion of . . . one's knowledge" (*VOS* 25) does not tell us which slice or aspect of reality we should focus on in any given situation. Reality is complex, and we can't possibly focus on all of it. In normal circumstances, it may be rational to analyze and write about Rand's definition of rationality. But if my toddler is screaming for help in the other room, the same action is irrational. Rand emphasized the importance of always being mindful of the context in all our activities. In the context I've just described, the rational thing to do is to tend to my toddler and figure out how best to comfort him. So it turns out that rationality must be a commitment to the fullest perception of the right things, at the right time, in the right way.

Bayer himself acknowledges in a footnote that the virtues "obviously have contextual applications. Being productive doesn't require working twenty-four hours seven days a week, and being honest doesn't require telling the truth to the murderer at the door." Exactly.

This is why it is necessary to state, for example, that honesty is being truthful about the right things, for the right reason, at the right time, and so on. Rand's own definition of honesty in *Atlas Shrugged* (1019) as a refusal to fake existence doesn't really tell us very much about what honesty amounts to as a character trait or what actions it requires. If we didn't already know that honesty is about being truthful, we could infer from Rand's statement that it's dishonest to paint a tree, because a painted tree fakes existence. Rand shows what honesty requires in various situations in the characters of her heroes, who are truthful with others about the right things, for the right reasons, at the right time, and so on, as well as truthful with themselves.

Again, Rand's definition of productive work as "the process by which man's consciousness controls his existence, a constant process of acquiring knowledge and shaping matter to fit one's purpose, of translating an idea into physical form, of remaking the earth in the image of one's values" (*Atlas* 1020) doesn't tell us that the matter we shape must belong to us and not others, or that what we produce must be objectively valuable rather than harmful, or that "a constant process of acquiring knowledge" doesn't imply that being productive means we may never sleep. Adding that productive work consists of shaping matter to fit one's purpose for the right reason, in the right way, at the right time, and so on, brings us closer to understanding the nature of this virtue. And observing Rand's heroes being productive shows us what these contextual requirements amount to. Of course, reading *Atlas Shrugged* or Rand's other novels is neither necessary nor sufficient for discovering what these contextual requirements amount to for any of the virtues. What is necessary is practical wisdom, for which we need life experience.

The upshot of this discussion is that all the virtues, and not only kindness and generosity, require us to keep the context of our actions in mind.

Another reason to acknowledge that kindness and generosity are virtues is that, as I argue at length in my paper, Rand's heroes possess them and her villains lack them. If you try to imagine any of her heroes without these virtues, you will find them unheroic and unattractive. Further, without these virtues a person cannot have justice or honesty either, because all the other-regarding virtues are based on the recognition that people are both agents and patients. As agents, they are autonomous beings with a right to live their lives as they wish, so long as they respect the rights of others. As patients, they are often in need of others' help or friendship. It is this recognition of individuals as both autonomous and vulnerable that is the shared foundation of all the other-regarding virtues: justice and honesty, as well as kindness and generosity.

Bayer rightly points out that, according to Rand, all the virtues "pertain to the relation of existence and consciousness: rationality, independence, integrity, honesty, justice, productiveness, pride" (*Atlas* 1018). But, he argues, it's "not at all obvious how kindness or generosity, even if conceived of as actions, are to be understood as the expression of a basic choice about the relationship between consciousness and existence." I think it's easy to see how.

Kindness is a response to an important aspect of human existence: our need for help and love, and our recognition of this need. Generosity expresses our love, friendship, or appreciation of others. Children would not survive to adulthood without kindness and generosity, and many of us would die miserable deaths in our old age without the kindness and generosity of family members or other caretakers.

Finally, in response to my claim that kindness and generosity may be required by integrity but can't thereby be reduced to integrity, Bayer asserts in effect that they can: "appropriate acts of kindness or generosity may be virtuous not because kindness and generosity as such are virtues but because they are cases of integrity and integrity is a virtue." By this argument, however, honesty and justice are also not virtues, because they too can be seen as cases of integrity. Arguably, *all* the virtues can be seen as cases of integrity, thereby leaving integrity as the sole virtue. Bayer is right to raise the issue of how to limit the number of virtues instead of letting them multiply beyond necessity.[2] The opposite problem I have just raised is the problem of how not to reduce all the virtues to one.

Other classical virtues missing from Rand's list, such as courage and temperance, are also responses to universal facts of human life. And practical wisdom (*phronesis*), the Aristotelian virtue that entails all the other virtues, is simply what Rand sometimes takes rationality to be: a grasp of the truth about important matters of human existence and one's own existence, and the intellectual-emotional disposition to act accordingly.

---

2. For discussion of this issue, see Russell 2009 and Swanton 2003.

Section V
SPIRITUAL VALUES
Art and Love

13
Ayn Rand's Aristotelian Literary Aesthetics
ROBERT MAYHEW

In *The Fountainhead* (1943), Howard Roark tells Steven Mallory: "I think you're the best sculptor we've got. I think it, because your figures are not what men are, but what men could be—and should be. Because you've gone beyond the probable and made us see what is possible" (329). In "The Goal of My Writing," Ayn Rand says of the passage from which this quote comes: "I was consciously and deliberately stating the essential goal of my own work—as a kind of small, personal manifesto" (*RM* 161), and a few paragraphs later, she says of Roark's words to Mallory: "This line will make it clear whose great philosophical principle I had accepted and was following and had been groping for, long before I heard the name 'Aristotle.' It was Aristotle who said that fiction is of greater philosophical importance than history, because history represents things only as they are, while fiction represents them 'as they *might be* and *ought to be*'" (*RM* 161–62). She refers to this "might be and ought to be" principle at least seven other times.[1] When did she learn that this was, as she puts it, a "great philosophical principle" of Aristotle's? In her 1945 letter "To the Readers of *The Fountainhead*," she explains her motive in becoming a novelist, and then she adds: "Later I discovered I had accepted as the

---

1. See "Basic Principles of Literature" (*RM* 71), "What Is Romanticism?" (*RM* 106), "Bootleg Romanticism" (*RM* 125), "Ninety-Three" (*Column* 56), *AOF* 114, and *Answers* 181.

rule of my life work a principle stated by Aristotle. Aristotle said that fiction is of greater philosophical importance than history, because history represents things only as they are, while fiction represents them 'as they might be and ought to be.' If you wish a key to the literary method of *The Fountainhead*, this is it" (*Letters* 669–70). An early draft of this letter indicates she made this discovery about a year earlier (i.e., late 1943 or early 1944), and thus before she began her systematic reading of Aristotle (probably in 1945).[2]

Instead, I think it certain that she encountered this principle indirectly, in Albert Jay Nock's *Memoirs of a Superfluous Man*, which was published the same year as *The Fountainhead*. Nock writes: "History, Aristotle says, represents things only as they are, while fiction represents them as they might be and ought to be; and therefore of the two, he adds, 'fiction is the more philosophical and the more highly serious'" (Nock 1943, 191).[3] In her copy of Nock's book, Rand underlined this passage and drew six perpendicular lines beside it in the margins, indicating supreme approval.[4]

So Rand saw her aesthetics as Aristotelian, at least with respect to one important principle (which she had accepted early and independently of reading Aristotle's *Poetics*). Any discussion of the Aristotelian nature of her aesthetics should cover this "might be and ought to be" principle. But as is clear from other chapters in this collection, she saw Aristotle as crucially important—and herself as Aristotelian—not (primarily) because of his aesthetics but for more fundamental philosophical reasons and especially for "the fact that he defined the *basic* principles of a rational view of existence and of man's consciousness" (*FTNI* 22).[5] So I think it is fitting to

---

2. The early draft is in *Papers* 092_08x_003_002. My thanks to Shoshana Milgram for bringing it to my attention. For when Ayn Rand began her reading of Aristotle, see her letter to Isabel Paterson (July 26, 1945): "I'm reading Aristotle in person" (*Letters* 179); letter to Hal Wallis (June 18, 1945): "You might like to know what was the first thing I did on regaining my freedom [i.e. temporarily stopping her work for Wallis as a screenwriter]: I went out and bought five dresses by Adrian and the complete works of Aristotle" (*Letters* 227). This last is actually McKeon 1941, which is not Aristotle's complete works, though it does include the complete *Poetics* (in the Bywater translation). Rand's copy is very lightly annotated but contains no marginalia in the *Poetics*. It is not known when or even if she ever read the *Poetics*.

3. In a footnote, Nock adds: "I hope I have not made too free with Aristotle's *noia genoito, ha*, but I think the implication is certainly there" (Nock 1943, 191n2). This mangles the Greek, *hoia an genoito* (*Poet.* 9, 1451b5), which Nock renders "things as they might be and ought to be." See also *Poetics* 17, 1455a34–b23.

4. I am grateful to the staff of the Ayn Rand Archives for sending me, back in 2005, a photocopy of the relevant page.

5. She goes on to explain what she means by this. For more on Rand's understanding

begin by comparing Aristotle and Rand on the rational nature of art (and specifically literature) and then proceed to related topics.

Literature as Rational

Prior to Aristotle, poetry (*poiēsis*, i.e., literary creation) was not generally considered a product of human reason.[6] Note the openings of the major works of Homer: "Sing, goddess, the anger of Achilles" (*Iliad*) and "Tell me, Muse, of the man of many ways" (*Odyssey*). Hesiod's *Theogony* and *Works and Days* begin with similar appeals to the Muses. Plato held a similar view: Poets create as a result of inspiration and mania, not reason (and therein lies poetry's danger). They do not know their subject matter; if a work of art is great, that is owing to divine inspiration. In the *Ion*, Plato has the character Socrates say: "all the good epic poets speak all those beautiful poems not from technical expertise (*ek technēs*), but through being divinely inspired and possessed (*entheoi ontes kai katechomenoi*), and likewise the good lyric poets" (533e).[7]

Aristotle's *Poetics* is in part a response to Plato.[8] Aristotle holds that poetry is a product of reason. The rational part of the soul, in his view, can be divided into two parts: the one that reflects on what cannot be otherwise—celestial objects, for example—and the one that reflects on what can be otherwise (see *EN* VI.1). What can be otherwise is the domain of action (*praxis*) and production (*poiēsis*) (*EN* VI.4 1140a1–6). The intellectual virtue in the realm of production is technical expertise (*technē*, see *EN* VI.4): "Every technical expertise is concerned with coming to be (*genesin*), and practicing the expertise and contemplating how something might come to be that is capable either of being or of not being, and the origin (*archē*) of which is in the producer and not in the thing produced.... Technical expertise is ... a state involving true reason concerned with production (*hexis tis meta logou alēthous poiētikē*)" (*EN* VI.4 1140a10–14, 20–21).

---

and evaluation of Aristotle's "view of existence and of man's consciousness" (*FTNI* 22), see the first five chapters in the present volume.

6. I often follow tradition and translate the Greek *poiēsis* and cognates with "poetry," "poet," and "poem," and so on, though I think "literary creation," "fiction writer," "work of literature," and so forth would in fact be more accurate.

7. Translations from the Greek are my own. See also Plato *Apology* 22a–c. Ion, who claims to be an expert on Homer, is said to lack knowledge (*Ion* 532b–c, 533d–e, 536b–c). For more on Plato's critique of representational art, see *Republic* I–II, X.

8. See Halliwell 1998, 19–27; Janko 1987, x–xiv; and Mayhew 2019b, 6–9. In the case of Homer, Aristotle is responding not only to Plato, but to the attempts to understand Homer allegorically (see Mayhew 2019b, 3–6 & ch. 10).

Although Aristotle does not stress the difference between what we would call the fine arts and other forms of technical expertise (such as shipbuilding, shield-making, or speechwriting), he does distinguish them.[9] Music, sculpture, painting, dancing, and acting are all kinds of *mimetic* (i.e., representational) technical expertise, as is poetry (i.e., literature).[10] Representation is essential to poetry: a medical treatise written in verse, Aristotle says, is not poetry.[11]

But like the other forms of technical expertise, representational art is the proper object of rational study. That poetry is, is clear from the *Poetics* as a whole. Consider its opening passage: "Concerning both poetics (*poiētikēs*) itself and its kinds, and what potential [or 'power,' *dunamin*] each has, and how plots should be constructed if the creation (*poiēsis*) is to be beautiful, and further out of how many and what sort of parts it is [constituted], and similarly too concerning all of the other [aspects] of the same method of inquiry (*methodou*)—we shall speak, beginning according to nature first from the first [things] (*arxamenoi kata phusin prōton apo tōn prōtōn*)" (*Poet.* 1 1447a8–14).[12] Aristotle holds that a science of literature is possible. For Aristotle, as Halliwell writes, "poetic mimesis is an art susceptible of rational and objective analysis, which will produce a theory of its principles, standards, and aims" (Halliwell 1987, 76). Once its basic principles are known, one can show objectively that there are good ways and bad ways of creating literary works.[13] There are limits to what counts as literature—his law of non-contradiction applies here as it does to the rest of reality—and there are rational standards that it must live up to in order to be good.

9. See the appendix to this chapter for how precisely Aristotle would distinguish them.

10. See *Poetics* 1 1447a13–28, *Rhetoric* I.11 1371b6, III.1 1404a21. Randall writes: "for Aristotle there is no distinction at all between what have come to be called in modern times the so-called 'fine arts' and the 'practical arts.' . . . The different and separate arts are distinguished only by the fact that they make different kinds of thing: the shipbuilder makes ships, the physician makes health, the poet makes plays" (1960, 278–79). In a marginal comment on this passage, Rand wrote: "All this is primitive thinking—and disastrously bad psychology on the part of Aristotle" (*Marginalia* 32). I think, however, that Randall gets Aristotle wrong here.

11. See *Poetics* 1 1447b13–20, and compare 9 1451b2–4. Aristotle writes that the representational technical expertise "that uses either plain language or verses [i.e., prose or poetry] remains at present unnamed" (1 1447a28–b9). If pressed, he might define this unnamed *technē* (which is close to our concept of literature) as representational technical expertise that represents through language (*logōi*, 1 1447a22). Again, see the appendix.

12. For the text of the *Poetics*, I have used Tarán and Gutas 2012.

13. For example, Aristotle says that to write a good tragedy, you should not show "wicked men passing from misfortune to good fortune . . . nor a thoroughly villainous person falling from good fortune into misfortune" (*Poet.* 13 1452b36–53a2).

Ayn Rand and Aristotle are in agreement here. Now she was opposed not only to the traditional view that art is the nonrational product of inspiration, but also to the twentieth-century contempt for rationality and objectivity in art, and for any need for or possibility of a definition of art or aesthetic standards. (Recall, for instance, Andy Warhol's "Art? Isn't that a man's name?")[14] In "The Psycho-Epistemology of Art," she writes: "While physics has reached the level where men are able to study subatomic particles and interplanetary space, a phenomenon such as art has remained a dark mystery, with little or nothing known about its nature, its function in human life or the cause of its tremendous psychological power.... While, in other fields of knowledge, men have outgrown the practice of seeking the guidance of mystic oracles whose qualification for the job was unintelligibility, in the field of esthetics this practice has remained in full force and is becoming more crudely obvious today" (*RM* 3–4).[15]

As with any productive endeavor, artistic creation is the product of reason. She makes this point in *Atlas Shrugged*: "Whether it's a symphony or a coal mine, all work is an act of creating and comes from the same source: from an inviolate capacity to see through one's own eyes—which means: the capacity to perform a rational identification—which means: the capacity to see, to connect and to make what had not been seen, connected and made before" (*Atlas* 728). Symphonies and coal mines are both products of reason, and both promote human life; and the difference in how they promote life points to the fundamental difference between the fine arts and other forms of creativity:

> One of the distinguishing characteristics of a work of art (including literature) is that it serves no practical, material end, but is an end in itself; it serves no purpose other than contemplation—and the pleasure of that contemplation is so intense, so deeply personal that a man experiences it as a self-sufficient, self-justifying primary.... Art *does* have a purpose and *does* serve a human need; only it is not a material need, but a need of man's consciousness. Art *is* inextricably tied to man's survival—not to his physical survival, but to that on which his physical survival depends: to the preservation and survival of his consciousness. ("Psycho-Epistemology of Art," *RM* 4–5)

14. Quoted in Gayford and Wright 2000, 561.
15. In this article, Rand defines "psycho-epistemology" (a term she coined) as "the study of man's cognitive processes from the aspect of the interaction between the conscious mind and the automatic functions of the subconscious" (*RM* 6).

Rand defines art as "a selective re-creation of reality according to an artist's metaphysical value-judgments" (*RM* 8).[16] I hope to make clearer "the distinguishing characteristics of a work of art"—and the last part of this definition—when I later discuss literature and philosophy. For now, note that the "re-creation" part indicates another similarity with Aristotle: they both believe literature must be representational. Rand writes: "As a re-creation of reality, a work of art has to be representational; its freedom of stylization is limited by the requirement of intelligibility; if it does not present an intelligible subject, it ceases to be art" ("Art and Cognition," *RM* 66).[17] Like Aristotle, Rand holds that literature is definable—it is that art which "re-creates reality by means of language" (*RM* 36)—and aesthetics can offer advice for one attempting to practice this art.[18]

"Might Be and Ought to Be," and Literature as Philosophical

Ayn Rand (*Marginalia* 33) provides the following (off the cuff) summary appraisal of Aristotle's literary aesthetics, as presented by Randall (1960, 290–93): "Good ideas by A. on literature: poetry as more important than history—men 'as they ought to be'—plot as the most important element of a play—'Characters exist "for the sake of action," not vice versa.' (R.)" These four points are in fact all related. In what follows, I focus on the first two, which, as we have seen, are taken together and singled out by Rand for their significance to her.

I begin with a fairly literal translation of the relevant passage (*Poet.* 9

---

16. Regarding "metaphysical value-judgments," on the previous page she writes:

> Is the universe intelligible to man, or unintelligible and unknowable? Can man find happiness on earth, or is he doomed to frustration and despair? Does man have the power of *choice*, the power to choose his goals and to achieve them, the power to direct the course of his life—or is he the helpless plaything of forces beyond his control, which determine his fate? Is man, by nature, to be valued as good, or to be despised as evil? These are *metaphysical* questions, but the answers to them determine the kind of *ethics* men will accept and practice; the answers are the link between metaphysics and ethics. And although metaphysics as such is not a normative science, the answers to this category of questions assume, in man's mind, the function of metaphysical value-judgments, since they form the foundation of all of his moral values. ("Psycho-Epistemology of Art," *RM* 7)

17. For Rand's elaboration on this, see *RM* 67–70. In *The Fountainhead*, the Council of American Artists, who "rebelled against the tyranny of reality and of the objective" (313–14), illustrates her conception of modern abstract visual artists. (Similar criticisms of modern painting, from a different perspective, can be found in Wolfe 1975.) The Council of American Writers does the same for modern (non-objective) literature. Its chairman, Lois Cook, is clearly based on Gertrude Stein, and in her notes to *The Fountainhead* Rand sometimes refers to her as Gertrude (*Journals* 210–11; see also *AOF* 11–12).

18. See "Basic Principles of Literature" (*RM*) and especially *AOF*.

1451a36–b11), which is part of Aristotle's lengthy discussion of plot in the *Poetics* (chs. 7–14):

> It is also obvious from what has been said that the function of the poet is not to present what has happened (*ta genomena*), but what sorts of things might happen (*hoia an genoito*), and [or "that is," *kai*] what is possible according to probability or necessity. For the historian and the poet do not differ by presenting with meter or without meter (since the works of Herodotus could be put into meter and they would be no less some sort of history with meter than without meter); but it differs in this: the one presents what has happened (*ta genomena*), the other what sorts of things might happen (*hoia an genoito*).[19] This is why poetry is more philosophical and more serious (*philosophōteron kai spoudaioteron*) than history: for poetry presents the universals (*ta katholou*) more, history the particulars (*ta kath' hekaston*). And a universal is: the sorts of things it goes with a sort of person to say or to do according to probability or necessity, which is what poetry aims at, though it attaches names; while the particular is: what Alcibiades did or what he experienced.[20]

Aristotle immediately makes it clear that this passage applies to comedy as well as to tragedy (see *Poet.* 9 1451b11–26). This is relevant, as comedy, he tells us, presents people who are "worse than those who exist" (see *Poet.* 2 1448a16–18, 5 1449a32–37).[21]

Poetry represents human action by presenting the kinds of things

---

19. The "might happen" here and a few lines earlier is a translation of *an genoito*, a potential optative. The potential optative expresses possibility, though according to Smyth it may also carry a normative flavor (§ 1824): "The potential optative with *an* states a future possibility, propriety, or likelihood, as an opinion of the speaker; and may be translated by may, might, can (especially with a negative), must, would, should" (1956, 407; italics in the original). This combination of possibility and propriety is no doubt what Nock was aiming for in translating the Greek "might be and ought to be." There is nothing specifically like this, however, in van Emde Boas et al., which states that the potential optative with *an* "is used to express a range of nuances: to describe actions that **might hypothetically occur**, or to make a **weak assertion** (i.e., to state something more cautiously than with the indicative)" (2019, 441; emphasis in the original). But the propriety of translating *an genoito* as "might be and ought to be" (strictly speaking it is not an accurate translation) is not important for the case I want to make here regarding the similarity between Rand and Aristotle.

20. For more on literature as presenting universals, and on "attaching names," see *Poetics* 17, 1455a34–b23.

21. On this subject generally, see Janko 1984. Aristotle's views are consistent in that he holds that epic, tragedy, and also comedy should all take good people seriously and treat them appropriately (in the last case by not subjecting them to comic abuse).

that might happen to certain kinds of people.[22] Aristotle says that "might happen" refers to what is in accordance with probability and necessity. Poetry is more philosophical than history because it presents the kinds of things that might happen—or to put it another way, it presents what is universal.[23] A universal in this context refers to what a certain kind of person (a certain *character*) would say or do according to probability or necessity. Philosophy involves universal knowledge of human things and the highest things.[24] History is less philosophical because it deals with particular people and particular events that have happened.

Ayn Rand agrees with Aristotle that literature is more philosophical than history. I will have more to say about why she does so after I discuss the "might be and ought to be" principle.

In light of Rand's acceptance of this principle, and her conviction that it is Aristotelian, the *Poetics* 9 passage raises a couple of questions. In that passage, "might be" (or "might happen") seems to refer to the need (literally) for characters to be certain types, whose actions must follow by probability or necessity. But Rand speaks of what might be *and ought to be*, and she has in mind the need for the artist to present man as he morally should be. So, before one can conclude that Rand is Aristotelian here, two questions need to be answered: (1) Does Aristotle think that literature should present people as they ought to be? (2) Does Rand think a writer should present characters that are universal types whose actions follow from probability and necessity?

In answer to the second question, I shall merely mention that Tore Boeckmann (2007b) has in my view argued convincingly that Rand does in effect hold this. Briefly, he shows that presenting characters that are universal moral types whose actions follow from necessity is, for Aristotle and for Rand, the essence of plot construction, and the means by which a

---

22. Actions that have happened are in a sense actions that might happen, so Aristotle must have in mind more than mere possibility. In *Poetics* 9, he writes: "things that have happened are obviously possible" (1451b17–18). See also 9 1451b29–32 and 18 1456a24–25.

23. Aristotle's conviction that literature is more philosophical than history is in part a response to Plato. In the *Republic*, Plato complains that representational art is twice removed from reality—from the Forms (10.595a–608b). Physical objects are already imitations of the Forms, and an artist—in painting a picture or narrating human action—is thus making a copy of a copy. So representational art is in a sense the opposite of philosophy, for the mind of the philosopher moves away from the physical world (the world of the senses) and toward the Forms. For Aristotle, however, representational art is not the mere copying of particulars. It is highly selective, dealing as it does with essential features of human action and character.

24. See, for example, *EN* VI.7 1141a18–20, X.9 1181b15. Note that for Rand, "human things" are the highest things.

plot writer accomplishes the presentation of any kind of character, including a morally good one.[25] This is why Rand calls the "might be and ought to be" principle the key to the literary method of *The Fountainhead*—and by implication of her other novels as well.

Turning to the first question—does Aristotle think literature should present people as they ought to be?—the answer is clearly (a qualified) Yes. Aristotle believes the poet should present universal types that act consistently,[26] and that this is required for the presentation of any type of character (*ēthos*).[27] The characters in a play will include villains and ordinary people (though arguably even these should be larger than life); but—setting aside comedy—the (or a) main character of a tragedy or epic should be a hero: not reflecting people as they are, but (in some sense) people as they ought to be. (As we shall see shortly, this does not mean that such heroes are or should be ethically perfect paradigms.)

Aristotle recognized that not all poets portray people in the same way. Poets present people, he says, the way *they are*, or the way *people think they are*, or the way *they ought to be*. For example, "Sophocles said that he himself portrayed people as they should be (*dei poiein*), but Euripides portrayed them as they are (*eisin*)" (*Poet*. 25 1460b33–35; see also 2 1448a1–18, 25 1460b8–11). But Aristotle has an opinion about

---

25. Both Aristotle and Rand emphasize the importance of plot. For instance, Aristotle: "plot (*muthos*) is the origin [or "first principle," *archē*] and as it were the soul of tragedy, and the characters are secondary" (*Poet*. 6 1450a38–39); Rand: plot is "the crucial attribute of a novel" ("Basic Principles of Literature," *RM* 73). For her full discussion of plot, see "Basic Principles of Literature," *RM* 73–78.

26. A clarification regarding consistency is in order. In *Poetics* 15, Aristotle says that, concerning characterization, there are four things the poet ought to aim at (more on the first one shortly), the last of which is relevant here: "Fourth, it should be consistent (*homalon*). For even if the one who is the basis for the representation is someone inconsistent (*anōmalos*) and such a character is assumed, even so it ought to be consistently inconsistent (*homalōs anōmalon*)" (*Poet*. 15 1454a26–28). (For elaboration, including discussion of ancient scholarship on the purported inconsistency of Homer's Achilles, which Aristotle may have discussed in a lost work, see Mayhew 2019a.) Rand has a strikingly similar view ("Basic Principles of Literature," *RM* 80): "Consistency is a major requirement of characterization. This does not mean that a character has to hold nothing but consistent premises—some of the most interesting characters in fiction are men torn by inner conflicts. It means that the author has to be consistent in his views of a character's psychology and permit him no inexplicable actions, no actions unprepared by or contradictory to the rest of his characterization. It means that a character's contradictions should never be unintentional on the part of the author."

27. See *Poetics* 6 1449b36–38, 1450a5–7; 15 1454a33–b2. When Aristotle speaks of a character, he means a certain moral type, not the categories of character that later (especially certain nineteenth- and twentieth-century writers) employed—for instance, naturalistic or psychological types. See Halliwell 1998, ch. 5 (esp. 150–52), and Halliwell 1987, 75, 94, 139–40.

which approach is best: "Since tragedy is an imitation of people better than we are, [the tragic poet] ought to imitate good portrait painters. For in rendering the particular form, while making [people] lifelike, they in fact paint them more beautiful [than they are]. So too the poet, in imitating [people who are] irascible or lazy or possessing the other such traits, [ought] to make those who are such [sc. irascible, lazy, etc.] decent (*epieikeis*) in their characters; for instance, Agathon and Homer [made] Achilles an example of harshness" (*Poet.* 15 1454b8–15).[28] Aristotle says, concerning characterization (*peri ta ēthē*) in tragedy: "first and foremost, [the characters] should be good (*chrēsta*)" (15 1454a16–17). Discussing epic, he writes: "it may be impossible that there are people like those Zeuxis painted, but it is better so, for [the artist] should improve on his model" (25 1461b11–13).[29]

So, Ayn Rand's claim that according to Aristotle "history represents things only as they are, while fiction represents them 'as they *might be* and *ought to be*'" is accurate—though she should have left off the quotation marks (the result of a reliance on Nock's too loose rendering of the Greek).

Now, that Aristotle and Ayn Rand agree that a literary work should present man as he ought to be does not mean that they agree about art's purpose in presenting man this way. The goal of her writing is not necessarily what she takes to be the goal of all legitimate or great writing. The goal of her writing, she tells us, is the projection or presentation of an ideal man, as an end in itself, purely for the pleasure of the contemplation of such.[30]

Aristotle agrees that the purpose of representational art is pleasure (see especially *Poet.* 13, also 4 1448b4–24 and *Rhet.* I.11 1371a24–b12), but it

---

28. The last line as it comes down to us in the manuscripts (*paradeigma sklērotētos hoion ton Achillea agathon/Agathōn kai Homēros*) is generally considered corrupt and has been widely emended by scholars. I was, however, convinced by Christian Wildberg (private correspondence) that, keeping in mind that the *Poetics* is almost certainly a set of lecture notes and not a polished treatise, there is no need to tamper with the text. I defend my reading of the passage in Mayhew 2019a, 6–8.

29. That Aristotle often compares poets and painters may mean that he considered the purpose of painting the same as or similar to that of fiction (or some genres of fiction at any rate).

30. "The Goal of My Writing" (*RM*). See also Peikoff 1991, 443. Consider Victor Hugo, the novelist Rand most admired. She claims that, although there is grandeur in Hugo's presentation of man, because of his philosophical (and religious) premises he was unable successfully to project an ideal man, and one suspects that this was not his major aim. See "What Is Romanticism?" (*RM* 106–7).

is unclear precisely what he has in mind, and there is no reason to think that his conception of the aim of literature is the same as the goal of Rand's writing. In fact, he holds that tragedy requires the presentation of a hero, but one who is brought down by an error or breach of morality (*hamartia*), for only this can properly serve the purpose of tragedy: "Tragedy . . . accomplishes by means of pity and terror the *catharsis* of such emotions" (*Poet.* 6 1449b25–28), and "the [tragic] poet should use imitation to produce the pleasure arising from pity and terror" (14 1453b11–13).[31] Epic, too, should present man as he ought to be, though it is not clear what Aristotle takes to be epic's purpose. It could be the pleasure connected with *catharsis*, or the contemplation of heroic action—to aid in moral education and/or for its own enjoyment.[32]

I have more to say about literature and moral education, but before turning to that topic, let me point out another similarity between Rand's aesthetics and the content of *Poetics* 9. I believe the following passage (from "Psycho-Epistemology of Art") has much in common with Aristotle's claims about characterization and universals:

> It is very difficult to isolate and integrate human traits even into purely *cognitive* abstractions and to bear them all in mind when seeking to understand the men one meets. Now consider the figure of Sinclair Lewis's Babbitt. He is the concretization of an abstraction that covers an incalculable sum of observations and evaluations of an incalculable number of men of a certain type. Lewis has isolated their essential traits and has integrated them into the concrete form of a single character—and when you say of someone, "He's a Babbitt," your appraisal includes, in a single judgment, the enormous total conveyed by that figure. (*RM* 20–21)

---

31. I have, in the course of a couple of lines, mentioned in passing the two most controversial concepts in Aristotle's aesthetics: *hamartia* and especially *catharsis*. Regrettably, I cannot discuss either here. Some scholars plausibly take *catharsis* to be an aid in getting the soul into a proper moral state. See, for example, Janko 1992. On *hamartia*, see Halliwell 1998, ch. 7 (esp. 215–30).

32. The most fundamental difference between epic and tragedy is that epic is narrated (see *Poet.* 5 1449b9–12). Connected to this is another difference: epics are longer (see 17 1455b15–23, 24 1459b17–18). In *Poetics* 23, Aristotle refers to the "proper pleasure" (*oikeian hedonēn*) in the case of epic, but he does not specify what this is (1459a21). Else (1957, 573) is confident (too much so, in my view) that this pleasure has no connection to the pleasure of tragedy and is likely therefore "purely an aesthetic matter." In *Poetics* 25, Aristotle says that the end or aim of poetry is astonishment (1460b24–26), but it is unclear whether he includes tragedy here (and thus pity and terror) or whether this is particularly the aim of epic (the topic of *Poet.* 25). At the very end of the *Poetics*, he seems to claim that epic and tragedy have the same end, but that tragedy can achieve it more effectively (26 1462b12–15).

But according to Rand, not only is literature more philosophical than history, art generally is by its nature the concretization of philosophy (specifically, metaphysics):

> By a selective re-creation, art isolates and integrates those aspects of reality which represent man's fundamental view of himself and of existence.[33] Out of the countless number of concretes—of single, disorganized and (seemingly) contradictory attributes, actions and entities—an artist isolates the things which he regards as metaphysically essential and integrates them into a single new concrete that represents an embodied abstraction. . . . Art is a concretization of metaphysics. *Art brings man's concepts to the perceptual level of his consciousness and allows him to grasp them directly, as if they were percepts.* (RM 8)

That art (including literature) is philosophical—or, as Rand would put it, is the concretization of philosophy—makes possible what, in her view, is its primary purpose: Art serves a rational human need by providing "the experience of living in a world where things *are as they ought to be*. This experience is of crucial importance to [man]: it is his psychological life line" ("The Goal of My Writing," *RM* 163).[34] Further, the philosophical nature of literature makes possible its moral educational value (so to speak).

Art and Moral Education

In the *Politics*, Aristotle says that "music" (*hē mousikē*, which likely includes literature) should be part of an education the aim of which is not what is useful or necessary but, rather, what is appropriate to a free and noble man (VIII.3 1338a30–33). Music is for the sake of three things: for the moral education of the young, for catharsis, and "third, for pastime (*diagōgēn*)—for both relaxation and rest from strain" (VIII.7 1341b38–41). I want to discuss the first of these.

In the *Nicomachean Ethics*, Aristotle claims that the young are not ready for the study of ethics; they are guided more by feelings—by pleasure and pain—than by reason (*EN* I.3 1095a2–11). They need to acquire moral character through proper habituation. In the *Politics*, he says that the first things we hear or see are the things we remember and like; there-

---

33. She is referring in effect to the "metaphysical value-judgments" mentioned earlier, in her definition of art, in "Psycho-Epistemology of Art," *RM* 7–8.

34. Rand believes that irrational people, too, rely on art, though in different ways (as do people of mixed premises, who fall between the fully rational and the extremely irrational). See especially "Art and Sense of Life" (*RM* 29–30).

fore, the young should not be exposed to depravity and malice (*Pol.* VII.17 1336b31–35). More fundamentally, Aristotle claims that virtue is connected to feeling what a rational person should feel: the right things, at the right time, in the right way, and so forth. In virtuous people, this is second nature: one acts the right way and feels the right things naturally. But to become virtuous, one must be habituated to feeling what one ought to at the right times; one must associate pleasure with virtuous actions and pain with vicious ones (see *EN* 2.1–6).

How does representational art help here? Aristotle tells us in *Politics* VIII.5. Music (and the other representational *technē*) involve a natural pleasure—there is something naturally pleasant about hearing music, seeing a play, looking at paintings and statues. This is agreeable to all ages and characters. Most important with respect to education is that we can, in a sense, take on the quality of a certain moral character when we hear music, see a play, and so on. "Getting into the habit of being pained or pleased by likenesses is close to being in the same condition with respect to the truth" (*Pol.* VIII.5 1340a23–25). For example, certain tunes evoke the emotions that one associates with courage or moderation or spiritedness, and so forth; other tunes evoke the opposite. Songs, stories, and images that we become used to are the ones we find (or will come to find) pleasant. And when we feel an emotion that is associated with courage, say, then we are, while experiencing the emotion, like a courageous person. If we experience this often enough, we gradually and more naturally become (or tend to become) courageous. Aristotle believes the same sort of thing also occurs in the case of other kinds of representational art (see *Pol.* VIII.5 1340a28–38).

How do Aristotle and Ayn Rand compare on these issues? In "The Psycho-Epistemology of Art," Rand writes: "*Art is not the means to any didactic end.* This is the difference between a work of art and a morality play or a propaganda poster" (*RM* 11).[35] But she agrees with Aristotle that literature can indeed help to connect pleasure and virtue. In "The Objectivist Ethics," she writes: "By what means does [a person] first become aware of the issue of '*good and evil*' in its simplest form? By means of the physical sensations of *pleasure* and *pain*.... The physical sensation of pleasure is a signal indicating that the organism is pursuing the *right* course of action" (*VOS* 17). In "Art and Moral Treason," she explains how this is connected

---

35. As an illustration of didactic art, which Rand was exposed to in her youth, see her parody of Soviet art in *We the Living* (120, 157–58, 361–67). I discuss this briefly in Mayhew 2012, 353–54.

to literature—and particularly Romantic literature, the literary school she favors and is an advocate for: "It is not abstract principles that a child learns from Romantic art, but the precondition and the incentive for the later understanding of such principles: the emotional experience of admiration for man's highest potential, the experience of *looking up* to a hero—a view of life motivated and dominated by values, a life in which man's choices are practicable, effective and crucially important—that is, a *moral* sense of life. While his home environment taught him to associate morality with *pain*, Romantic art teaches him to associate it with *pleasure*" (*RM* 140).[36] So, for both Aristotle and Rand, literature that presents man as he ought to be can play a role in a child's moral education, though for Rand this is not the purpose or primary function of literature (and they differ on what literature ought to teach or show the young). It is not entirely clear to me what precisely Aristotle thought was the primary purpose of literature, but moral education is certainly one of its purposes.

There are other connections between Aristotle's aesthetics and Ayn Rand's that are worth exploring, the most important being their views on the role and nature of plot, as indicated above (see Boeckmann 2007b). But judging from the issues I have discussed, I think it clear that Aristotle and Rand have similar views about aesthetics, at the level of essentials, and that many of the differences between them are a reflection of the fact that he is discussing ancient epic and drama, whereas she is primarily concerned with literature in the modern era. That her literary aesthetics is Aristotelian is especially interesting given that it came to be so independently of her having read the *Poetics*.[37] This does not mean that the connections between her aesthetics and Aristotle's are accidental; rather, it points to deeper philosophical connections—the kinds of connections discussed elsewhere in the present volume.

---

36. The entire essay is important on the present issue. Re. "his home environment taught him to associate morality with pain," Rand had, earlier in the essay, written:

> Apart from its many other evils, conventional morality is not concerned with the formation of a child's character. It does not teach or show him what kind of man he ought to be and why; it is concerned only with imposing a set of rules upon him—concrete, arbitrary, contradictory and, more often than not, incomprehensible rules, which are mainly prohibitions and duties. A child whose only notion of morality (i.e., of values) consists of such matters as: "Wash your ears!"—"Don't be rude to Aunt Rosalie!"—"Do your homework!"—"Help papa to mow the lawn (or mama to wash the dishes)!"—faces the alternative of: either a passively amoral resignation, leading to a future of hopeless cynicism, or a blind rebellion. (*RM* 138–39)

37. In contrast to the Italian and French Classicists, who read Aristotle religiously and claimed to be Aristotelian but (I would argue) were not.

Appendix

Table 13.1. Aristotle's Classification of Literature and Its Kinds

Technical Expertise (*technê*) E.g. ship-building, shield-making, rhetoric (writing speeches), tragedy	vs. the other intellectual virtues, e.g. wisdom (*sophia*) and prudence (*phronêsis*)
Representational Technical Expertise The *technai* that produce tragedy, epic, comedy, music, painting, sculpture, etc.	vs. the kinds of technical expertise the products of which are not representations; e.g. ship-building, shield-making, medicine, rhetoric
"Literature" Representational technical expertise that represents via language (*en logôi*). (Aristotle says that this kind of *technê* has no name.) Includes fiction in both prose (e.g. Plato's dialogues) and in meter (e.g. tragedy, epic)	vs. the kinds of representational technical expertise that represent through some other medium (e.g. painting, sculpture, dancing, music)
The Major Kinds of Literature Discussed in the *Poetics* (differentiated by the modes and objects of representation)		

Epic Mode: narration Object: better people	Tragedy Mode: dramatization Object: better people	Comedy Mode: dramatization Object: worse people

Acknowledgements

I wish to thank Tore Boeckmann, John Cooper, Allan Gotthelf, Jim Lennox, Fred Miller, and Greg Salmieri for discussion of my ideas on this topic before I began writing the paper, and/or for comments on an earlier draft.

14
Love and Philosophy
Aristotelian versus Platonic
ALLAN GOTTHELF[1]

What is love?
Why does love make us so happy?
Why are we attracted to the people we are attracted to?
What is the connection between a person's attitude towards love and his or her personal philosophy?

We all know what we mean by "Platonic love": a relationship that's *close*, but not *sexual*. We usually mean a man–woman relationship, and one that involves a sharing of intellectual, esthetic, or other "spiritual" interests. But why is a type of love named after a philosophy? And why is a *philosopher* speaking about love—and why does his title suggest that he's going to talk about *another* type of love, named after *another* philosopher?

Well, the subject of love fascinates me—and what also fascinates me is the not-very-much-noted connections between a person's attitudes toward love and his or her personal philosophy, his basic view of the kind of world it is, the kind of people we are, the kind of life we should

1. Editors' Note: On May 1, 1975, Allan Gotthelf spoke on "Love and Metaphysics" at Swarthmore College, where he was then a visiting professor. This may have been the first iteration of a lecture that became a staple of Gotthelf's repertoire. In 2004 he wrote that the "lecture, first written in 1975 and revised many times since, has been given on over twenty-five occasions, at colleges and universities and to private groups, throughout the U.S., and in several other countries, including at: Hunter College, Douglass College, Stanford University, University of Michigan, University of Maryland, Georgetown University, George Washington University, The College of New Jersey, the University of Texas at Austin, the Honors College of the University of Pittsburgh, McGill University and Mount Royal University

live, and what we can expect of such a life in such a world. And there is much to learn about love and its connection to philosophy by studying—you guessed it—the view of love of the great philosophers, Plato and Aristotle.

So, what I want to do today is to discuss with you the differing views of love of Plato and Aristotle—and they are *dramatically* different—and the way these differences derive from more basic parts of their philosophies. I will be somewhat briefer with Plato's views, so that I can give more time to the lesser known but very exciting view of Aristotle's, which I call: *Aristotelian love*. My real theme, however, is the connections between love and philosophy, in your case and mine as much as in Plato's and Aristotle's.

The term "Platonic love" originated in the Renaissance. Then, as today, it stood for a man-woman relationship, involving the sharing of spiritual values, in which all intimate sexual contact was absent. There was, however, one major difference. To call a relationship "Platonic" today is to view it as limited or partial: "It's *only* Platonic," we say. For most of us the ideal love relationship is one that combines the deep personal intimacy that some Platonic relationships have with an intense mutual sexual attractiveness. For the Renaissance thinkers who coined the term, however, Platonic love was the *ideal* relationship, and this was because of two things. For one, sex was viewed by most people of that time as impure and base; the ideal relationship would be free of so degrading an interaction. (Not that the average person avoided sex; he just viewed his relationships and desires as much less than ideal, and himself as weak and imperfect for having them.) Secondly, the Renaissance thinkers believed that love had a higher purpose, and that this purpose was best fulfilled by a Platonic relationship.

The higher purpose of Renaissance Platonic love was something that transcended *human* relationships altogether. All interpersonal love was seen as a stepping stone, a means to one's moral and religious improve-

---

(Canada), University of Oslo (Norway), University of Freiburg (Germany), Central European University (Hungary), and Kobe University and Hokkaido University (Japan)." Its delivery at Central European University in 2002 was in connection with a seminar for graduate students of ancient philosophy who were sent the text of the lecture in advance. Because the lecture had been "written for a more general audience, with limited analysis and documentation," and because the students had recently read John Cooper's (1980) essay on "Friendship and the Good" in Aristotle, Gotthelf's cover letter to these students included a discussion of the differences between his and Cooper's interpretations of the first argument in *Nicomachean Ethics* IX.9 (1169b28–70a4). We have adapted this discussion into an appendix.

ment. Morton Hunt, in his fascinating book *The Natural History of Love* writes that,

> The fundamental theme [of Renaissance Platonic love] is that love is the source of all sweetness and moral virtue, since it leads men to concentrate on beauty, and beauty leads the mind towards the contemplation of divinity. It was therefore clear that the lover and the lady had to see and converse with each other frequently . . . but their love, to be finest and most ennobling, had to remain chaste and free of actual physical union (Hunt 1959, 181–182).

The Renaissance thinkers called this conception which they practiced (and these thinkers did try to practice it) "Platonic love" because, though they developed it in certain ways on their own, basically they got it from Plato.

Plato, too, viewed love relationships as ideally spiritual, and as a stepping stone to something higher. But let's ask: a stepping stone to what? (And *from* what?) Here we meet Plato's view of reality. Plato viewed the world we live in and everything in it—including human beings—as radically imperfect and incomplete. As an example, Plato would say, consider the beauty you find in other people you love. Whether it be a physical or a spiritual beauty, does the person you love possess it fully and perfectly, at all times and in every way? No, he would say—no one and no thing in this world is purely and perfectly beautiful, purely and perfectly good—or purely and perfectly anything. When we call something beautiful—or even circular, for example—we recognize, he said that it is *incompletely* so, that it falls short of our idea of what beauty—or circularity—really is. The things that correspond to our ideas of beauty, goodness, and circularity must be, not the imperfect, incomplete, things of this world, but perfect entities in another, nonmaterial dimension, entities he called "Forms."

Things in this world, Plato said, "participate in" the Forms, they are deficient *copies*, or *images*, of the Forms. As your shadow or mirror-image is you (right?), but never perfectly, exactly or completely you—it's only an image—so the characteristics of things in this world are images, impure copies of their pure and perfect versions in the world of Forms. Such is our incompleteness as *persons*, Plato thought. We are, inevitably, mixtures of beauty and ugliness, goodness and evil, unable to achieve the perfect beauty and goodness of the Forms of Beauty and Goodness; we know with humility our inability to achieve perfection, but—and this was crucial—we yearn for the perfection nonetheless. This is where love comes in. Love, Plato said, is the expression of this yearning for completeness, for the beauty and goodness we lack and can never fully achieve. When we love another person, he held, we love him for some beauty we perceive in him and feel we lack. But what is it we actually love, Plato asked? If you fell in love with the image of a person you saw in an imperfect photograph, it would be the actual person and not the photographic image that you were in love with. In the same way, he believed, when we love some imperfect human being for the beauty he or she imperfectly embodies—a beauty which is an imperfect copy of the perfect beauty of the Form of Beauty—it is this Form and its perfection that we really love. Plato called this Form "Beauty Itself."

Of course, Plato said, most of us do not know that it is "Beauty Itself" that we are really in love with. To come to be aware of Beauty Itself—and to experience the fullest intensity of love—requires an intellectual and spiritual training and progression. This progression, Plato said, moves from the love of a body we find beautiful, expressed in sexual desire (the lowest level), to a love of "the beauty that exists in souls" (*Symposium* 210b6–7) to the beauty of good actions and laws, to the beauty of mathematics and philosophy, to—finally—the "miraculous beauty" of Beauty Itself, which exists "by itself," "eternally," and perfectly (210e–11b). "Here above all places," said Plato, "is the life worth living for man, lived in the contemplation of Beauty Itself" (211d). Our love for others comes at the lower levels of the progression, and is "petty" compared to the love we can develop for the Form; our love for others is a stepping stone to that higher and truer love.

Now, Plato viewed the transcending of sexual desire and the pursuit of the Form of Beauty as central to his understanding of love, and these doctrines *are* central to the particular conception of love he put forth. But this conception exhibits a certain pattern and expresses a certain psychological perspective on love, and this broader pattern and perspective has appeared in many forms through the ages and continues to occur in today's world. It is this pattern, the Platonic *perspective* on love, that I want to focus our attention on and to try to define.

> PLATONIC LOVE is that conception of love according to which love of another human being (i) stems from a fundamental incompleteness of person, and (ii) is aimed at some higher goal and value beyond the love relationship itself, through which the desired completeness is approached.

Psychologically, it involves an awareness of one's incompleteness, a basic humility of person; and it has as its goal the achievement of a greater moral and spiritual stature, a sense of oneself as a fuller, more complete or more adequate person.

That's the Platonic view of love. You can see how it depends on Platonic philosophy—on a view of human beings as fundamentally incomplete and imperfect, as dependent in some basic way on a realm or world greater than ourselves, in relation to which in individual things around us are dependent and secondary.

If that is the Platonic view of life, and its underlying philosophy, what would be its opposite? Wouldn't it be a view of reality, man, and love which holds:

—that there is nothing higher or more real than the individual things of this world;

—that a human being is a basically complete being, not an imperfect, semi-real one;

—that he is able to achieve full virtue of character and lasting fulfillment on earth;

—that when he has achieved this a person takes pride in himself, even *loves* who he is, and this is profoundly *good*;

—that his love of certain special, selected others is an expression of this self-love;

—and that the happiness of such a relationship is an end in itself and not a means to any greater end, because there is no greater end for a human being than his own happiness on earth?

Would this not be a fundamental alternative to the Platonic view?

It would be—and it *is*. What I have just given you (with one, partial exception) is an accurate summary of the philosophical foundations and defining essentials of Aristotle's view of love, the view I call *Aristotelian love*. (The partial exception has to do with the place of the "Prime Mover" in Aristotle's thought, a Platonic element which does not materially affect this new conception of Aristotelian love.) Let's explore it point by point.

In opposition to Plato, Aristotle maintained that it is the things of the world that are real: "We can dispense with the Forms, for the [theory] is just chatter, just sound without sense" (*APo.* I.22 83a32–35).

Aristotle insisted that perfection—in the realistic meaning of *completion*—full, mature self-development—could be found in the world in which we live—the one reality there is. He suggested that Plato had *arbitrarily* defined standards of perfection that were impossible to achieve, standards not based on the nature of things nor on human nature, and that if one's standards conflict with actual reality, it is the standards that have to go, and not our respect for the world. (This is a very important point, and we can bring it home with an example. In bowling, the highest possible score is 300. If someone decided to define a perfect game as a score of 301 and then bemoaned "man's inability to bowl a perfect game," it's not the human potential that Aristotle would lose respect for.)

Human beings are not, Aristotle asserted, incomplete by nature, not a pale reflection of something higher. Like anything else, humans have a definite nature and definite characteristics in our own right. We are, Aristotle said, *the rational animal*. The ability to think is our essential characteristic, that which distinguishes us from every other animal and is the core of our human nature. Our emotional capacity is able to function in harmony with our reasoning capacity and will do so if we use our reasoning capacity correctly.

This view of man is at the base of Aristotle's moral philosophy—and of his view of the nature of love and its role in human life. The good life for a human being, according to Aristotle, involves the fullest, most excellent use of reason. Since our rational nature manifests itself both in our intellectual activity and in our character, there are for Aristotle virtues of intellect and virtues of character. The intellectual virtues are the main thinking skills and the commitment to their use, both those involved in more theoretical thought and those involved in practical life. The character virtues include such qualities needed for successful living as bravery, temperance, truthfulness, generosity, friendliness, justice, and pride.

These virtues, Aristotle said, and the personal fulfillment they bring are fully achievable by man: "Happiness . . . is not godsent but attained through virtue and some sort of learning or cultivation. . . . [Since happiness depends on virtue,] it will be shared by many people, for study and effort will make it accessible to anyone whose capacity for virtue is unimpaired" (*EN* I.9 1099b15–20).

A person who is fundamentally virtuous, fundamentally good, he held, will and should find full pride in himself. (The Greek word for pride literally meant "greatness of soul.") "Pride, as its very name suggests, seems to be concerned with great and lofty matters. . . . A man is regarded as proud when he thinks he deserves great things and actually deserves them.... It follows that a truly proud man must be good. And what is great in each virtue would seem to be the mark of a proud person.... Pride thus is the *crown*, as it were, of the virtues: it magnifies them, and it cannot exist without them. Therefore, it is hard to be truly proud, and, in fact impossible without nobility of person" (*EN* IV.3 1123a34–24a4).

Such a human being, Aristotle explained, would actually love the person he is, and this, he believed, was profoundly right: "A [good] man is his own best friend and therefore *would* have the greatest affection for himself" (*EN* IX.8 1168b8–10; emphasis added). "A man like that... wishes to spend his time with himself, for he does so with pleasure. The memory of his achievements gives him delight, and his hopes for the future are good" (IX.4 1166a23–26).

"And so a good man *should* be a self-lover" (*EN* IX.8 1169a11; emphasis added). A person's love of himself, Aristotle is saying, is a direct expression of his pride, which is a consequence of his virtue. A person's love of others, according to Aristotle, is a direct expression of his love of himself: "All love for others is an extension of the love one has for oneself" (*EN* IX.4 1166a10, cf. IX.8 1168b5). "[The good man] has the same attitude toward the one he loves as he does toward himself, for his friend really is another self" (IX.4 1166a30–32).

Aristotle examined a range of positive emotional bonds between human beings, from the mild benevolence one feels for a chance acquaintance to the deepest personal love, and distinguished various types of friendship and love. He did not separate out and discuss what we would call romantic love—the concept as we know it had not yet developed—but wrote rather of the wider category of deep personal love that includes very close personal friendships—where friends truly love one another—and would include authentic romantic love in our sense. It is Aristotle's discussion of this wider category of friendship and love that we'll take a look at. (We will have to draw from it ourselves the implications for romantic love, and they will be *very* interesting.)

In this category of relationship, according to Aristotle, the basis of love—that about the person which leads you to love him—is his goodness, his personal *virtues*, what he is *as a person*. And it is in *this* type of relationship that you love the person "for himself." (To love a person *for himself*, does not mean for Aristotle to love him "unselfishly"— for himself rather than for yourself. No, of course you want to benefit from the relationship, and you pursue it for that reason. To love a person "for himself" in Aristotle's meaning is to love him for what he is *as a person*, rather than for something much less important and much more inessential, such as his wealth, or his professional standing, or his "connections.")

In contradistinction to Plato, Aristotle held that a love relationship is an end in itself and not a means to some higher goal outside the relationship. And its driving force is not a sense of humility and a search for moral and spiritual improvement but precisely the opposite: according to Aristotle, the driving force of love is an *already acquired* pride and self-value. As I quoted just before: "All love for others is an extension of the love one has for oneself. . . . [The good man] has the same attitude toward the one he loves as he does toward himself, for his friend really is another self" (*EN* IX.4 1166a10, a30–32).

As far as we know, it was Aristotle who originated the saying, A "friend . . . is another self," and its meaning is central to his explanation of the *motivational root* of love.

What, then, *is* the root of love? Why do we need friendships and love relationships? Why do they make us so happy? To answer this, Aristotle looks first at the mature, fully developed human being. Why would an otherwise fulfilled person, with a developed moral character and pride—the sort of person Aristotle called "self-sufficient"—need someone to love?

> The self-sufficient man *will* need someone to love. . . . [For] it is both a most difficult thing, as some of the sages have said, to attain a knowledge of oneself, and also a most pleasant thing. . . . And so, as when we wish to see our own face, we do so by looking into the mirror, in the same way when we wish to know ourselves we can obtain that knowledge by looking at the one we love. For the one we love is, as we say, another self. If, then, it is pleasant to contemplate oneself, and it is not possible to do this without having someone else whom one loves, the self-sufficient man *will* need someone to love. (*MM* II.15 1213a13–26)[2]

According to Aristotle there are two facts about human nature at the root of a self-sufficient person's desire for love. First is the fact that a certain kind of self-experience or self-awareness—*a certain perspective on your character and the sort of person you are*—is a source of profound happiness; and, second, the fact that this particular kind of self-experience is possible *only* through love. Aristotle is not saying that without

2. On whether the *Magna Moralia* is indeed by Aristotle, see the next note below.

someone like myself to love I cannot know my own character or be happy at all; definitely not. Rather, there is a certain perspective on myself and my character, and the distinctive pleasure that that perspective brings, which I cannot have by myself. What *is* that special perspective, and special kind of self-experience, that love provides, and *why* is it possible only through love?

Aristotle answered as follows: "We stated at the beginning that happiness, a fulfilled life, is some kind of *activity*, and an activity clearly is something that comes into being across time and not something that is there already completed, as a possession or piece of property is" (*EN* IX.9 1169b29–31).

Because our life is an activity, Aristotle is saying, we can't observe it all at once, the way we can observe a thing, such as a house we have built or bought. Yet, a good person will want to see in every way the sort of person he is—and Aristotle is saying, it would be a great source of pleasure to see oneself the way one sees his house. While a person cannot get that perspective on his personal virtues by himself (since he is to himself an activity), he *can* get that perspective from being with the person he loves. Why?

Aristotle explains: "We are better able to observe our neighbors than ourselves, and their actions better than our own; and the actions of a person of high moral character are a source of pleasure to a good man who loves him, in that they possess both qualities which are pleasant by nature [namely, they are good actions and they are like his own]" (*EN* IX.9 1169b34–70a2).

The person we love, says Aristotle, is a spiritual mirror. As another self, yet a separate self, he or she gives us a unique perspective on ourselves, and our deepest personal values, a perspective we cannot get by ourselves—a joyous perspective and experience, to the extent to which we authentically like and value ourselves.

This heightened self-experience is at the root of love, according to Aristotle, and it is expressed in action most of all in the desire to be with, to spend one's time and life with, the person or persons one loves:

> What [sexual partners] love most is to see one another, and they prefer sight to all other senses, because love exists and is generated by sight more than by any other sense. . . . [Likewise for friends who love one another.] But only by living together can the perception of a friend's existence be activated, so that it is natural that lovers aim at living together.

And whatever his existence means to each partner individually or whatever it is for the sake of which he lives, he wishes to pursue this together with those he loves. Hence, some friends drink together, others play dice, while others do gymnastics or go hunting or do philosophy. (*EN* IX.12 1171b29–72a5)

That's ARISTOTELIAN LOVE.

On this conception, love of another human being:

(i) stems from a fundamental *completeness* of person—an achieved moral character and its concomitant, an authentic self-love; and

(ii) is aimed at a heightened, and joyous, self-experience, as an end in itself, not a means to some greater end—because there is no greater end for a human being than his own happiness on earth, and such love is a source of profound happiness.

(As for Aristotle's view of romantic love, and sex, in particular, while his philosophy provides the basis for a positive view of sex and of romance, he actually said very little about it in writings of his which have survived. We'll look at the place of sex in an Aristotelian approach to love very shortly.)

I hope, parenthetically, that it is clear that Aristotle's view of love is not "narcissistic." Aristotle is not saying that what we actually love is ourselves and not the other person. Of course, it is the other person, in all of his or her uniqueness, that we love, and Aristotle is fully aware of this. His theory is aimed rather at explaining the *causes* of that love, the reasons why we love those unique individuals we do, the things about those individuals that generate our love *for them*, and it is *here* that he brings in our feelings for ourselves and our personal values.

Finally, I should anticipate the worry that Aristotle's view of love applies only to fully developed adults in their thirties and forties and fifties (and is *anyone* ever *fully* developed, in the sense of having no place for more growth?). In his view there will be a form of Aristotelian love appropriate to one's age and the stage of one's personal development. Furthermore, an Aristotelian love will be possible even to individuals who have deep self-doubts, so long as their relationship is not *based on* those self-doubts but on shared positives. It is also worth acknowledging (and even celebrating) the fact that love relationships do provide opportunities for learning more about oneself and for moral growth; what Aristotle is claiming, however, is that these are not the primary driving force and function of love, just delightful side-benefits of a relationship whose center and motor is as I have described it.

We have seen that the Platonic conception of love depends on a certain basic philosophy. It views love as stemming from a perceived incompleteness of person, and as aimed at a sense of oneself as a fuller, more complete person, *because* it views people, and the things of this world in general, as inherently incomplete and imperfect, and as dependent on and secondary to something greater. The Aristotelian conception of love also depends on an underlying philosophy.

Aristotle's view that love is an expression of a fundamental *completeness* of person and is aimed at an enjoyment of self and other, depends on a view of the individual things of the world as potentially *complete*—as *not* dependent on anything higher, and of the human individual as *not* essentially imperfect, but able to achieve solid goodness and beauty of person. (Not Platonic "perfection," but human completeness—development, maturity, self-realization.)

Our conception of love depends on our philosophy. If we hold a view of the world as inherently incomplete and defective, and a view of the human (and thus of *ourselves*) as weak and imperfect, an Aristotelian love will be outside our reach and our relationships will be fundamentally Platonic. If we hold on to an Aristotelian view of the world and the human potential, and work to fulfill that potential in ourselves, we will not limit ourselves to the incompleteness, and in my view the ultimate emptiness, of Platonic-type relationships.

Now, in saying this I am not only declaring agreement with the essentials of Aristotelian philosophy and Aristotelian love, while rejecting their Platonic counterparts; I am also implying that the fundamental choice between conceptions of love is a choice between the Aristotelian and the Platonic, that these are not just two differing historical viewpoints, but two *archetypes*—two *fundamental* alternatives on the nature of love. I want to explain this by means of certain ideas in the writings of a contemporary Aristotelian. The twentieth-century thinker who is the most Aristotelian is the novelist-philosopher Ayn Rand, best known for her novels *Atlas Shrugged* and *The Fountainhead*.

The key idea of hers here is *self-esteem*, your respect for the ability of your mind to guide your life and achieve your happiness. She defines self-esteem as the "inviolate certainty that [one's] mind is competent to think and [one's] person is worthy of happiness, which means: is worthy of living" (*Atlas* 1018). In her great novel *Atlas Shrugged*, from which I've taken that definition, Ayn Rand shows that self-esteem is a fundamental need of ours and that its comparative presence or absence has a basic effect on the way we live and act. But a person is not born with self-esteem; it must be developed, and its development requires both a policy of thinking for yourself and acting on your own judgment, *and* a deep commitment to your own happiness. A person who significantly lacks self-esteem still needs it, and, if he does not act to correct his deficiency with the sort of self-respecting behavior I've just described, he will seek *substitutes* for self-esteem; he will seek through irrational means to convince himself that he has the self-esteem his deeper feelings tell him he lacks. (It is interesting to note, by the way, that Ayn Rand was writing of the centrality of self-esteem, and of unsuccessful searches for substitutes for self-esteem, long before these ideas became the staple they now are of the psychological literature.)

In the realm of love, the person with a firm self-esteem and the person of limited self-esteem take basically different approaches. The person of self-esteem comes to the realm of love, as Aristotle discussed, with a desire to find "another self," someone fundamentally like himself, for the heightened self-awareness and enjoyment we have discussed. The person predominantly lacking in self-esteem comes to the realm of love with a need to prove to himself that he has that thing his deeper feelings tell him he lacks—he comes with a need to fill a void and somehow make himself feel *adequate* or complete as a person. He views love as a *means* to a higher goal and value beyond the relationship itself, through which he will fill that void and approach that completeness. He is, in other words, a *Platonic* lover. And the converse, I want to suggest, is also true: the way to understand the Platonic sort of love, in all its forms, from the more attractive, "idealistic" version of Plato's to the very unattractive one we will discuss in a moment, is by reference to its attitude toward self-esteem, its view of love relationships as *attempts to acquire a not-yet-possessed self-esteem.*

If we understand "Platonic" love, not as Plato himself presented it (and not in the everyday meaning), but in this broader manner, we can see the fundamentally Platonic character of many approaches to love and sex which at first appear non-Platonic. In Plato's own philosophy, sex was to be transcended, because it was thought to lack the spiritual or nonmaterial character of the higher world of Forms. But, in this broader sense of Platonic love, one can have a Platonic view of love *with* sex, and without a world of Forms.

As an example, consider the advocates of promiscuous sex without love, without closeness or authentic respect. The man—or woman—who will sleep around, as a "release," "for the pleasure," who sees sex as "just a natural, bodily function." Is their sex really a joyous end in itself as they claim, or is it a means to something "higher"—something they care about more than they care about their partners? Something often called "ego," which really means "lack of ego"? I want to suggest that for sexually promiscuous people, sex is *not* an end in itself, it is rather a means to something else: it is a desperate search for a self-esteem they lack. They want to feel, not an ecstatic intimacy with a deeply special person they know and love, but like "somebody"—"I'm somebody because they'll sleep with me, because they respond to me, and because my friends, when I tell them about it, will envy me." That this is the underlying motive can be seen from many things: from the emotional distance between the partners after it's over; from how they feel about themselves afterwards; from the frequent need to fantasize during; from the frequent changing of partners; from the compulsiveness of it all—and from the introspective testimony of those who are able and willing to look. It *is* fundamentally a search for a sense of self-esteem. And that is the Platonism of promiscuous sex—and it *is* a form of Platonism, even if Plato himself wouldn't have approved of it.

But, as we all really know, a search for self-esteem through love or sex can't succeed. Ayn Rand put it this way in *Atlas Shrugged*: "The man who despises himself tries to gain self-esteem from sexual adventures—which can't be done, because sex is not the cause, but an effect and an expression of a man's sense of his own value" (*Atlas* 489).

Ayn Rand was the first to identify explicitly what is implicit in the clash between Aristotle and Plato on love: that the fundamental opposition between conceptions of love is between those that see love as an expression of an *already acquired self-esteem* and those that see it as an *attempt to acquire a self-esteem not yet possessed*. Listen to Francisco D'Anconia, that wonderful character in *Atlas Shrugged*:

> Love is blind, they say; sex is impervious to reason and mocks the power of all philosophers. But, in fact, a man's sexual choice is the result and the sum of his fundamental convictions. Tell me what a man finds sexually attractive and I will tell you his entire philosophy of life. Show me the woman he sleeps with and I will tell you his valuation of himself.... He will always be attracted to the woman who reflects his deepest vision of

himself, the woman whose surrender permits him to experience—or to fake—a sense of self-esteem. (*Atlas* 489-90)

This is of course a literary abstraction, and there is much more to be said about the matter and there are many questions that arise, but the principle is deeply and exactly right.

Thus, as the promiscuous approach to love is in essence Platonic, so Ayn Rand's is in essence Aristotelian—it is a historic advance in the Aristotelian understanding of love.

For, not only does Ayn Rand make clearer how love is an expression of self-esteem, she also expands on the Aristotelian understanding of what exactly it is that one responds *to* in the person one loves. Love, she held, is indeed a response to the character and values of another person, but it is a response to them *as they are embodied* in something about a person that is even more basic and encompassing: what she called his "sense of life." By a "sense of life" she meant that emotional sum of a person's deepest personal philosophy, which each human being forms in the course of his life and choices—"an emotional, subconsciously integrated appraisal of man and of existence" (*RM* 24-25)—a personal perspective on what is true and important about life and about man, and thus about oneself and one's place in the world. In an essay explaining her concept of a sense of life, she comments that "There are two aspects of man's existence which are the special province and expression of his sense of life: love and art" (*RM* 21)—and about love, Ayn Rand writes:

> Love is a response to values. It is with a person's sense of life that one falls in love—with that essential sum, that fundamental stand or way of facing existence, which is the essence of a personality. One falls in love with the embodiment of the values that formed a person's character, which are reflected in his widest goals or smallest gestures, which create the *style* of his soul—the individual style of a unique, unrepeatable, irreplaceable consciousness. It is one's own sense of life that acts as the selector, and responds to what it recognizes as one's own basic values in the person of another. It is not a matter of professed convictions (though these are not irrelevant); it is a matter of much more profound, conscious *and subconscious* harmony. ("Philosophy and Sense of Life," *RM* 22)

Ayn Rand's view of love, as I say, is in essence Aristotelian and is a historic advance in the Aristotelian understanding of this fundamental aspect of human existence.

Aristotle's discussion, great as it is, has several important limitations. Part of what I have encompassed under the term "Aristotelian love" is present in Aristotle's writings only implicitly, and some elements of the fuller theory are not there at all, most notable the theory of romantic love and sex. Aristotle laid down the fundamentals on which a full understanding of the nature of love rests, but there was much to be done to complete his work. The central new ideas and the starting points for all future work are in my view to be found in the writings of Ayn Rand.

Let me stress, however: I come not to criticize Aristotle but to praise him.

His great achievement was to define the essentials of this grand conception, Aristotelian love, and the philosophy of self-sufficient individuals on which it rests.

And, more than to praise Aristotle, I have come to say that Platonic love, Aristotelian love, and every particular view of love—including your own, and the romantic choices that express it—depends fundamentally on a philosophy—on a view of the basic nature of a human being, and of our relationship to reality.

For, you know, Ayn Rand was right—in the deepest philosophical sense—when she wrote in the novel *The Fountainhead* (388):

Before one can say 'I love you' one must know first how to say the 'I.'

Appendix: Self-Awareness versus Self-Knowledge as the Root of the Value of Friendship

Ayn Rand has, for the most part, gotten very little attention, and less admiration, both for her literature and her philosophy from American academics, including philosophers, although there are signs of late of a slowly growing interest. I myself consider her a thinker of the first rank, with strikingly original views on many fundamental issues in philosophy—views which, I may say, often have the added advantage of being true! I am in fact working on several projects aimed at expounding, for academic philosophers, some of these views and the evidence and argument that lie behind them. In the context of the above lecture, the significant point is perhaps Rand's great affinity to Aristotle on the matters of friendship and love. And her success (or so I suggest) in developing an Aristotelian view of sex, and elaborating Aristotle's view of the roots of our love-responses in directions that help explain the particularized character of our response.

The basic argument Aristotle gives in *EN* IX.9, as to why a flourishing life must include individuals one loves, is one I think she would essentially endorse, if the argument is interpreted correctly. The interpretation I sketch in my lecture is very different from the one given by John Cooper in his otherwise excellent papers on friendship and the good in Aristotle. I would like to indicate why I do not accept his interpretation, something I do not discuss in the lecture, because of the nature of its original audience.

Cooper (1980, 317–24) raises the question of why, according to *EN* IX, character-friendship is a necessary constituent of a flourishing life. He claims that the long argument from 1170a13 presupposes that one already has character-friends, but he gives no reason why, if one's aim is to flourish, one should acquire them in the first place. Cooper's rejection of the long argument in *EN* IX.9 is crucial to his rejection of the shorter, first argument in IX.9 (1169b28ff.).

However, Cooper says, a reason why a virtuous man needs to acquire character-friends in the first place, if he is to flourish, *is* provided in a passage in the corresponding section of the *Magna Moralia* (1213a10–26), which he quotes (1980, 320). And it is, he says, a very good reason. Cooper refers to the claim of the *MM* passage (the source of which may be either a younger Aristotle, or a later Peripatetic) that what a character-friend provides one with is self-*knowledge*, not possible easily or well without interaction with one's friend. The passage, then, offers the idea that "character-friendship provides the best means available to a human being for arriving at as secure a knowledge of his own life and character as such a creature can manage" (322–23). Cooper thinks such a rationale for having character-friendships is plausible. Indeed a few lines later he writes that "the recognition, which lies at the center of this argument, of the social basis of a secure self-concept and of the role intimacy plays in providing the means to this is a notable achievement" (323).

Cooper then observes that the first *EN* argument (referred to above) has "pronounced affinities" to the argument just examined. This is the argument which I make the centerpiece of my own analysis of the Aristotelian account of our need of character-friends (and indeed, people to love), but Cooper finds the argument sadly wanting. (On page 323 he quotes the entire passage [1169b28–1170a4], while I only excerpt from it; so we should consult it in his article.) He complains (324) that while the argument speaks of studying (or contemplating, *theorein*) the good actions of one's own and one's friend's, it never explains why the good person should want to do that, or what contribution it might make to his flourishing.

Cooper observes correctly that there is *no* mention here of self-knowledge as the aim of the good person's contemplation of the good acts of his friend and his own (324), and no mention of knowledge in the later long argument (320). Instead, the long argument speaks of what Cooper calls "self-consciousness," with repeated use of the verb *aisthanesthai*: with a friend we are better able (as I put it in my lecture) to perceive ourselves, we have *"a heightened self-awareness."* The *Magna Moralia* passage, on the other hand, makes no use of this verb but uses only verbs of self-*knowing*.

Well, in my lecture I give two reasons why a good man will want to contemplate (i.e., to be aware of) his own actions and thus the actions of his character-friends—the very reasons Aristotle himself gives in the passage. And to illuminate this, I borrow the language, not of self-knowledge from far-off *Magna Moralia*,[3] but of heightened "self-awareness," "self-perception" from the long argument only one page later, an argument mistakenly dismissed by Cooper.

I leave it to you to keep these issues in mind, while reading my lecture, when you reach the point at which I make use of this *EN* IX.9 argument to construct my own picture of Aristotle's view of the contribution. See how I do it, and whether you think it a more plausible reading of that argument than Cooper's, or not. And while you're thinking about it, consider one final question. Whatever Aristotle may have thought about a child's acquisition of a "secure self-concept" (Cooper 1980, 323), can you imagine that he thought that the "great-souled" man, the *megalopsuchos*, the man of pride of *EN* IV.3, could be someone whose continu-

---

3. I myself in the lecture use the *MM* passage only as a jumping-off point. My own view is that *MM* is either a younger Aristotle's first attempt at the issue, or a later Peripatetic's less secure attempt, confusing the later Aristotle's enjoyment of already secure self-esteem with the Peripatetic's own longing for a more secure self-esteem. One small point in favor of *MM* being early Aristotle is that the contrast between its use of verbs of self-*knowing* and *EN*'s use of verbs of self-perception (or self-awareness) is mediated by the corresponding passage in what would be the *middle treatise*, the *Eudemian Ethics*. At *EE* VII.12 1245a35–37, Aristotle, perhaps on his way from the *Magna Moralia* understanding of the contribution character-friends make to a flourishing life to the *Nicomachean Ethics* understanding, uses *both* verbs, when he writes: "To perceive (*aisthanesthai*) a friend, therefore, is necessarily in a way to perceive (*aisthanesthai*) oneself and in a way to know (*gnorizein*) oneself." So perhaps we are detecting another case of the sort of evolution from *MM* through *EE* to *EN* that Cooper, in his paper on the authenticity of the *MM*, took as a sign of that authenticity.

ing sense of his own worth depends on his continuing interactions with his friends? If not, then the contribution Aristotle surely believes friends make to the flourishing of a man with such pride must be of a very different nature—a nature closer to the account I give in the above lecture.

15
Reflections on Allan Gotthelf's "Love and Philosophy"
GREGORY SALMIERI

Although it is being published here for the first time, Allan Gotthelf's lecture "Love and Philosophy" has the status of a classic in Objectivist circles. It was delivered dozens of times over fifty years in both academic and popular contexts, has long been commercially available as an audio recording, and has circulated informally as a typescript. I know one man who attributes his decades-long marriage and happy family life to the talk's influence on him as a young man deliberating about an earlier and less fulfilling relationship. Allan often assigned the typescript in his undergraduate courses (which is where I first encountered it in the late 1990s), and it has been assigned occasionally by other professors (myself included).

Many of the key claims in the paper are adapted from Francisco d'Anconia's speech about the "Meaning of Sex" in *Atlas Shrugged* (489–93, cf. *FTNI* 109–12) or from other Objectivist sources. This is so for the paper's central theme that a person's romantic desires and choices reflect a view of love that in turn is an expression of one's metaphysical views of the nature of human beings and of reality, and an expression of one's own self-assessment.[1] It is true also for the thesis that Platonic love, understood

---

1. On the relation between sense of life (as an implicit metaphysics) and self-esteem (as a metaphysical self-assessment), see Ghate (2016) 116–23.

as a "pure" Romantic love devoid of sexual desire, is of a piece with "the depravity of a desire devoid of love" (*Atlas* 491).

Objectivism is also an influence (though less obviously so) on Allan's interpretation of Aristotle's view of friendship—especially in the respects in which this interpretation differs from that of Cooper (1980). The position that Allan attributes to Aristotle (correctly, in my view) is essentially Rand's view of what we might call (adapting the title of one of her essays on art) "the psycho-epistemology of love."

For Cooper's Aristotle, friendship's function is essentially *heuristic*: through the relationship each friend learns things about himself that enable him to improve his character. On Allan's interpretation, by contrast, the value of an Aristotelian friendship lies not in anything one can learn from interaction with one's friends but simply in the fact that sharing one's life with them affords one a certain sort of profound and pleasurable experience, which is an end in itself.

But although these friendships are not means to any such end as self-improvement, their value does derive from a contribution they make to the rest of one's life. They are "ends in themselves" in the sense in which Rand applied this phrase to art. "It serves no practical, material end, but is an end in itself; it serves no purpose other than contemplation—and the pleasure of that contemplation is so intense, so deeply personal that a man experiences it as a self-sufficient, self-justifying primary and, often, resists or resents any suggestion to analyze it" ("The Psycho-Epistemology of Art," *RM* 4–5).

For Rand, no values (and no emotions) are "irreducible and unrelated ... to the needs of a living entity's survival," and art "does serve a human need; only it is not a material need, but a need of man's consciousness" (*RM* 5). The specific need art serves is that of enabling a human being to encounter *in perceptible form* his metaphysics—his "fundamental view of himself and of existence" (*RM* 8). Because human choices presuppose stances on metaphysical issues, everyone must (at least implicitly) form a metaphysics that he relies on to navigate the world. But the complexity and abstractness of a metaphysics makes it impossible for anyone to "hold it all in the focus of his immediate conscious awareness" (*RM* 7). To orient ourselves and maintain our motivation, we need a way to contemplate our metaphysics in the form of an object distinct from ourselves that we can directly experience. An artwork is a perceptible object that embodies a worldview and thereby makes it available for contemplation. "The reason why art has such a profoundly personal significance" is that when an artwork supports one's own fundamental view of reality, it confirms the efficacy of one's consciousness (*RM* 12).

In an essay written under Rand's editorship, Nathaniel Branden ascribes a similar function to human relationships:

> Since man is the motor of his own actions, since his concept of himself, of the person he has created, plays a cardinal role in his motivation—he desires and needs the strongest possible experience of the reality and objectivity of that person, of his *self*.
>
> When a man stands before a mirror, he is able to perceive his own face as an object in reality, and he finds pleasure in doing so, in contemplating the physical entity who is himself. . . . Is there a mirror in which man can perceive his *psychological* self? In which he can perceive his own soul? Yes. The mirror is another consciousness. (Branden, "Self-Esteem and Romantic Love," *TO* 372)

Unlike the esthetic value of an artwork, which one simply contemplates, the value of the self-experience one gets from human relationships derives specifically from interacting with the consciousness of another. The other party's awareness of and response to oneself is essential to the experience of self-awareness, which Branden calls "visibility" (*TO* 374), that one human being can get from interacting with another.

Branden goes on to note that an interaction will provide visibility only to the extent that there is a "mutuality of mind and values" between the two people and that such interactions can only yield visibility for a person to the extent that "his inner view of himself is consonant with the personality projected by his behavior" and so reflected in the other person's response to it (*TO* 374). It follows that this experience will be available most intensely to proud, virtuous people in relationships with others who share their moral virtues and many of their personal values—that is, to the sorts of people who Aristotle thinks enjoy friendships of character. Branden goes on to discuss romantic love as the most intense form of this relationship and to highlight the special sort of visibility that is possible through sex.

Although articulated first in nonfiction form by Branden, this view of "visibility" is clearly present in the characterization of the friendships and romances in *Atlas Shrugged*. Consider especially the scene in which Dagny and Galt consummate their relationship:

> Just as her eyes had the power to translate wave lengths of energy into

sight, just as her ears had the power to translate vibrations into sound, so her body now had the power to translate the energy that had moved all the choices of her life, into immediate sensory perception. It was not the pressure of a hand that made her tremble, but the instantaneous sum of its meaning, the knowledge that it was his hand, that it moved as if her flesh were his possession, that its movement was his signature of acceptance under the whole of that achievement which was herself—it was only a sensation of physical pleasure, but it contained her worship of him, of everything that was his person and his life . . . it contained her pride in herself and that it should be *she whom he had chosen as his mirror*, that it should be her body which was now giving him the sum of his existence, as his body was giving her the sum of hers. These were the things it contained—but what she knew was only the sensation of the movement of his hand on her breasts.

He tore off her cape and she felt the slenderness of her own body by means of the circle of his arms, as if his person were only a tool for her triumphant awareness of herself, but that self were only a tool for her awareness of him. It was as if she were reaching the limit of her capacity to feel, yet what she felt was like a cry of impatient demand, which she was now incapable of naming, except that it had the same quality of ambition as the course of her life, the same inexhaustible quality of radiant greed. (*Atlas* 956–57, emphasis added)

Notice not only the language of mirroring (present in Branden's essay and in *MM* II.15), but also the emphasis on how, through perceiving Galt's body on hers, Dagny experiences viscerally the specific qualities of soul that the two value in themselves and in one another. To characterize the act as one of learning or self-improvement would be to instrumentalize it, but in that moment Dagny isn't seeking anything beyond the act itself and the profound experience the act contains of the values for the sake of which she is living.

As contemplating art enables one to experience one's metaphysics in the form of an external object, so sex with someone one loves enables a person of self-esteem to experience what he values about himself in the form of the mate who is another self. Making love and the contemplation of the artwork are both experienced as ends in themselves, rather than as means to knowledge or to any other specific ends. But the value of such experiences derives from the role they play in sustaining a person's motivation. This role, in turn, derives from facts about what Rand calls our psycho-epistemology—that is, about the psychological mechanisms by which human beings form, hold, and use knowledge, especially insofar as these mechanisms concern the relation between the conscious and subconscious mind and the perceptual and conceptual levels of consciousness.

Aristotle, of course, does not discuss sex in this way. But, if Allan's interpretation of him is correct, his account of the value of "living with" a friend is similar in character. Its essential value lies not in anything one might learn (or otherwise gain) from the interaction, but in the pleasurable experience of it, and in the contribution that the enhanced pleasure of sharing a beloved activity with a friend makes to the activity itself. For Aristotle, the pleasure one takes in an activity perfects the activity (*EN* X.4), which includes motivating and enabling one to engage in it more intently.

This aspect of Aristotelian friendship also looms large in Rand's characterizations, both of lovers and of friends. It is especially salient in her narration of Rearden's thoughts as he and Francisco leap into action in response to an emergency:

> There was no time to form words, to think, to explain, but he knew that this was the real Francisco d'Anconia, this was what he had seen from the first and loved—the word did not shock him, because there was no word in his mind, *there was only a joyous feeling that seemed like a flow of energy added to his own.*
>
> To the rhythm of his body, with the scorching heat on his face and the winter night on his shoulder blades, he was seeing suddenly that this was the simple essence of his universe: the instantaneous refusal to submit to disaster, the irresistible drive to fight it, the triumphant feeling of his own ability to win. He was certain that Francisco felt it, too, that he had been moved by the same impulse, that it was right to feel it, right for both of them to be what they were—he caught glimpses of a sweat-streaked face intent upon action, and it was the most joyous face he had ever seen. (*Atlas* 457–58, emphasis added)

Rearden's "joyous feeling" is akin to the enervating effect of an artwork that affirms one's worldview. It makes manifest to him "the simple essence of his universe." But this experience comes not from *contemplating* Francisco as one might contemplate either a work of art or an inspiring act in which one is not a participant. It is the feeling of *cooperating* with Francisco in a joint activity undertaken in (what Branden called) "a mutuality of mind and values" (*TO* 374). The joy is a pleasure that perfects the activity, enhancing and sustaining Rearden's motivation, like a "flow of energy added to his own." *This* is what Aristotelian friendship adds to the beloved activities that constitute the lives of virtuous people. This is why "what friends find most choiceworthy is living together" (*EN* 1171b31–33) and why "whatever existing consists in for each sort of person, whatever it is for the sake of which he chooses to live, this is what he wishes to pass his time doing in the company of his friends" (1172a1–3). It is in this way that friends "share the actions in which they find their common life" (1172a7–8), for (as a friend tells Dagny) "man *is* a social being, but not in the way the looters preach" (*Atlas* 747)—that is, we are social, not primarily as beneficiaries of one another's care (much less of one another's sacrifices) but as self-sufficient, creative individuals whose joyous and self-sustaining activity is reinforced by the similar activities of others like ourselves. This activity is enhanced immeasurably when shared with those we love.

One of the things that Aristotle tells us that the best friends share is philosophy. I know I can speak for my coeditor as well as myself in saying that it was a great joy to pass many years in this activity with Allan Gotthelf. It is a privilege to be able to close this volume with these reflections on one of my friend's favorite lessons about the two philosophers to whom he devoted his life's work. For, as he wrote for his epitaph, "What better life—some precious loves aside—than to have spent my time with the minds of Aristotle and Ayn Rand. . . . And to have brought their wisdom to the world!"

CONTRIBUTORS

James G. Lennox is professor emeritus of history and philosophy of science, University of Pittsburgh. He has published widely on the history and philosophy of biology with a special focus on Aristotle, Charles Darwin, and evolutionary biology. His books include *Aristotle: On the Parts of Animals I–IV*, a translation and commentary (Oxford, 2001), *Aristotle's Philosophy of Biology* (Cambridge, 2001), *Aristotle on Inquiry* (Cambridge 2021), and many coedited volumes, including *Philosophical Issues in Aristotle's Biology* (Cambridge, 1987), *Self-Motion from Aristotle to Newton* (Princeton, 1994), and *Concepts and Their Role in Knowledge: Reflections on Objectivist Epistemology* (Pittsburgh, 2013).

Gregory Salmieri is senior fellow at the Civitas Institute at the University of Texas, Austin, where he teaches in the Philosophy Department. He previously held research and teaching positions at Rutgers University, Boston University, and the University of North Carolina, Chapel Hill. He is the coeditor (with Allan Gotthelf) of *A Companion to Ayn Rand* (Wiley-Blackwell, 2016) and (with Robert Mayhew) *Foundations of a Free Society* (University of Pittsburgh Press, 2019). His papers on Aristotle have appeared in *Ancient Philosophy*, *Apeiron*, and *Metascience*, and he has contributed papers on Rand and objectivism to numerous collections and reference works.

Neera K. Badhwar is professor emerita of philosophy at the University of Oklahoma and senior fellow at the Mercatus Center, George Mason University. She has published in the *Journal of Philosophy*; *Ethics*; *Nous*; *Philosophy and Phenomenological Research*; *Politics, Philosophy, and Economics*; *Social Philosophy and Policy*; and other journals. Her book *Well-Being: Happiness as the Highest Good* was published by Oxford University Press in 2014, and her anthology *Friendship: A Philosophical Reader* by Cornell University Press in 1993. She has received fellowships from the University Center for Human Values at Princeton University, the Social Philosophy and Policy Center at Bowling Green State University, and the Earhart Foundation. Her first children's book, *Kali the Elephant Learns from Socrates the Philosopher*, is forthcoming.

Ben Bayer is fellow and director of content at the Ayn Rand Institute, where he teaches and writes for ARI's online publication, *New Ideal*. He has taught philosophy at Loyola University Chicago, Colorado College, Metropolitan State University of Denver, and Loyola University New Orleans. He has published scholarly articles in *American Philosophical Quarterly*, *Synthese*, *Philosophia*, and *Acta Analytica*, among others. He has also contributed essays to *Concepts and Their Role in Knowledge: Reflections on Objectivist Epistemology* and *Essays on Ayn Rand's "The Fountainhead."*

Andrea Falcon is professor emeritus at Concordia University, Montreal, and is currently lecturing in the Department of Philosophy at the University of Milan, Italy. He writes extensively on Aristotle and the Aristotelian tradition. His two most recent monographs are *The Architecture of the Science of Living Beings: Aristotle and Theophrastus on Animals and Plants* (Cambridge University Press, 2024) and (together with Klaus Corcilius and Robert Roreitner), *Aristotle on the Essence of Human Thought* (Oxford University Press, 2024).

Allan Gotthelf (1942–2013) was Anthem Foundation Distinguished Fellow for Research and Teaching in Philosophy at Rutgers University and professor emeritus of philosophy at the College of New Jersey. Between 2003 and 2012, he was a visiting professor of history and philosophy of science at the University of Pittsburgh. He is a cofounder of the Ayn Rand Society, the longest-serving chair of its steering committee, and the founding editor of this series. A collection of his papers on Aristotle has been published as *Teleology, First Principles, and Scientific Method in Aristotle's Biology* (Oxford University Press, 2012). His (co)edited volumes include *Aristotle on Nature and Living Things* (Mathesis, 1985), *Philosophical Issues in Aristotle's Biology* (Cambridge University Press, 1987), *Metaethics, Egoism, and Virtue* (Pittsburgh, 2011), *Concepts and their Role in Knowledge* (University of Pittsburgh Press, 2013), and *A Companion to Ayn Rand* (Wiley-Blackwell, 2016).

Joseph Karbowski is currently a data scientist for PNC Financial Services. Previously he was assistant professor at the University of Notre Dame, visiting assistant professor at Northwestern University and the University of Pittsburgh, and Humboldt Fellow at LMU-Munich. He published articles on various aspects of Aristotle's ethics, politics, and philosophy of science, and his book *Aristotle's Method in Ethics: Philosophy in Practice* explores Aristotle's conception of the nature of philosophy and its application to the domain of ethics.

Robert Mayhew is professor of philosophy at Seton Hall University. His primary research interests are in ancient philosophy, especially Aristotle and other Peripatetics. His most recent books in this field are *Aristotle's Lost Homeric Problems* (Oxford University Press, 2019) and (as coeditor) two collections of essays on the Aristotelian *Mirabilia* (Routledge, 2023–2024). He is currently working on editions of the fragments of two lost works of Aristotle as well as an edition of the *Eudemian Ethics* for the Loeb Classical Library. He has a serious interest in Ayn Rand, his many publications on her including (as coeditor, with Gregory Salmieri) *Foundations of a Free Society: Reflections on Ayn Rand's Political Philosophy* (in the present series).

Fred D. Miller Jr. is research professor in social philosophy and policy at West Virginia University and professor emeritus of philosophy at Bowling Green State University. He is the author of *Nature, Justice, and Rights in Aristotle's Politics* and *Aristotelian Statecraft: Essays on Aristotle's Politics* and translations of works by Aristotle and his commentators. His coedited volumes include *A Companion to Aristotle's Politics*, *Reason and Analysis in Ancient Greek Philosophy* and *A History of the Philosophy of*

Law from the Ancient Greeks to the Scholastics. He is executive editor of *Social Philosophy and Policy* and former president of the Society for Ancient Greek Philosophy.

Michail Peramatzis is an associate professor at the Philosophy Faculty, University of Oxford, and the Hinton Clarendon Tutorial Fellow at Worcester College. He works on Aristotle's and Plato's theoretical philosophies but also has interests in logic, epistemology, metaphysics, and the philosophy of science. He is the author of *Priority in Aristotle's Metaphysics* (Oxford University Press, 2011) and many articles on Aristotle and Plato.

Jason Rheins is fellow and instructor at the Ayn Rand Institute. He has previously taught at University of North Carolina, Chapel Hill; St. John's University, New York; and Loyola University Chicago, and was a senior research fellow at Higher-Ground-Education Montessorium, investigating ancient pedagogy. His writings have appeared in journals including *Phronesis* and in volumes on Greek and Roman philosophy, Ayn Rand, and the philosophy of science. He is writing a monograph on Plato's theology, which he hopes to complete before the next Olympiad, Gods willing.

REFERENCES

Uniform Abbreviations of Works by Aristotle

APo.	Posterior Analytics
APr.	Prior Analytics
Cat.	Categories
DA	De Anima
EE	Eudemian Ethics
EN	Nicomachean Ethics
HA	History of Animals
Int.	De Interpretatione
Met.	Metaphysics
MM	Magna Moralia
PA	Parts of Animals
Phys.	Physics
Poet.	Poetics
Pol.	Politics
Rhet.	Rhetoric
Top.	Topics

Uniform Abbreviations of Works by Ayn Rand

There is no standard edition of Rand's works, and since much of her nonfiction is most readily available in mass-market editions with inconsistent pagination, referring to them can be a challenge. We have adopted the abbreviations for Rand's works that are used in Gotthelf and Salmieri 2016. Find them listed below paired with bibliographic information on the edition (and, when necessary, the printing) that is referenced in this volume.

Most of Rand's nonfiction was initially published in periodicals she edited or coedited, and much of it has been republished in books, some compiled by Rand during her lifetime and others compiled posthumously by other editors. Both Rand's periodicals and some of the books she compiled during her lifetime contain pieces by other authors, and she endorsed this material as representative of her philosophy. Some of the posthumously published collections of her essays contain additional essays written by other authors after her death, which do not share this endorsement. In the decades since her death, Rand's estate has also brought out editions of her unpublished stories, correspondence, and notes, and several books have been prepared based on material that she originally presented orally in various formats. All of this posthumously published material has been edited in various ways by other hands and, in any case, did not necessarily represent Rand's considered views. In the list below, volumes marked by a dagger (†) are comprised of such posthumously published material. Volumes marked by an asterisk (*) include both pieces Rand published in her lifetime and posthumously published material or pieces written by other authors after her death. Material marked by a double dagger (‡) is archival material that has not been published. (For more on the composition of Rand's corpus and the provenance of various pieces, see Salmieri 2016b.)

Answers†	*Ayn Rand Answers: The Best of Her Q&A*. Edited by Robert Mayhew. New American Library, 2005.
Anthem	*Anthem*. Centennial edition. Dutton, 2005.
Anthem38	*Anthem*. Cassell, 1938.
AOF†	*The Art of Fiction: A Guide for Writers and Readers*. Edited by T. Boeckmann. Plume, 2000.
AON†	*The Art of Nonfiction: A Guide for Writers and Readers*. Edited by R. Mayhew. Plume, 2000.
ARL	*The Ayn Rand Letter*. Bound edition. Second Renaissance Book, 1990.
Atlas	*Atlas Shrugged*. Centennial edition. Dutton, 2005.
Biographical Interviews.	*Ayn Rand Biographical Interviews, 1960–1961*. Transcriptions of taped interviews with Ayn Rand located in the Ayn Rand Archives.
Column	*The Ayn Rand Column*. Revised edition, edited by P. Schwartz. Second Renaissance Books, 1998.
CUI	*Capitalism: The Unknown Ideal*. Centennial edition, printing 50. Signet, 2005.
Fountainhead	*The Fountainhead*. (1943*): "Introduction" Introduction to the twenty-fifth anniversary edition of

REFERENCES

	The Fountainhead (New York: Bobbs-Merrill Co.; 1968).
FTNI	*For the New Intellectual: The Philosophy of Ayn Rand*. Centennial edition, printing 50. Signet, 2005.
Ideal†	*Ideal: The Novel and the Play*. Edited by R. Ralston and L. Peikoff. New American Library, 2015.
ITOE	*Introduction to Objectivist Epistemology*. Expanded second edition, edited by H. Binswanger and L. Peikoff. Meridian, 1990.
Journals†	*Journals of Ayn Rand*. Edited by D. Harriman. Dutton, 1997.
Letters†	*Letters of Ayn Rand*. Edited by M. Berliner. Dutton, 1995.
Marginalia†	*Ayn Rand's Marginalia: Her Critical Comments on the Writings of over 20 Authors*. Edited by R. Mayhew. Second Renaissance Books, 1995.
Papers‡	The Ayn Rand Papers collection of the Ayn Rand Institute. Materials in this collection are cited by their reference number.
"Playboy Interview"	"Playboy Interview: Ayn Rand," by Alvin Toffler. *Playboy* (March): 35–43. (Rand had the opportunity to edit the text of her answers; so the answers in this interview are neither extemporaneous nor adapted by another editor.)
Plays	*Three Plays*, printing 10. Signet, 2005.
PWNI	*Philosophy: Who Needs It*. Centennial edition, printing 30. Signet, 2005.
RM	*The Romantic Manifesto: A Philosophy of Literature*. Centennial edition, printing 30. Signet, 2005.
ROTP	*Return of the Primitive: The Anti-Industrial Revolution*. Edited by P. Schwartz. Meridian, 1999.
Russian Writings†	*Russian Writings on Hollywood*. Edited by M. Berliner, translated by D. Garmong. Ayn Rand Institute Press, 1999.
Speaking†	*Objectively Speaking: Ayn Rand Interviewed*. Edited by M. Podritske and P. Schwartz. Lexington Books, 2009.
TO	*The Objectivist*. Second Renaissance Books, 1990. (This bound edition of the periodical includes pieces by Rand and by other authors.)
TON	*The Objectivist Newsletter*. Bound edition. Second Renaissance Books, 1990.

Unconquered†   *The Unconquered with another, earlier adaptation of We The Living.* Edited by R. Mayhew. Palgrave Macmillan, 2014.

VOR   *The Voice of Reason: Essays in Objectivist Thought.* Edited by L. Peikoff. Meridian, 1990.

VOS   *The Virtue of Selfishness: A New Concept of Egoism.* Centennial edition, printing 70. Signet, 2005.

Workshops‡   "The Objectivist Workshops Transcript with Previously Omitted Sections." Transcribed by Benjamin Bayer for the Ayn Rand Archives. (Portions of an earlier version of this transcript have been published, in an edited form, as an appendix to the expanded second edition of *ITOE*.)

WTL   *We the Living.* 75th anniversary deluxe edition. New American Library, 2011.

WTL36   *We the Living.* Macmillan, 1936.

Secondary Sources

Ackrill, J. L. 1974. "Aristotle on Eudaimonia." *Proceedings of the British Academy* 60.

Alfano, Mark. 2013. *Character as Moral Fiction.* Cambridge University Press.

Badhwar, Neera. 1993a. "Altruism versus Self-Interest: Sometimes a False Dichotomy." *Social Philosophy and Policy* 5, no. 10 (January 1993): 90–117.

Badhwar, Neera. 1993b. "The Virtues of Benevolence: The Unnamed Virtues in *The Fountainhead*." Presented at The Ayn Rand Society, APA, for the fiftieth anniversary of the publication of *The Fountainhead*.

Badhwar, Neera. 1996. "The Limited Unity of Virtue." *Nous* 30, no. 3 (1996): 306–29.

Badhwar, Neera. 1999. "Is Virtue Only a Means to Happiness? An Analysis of Virtue and Happiness in Ayn Rand's Writings." *Reason Papers* 24: 27–44. https://reasonpapers.com/pdf/24/rp_24_2.pdf.

Badhwar, Neera. 2001. *Is Virtue Only a Means to Happiness? An Analysis of Virtue and Happiness in Ayn Rand's Writings.* Objectivist Center, 2001.

Badhwar, Neera. 2014a. "Reasoning about Wrong Reasons, No Reasons, and Reasons of Virtue." In *The Philosophy and Psychology of Character and Happiness*, edited by Nancy E. Snow and Franco Trevigno. Routledge.

Badhwar, Neera. 2014b. *Wellbeing: Happiness in a Worthwhile Life.* Oxford University Press.

Badhwar, Neera K., and Russell E. Jones. 2024. "Aristotle on the Love of Friends." In *The Oxford Handbook of Philosophy of Love*, edited by Christopher Grau and Aaron Smuts. Oxford University Press.

Badhwar, Neera, and Roderick Long. 2020. "Ayn Rand." In *Stanford Encyclopedia of Philosophy*. https://plato.stanford.edu/entries/ayn-rand/.

REFERENCES

Balme, David. 1987. "Aristotle's Biology Was Not Essentialist." In Gotthelf and Lennox 1987.

Barnes, Jonathan, ed. 1984. *The Complete Works of Aristotle: The Revised Oxford Translation*. Princeton University Press.

Barnes, Jonathan. 1993. *Aristotle: Posterior Analytics*. 2nd ed. Oxford.

Bayer, Benjamin. 2022. "That Radiant Selfishness of Soul: The Virtue of Pride." https://www.youtube.com/watch?v=RfZPpIic7-o/.

Bennett, Jonathan. 1974. "The Conscience of Huckleberry Finn." *Philosophy* 49: 123–34.

Binswanger, Harry. 1989. "Consciousness as Identification: The Nature of Cognition and Concept-Formation." Recorded lecture series. Second Renaissance.

Binswanger, Harry. 1990. *The Biological Basis of Teleological Concepts*. Ayn Rand Institute Press.

Binswanger, Harry. 1992. "Life Based Teleology and the Foundations of Ethics." *Monist* 75(1).

Binswanger, Harry. 2014. *How We Know*. TOF Publications.

Boeckmann, Tore. 2007a. "*The Fountainhead* as a Romantic Novel." In Mayhew 2007a.

Boeckmann, Tore. 2007b. "What Might Be and Ought to Be: Aristotle's *Poetics* and *The Fountainhead*." In Mayhew 2007a.

Boeckmann, Tore. 2008. "Caspar David Friedrich and Visual Romanticism." *Objective Standard*, Spring 2008.

Boeckmann, Tore. 2016. "Ayn Rand's Literary Romanticism." In Gotthelf and Salmieri 2016.

Bolton, Robert. 1991. "Aristotle's Method in Natural Science: *Physics* I." In *Aristotle's* Physics: *A Collection of Essays*, edited by L. Judson. Oxford University Press.

Bolton, Robert. 1994. "Aristotle's Conception of Metaphysics as a Science." In *Unity, Identity and Explanation in Aristotle's Metaphysics*, edited by T. Scaltsas, D. Charles, and M. L. Gill. Oxford University Press.

Bostock, David. 2000. *Aristotle's Ethics*. Oxford University Press.

Broadie, Sarah. 1991. *Ethics with Aristotle*. Oxford University Press.

Broadie, Sarah. 2012. "A Science of First Principles (Metaphysics A 2)." In Steel 2012.

Burnett, Francis Hodgson. 1907. *The Shuttle*. Frederick A. Stokes Company. https://www.google.com/books/edition/The_Shuttle/tZ6FdJkzfGsC?hl=en&gbpv=0/.

Cambiano, Giuseppe. 2012. "The Desire to Know (Metaphysics A 1)." In Steel 2012.

Charles, David. 2000. *Aristotle on Meaning and Essence*. Oxford Aristotle Studies. Oxford University Press.

Code, Alan. 1986. "Aristotle's Investigation of a Basic Logical Principle: Which

Science Investigates the Principle of Non-Contradiction?" *Canadian Journal of Philosophy* 16, no. 3 (September): 341–58.

Code, Alan. 1987. "Metaphysics and Logic." In *Aristotle Today: Essays on Aristotle's Ideal of Science*, edited by M. Matthen. Edmonton.

Code, Alan. 1996. "Owen on the Development of Aristotle's Metaphysics." In *Aristotle's Philosophical Development*, edited by William Wians. Rowman and Littlefield.

Code, Alan. 1997. "Aristotle's Metaphysics as a Science of Principles." *Revue Internationale de Philosophie* 51(3): 357–78.

Cohen, Marc J. 1986. "Aristotle on the Principle of Non-Contradiction." *Canadian Journal of Philosophy* 16, no. 3 (September 1986): 359–70.

Cooper, John M. 1975. *Reason and Human Good in Aristotle*. Harvard University Press.

Cooper, John M. 1980. "Friendship and the Human Good." In *Essays on Aristotle's Ethics*, edited by A. O. Rorty. University of California Press.

Cooper, John M. 1999a. "Contemplation and Happiness: A Reconsideration." In *Reason and Emotion*. Princeton University Press.

Cooper, John M. 1999b. "Some Remarks on Aristotle's Moral Psychology." In *Reason and Emotion*. Princeton: Princeton University Press.

Cooper, John M. 2004. "Metaphysics in Aristotle's Embryology." In *Knowledge, Nature, and the Good*. Princeton University Press.

Cooper, John M. 2012. *Pursuits of Wisdom*. Princeton University Press.

Crubellier, Michel. 2009 "Aporiae 1–2." In *Aristotle's* Metaphysics *Beta: Symposium Aristotelicum*, edited by Michel Crubellier and André Laks. Oxford.

de Liège, Tristan. 2023. "The Human Form of Life: Rand and Foot on Biological Foundations of Normativity." *Reason Papers* 43, no. 2 (Fall 2023): 44–68.

de Vere's, Maximilian Schele. 1871. *Americanisms: The English of the New World*.

Deci, Edward. 1995. *Why We Do What We Do*. Penguin.

Den Uyl, Douglas, and Douglas B. Rasmussen. 1978. "Nozick on the Randian Argument." *Personalist* 59: 184–205. Reprinted in *Reading Nozick*, edited by Jeffrey Paul. Rowman and Littlefield, 1981.

Drefcinski, Shane. 1996. "Aristotle's Fallible Phronimos." *Ancient Philosophy* 16 (1996): 139–54.

Else, Gerald. 1957. *Aristotle's* Poetics: *The Argument*. Harvard University Press.

Falcon, A. 2017. "*Physics* I.1." In *Aristotle's* Physics *I: A Systematic Exploration*, edited by D. Quarantotto. Cambridge University Press.

Falcon, A. 2021. "Aristotle on the Infant Mind." In *Le langage: Lectures d'Aristote*, edited by L. Gazziero. Peeters, Leuven.

Ferejohn, Michael. 1991. *The Origins of Aristotelian Science*. Yale University Press.

Franklin, Benjamin. 1996. *The Autobiography of Benjamin Franklin*. Mineola, NY: Dover Publications.

Fraser, Nancy. 2013. *Fortunes of Feminism: From State-Managed Capitalism to Neoliberal Crisis.* Verso.

Frede, Michael. 1987. "The Title, Unity, and Authenticity of the Aristotelian Categories." In *Essays in Ancient Philosophy*, edited by Michael Frede. University of Minnesota Press.

Freeman, Jan. 2011. "'Making Money': Good English or All-American?" *Throw Grammar from the Train: Notes from a Recovering Nitpicker.* https://throwgrammarfromthetrain.blogspot.com/2011/01/making-money-good-english-or-all.html.

Furth, M. 1986. "A Note on Aristotle's Principle of Non-Contradiction." *Canadian Journal of Philosophy* 16, no. 3 (September 1986): 371-82.

Gayford, Martin, and Karen Wright, eds. 2000. *The Grove Book of Art Writing.* Grove Press.

Geach, P. T. 1957. *Mental Acts.* Routledge and Kegan Paul.

Ghate, Onkar. 2009. "The Part and Chapter Headings of *Atlas Shrugged.*" In Mayhew 2009.

Ghate, Onkar. 2016. "A Being of Self-Made Soul." In Gotthelf and Salmieri 2016.

Gotthelf, Allan, ed. 1985. *Aristotle on Nature and Living Things.* Mathesis Publications and Bristol Classical Press.

Gotthelf, Allan. 1988. "The Place of the Good in Aristotle's Natural Teleology." *Boston Area Colloquium in Ancient Philosophy* 4: 113-39.

Gotthelf, Allan. 1997. "Division and Explanation in Aristotle's *Parts of Animals.*" In *Beiträge zur antiken Philosophie: Festschrift für Wolfgang Kullmann*, edited by H.-C. Günther and A. Rengakos. Steiner Verlag. Republished as Gotthelf 2012, ch. 9.

Gotthelf, Allan. 2000. *On Ayn Rand.* Wadsworth.

Gotthelf, Allan. 2011. "The Choice to Value." In Gotthelf and Lennox 2011.

Gotthelf, Allan. 2012. *Teleology, First Principles, and Scientific Method in Aristotle's Biology.* Oxford University Press.

Gotthelf, Allan. 2013. "Ayn Rand's Theory of Concepts: Rethinking Abstraction and Essence." In Gotthelf and Lennox 2013.

Gotthelf, Allan (completed by Gregory Salmieri). 2016. "The Morality of Life." In Gotthelf and Salmieri 2016.

Gotthelf, Allan, and James G. Lennox, eds. 1987. *Philosophical Issues in Aristotle's Biology.* Cambridge University Press.

Gotthelf, Allan, and James G. Lennox, eds. 2011. *Metaethics, Egoism, and Virtue: Studies in Ayn Rand's Normative Theory.* University of Pittsburgh Press.

Gotthelf, Allan, and James G. Lennox, eds. 2013. *Concepts and Their Role in Knowledge: Reflections on Objectivist Epistemology.* Pittsburgh University Press.

Gotthelf, Allan, and Gregory Salmieri, eds. 2016. *A Companion to Ayn Rand.* Wiley-Blackwell.

Greenwood, L. H. G. 1909. *Aristotle: Nicomachean Ethics Book VI*. Cambridge University Press.

Gregor, Mary J., ed. 1996. *The Cambridge Edition of the Works of Immanuel Kant: Practical Philosophy*. Cambridge University Press.

Gross, David. 2018. "The Ghost of Aristotle Interviewed by a Telepathic Tapeworm." Website: https://sniggle.net/TPL/index5.php?entry=29Nov18/.

Halliwell, Stephen. 1987. *The Poetics of Aristotle: Translation and Commentary*. University of North Carolina Press.

Halliwell, Stephen. 1998. *Aristotle's Poetics*. 2nd ed. University of Chicago Press.

Hardie, W. F. R. 1965. "The Final Good in Aristotle's Ethics." *Philosophy: The Journal of the Royal Institute of Philosophy* 40:154.

Hayduck, M., ed. 1891. *Alexandri Aphrodisiensis in Aristotelis Metaphysica Commentaria* (CAG 1). Berlin.

Hitz, Zena. 2020. *Lost in Thought*. Princeton University Press.

Hospers, John. 1961. *Human Conduct: An Introduction to the Problems of Ethics*. Harcourt, Brace and World.

Huemer, Michael. 1996. "Why I Am Not an Objectivist." https://spot.colorado.edu/~huemer/papers/rand.htm.

Huemer, Michael. 2002. "Is Benevolent Egoism Coherent?" *Journal of Ayn Rand Studies* 3(2).

Huemer, Michael. 2019. "Defending Liberty: The Commonsense Approach." In Salmieri and Mayhew 2019.

Hugo, Victor. 1864a. *William Shakespeare*. Librairie Internationale.

Hugo, Victor. 1864b. *William Shakespeare*. Hurst and Blackett. (Translation attributed to A. Baillot, though uncredited in the text.)

Hugo, Victor. 1887. *William Shakespeare*. Translated by Melville B. Anderson. A. C. McClurg and Company.

Hunt, Morton. 1959. *The Natural History of Love*. Knopf.

Hursthouse, Rosalind. 1999. *On Virtue Ethics*. Oxford University Press.

Irwin, Terence. 1980. "The Metaphysical and Psychological Basis of Aristotle's Ethics." In *Essays on Aristotle's Ethics*, edited by A. O. Rorty. University of California Press.

Irwin, Terence. 1988a. *Aristotle's First Principles*. Clarendon Press.

Irwin, Terence. 1988b. "Disunity in the Aristotelian Virtues." In *Oxford Studies in Ancient Philosophy*, edited by J. Annas. Supplementary volume. Clarendon Press.

Irwin, Terence, trans. 1999. *Nicomachean Ethics*. 2nd ed. Hackett.

Janko, Richard. 1984. *Aristotle on Comedy: Towards a Reconstruction of Poetics II*. Duckworth.

Janko, Richard. 1987. *Aristotle: Poetics with the Tractatus Coislinianus, Reconstruction of Poetics II, and Fragments of the On Poets*. Hackett.

Janko, Richard. 1992. "From Catharsis to Aristotelian Mean." In *Essays on Aristotle's* Poetics, edited by A. O. Rorty. Princeton University Press.

Joseph, H. W. B. 1916. *An Introduction to Logic*. Clarendon Press.

Kahn, Charles. 2009. "A Return to the Theory of the Verb *Be* and the Concept of Being." *Ancient Philosophy* 24: 381–405. Reprinted in his *Essays on Being*.

Karbowski, Joseph. 2019. *Aristotle's Method in Ethics: Philosophy in Practice*. Cambridge University Press.

Kelley, David. 2014. *Unrugged Individualism: The Selfish Basis of Benevolence*. Revised ed. https://atlassociety.org/sites/default/files/Unrugged_Ind.pdf; 2003/. The Atlas Society.

Kelsey, S. 2008. "The Place of I. 7 in the Argument of *Physics I*." *Phronesis* 53: 180–208.

Kenny, Anthony. 1977. "Aristotle on Happiness." In *Articles on Aristotle*, vol. 2. *Ethics & Politics*, edited by Barnes, Schofield, and Sorabji. Duckworth.

Keyt, David. 1983. "Intellectualism in Aristotle." In *Essays in Ancient Greek Philosophy*, vol. 2, edited by John P. Anton and Anthony Preus. SUNY Press.

Kosman, Aryeh. 2013. *The Activity of Being*. Harvard University Press.

Kraut, Richard. 1991. *Aristotle on the Human Good*. Princeton University Press.

Lear, Gabriel R. 2004. *Happy Lives and the Highest Good*. Princeton University Press.

Lear, Jonathan. 1980. *Aristotle and Logical Theory*. Cambridge University Press.

Lennox, James G. 1985. "Are Aristotelian Species Eternal?" In Gotthelf 1985.

Lennox, James G. 1987. "Kinds, Forms of Kinds, and the More and the Less." In Gotthelf and Lennox 1987.

Lennox, James G. 2001a. *Aristotle on the Parts of Animals I-IV*. Oxford University Press.

Lennox, James G. 2001b. *Aristotle's Philosophy of Biology*. Cambridge University Press.

Lennox, James. G. 2021. *Aristotle on Inquiry: Erotetic Frameworks and Domain-Specific Norms*. Cambridge.

Lewis, John, and Gregory Salmieri. 2016. "A Philosopher on Her Times." In Gotthelf and Salmieri 2016.

Lewis, Sinclair. 1920. *Main Street: The Story of Carol Kennicott*. Grosset and Dunlap.

Liberman, Mar. 2006. "Ayn Rand, Linguist?" Language Log. http://itre.cis.upenn.edu/~myl/languagelog/archives/002929.html.

London, Jack. 1956. *Jack London's Tales of Adventure*. Edited by Irving Shepard. Hannover House.

London, Jack. 2015. *The Collected Works of Jack London: The Complete Works*. Pergamon Media. Kindle Edition.

Long, Roderick. 2000. *Reason and Value: Aristotle versus Rand*. Objectivist Center.

Long, Roderick. 2010. "The Winnowing of Ayn Rand." *Cato Unbound*. www.cato-unbound.org/2010/ 01/20/roderick-t-long/winnowing-ayn-rand/.

Long, Roderick. 2016. "Rational Animals, Productivity, and Constitutive Virtues. *Cato Unbound*. www. cato-unbound.org/2016/11/03/roderick-t-long/rational-animals-productivity-constitutive-virtues/.

Long, Roderick. 2020. "From Defiant Egoist to Submissive Citizen: Is There a Bridge? Why the Hell Is There a Bridge?" *Journal of Ayn Rand Studies* 20(2).

Mack, Eric. 1984. "The Fundamental Moral Elements of Rand's Theory of Rights." In *The Philosophic Thought of Ayn Rand*, edited by Douglas Den Uyl and Douglas Rasmussen. University of Illinois Press.

Mack, Eric. 2003. "Problematic Arguments in Randian Ethics." *Journal of Ayn Rand Studies* 5, no. 1 (Fall): 1–66.

Matthen, M. ed. 1987. *Aristotle Today: Essays on Aristotle's Ideal of Science*. Academic Printing and Publishing.

Mayhew, Robert. 2004. "*We the Living* '36 & '59." In *Essays on Ayn Rand's* We the Living, edited by Robert Mayhew. Lexington Books.

Mayhew, Robert, ed. 2005. *Essays on Ayn Rand's* Anthem. Lexington Books.

Mayhew, Robert, ed. 2007a. *Essays on Ayn Rand's* The Fountainhead. Lexington Books.

Mayhew, Robert. 2007b. "Humor in *The Fountainhead*." In Mayhew 2007a.

Mayhew, Robert, ed. 2009. *Essays on Ayn Rand's* Atlas Shrugged. Lexington Books.

Mayhew, Robert. 2012. "Kira Argounova Laughed: Humor and Joy in *We the Living*." In *Essays on Ayn Rand's* We the Living, 2nd ed., edited by Robert Mayhew. Lexington Books.

Mayhew, Robert. 2019a. "Achilles' Inconsistency in Aristotle's Lost *Homeric Problems*: A Fresh Look at Four bT-scholia of the *Iliad*." *Hyperboreus: Bibliotheca Classica Petropolitana* 25(1): 5–26.

Mayhew, Robert. 2019b. *Aristotle's Lost* Homeric Problems: *Textual Studies*. Oxford University Press.

McDowell, John 1980. "The Role of Eudaimonia in Aristotle's Ethics." In *Essays on Aristotle's Ethics*, edited by Amelie Rorty. University of California Press.

McDowell, John. 1994. *Mind and World*. Harvard University Press.

McDowell, John. 1998. *Mind, Value and Reality*. Harvard University Press.

McKeon, Richard, ed. 1941. *The Basic Works of Aristotle*. Random House.

Merritt, Maria, John Doris, and Gilbert Harman. 2010. "Character." In *The Moral Psychology Handbook*, edited by John Doris and The Moral Psychology Research Group. Oxford University Press.

Mignucci, Mario. 1975. *L'argomentazione dimostrativa in Aristotele*. Antenore.

Mill, J. S. 1871. *Utilitarianism*. London: Longman, Green, Reader, and Dyer.

Miller, Casey, and Kate Swift. 1976. *Words and Women*. Anchor Press/Doubleday.

Miller, Fred D., Jr. 2013. "Aristotle on Belief and Knowledge." In *Reason and Analysis in Ancient Greek Philosophy*, edited by Georgios Anagnostopoulos and Fred D. Miller Jr. Springer.

Moosavi, Parisa. 2019. "From Biological Functions to Natural Goodness." *Philosophers' Imprint* 19:51.

Moss, Jessica. 2011. "Virtue Makes the Goal Right." *Phronesis* 56(3): 204–61.

Moulton, Janice. 1981. "The Myth of the Neutral 'Man.'" In *Sexist Language: A Modern Philosophical Analysis*, edited by Mary Vetterling-Braggin. Littlefield, Adams.

Nederman, Cary J. 2008. "Men at Work: *Poesis*, Politics and Labor in Aristotle and Some Aristotelians." *Analyse & Kritik* 30.

Nock, Albert Jay. 1943. *Memoirs of a Superfluous Man*. Harper and Brothers.

Nozick, Robert. 1971. "On the Randian Argument." *The Personalist* 52: 282–304. Reprinted in *Reading Nozick*, edited by Jeffrey Paul. Rowman and Littlefield, 1981. Also reprinted in *Socratic Puzzles*, edited by Robert Nozick. Harvard University Press, 1997.

Øversveen, Emil. 2022. "Capitalism and Alienation: Towards a Marxist Theory of Alienation for the 21st Century." *European Journal of Social Theory* 25 (3).

Owen, G. E. L. 1960. "Logic and Metaphysics in Some Earlier Works of Aristotle." In *Aristotle and Plato in the Mid-fourth Century*, edited by I. Düring and G. E. L. Owen. Humanities Press. Reprinted in G. E. L. Owen, *Logic, Science, and Dialectic*. Cornell University Press, 1986.

Peikoff, Leonard, 1976. *The Philosophy of Objectivism*. Recorded lecture series, available at https://estore.aynrand.org/products/the-philosophy-of-objectivism-mp3-download/.

Peikoff, Leonard. 1991. *Objectivism: The Philosophy of Ayn Rand*. Penguin Books.

Peikoff, Leonard. 1998. *Objectivism through Induction*. Recorded lecture series. Second Renaissance.

Peramatzis M. 2010. "Essence and *per se* Predication in Aristotle's *Metaphysics* Z.4." *Oxford Studies in Ancient Philosophy* 39: 121–82.

Politis, V. 2004. *Routledge Philosophy Guidebook to Aristotle and the Metaphysics*. Routledge.

Randall, John Herman, Jr. 1960. *Aristotle*. Columbia University Press.

Rasmussen, Douglas. 2002. "Rand on Obligation and Value." *Journal of Ayn Rand Studies* 4: 69–86.

Rasmussen, Douglas. 2006. "Regarding Choice and the Foundations of Morality: Reflections on Rand's Ethics." *Journal of Ayn Rand Studies* 7(2): 309–28.

Rasmussen, Douglas. 2007a. "The Aristotelian Significance of the Section Titles of *Atlas Shrugged*: A Brief Consideration of Rand's View of Logic and Reality." In *Ayn Rand's* Atlas Shrugged: *A Philosophical and Literary Companion*, edited by Edward W. Younkins. Ashgate.

Rasmussen, Douglas. 2007b. "Rand's Metaethics: Rejoinder to Hartford." *Journal of Ayn Rand Studies* 8(2): 307–16.

Reeve, C. D. C. 1992. *Practices of Reason: Aristotle's Nicomachean Ethics*. Oxford University Press.

Reeve, C. D. C. 2013. *Aristotle on Practical Wisdom: Nicomachean Ethics VI*. Harvard University Press.

Rheins, Jason. 2016. "Objectivist Metaphysics: The Primacy of Existence." In Gotthelf and Salmieri 2016.

Robinson, Cedric 2019. *On Racial Capitalism, Black Internationalism, and Cultures of Resistance*. Pluto Press.

Ross, W. D., trans. 1915. *Nicomachean Ethics*. In *The Works of Aristotle Translated into English*, vol. 9, edited by J. A. Smith and W. D. Ross. Oxford University Press.

Ross, W. D. 1949. *Aristotle's Prior and Posterior Analytics*. Oxford University Press.

Ross, W. D. 1953. *Aristotle's Metaphysics*. Vol. 1. Oxford University Press.

Russell, Daniel C. 2009. *Practical Intelligence and the Virtues*. Clarendon Press.

Salmieri, Gregory. 2005. "Prometheus' Discovery: Individualism and the Concept 'I' in *Anthem*." In Mayhew 2005.

Salmieri, Gregory. 2007. *Atlas Shrugged as a Work of Philosophy*. Lecture Course available online at https://courses.aynrand.org/campus-courses/atlas-shrugged-as-a-work-of-philosophy/.

Salmieri, Gregory. 2008. *Aristotle and the Problem of Concepts*. Dissertation, University of Pittsburgh.

Salmieri, Gregory. 2009a. "Aristotle's Non-'dialectical' Method in the *Nichomachean Ethics*." *Ancient Philosophy* 29: 311–35.

Salmieri, Gregory. 2009b. "*Atlas Shrugged* on the Role of the Mind in Human Existence." In Mayhew 2009.

Salmieri, Gregory. 2009c. "Discovering Atlantis: *Atlas Shrugged*'s Demonstration of a New Moral Philosophy." In Mayhew 2009.

Salmieri, Gregory. 2012. "Aristotle's Conception of Universality." https://doi.org/10.13140/RG.2.2.15064.30728.

Salmieri, Gregory. 2013. "Conceptualization and Justification." In Gotthelf and Lennox 2013.

Salmieri, Gregory. 2016a. "The Act of Valuing (and the Objectivity of Values)." In Gotthelf and Salmieri 2016.

Salmieri, Gregory. 2016b. "Annotated Bibliography of Primary and Quasi-Primary Sources." In Gotthelf and Salmieri 2016.

Salmieri, Gregory. 2016c. "Egoism and Altruism." In Gotthelf and Salmieri 2016.

Salmieri, Gregory. 2016d. "The Objectivist Epistemology." In Gotthelf and Salmieri 2016.

Salmieri, Gregory. 2019. "Selfish Regard for the Rights of Others." In Salmieri and Mayhew 2019.
Salmieri Gregory. 2023. "Capitalism: The Only Moral Social System." https://www.youtube.com/watch?v=AAUqnNyMO2c/.
Salmieri, Gregory, and Benjamin Bayer. 2014. "How We Choose Our Beliefs." *Philosophia* 42: 41–53.
Salmieri, Gregory, and Robert Mayhew, eds. 2019. *Foundations of a Free Society*. University of Pittsburgh Press.
Sandel, Michael. 2013. *What Money Can't Buy: The Moral Limits of Markets*. Penguin.
Scaltsas, T., D. Charles, and M. L. Gill, eds., 1994. *Unity, Identity and Explanation in Aristotle's Metaphysics*. Oxford University Press.
Scott, D. 2015. *Levels of Argument: A Comparative Study of Plato's* Republic *and Aristotle's* Nicomachean Ethics. Oxford University Press.
Shields, Christopher. 1999. *Order in Multiplicity: Homonymy in the Philosophy of Aristotle*. Oxford University Press.
Smith, Tara. 2000. *Viable Values*. Rowman and Littlefield.
Smith, Tara. 2006. *Ayn Rand's Normative Ethics: The Virtuous Egoist*. Cambridge University Press.
Smyth, Herbert. 1956. *Greek Grammar*. Rev. ed. Harvard University Press.
Stasz, Clarice. 1999. "Jack London's 'Credo'" http://london.sonoma.edu/credo.html. Site now defunct, archived at https://archive.ph/20121215010151/http://london.sonoma.edu/London/credo.html#selection-157.25-157.61/.
Steel, Carlos, ed. 2012. *Aristotle's* Metaphysics Alpha: *Symposium Aristotelicum*. Oxford University Press.
Swanton, Christine. 2003. *Virtue Ethics: A Pluralistic View*. Oxford University Press.
Tarán, Leonardo, and Dimitri Gutas. 2012. *Aristotle, Poetics: Editio Maior of the Greek Text with Historical Introductions and Philological Commentaries*. Leiden.
Tolstoy, Leo. 2000. *Anna Karenina*. Translated by Richard Pevear and Larissa Volokhonsky. Penguin.
van Emde Boas, Evert, Albert Rijksbaron, Luuk Huitink, and Mathieu de Bakker. 2019. *The Cambridge Grammar of Classical Greek*. Cambridge University Press.
Wallace, James. 1978. *Virtues and Vices*. Cornell University Press.
Warren, Virginia L. 1986. "Guidelines for Non-sexist Use of Language." *Proceedings and Addresses of the American Philosophical Association* 59(3).
Wheeler, Jack. 1984. "Rand and Aristotle: A Comparison of Objectivist and Aristotelian Ethics." In *The Philosophic Thought of Ayn Rand*, edited by Douglas Den Uyl and Douglas B. Rasmussen. University of Illinois Press, 1984.

Wilde, Oscar. 1891. "The Soul of Man Under Socialism." Boston: John W. Luce and Company.

Wilson, Timothy D. 2002. *Strangers to Ourselves*. Harvard University Press.

Wolfe, Tom. 1975. *The Painted Word*. Picador.

Wood, Gordon S. 1991. *The Radicalism of the American Revolution*. Knopf.

Wright, Darryl. 2005. "Needs of the Psyche in the Early Ayn Rand." In Mayhew 2005.

Wright, Darryl. 2009. "Ayn Rand's Ethics from *The Fountainhead* to *Atlas Shrugged*." In Mayhew 2009.

Wright, Darryl. 2011. "Reasoning about Ends: Life as a Value in Ayn Rand's Ethics." In Gotthelf and Lennox 2011.

Wright, Darryl. 2019. "The Scope and Justification of Rand's Non-initiation of Force Principle." In Salmieri and Mayhew 2019.

INDEX

Note: References following "n" refer notes.

A is A (phrase), 6–7, 28–29, 204. *See also* identity, law of
absolutism, contextual, 210n7. *See also* essence: Rand's view of
abstraction. *See* concept
Achilles, 251n26, 252
actions: as under direct control, 205–6, 208–9, 226, 228–30
Agathon, 252
agency, 108n33, 195–96
akrasia, 150–51, 165, 174, 215
Alexander of Aphrodesias, 15n19
algebra, 17–18, 66
altruism, 190–93
analysis (*diairēsis*), 80
Answers, 106
Anthem, 123–24, 127
aporia. *See* puzzle
appearance vs. reality, 10–11. *See also* change: problem of
Aquinas, Thomas, 104
Argounova, Kira, 121–22, 123n23, 127–28, 179, 182, 187
art (technical expertise). *See* technē
art: as concretization of metaphysics, 254, 277–78; as concretizing an ideal, 136–37; as rational, 245–48; definition of, 248; educational role of, 254–56; purpose of, 128, 247, 252–54; representational, 246, 248, 257; similarities to love, 277–80. *See also* literature
Art of Fiction, The, 69n9, 70, 133n35
Art of Nonfiction, The, 46, 52, 133n34
Atlas Shrugged, 6–7, 122, 125, 127–28; Aristotelian references, 5–7, 16, 28–29, 63n1, 126n26; Galt's speech, 29, 111n1, 203–5, 224; "The Meaning of Money" (Francisco's speech), 113n5; "The Meaning of Sex" (Francisco's speech), 270–71, 276–77; nature of heroes in, 134, 178, 185n28, 186, 187–88, 192–93, 200; nature of villains in, 178, 186–87, 199; on friendship and romance, 136, 142, 179, 181–82, 197–98, 215n12, 278–81; on metaphysics, 16, 28, 34, 204; on morality, 96, 97, 104, 111, 125, 141, 205; on productivity and creation, 184, 186, 237–38, 247; on self-esteem and pride, 217–18, 224, 268–69; on sense of life, 195, 215–16; on virtue, 137n42, 180, 185, 203, 210n7, 222–23, 238
Ayn Rand Letter, The, 143

axiomatic concepts. *See* axioms; concepts: axiomatic

axioms: abstractness of, 17–19; function and need for, 7–8, 13–14, 17–18, 22–25, 33–35; reference of, 10–13, 18–22, 33–34; validation of, 14–17, 25–26, 34; vs. axiomatic concepts, 27–28, 32, 35–41; vs. posits, 7, 35. *See also* concepts: axiomatic; Excluded Middle, Principle of; identity; Non-Contradiction, Principle of

Bacon, Francis, 160, 221

Balme, David, 74

beauty, 175, 232; Platonic form of, 260–61

being, 29, 46–50, 54–57. *See also* existence; substance

benevolence, 189–200, 203, 236–39. *See also* kindness

benevolent universe premise, 195. *See also* sense of life

best within us, the (phrase), 122

bias, 170–71

Binswanger, Harry, 66

Biographical Interviews, 29

biology: relationship to ethics, 143–45, 151–52, 158. *See also* ethics: Aristotelian, as biocentric

Boeckmann, Tore, 250

Bolton, Robert, 14–15, 45

Boswell, James, 113n5

Boyle, Orren, 186

Branden, Nathaniel, 190–91, 214, 278–80

bravery, 167–68

Burnett, Francis Hodgson, 120, 123

Cameron, Henry, 136n41, 188, 198, 200, 235

capitalism, 89n3, 118, 123, 160

caretakers, dependence on, 196–97, 239

Carnap, Rudolf, 41

caste system: in Aristotle's ethics, 117

Categories, 48, 50, 52, 57

categorical imperative, Kantian, 105–6

categories, Aristotelian, 11–12, 21–22, 36, 46–57

catharsis, 253n31, 254

causality, law of, 28

causation, final, 99n14, 106, 110

central idea, 126n27, 133–34

change: Aristotle's theory of, 80–83; problem of, 39n2, 207. *See also* appearance vs. reality

character, 177, 211–12. *See also* virtue: characterological

characterization. *See* literature: characterization

charity, 189–91, 228

choice, 103–10, 134, 156, 204–6, 224, 228–29. *See also* free will; live, choice to

Code, Alan, 15, 45

comedy. *See* literature: comedy

concept-formation, 18–22, 53, 64–68, 74–75; as illuminating complexity, 78, 83

concepts: as affections in the soul, 70; axiomatic, 17–28; definition of, 67; explanatory power of, 78; issue of, 18–19; Rand's theory of, 63–68; theoretical vs. ordinary, 84–85; vs. propositions, 32, 35–41, 42–43

conceptual common denominator, 20

confirmation bias. *See* bias

consciousness: as an active process, 24; as axiomatic concept, 18–19, 20–21, 27–28 (*see also* concepts: axiomatic; Primacy of Consciousness; Primacy of Existence)

consequentialism, 202

contemplation: Aristotle's ideal life, 112, 115–16, 168. *See also* leisure, life of; as divine, 117–18; vs. deliberation, 114–15, 245

Cook, Lois, 248n17

Cooper, John, vii, 74, 92, 95, 258n1, 273–75, 277

courage, 168, 255

Cratylus, 15n16

creativity, 129–30, 141

creator (Roarkian), 125–26. *See also* Roark, Howard: on building and creation

Capitalism: the Unknown Ideal: "What Is Capitalism?," 109, 113, 118, 129n30, 191

d'Anconia, Francisco, 187, 221; and

Dagny Taggart, 141n47, 179, 183, 216n13; and Hank Rearden, 210, 218, 222n17, 280; and John Galt, 136n40; Speech on the meaning of money (*see Atlas Shrugged*, "The Meaning of Money"); Speech on the meaning of sex (*see Atlas Shrugged*, "The Meaning of Sex")

De Anima, 93; Book II: 30, 48n7, 93, 114, 125; Book III: 70, 72, 100

Danneskjöld, Ragnar, 5, 7, 12

De Caelo, 59

definition, 53, 75; purpose of, 67–68. See also essence

deliberation (vs. contemplation), 114–15, 245

demonstration: Aristotelian, 7–9, 11, 14–17; premise vs. presupposition of, 8

deontology, 189, 202

determinate signification, principle of, 39, 41–42

De Interpretatione, 70

dialectic, 9, 14–17, 154n1

Donnigan, Mike, 186

Eudemian Ethics, Book I: 112, 114, 130; Book II: 114; VII: 93, 274n3

egoism vs. altruism, 190–93

Either-or (phrase), 6–7

elenctic demonstration, 14–17, 34, 43–44, 46fn2. See also Non-contradiction, Principle of: validation; reaffirmation through denial

emotional disposition, 170, 179, 181, 203, 218–19

emotions: as dependent on value judgments, 166, 176–79, 211–13, 234–35; as not tools of cognition, 179, 214–16; vs. reason, 176–79, 214–16, 234–35

endoxa, method of, 93, 150–51, 153–54, 157

enkrateia, 165, 174, 215–16

entity, 50–52, 55, 57, 68–69. See also substance

epic. See literature: epic

epistēmē, 7–8, 47, 72, 94, 114

epistemological vs. metaphysical distinction, 21–25, 51–53, 55, 68, 75, 97

epistemology: need for, 209–10

essence: Aristotle compared to Rand, 18n25, 29, 52–53, 57, 68, 75; Aristotle's metaphysical view of, 36–38, 40–44, 70–74; as the fundamental distinguishing characteristic, 67–68; Rand's view of, 63–68; vs. accident, 48n7, 57

eternalism, 59

ethical methodology, 149–50; Aristotle's, 153–58; Rand's, 161

ethics: Aristotelian, as biocentric, 100, 110; as founded on prescientific experience, 140–41, 151, 154–55, 158; objectivity of, 90–95, 137–47, 154–55, 229; of emergencies, 190; purpose of, 94, 139, 229–30; Rand's view of Aristotelian, 89–95; Rand's views as more abstract than Aristotle's, 146–47; relationship to biology, 143–45, 151–52, 158

eudaimonia, 99–101, 103–4, 108, 119n17, 185

Euripides, 251

evasion, 199, 223–24

evolutionary psychology, 156

Excluded Middle, Principle of (PEM), 7–17, 26–29. See also axioms; Either-or

existence, 18–19, 20–21, 27–28, 54–57, 155. See also being; concepts: axiomatic; Primacy of Existence

fact: meaning of, 55n19

Ferris, Floyd, 199–200

fiction. See art: literature

first philosophy. See metaphysics

flourishing. See *eudaimonia*

Foot, Philippa, 137

form: human (*see* Man's life); vs. kind, 73–75; vs. matter, 48, 50, 56, 77, 80–83, 96

forms, Platonic, 53, 72, 260–62, 269. See also realism (about concepts)

Fountainhead, The, 122, 126, 129, 137, 179–80, 243, 272; literary method of, 243–44, 248n17, 251; psychological plausibility of characters in, 180n20; Roark's courtroom speech, 113, 123–25, 135, 193n42

Francon, Dominique, 174, 179–80, 199, 216n13, 221

Franklin, Benjamin: list of virtues, 206–7

free will, 126, 205, 229. See also choice

friendship, 128, 172, 264–65, 272–75, 277, 280–81. *See also* love
For the New Intellectual, 58, 69n8, 89n2, 113, 125, 175n14, 244
function argument, Aristotle's, 92, 150–51, 158–59
Furth, Montgomery, 15
Generation of Animals, Book II: 100n18; Book IV: 74
Galt, John, 136, 187, 221; and Dagny Taggart, 134, 136n40, 278–79; and Francisco d'Anconia, 136n40. *See also Atlas Shrugged*: Galt's speech
Generation and Corruption, 100n18
Geach, Peter, 69
generalization, false, 85
generosity, 167–68, 194–98, 201, 226–28, 236–39
God: Aristotelian, 59, 117–18, 135–36; belief in, 161, 188, 223
good, ultimate. *See* value: ultimate
goodness, as property vs. action, 175, 207–8
Gotthelf, Allan, 100n18, 103n27, 106–8, 281
government controls, 187
gratification, life of, 112n4
Historia Animalium, 73, 79
Halliwell, Stephen, 246
hamartia, 253n31
happiness, 98–99, 180, 195–96, 219–20; and love, 262–63, 267; and self-esteem, 219, 268–69; vs. survival, 175n13 (*see also* living vs. existing; living well vs. mere living). *See also* eudaimonia; survival
health, 47n6, 208n3
Heraclitus, 15n16
hero-worship, 256
Herodotus, 249
heroes: as efficacious, 123, 183, 186–87; Rand's, 123, 128, 136, 175n13, 200, 233. *See also* creator (Roarkian), magnanimous man (Aristotelian)
Hesiod, 92, 245
Himmler, Heinrich, 179
Hippocrates, 102

history vs. fiction, 243–44, 249–50
Homer, 92, 184, 245, 252
homosexuality, 144, 171, 182
honesty, 98, 141, 175, 184–85, 224–25. *See also* virtues
honor, 130
Hopkins, Ernest J., 120n20
Hospers, John, 129n35
Hugo, Victor, 119, 123, 252n30
human being: as ends in themselves, 193–94, 196–97; as rational animal, 127–28, 142–43, 263; as social animal, 142. *See also* Man's Life
Hunsacker, Lee, 186
Hunt, Morton, 260
Hursthouse, Rosalind, 202
identity: axiomatic concept of, 18–19, 20–21, 27–28, 41, 54–57; law of, 6n1, 28, 29n39, 41–42, 52. *See also* A is A; axioms; concepts: axiomatic
immovable mover. *See* Prime Mover
implicit knowledge, 19–20, 22, 56
incompetence: in relation to vice, 186–87
independence, 184, 224–25. *See also* virtues
individuality, 124, 129–30, 148–49
induction, 9, 17n22, 26, 150–51
Industrial Revolution, 160
infallibility, 209–10
infinite regress, 14, 33, 99
integration, need for cognitive, 64
integrity, 98, 175, 184–85, 224–25, 239. *See also* virtues
Irwin, Terence, 150, 153–54, 169
is-ought problem, 97
Introduction to Objectivist Epistemology, 17–25, 64–70, 98, 100, 128, 210; Foreword, 53, 63–64; Ch.1, 56; Ch.2, 65–67; Ch.5, 67–69, 98, 100, 128; Ch.6, 26n34, 27, 34–35, 53, 54, 56; Ch.8, 210n6; Workshops, 6n1, 21, 20n27, 23–25, 51–55, 57, 65
Johnson, Samuel, 113n5
Joseph, H. W. B., 28n38
Journals of Ayn Rand, The, 17, 18n24, 19n26, 105, 135n40, 248n16

justice, 98, 141, 168, 176, 184–85, 224–25. *See also* virtues
Kant, Immanuel, 56, 69, 75, 105, 202n1, 229, 233
Keating, Peter, 129, 174, 176n15, 181n23, 198–99
Kelley, David, 196
kind vs. form, 73–75
kindness, 194–98, 201, 226–28, 236–39. *See also* benevolence
knowledge: first to us vs. first in nature, 78–79, 83, 84
Kosman, Aryeh, 29n40
Larkin, Paul, 186
Laws of logic (Aristotelian), 5–17
Lawson, Eugene, 186
Lear, Gabriel Richardson, 116n6
Leibniz, Gottfried Wilhelm, 41
leisure, life of, 112, 114–28. *See also* contemplation; life: ideal form of
Lennox, James (Jim), 74, 281
Letters of Ayn Rand, The, 129n30, 244
Lewis, Sinclair, 121, 253
life: analogies to artistic composition, 133–34, 142; as an activity, 111, 114; as standard of value, 97–99, 101–3, 130–32, 139, 140–41, 146; as ultimate value, 96–97, 128, 129n30, 175n13 (*see also* value: ultimate); ideal form of, 111–12, 124–28, 185–86; similarities between Aristotle's and Rand's ideal, 119–24, 168; spiritual meaning of, 122 (*see also* living vs. existing; living well vs. mere living)
literature: Aristotle's classification of, 257; characterization, 251n26, 252, 253; comedy, 249, 257; epic, 249n21, 251–53, 256, 257; epic vs. tragedy, 253n32, 257; plot, 248–51; plot-theme, 133n35; Romanticism, 134–35, 256; tragedy, 249, 251–53, 257; vs. history, 243–44, 249–50. *See also* art
live, choice to, 105–8
living vs. existing, 119–21, 122–23
living well vs. mere living (phrase), 112, 114, 118
Locke, John, 89n3

London, Jack, 120, 123
loneliness, 174, 216n13
love: Aristotelian, 262–67, 277; Aristotelian vs. Platonic, 268–69; as expression of self-love, 263–65, 270–72; as spiritual mirroring, 265–67, 278–79; Platonic, 258–62; relation to philosophy, 258–59, 268–72, 276–77; romantic, 128, 220, 264, 270–71, 276–79; root of, 260–62, 265–67; similarities to art, 277–80; types of, 264. *See also* friendship
Mack, Eric, 102, 103n26, 106
magnanimous man, 168. *See also* pride
Mallory, Steven, 198, 243
Man's Life: Aristotle's view of, 114–18, 146–47; Rand's view of, 118–29, 146–47; vs. 'human life' (term), 111n2
Man's Life: vs. animal life, 97, 114, 132. *See also* human being
Marginalia, Ayn Rand's, 246n10, 248
Marx, Karl, 118n15
mathematical axiom, 6n1, 12–13, 17–18
mathematics, 17–18, 34, 94, 125
matter (vs. form), 48, 50, 56, 77, 80–83, 96
McDowell, John, 69, 92, 140n44
means-to-end, relationship, 126–28
measurement, implicit, 65
measurement-omission, 21–22, 65–67
metaphysical value-judgments, 195, 219, 234–35, 248n16, 254n33
Metaphysics, Book A: 10, 95, 116; Book B: 10–12, 46n3, 71; Book Γ: 6n1, 10–17, 33, 43, 45–50; Γ.1: 11, 47n4, 102; Γ.2: 2, 47–49, 102n25; Γ.3: 12–14, 37, 38, 47; Γ.4: 8, 14–15, 38, 39n2, 40, 42, 94; Γ.5: 15n16, 16, 30, 39n2, 59; Γ.6: 8n3, 49n10; Γ.7: 16; Γ.8: 27; Book Δ: 41, 73n15; Book E: 94, 102; Book Z: 12n12, 36, 41, 48n7, 84n6; Book H: 36, 48n7; Book Θ: 38, 48; Book I: 41, 73; Book K: 94; Book Λ: 59, 117n13
metaphysics, 10–13. *See also* art: as concretization of metaphysics
mildness, 115
Mill, J. S., 202n1

Milton, John, 200
mistakes: in relation to rationality, 181–83, 209–10
Magna Moralia, 265, 273, 274n3, 279
money, to make money (phrase), 113n5
moneymaking: life of, 112, 118
moral progress, 159–60
Motion of Animals, 104
Mulligan, Pat, 225
natural selection, 143–44
Nicomachean Ethics, 114–18, 132; Book I.1: 99; Book I.2: 99, 107, 131; I.3: 95, 140, 254; I.4: 151; I.5: 112; I.7: 92, 99, 100, 101n23, 104, 108, 114, 151, 158; I.8: 167; I.9: 263; Book II: 90–91, 166–67; Book III: 108–9, 156, 167, 180; Book IV: 109, 115, 168, 173, 263–64, 274; Book VI: 94n11; VI.1: 91, 131, 245; VI.2: 94; VI.4: 245; VI.5: 91, 94, 167, 169, 172; VI.7: 250n24; VI.8: 156, 171; VI.12: 101, 109, 167; VI.13: 91, 166–67; Book VII: 93, 150–51, 174; Book VIII: 172; Book IX.3: 172; IX.4 174, 264; IX.7: 100; IX.8: 264; IX.9: 100, 266, 273–74; IX.12: 172, 266–67, 281; Book X: 93–94, 117, 250n24, 280
Nock, Albert Jay, 244, 249n19, 252
nominalism, 65
Non-Contradiction (phrase), 6–7
Non-Contradiction, Principle of (PNC): Aristotle's view, 6, 7–15, 49–50; definition and formulation, 12, 36–38, 49–50; Rand and Aristotle, 6, 16, 26–29, 50; relation to essence and substance, 38, 40, 49; validation, 14–16, 26, 33–34, 42–44 (*see also* elenctic demonstration; reaffirmation through denial). *See also* axioms
nous. See reason
Objectivist, The: "Emotions and Values," 212; "Self-Esteem and Romantic Love," 278, 280–81
"Objectivist Ethics, The," 95–103, 107, 203; introduction (VOS, 13–14), 89, 90, 95–96, 130, 139, 229; dependence of value on life (15–18), 96, 97, 98n14, 99, 107, 125, 131, 207, 255; consciousness (18–20), 180; reason and volition (20–22), 100, 176 100, 176; reason and survival (22–24), 101, 103; morality's function, standard, and purpose (25–27), 98, 101, 139, 175, 199, 225n19, 232, 237; morality's essential content (27–30), 132, 176, 177, 209, 217, 218, 221n16, 234; reason and emotion (30–34), 179, 180, 197, 213, 235
Objectivist Newsletter, The: "Benevolence versus Altruism," 190
objectivity. *See* axioms: function and need for; ethics: objectivity of; similarity: as objective
omniscience, 209–10
oneness, numerical, 41
original sin, doctrine of, 205
Ortega y Gasset, José, 17
ousia. See substance
Owen, G. E. L., 153
Parts of Animals, 8, 73, 74, 100
Papers, 133; *Moral Basis for Individualism, The*, 105
Parmenides, 10
passion, 141
patiency, 195
Peikoff, Leonard, 26, 29, 189, 195, 220, 223
perception, 9, 26, 30, 64
perfection: moral, 171–72, 185n28, 217–19, 260–63; standard of, 262–63
Pericles, 172
philosophy, hierarchy of, 155
Philosophy Who Needs It: "Causality versus Duty," 98n14, 105–7, 204; "The Metaphysical Versus the Man-Made," 28n36, 58n24; "The Missing Link," 188, 220n15, 236; "Philosophy: Who Needs It?," 58n24, 95
phronēsis, 109, 114–15, 146, 165–67, 237; as unity, 166–67, 169–70, 200; definition, 91; in neo-Aristotelian virtue ethics, 139–40; in relation with rationality, 181, 239; translation of, 115n8. *See also* virtues, characterological
phronimos, Aristotelian, 90–91, 109, 139–40
Physics, 78, 80–84

INDEX   307

Plato: Aristotle speaking approvingly of, 92; on epistemology, 36, 39, 57n22, 71–72; on literature, 245, 250n23; on metaphysics, 10–11, 82; on virtue, 165; Rand on, 53, 56, 58–59, 69, 75
"Playboy Interview," 235
Poetics, 135n36, 244–46, 248–53
poetry. *See* art; literature
Politics, 114, 166; Book II: 100n19; Book III: 172; Book VII: 185, 255; Book VIII: 186, 254–55
political life, Aristotelian, 112, 115–16
posits vs. axioms, 7, 35
Posterior Analytics, 46, 74; Book I: 7–9; I.1: 7, 35; I.2: 7, 11, 13, 35, 37, 72; I.3: 7, 8, 14n15; I.7: 35; I.10: 35, 37, 47, 74n17; I.11: 8n5, 9n6; I.18: 17n22; I.22: 72, 262; I.32: 35; Book II: 25n32; II.10: 74n17; II.14: 74n17; II.19: 9, 14n15, 27n35, 72, 17n22
pride, 98, 185, 217–22, 224–25, 228; as crown of the virtues, 168, 263–64; Rand vs. Aristotle, 185n28; relation to romance, 215n12, 263–64. *See also* creator (Roarkian); magnanimous man (Aristotle); virtues
Primacy of Consciousness, 53, 56, 59. *See also* consciousness; existence; Primacy of Existence
Primacy of Existence, 24, 56, 57–60. *See also* consciousness; existence; Primacy of Consciousness
primary category of being, 11–12, 46–54
primary philosophy. *See* metaphysics
Prime Mover, Aristotelian, 125–26, 135–36, 262
Prior Analytics, 9, 17
privation, 77, 80–83
production: Rand's ideal life, 112–13, 118 (*see also* life: ideal form of); relationship to things produced, 116, 126–28; vs. leisure, 114–28
productiveness, 98, 141, 183–86, 224–25; requirements of, 196, 224–25, 237–38. *See also* production; work
promiscuity, 144, 269
proposition (vs. concept), 32, 35–41, 42–43

Protagoras, 16, 30
psycho-epistemology, 219–21, 279–80
psychological time measurements, 21–22, 23–24, 45n1
psychology: relationship to philosophy, 144–46; sexual (relations between the sexes), 111n2
purpose, 98, 126, 176, 221; central, 183–84; vs. standard, 98, 129–37. *See also* values: cardinal
puzzle (*aporia*), 10–12, 150–51; about genus, 46–50.

Rand, Ayn: early vs. mature, 119–22
Randall, John Herman, 89, 246n10, 248
Rasmussen, Douglas B., 106–8, 119n17
rationality, 98, 175–76, 199, 221n16; and forming values, 91–92, 106–9, 125, 128, 209–10, 213; as an action, 223–25; as not a moral virtue, 181–83, 199, 209, 233–34; contextual application of, 227, 236–37; definition of, 231–33; relation to *phronēsis*, 181. *See also* art: as rational; human being: as rational animal; reason; virtues: as forms of rationality
reaffirmation through denial, 19, 26, 43–44. *See also* elenctic demonstration; Principle of Non-contradiction: validation
realism (about concepts), 52–53, 65–66, 68, 72–76. *See also* forms: Platonic
reality: as interconnected, 189, 223–24
Rearden, Hank, 181–82, 188–89, 200, 209–10, 214–16, 218, 222n17, 234–35; and Dagny Taggart, 192–93, 198; and Francisco d'Anconia, 280
Rearden, Lillian, 159, 182, 215–16, 218
reason: Aristotelian starting point of knowledge, 8–9, 80; as cardinal value, 98; as man's basic tool of survival, 97, 103, 125; as productive and valuing faculty, 127–28, 204–5; choice to live and, 97, 103–4, 205; definition of, 97, 100; in choosing ends, 106, 132–34, 143; psycho-epistemology and, 221; relation to virtue, 91, 114, 225n19; repurposing faculties through, 143,

156; volitional nature of, 204–6; vs. emotion, 176–79, 214–16, 234–35, 263. *See also* rationality; values: cardinal

reputation, 130

Return of the Primitive, The: "The Age of Envy," 215; "The Inexplicable Personal Alchemy," 195

Rhetoric: 95, 135n36, 246n9, 252

rights, 143, 161

Roark, Howard: and Wynand, 180, 216, 226, 235; benevolence of, 198; heroism of, 137, 159, 185, 187, 221; on building and creation, 122, 125–25, 129, 136, 186, 193, 243

Romantic Manifesto, The: "Art and Cognition," 248; "Art and Moral Treason," 256; "Art and Sense of Life," 135n38, 248; "Basic Principles of Literature," 125, 133n35, 243n1, 251n25, 251n26; "The Goal of My Writing," 230, 243, 252n30, 254; "Introduction to Ninety-Three," 119; "Philosophy and Sense of Life," 135, 177, 178–79, 195, 200, 211–13, 234–35, 271, 277–78; "Psycho-Epistemology of Art," 136–37, 247–48, 248n16, 253–54, 255, 277

Romanticism, 134–35

Russell, Bertrand, 41

said-of vs. present in, 48fn7

Salmieri, Gregory, 52n15, 74, 105, 108n33, 176, 209

sameness, numerical, 41

science: Aristotelian, 47, 114–15, 141; relationship to philosophy, 145–46, 150–51; role in human life, 128, 160; theoretical vs. practical, 94

scientific knowledge, 11; process of forming, 78–79; starting point of, 7–9, 78–79

scientism, 151, 155

Scott, Dominic, 154–55

Sophistical Refutations, 14–15

second-hander, 125–26

self-awareness, 265–66, 272–75, 278

self-esteem, 98, 217–21, 222; in relation to love, 269–71, 274n3, 276–77; in relation to sex, 144, 269–71, 279. *See also* love:

Aristotelian vs. Platonic; values, cardinal

self-knowledge, 170, 272–75

sense of life, 135, 177, 211–13, 219–21, 234–35, 271

sense perception. *See* perception

sex, 128, 144, 278–80; in relation to Aristotelian love, 270–71; in relation to Platonic love, 258–61, 269–70; nonprocreative, 140, 143–44; forms of practice, 144–45

sexism, 117n12, 169

similarity: as objective, 64–65

slavery, 118, 138, 161, 169, 171

social hierarchy, 117

Solon, 92

sophia: Aristotelian science, 114, 257

Sophocles, 251

Spinoza, Baruch, 17, 59

standard (vs. purpose), 98, 129–37

Stein, Gertrude, 248n17

Stoicism, 219, 229

substance, 10–12, 36–38, 46–52, 57, 82. *See also* being; entity

survival: momentary vs. qua man, 101–3, 139. *See also* life

Taganov, Andrei, 123, 179, 182, 188, 234, 235

Taggart, Cheryl, 198

Taggart, Dagny, 134, 159, 178–79, 186–87, 192–93, 198; and Francisco d'Anconia, 183, 216n13; and Hank Rearden, 182–83, 215–16, 218; and John Galt, 136n40, 278–79

Taggart, James, 159, 178, 186, 199

target, Aristotelian metaphor, 112, 114, 130–31

Tchaikovsky, 136

technē (art), 114–15, 116n10, 125, 187, 245–46, 257

teleological measurement, 98, 157

temperance, 206–7, 228

Theophrastus, 134

Thrasymachus, 159

Timoshenko, Stepan, 123

Tolstoy, Leo, 119

Toohey, Ellsworth, 179, 199–200

Topics, Book I: 41, 93; Book VI: 79n1, 94; Book VII: 41
trader principle, the, 141–42
tragedy. *See* literature: tragedy
unit (in concept-formation), 18–19
universal predication of singulars, 71–74. *See also* concept
universality: in scope vs. in form, 33
unmoved mover. *See* Prime Mover
validation (vs. proof), 25–26. *See also* axioms: validation of; Non-contradiction, Principle of: validation of
value judgments: as products of rational action, 213. *See also* metaphysical value-judgments
value, standard of: divine vs. human, 117–18; vs. ultimate value, 98. *See also* life: as standard of value
values: cardinal, 98, 100–101, 180, 219, 221–22, 225n19; definition of, 96; dependent on life, 96; intrinsic, 108–9, 128–29, 157; intrinsic vs. instrumental, 116–17, 138; intrinsic-subjective-objective (trinity), 108–9; personal, 124, 132, 135, 266–67, 278; spiritual vs. material, 118; ultimate, 97, 100–101, 131–32 (*see also* life: as ultimate value)
vice, 173–74, 199–200
virtue ethics, 139–40, 189, 202–3, 206–7
virtues: Aristotle's general view of, 114–15; as action vs. character-trait, 175–76, 203–11, 228–29, 231–33; as dealing with relationship of consciousness and existence, 180, 224, 227–28, 238; as forms of rationality, 166, 175, 180–81, 206, 225, 227; as global, 166, 169–72, 187–89, 200, 223–24; as golden mean, 91n5, 115, 167–68; as involving long-range commitment, 175–76, 209; as means to values, 98, 100–101, 174–75, 180, 204–6, 218; as principles, 137n42, 146; as unity, 166, 183–89, 197, 200, 222–26, 235–36; as unqualified, 226–27, 236–38; belonging to distinct spheres, 167–68; cardinal, 98, 206, 255n19; characterological, 114–15, 146, 165–67, 170, 200, 218–19, 255; compartmentalization of, 166, 187–89, 201, 222–23; definition of, 175–76, 206–7, 231–32; perfect (*see* perfection): moral; Rand's seven, 175–76, 180–81, 205–6, 224–26, 235–36. *See also* courage; honesty; independence; integrity; justice; *phronēsis*; pride; productivity; rationality
visibility, 278–79. *See also* love: as spiritual mirroring
Virtue of Selfishness, The: "The Ethics of Emergencies," 184–85, 189–90, 228; "Man's Rights," 193, 196; "The Objectivist Ethics." *See also* "Objectivist Ethics, The"
Voice of Reason, The: "Psychology of Psychologizing," 206; "Review of Aristotle by John Herman Randall, Jr." vii, 27, 64, 89–90, 100
Wallace, James, 197
Warhol, Andy, 247
We the Living, 121–23, 179, 255n35
wealth, 130
what gives rise to the need for (question), 22–23, 30–31, 35, 96
what might be and ought to be (phrase), 243–44, 248–54
Whitehead, Alfred North, 41
Wilde, Oscar, 119n18, 120, 123
Willers, Eddie, 122, 178
wisdom, practical. *See phronēsis*
wit, 115
work, 121, 183–86, 237–38, 247. *See also* production
Wynand, Gail, 176n15, 179–80, 226, 235; and Dominique Francon, 216n13; and Howard Roark, 186, 198–99